28th Modern Artificial Intelligence and Cognitive Science Conference (MAICS 2017)

Fort Wayne, Indiana, USA
28 - 29 April 2017

ISBN: 978-1-5108-5002-6

Printed from e-media with permission by:

Curran Associates, Inc.
57 Morehouse Lane
Red Hook, NY 12571

Some format issues inherent in the e-media version may also appear in this print version.

Printed by Curran Associates, Inc. (2018)

MAICS
c/o Anca Ralescu
EECS Dept. ML 0030
University of Cincinnati
Cincinnati, OH 45221-0030
USA

Phone: (513) 556-4752
Fax: (513) 556-2569

anca.ralescu@uc.edu

Additional copies of this publication are available from:

Curran Associates, Inc.
57 Morehouse Lane
Red Hook, NY 12571 USA
Phone: 845-758-0400
Fax: 845-758-2633
Email: curran@proceedings.com
Web: www.proceedings.com

TABLE OF CONTENTS

Foreword

We are pleased to introduce the proceedings for the 28th Modern Artificial Intelligence and Cognitive Science conference (MAICS 2017), hosted at Indiana University – Purdue University Fort Wayne (IPFW) from April 28-29.

A conference such as this could not have been organized successfully without the help of many people and organizations. First, we must thank IPFW's Office of the Vice Chancellor for Academic Affairs, and the Institute for Research Scholarship, and Creative Endeavors, for their extremely generous financial support of this conference. Their support allowed us to offer more opportunities for students and junior faculty opportunities to participate in this conference. Many of these students have come up to us personally, sincerely thanking us for allowing them to participate in this conference and being introduced to the exciting world of academic research.

We also wish to thank the IPFW Sigma Xi chapter, and the IPFW computer science department, for their financial support.

The little details matter tremendously in planning events like these, and those details were meticulously taken care of by Makaylia Rosebrock, an IPFW undergraduate student who worked for months to help plan the conference.

We thank our speakers, Dr. Selmer Bringsjord and Dr. John E. Hummel, for not only giving highly engaging and fascinating talks, but for participating in a panel discussion that will be remembered for years to come.

Finally, thanks again to all of our program committee members, particularly Michael Glass, who went above and beyond his responsibilities as a program committee member. These proceedings were compiled by Michael, and he offered us lots of helpful advice that made organizing this conference much easier.

Dr. John Licato
Dr. Aleshia Hayes
MAICS 2017 Conference Chairs

MAICS 2017

April 28-29, 2017
Indiana University/Purdue University – Fort Wayne (IPFW)
Fort Wayne, IN

KEYNOTE SPEAKERS

Dr. Selmer Bringsjord

Chair of Cognitive Science Department, Rensselaer Polytechnic Institute
Director of the Rensselaer AI and Reasoning (RAIR) Lab

"Inaugurating the Formal Science of Darwin's Mistake"

In their bold "Darwin's Mistake," Penn, Holyoak, & Povinelli (PHP; 2008) argue that Darwin profoundly erred in holding that there is no discontinuity between the cognitive capacities of nonhuman animals (e.g. dogs, the cognitive powers of which he repeatedly exalted, and also e.g. chimpanzees) versus those of *Homo sapiens*.[1] Predictably, many refuse to concede that PHP are right. This debate, which continues, is to this point in time a decidedly and thoroughly *informal* affair --- one based in part on evidence, yes; and indeed evidence that comes at least in part from science, but from *empirical* science (comparative psychology, mostly). I begin to recast the debate in the language of the *formal* sciences, which are based directly on formal logic and mathematics and are theorem-driven. The ultimate upshot expected from this recasting is the result that Darwin's continuity position, which is the very foundation of his *Descent of Man*, is *provably* wrong. My recasting, among other things, supplants PHP's reference to "physical symbol systems" with formalisms used in order to be precise about what computation is, and supplants helpful talk of various cognitive capacities (e.g., "relational reasoning") with precise forms of reasoning over rigorous defined formulas and equations.

[1]I have long maintained that Darwin's /Descent of Man/ is painfully illogical. See e.g. "How Logical is Darwin's /Descent of Man" (2009): http://kryten.mm.rpi.edu/PRES/DESCENT111909/SB_Darwin_Descent.pdf. A nd I have pointed out that Pinker's reply to Wallace's Paradox, on formal grounds, doesn't work: see (Bringsjord 2001).

- Bringsjord, S. (2001) "Are We Evolved Computers? A Critical Review of S Pinker's /How the Mind Works/" /Philosophical Psychology/ 2: 227—243. A preprint is available at http://kryten.mm.rpi.edu/selmer.wallaceparadox.pdf.
- Darwin, C. (1997/1871) /Descent of Man/ Amherst, NY: Prometheus.
- Penn, D., Holyoak, K. & Povinelli, D. (2008) "Darwin's Mistake: Explaining the Discontinuity Between Human and Nonhuman Minds" /Behavioral & Brain Sciences/ *31*: 109--178.

Dr. John E. Hummel

Professor of Psychology, University of Illinois at Urbana-Champaign
Director of the Relational Reasoning Laboratory

"What Happened to the Human Brain?"

Humans are unique among the great apes in our capacity to reason explicitly about relations—an ability that underlies our capacity for mathematics, science, engineering and everything else that distinguishes us as a species. Reasoning about relations requires us to represent relations as entities in their own right, to bind arguments to those relations, to map systems of structures based on shared relations and to use the resulting mappings to constrain inference and learning. During human evolution something happened to our brains that makes it possible for us to do these things. I will discuss simulations of how the human brain accomplishes these tasks, and how the resulting algorithms account for aspects of human thinking, especially those that make us unique among the great apes.

For more information: http://ipfw.edu/maics
Contact: MAICS@ipfw.edu

Automated IQ Estimation from Writing Samples

Austin Hendrix, Roman Yampolskiy
University of Louisville
Louisville, KY 40208
austin.hendrix@louisville.edu, roman.yampolskiy@louisville.edu

Abstract

The primary focus of this research is to introduce a method of measuring an individual's IQ by analyzing the vocabulary in said individual's writing. In this paper, we show that the ratio of SAT words in a dataset of writing samples is roughly normally distributed, though with an obvious left skew. We go on to show a method that can be used to calculate an individual's IQ with this ratio and provide samples with measured accuracy. The conclusion suggests ways to increase accuracy in order to further develop the research along with applications of doing so.

1 Introduction

Stylometry is the statistical analysis of differences in literature between authors (Franking, 1988). As early as 1880, the study of stylometry has been used as a method of authorship identification on disputed texts. With the development of computers and automation techniques, sylometric analysis has become easier. An early example of software defined stylometry was used to identify the author of the disputed papers amongst the "Federalist Papers" (Tweedie, Singh, Holmes; 1996). This work demonstrated that stylometric analysis using automation is, at least in this application, able to draw similar conclusions about the authorship of these papers as previous work on the subject. In recent years, stylometry has taken on a broad range of applications. More specifically, stylometry has been used in the identification of chat bots (Ali, Hindi, Yampolskiy; 2011). Further research was done to show that when a chat bot changes behavior over time, the stylometry approach becomes more difficult (Ali, Schaeffer, Yampolskiy; 2012). In addition, it has been demonstrated that stylometric author identification processes can be used on a single author that is capable of writing in multiple languages. (Ali, Yampolskiy, 2014). This is significant in that it demonstrates certain writing trends are independent of the authors' language and are therefore likely stronger candidates for comparing authors that write in different languages.

As there is no true scientific measurement that is currently used to quantify someone's intelligence, many different measurements have been used. Intelligence tests have often been a common way to determine an individual's intelligence relative to others. There have been many negative and controversial opinions on these tests, yet experts still agree on their overall usefulness (Snyderman, Rothman; 1989). Further studies have shown that a standard intelligence test provides the best single, reliable predicator of academic aptitude (Bullerdieck, 1985). One popular example of standard intelligence tests measures an individual's Intelligence Quotient (IQ). The assumption behind this system of measurement is that if a large sample of IQs are mapped together, the distribution will be normal. It has been shown that there are issues with the structure and quality of the standard IQ test (Lawler, 1977). Still, the IQ test can be a useful way for individuals to compare intelligence. For this paper, we will act under the assumption that an individual's IQ score relates directly to their true intelligence level.

This preliminary research project is focused on exploring whether an individual's IQ can be determined by using software defined stylometry. The novelty of this process is that it is not centered around author identification. Instead, stylometry will be used to determine the relative writing quality of a known author. The process will involve analyzing an attribute of a known author's writing to determine said author's IQ. There are multiple attributes of writing that are potential candidates for this application. For the beginning of this research, we will focus on the individual in question's vocabulary. Other research has been done to discuss other attributes with possible merit. These attributes include, but are not limited to, word-length, syllables, sentence-length, and distribution of parts of speech (Holmes, 1994).

2 Collegiate Word Ratio

To determine an individual's IQ based on their vocabulary, a quantitative way to measure the quality of their vocabulary is necessary. For the purposes of this project, we will define a "Collegiate Word" as a word the SAT considers a part of strong vocabulary usage.[1] The College Word Ratio (CWR), which we will refer to through this paper, is therefore defined as:

Collegiate Word Ratio = Collegiate Word Count / Total Word Count

The CWR of each sample will be measured by software and then compared to the rest of the samples to determine its relative quality by use of a distribution. A pseudo-code for calculating the CWR of a sample is shown in Figure 1.

```
for SampleWord in Sample:
        for CollegiateWord in CollegiateWordList:
                if SampleWord == CollegiateWord:
                        CollegiateWordCount++

CollegiateWordRatio = (CollegiateWordCount /
SampleWordCount)
```

Figure 2: Calculating CWR Pseudo-code

Now that we have a clearly defined a process for calculating the CWR of a sample, we need to execute this software on a large dataset. An ideal dataset would consist of writing samples by many randomly selected individuals. Along with this, each writing sample would represent each individual's average writing ability. As such a dataset was not available to the authors of this project, another source had to be found.

The Common Crawl is a corpus containing raw web page data, extracted metadata and text extractions.[2] The text extractions from this corpus contain the raw text taken directly from websites. We are acting under the assumptions that the text extractions are all written by humans and likely contain that individual's average writing. To help increase the accuracy of results under this assumption, only samples with more than 100 words were used. After collecting a large number of samples from the Common Crawl corpus, each sample's CWR was stored and mapped onto a distribution (Figure 2). The distribution is fairly normal, though there is a slight skew to the left. This implies that on a large number of samples, the distribution of CWR is fairly normal and resembles the distribution of IQs.

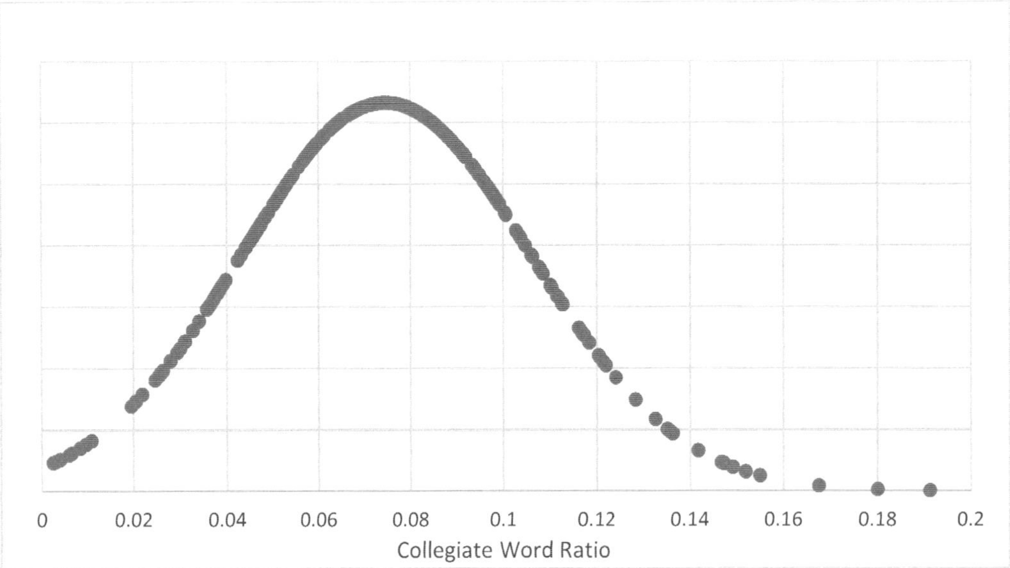

Figure 1: Collegiate Word Ratio Distribution

[1] The full list of words used for this project can be found at www.freevocabulary.com.

[2] https://aws.amazon.com/public-datasets/common-crawl/

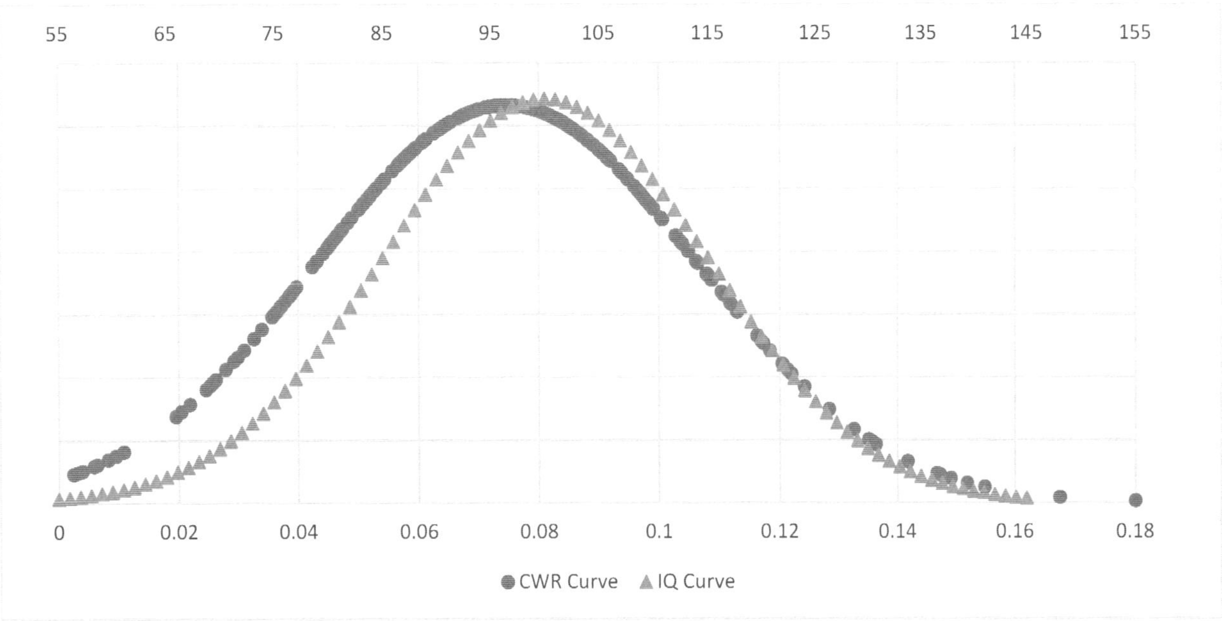

Figure 3: CWR VS IQ Distribution

3 Determining IQ from CWR

We have shown the distribution of CWR is fairly normal, and now we will demonstrate the process of using CWR to calculate an individual's IQ. A graph showing these two distributions overlaid is located below (Figure 3).

The IQ curve shown is the ideal expected IQ distribution. It is perfectly normal with a mean of 100. The CWR distribution, though skewed slightly left, is mapped very closely to the IQ distribution for the second and third positive standard deviation from the mean. For the purposes of this analysis, we will assume that this indicates the CWR in this area will map onto its corresponding IQ. This will result in a certain amount of error when calculating IQ from CWR. Nevertheless, the distributions are close enough that the process should give a good estimation of an individual's IQ.

To begin the process of transferring between the two curves, we need to know the standard deviation and mean of both distributions. For the IQ curve, these are fixed values. The mean IQ value of all individuals is said to be 100 and the standard deviation of all IQ values is said to be 15. For our data set, the mean CWR is 0.074759005 and the standard deviation is 0.031552108.

Using these values and an induvial data point's CWR, a corresponding IQ score can be calculated. Performing this calculation involves finding the z-score of the data point. This is done by the following:

Z-Score = (CWR Data Point – CWR Mean) / CWR Standard Deviation

Sample World Length	Sample Collegiate Word Count	Sample CWR	Expected IQ	Measured IQ	% Error
752	94	0.1250	153	123.88	19.03
412	51	0.1238	130	123.31	5.15
136	22	0.1618	141	141.36	0.26
3279	433	0.1321	129	127.24	1.36

Table 1: Predicted VS Measured IQ

This z-score represents the number of standard deviations, positive or negative, that the data point is away from the mean. Since we know the standard deviation and mean of all IQ scores, the corresponding IQ can be calculated as follows:

Corresponding IQ = (Z-Score * IQ Standard Deviation) + IQ Mean

4 Testing IQ Estimation Software

Now that a sample of writing can be used to determine the IQ of an individual from their CWR, we must determine if the IQ is accurate. The process of doing this is straightforward, though difficult to accomplish. For it to be reliably said that CWR can be used to calculate an individual's IQ, we must find multiple individuals with a known IQ and access to writing that is their own. The pseudo-code for the software used to map the CWR of samples on to a corresponding IQ is shown in Figure 4.

Using social media contacts, we located several individuals willing to give their IQ and a sample of their writing for the purposes of testing our software. It should be noted that there is no external verification that these individuals gave an accurate IQ, but these samples are a good starting point for testing the reliability of this software. The data collected from these samples is shown in Table 1. Regardless of the large error in the first sample, the accuracy of the rest of the samples provide support for this approach for calculating IQ.

```
Sample_Z_Score = (CWR_Sample – CWR_Mean) /
CWR_Standard_Deviation
Sample_IQ = (Sample_Z_Score *
IQ_Standard_Deviation) + IQ_Mean
```

Figure 4: Calculating IQ Pseudo-code

5 Conclusions and Future Work

Though our first sample produced a result with a moderate error, there still seems to be merit to looking further into this methodology. It should be noted that the samples used were approximately 2 standard deviations above the mean. Further sampling should include data on both ends of the curve. There may not ultimately be a cause effect relationship between intelligence level and vocabulary usage, but this research does indicate the two are correlated. The normality of the distribution of CWR may be significant in other applications, and should be noted regardless of the final merits of this approach to calculating intelligence.

This research paper is intended to be purely preliminary and simply introduce the concept and one possible implementation of using an individual's vocabulary to determine IQ levels. To further develop this research, the authors suggest a larger dataset be used to create a more accurate distribution. In addition, a more reliable dataset is necessary to test the accuracy of these methods. For the strongest possible results, self-reported IQ scores should not be used. Ideally, the next stage in research will include an IQ test along with a specific writing prompt on which to run our software. Lastly, there is likely merit in exploring the analysis of the other attributes of writing that are mentioned at the introduction to this piece. It is possible that one or all of these attributes may provide a better avenue for calculating an individual's intelligence level.

The ability to analyze the intelligence of individuals is a very useful tool. It has been shown in previous research that numerous factors influence whether an intellectually gifted child will ultimately lead a successful life (Tomlinson-Keasey, Little; 1990). Earlier identification of these children, through application of this research, has the potential to allow these children to be guided down a positive path that will lead to their personal success. In addition, this research could play a role in evaluating the abilities of persons currently prominent in the political and scientific realms. Nevertheless, further research must be done in this area of study before anything truly conclusive can be said.

6 References

Ali, Nawaf; Hindi, Musa; Yampolskiy, Roman. (2011). Evaluation of authorship attribution software on a Chat bot corpus. Information, Communication and Automation Technologies (ICAT), 2011 XXIII International Symposium on, IEEE.

Ali, Nawaf; Schaeffer, Derek; Yampolskiy, Roman. (2012). Linguistic Profiling and Behavioral Drift in Chat Bots. MAICS, 27-30.

Ali, Nawaf; Yampolskiy, Roman. (2014). BLN-Gram-TF-ITF as a Language Independent Feature for Authorship Identification and Paragraph Similarity. 9th Cyber and Information Science research Conference, Oak Ridge, Tennessee.

Bullerdieck, K. Kelly McK. (1985). Considerations in Defining the Gifted. http://journals.sagepub.com/doi/abs/10.1177/107621758500800607

Franking, Holly. (1988). Stylometry: A statistical method for determining authorship, textual integrity, and chronology. University of Kansas, ProQuest Dissertations Publishing.

Holmes, D. (1994). Authorship Attribution. Computers and the Humanities, 28(2), 87-106. http://www.jstor.org/stable/30200315

Lawler, James. (1977). IQ: Biological Fact or Methodological Construct? Science & Society, vol. 41, no. 2, pp. 208–218. www.jstor.org/stable/40402014.

Snyderman, M., & Rothman, S. (1987). Survey of expert opinion on intelligence and aptitude testing. American Psychologist, 42(2), 137-144.

Tomlinson-Keasey, Carol; Little, Todd D. (1990). Predicting educational attainment, occupational achievement, intellectual skill, and personal adjustment among gifted men and women. Journal of Educational Psychology, vol. 82(3), pp. 442-455.

Tweedie, F., Singh, S., & Holmes, D. (1996). Neural Network Applications in Stylometry: The "Federalist Papers" Computers and the Humanities, 30(1), 1-10. Retrieved from http://www.jstor.org/stable/30204514

Morphognosis: the shape of knowledge in space and time

Thomas E. Portegys
Ernst & Young LLP New York, NY, USA
tom.portegys@ey.com

Abstract

Artificial intelligence research to a great degree focuses on the brain and behaviors that the brain generates. But the brain, an extremely complex structure resulting from millions of years of evolution, can be viewed as a solution to problems posed by an environment existing in space and time. The environment generates signals that produce sensory events within an organism. Building an internal spatial and temporal model of the environment allows an organism to navigate and manipulate the environment. Higher intelligence might be the ability to process information coming from a larger extent of space-time. In keeping with nature's penchant for extending rather than replacing, the purpose of the mammalian neocortex might then be to record events from distant reaches of space and time and render them, as though yet near and present, to the older, deeper brain whose instinctual roles have changed little over eons. Here this notion is embodied in a model called *morphognosis* (*morpho* = shape and *gnosis* = knowledge). Its basic structure is a pyramid of event recordings called a *morphognostic*. At the apex of the pyramid are the most recent and nearby events. Receding from the apex are less recent and possibly more distant events. A morphognostic can thus be viewed as a structure of progressively larger chunks of space-time knowledge. A set of morphognostics forms long-term memories that are learned by exposure to the environment. A cellular automaton is used as the platform to investigate the morphognosis model, using a simulated organism that learns to forage in its world for food, build a nest, and play the game of Pong.

1 Introduction

The human brain is the seat of intelligence. Thus when we attempt to craft intelligence, naturally we turn to it as a guide. Fortunately, neuroscience is proceeding at an astounding pace [Kaiser, 2014; Stetka, 2016], methodically unpacking its mysteries. Yet the complexity of the brain, with billions of neurons and trillions of synapses, remains daunting. Teasing apart which aspects and features of the brain are essential to the function of intelligence and which are incidental is a crucial and difficult task. Krakauer *et al.* [2017] recommend that neuroscience work takes place after the study of related behaviors.

Unfortunately, the prospects of understanding complex systems through examination and dissection are questionable [Jonas and Kording, 2016]. And as for constructing a complete precise brain model, it is possible, as John von Neumann believed [Mühlenbein, 2009], that at a certain level of complexity the simplest precise description of a thing is the thing itself. In reaction to this, some efforts, such as The Human Brain Project [2015] and Numenta [Hawkins, 2004; White paper, 2011], have taken the position that analysis must be complemented with synthesis and simulation to achieve a satisfactory level of understanding.

From an artificial intelligence (AI) viewpoint, we must keep in mind that the purpose of a brain is to allow an organism to navigate and manipulate its environment. Thus it is a solution to problems posed by the environment. While the earlier days of AI seemed more focused on this viewpoint, recently neuroscience has assumed perhaps an outsized role in directing AI, even to the extent of governmental encouragement [Vogelstein, 2014].

Some researchers maintain that the environment largely consists of a body for the brain to interact with. The embodied brain will thus leverage the sensory and motor capabilities of a body that are adapted to an environment. Robotics researchers such as Brooks [1999], Hoffmann and Pfeifer [2011] have argued that true artificial intelligence can only be achieved by machines that have sensory and motor skills and are connected to the world through a body. However, this approach belies the problem since the body, like the brain, is also a solution to its environment.

Determining a model of an organism's environment is more tractable than creating a brain model of an environmental model. But it requires settling on what is in the world that produces sensory events and reacts to motor responses. Confounding this is that we of course must use our brains to do this. There is a common and somewhat ironic tendency to describe AI inputs and outputs in human cognitive terms, i.e. post-processed brain output, such as symbolic variables.

Hoffman [2009] argues that evolution has shaped our senses and perceptual machinery to only provide information on events that are ancestrally significant, such as finding food and safety. Other events in the environment that we cannot directly sense must be mapped through technology onto our sensory capabilities. For example, in the age of science the existence and use of X-rays is important, but we sense them only indirectly, as shadows on photographic film. Indeed, Hoffman argues that reality may be more radically alien than we can imagine.

Epistemological offerings would seem at best too abstract to be useful for framing a sensory-response environment, and at worst useless, as in the cases of nihilism and solipsism. And physics has in recent times become increasingly muddier on the "true" nature of reality:

- The arrow of time may be related to the perception of entropy [Halliwell, 1994]
- String theory demands a number of extra infinitesimal dimensions [Rickles, 2014].
- The perception of space may be a holographic projection [Bousso, 2002].
- Reality could be a cellular automaton [Wolfram, 2002], a graph [Wolfram, 2015], or a simulation [Moskowitz, 2016].

Despite these hazards, people universally experience the environment as a space-time structure. And even if there is a different underlying substructure, the model is empirically effective. The presence of mammalian brain structures for mapping spatial events [Vorhees and Williams, 2014] provides evidence for the processing of this type of information. Similarly, brain structures for sensing the passage of time have also found support [Sanders, 2015].

Using space-time as a model, it can be speculated that higher intelligence is the ability to process information arising from a larger extent of space-time. And in keeping with nature's penchant for extending rather than replacing, the purpose of the mammalian neocortex might then be to record events from distant reaches of space and time and render them, as though yet near and present, to the older, deeper brain whose instinctual roles have changed little over eons. If this is so, these structures would be repurposed to embody language and abstract concepts.

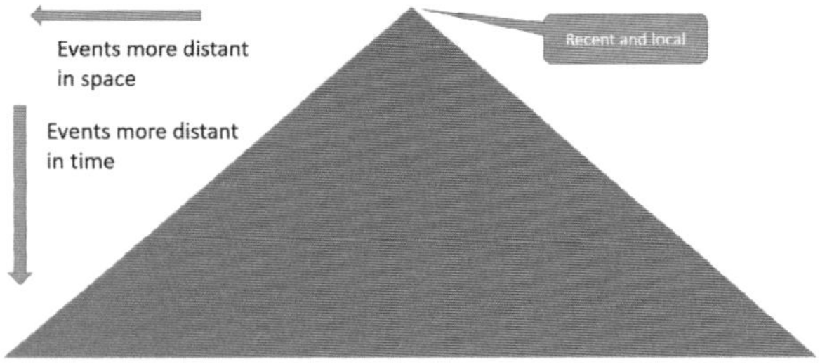

Figure 1 – Morphognostic event pyramid

Building an internal spatial and temporal model of the environment allows an organism to navigate and manipulate the environment. This paper introduces a model called *morphognosis* (morpho = shape and gnosis = knowledge). Its basic structure is a pyramid of event recordings called a *morphognostic*, as shown in Figure 1. At the apex of the pyramid are the most recent and nearby events. Receding from the apex are less recent and possibly more distant events.

Morphognosis is partially inspired by an abstract morphogenesis model called *Morphozoic* [Portegys *et al.*, 2017]. Morphogenesis is the process of generating complex structures from simpler ones within an environment. Morphozoic is based on hierarchically nested neighborhoods within a cellular automaton. Morphozoic was found to be robust and noise tolerant in reproducing a number of morphogenesis-like phenomena, including Turing diffusion-reaction systems [Turing, 1952], gastrulation, and neuron pathfinding. It is also capable of image reconstruction tasks.

2 Description

The morphognosis model is demonstrated in three 2D cellular environments: (1) a food foraging task, (2) a nest building task, and (3) the game of Pong. The food foraging task is used as a venue to further define the model.

2.1 Food foraging

In this task a virtual creature called a *mox* finds itself in a 2D cellular world as shown in Figure 2. To find food the mox must navigate around various obstacles of various types (colors).

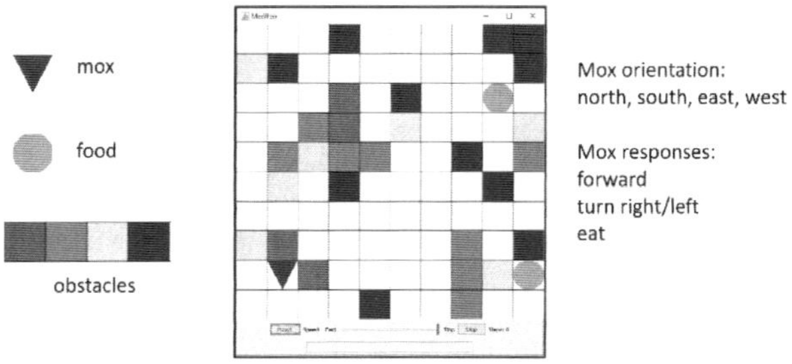

Figure 2 - Mox food foraging in a 2D cellular world.

Figure 3 shows a snapshot of a morphognostic describing the space-time events, in this case obstacle encounters, while the mox forages. In this case a neighborhood is configured as a 3x3 set of sectors.

Cell type densities are stored instead of raw cell values to allow linear scaling of information as the hierarchy increases since storing individual cell values would result in a geometric growth. The cell type density is only one of a number of possible statistical or aggregation functions that could be used. An alternative might be to look at the distribution of cell types as an image processing operation, such as taking a Laplacian, Sobel or other image operator.

2.1.1 Morphognostic spatial neighborhoods

A cell defines an elementary neighborhood:

$$neighborhood_0 = cell$$

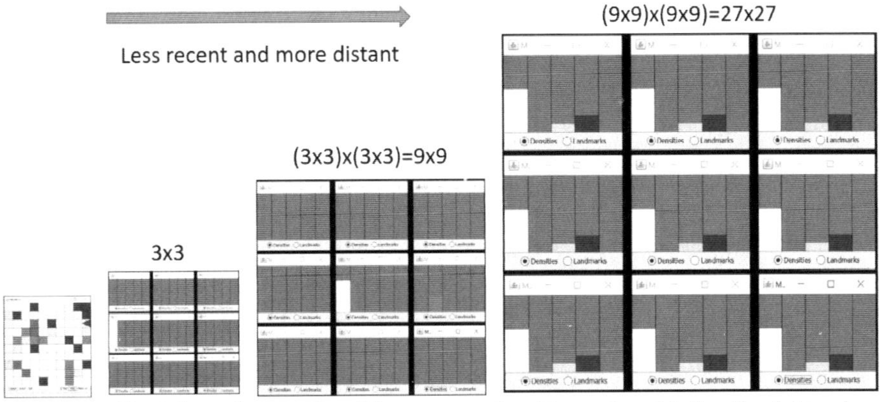

Figure 3 - Pyramid of obstacle type densities arranged as hierarchy of 3x3 cell neighborhoods.

A non-elementary neighborhood consists of an *NxN* set of *sectors* surrounding a lower level neighborhood:

$$neighborhood_i = NxN(neighborhood_{i-1})$$

where N is an odd positive number.

The value of a sector is a vector representing a histogram of the cell type densities contained within it:

$$value(sector) = (density(cell\text{-}type_0), density(cell\text{-}type_1), \ldots density(cell\text{-}type_n))$$

The number of cells contributing to the density histogram of a sector of $neighborhood_i = N^{i-1}xN^{i-1}$

2.1.2 Morphognostic temporal neighborhoods

A neighborhood contains events that occur between time *epoch* and *epoch + duration*:

$$t1_0 = 0$$
$$t2_0 = 1$$
$$t1_i = t2_{i-1}$$
$$t2_i = (t2_{i-1} * 3) + 1$$
$$epoch_i = t1_i$$
$$duration_i = t2_i - t1_i$$

2.1.3 Metamorphs

In order to navigate and manipulate the environment, it is necessary for an agent to be able to respond to the environment. A *metamorph* embodies a morphognostic→response rule. A set of metamorphs can be learned from a manual or programmed sequence of responses within a world.
Metamorphs establish an important feedback:

- Learned morphognostics shape responses.
- Responses shape the learning of morphognostics.

Metamorph "execution" consists generating a morphognostic for the current mox position and orientation then finding the closest morphognostic contained in the learned metamorph set, where:

$$distance(metamorph_i, metamorph_j) = \sum_{x}^{neighborhoods} \sum_{y}^{sectors} \sum_{z}^{cell\,types} abs\begin{pmatrix} cell\,type\,density_{i,x,y,z} - \\ cell\,type\,density_{j,x,y,z} \end{pmatrix}$$

2.1.4 Artificial neural network implementation

In a complex environment, generating a large number of metamorphs may be prohibitive in terms of storage and search processing. Alternatively, metamorphs can be used to train an artificial neural network (ANN), as shown in Figure 4, to learn responses associated with morphognostic inputs. During operation, a current morphognostic can be input to the ANN to produce a learned response. The ANN also has these advantages:

- Faster.
- More compact.
- More noise tolerant.

2.1.5 Results

The mox were trained in worlds featuring a number of randomly placed obstacles of various types. Training was done by "autopiloting" the mox along an optimal path to the food. This generated a set of metamorphs suitable for testing. Table 1 shows the results of varying the neighborhood hierarchy depth in a 10x10 world. Success indicates the mean amount of food eaten, so 1 is a perfect score. It can be observed that more obstacles tend to improve performance. This is because they tend to form unique landmark configurations to guide the mox. Larger neighborhoods also tend to improve performance.

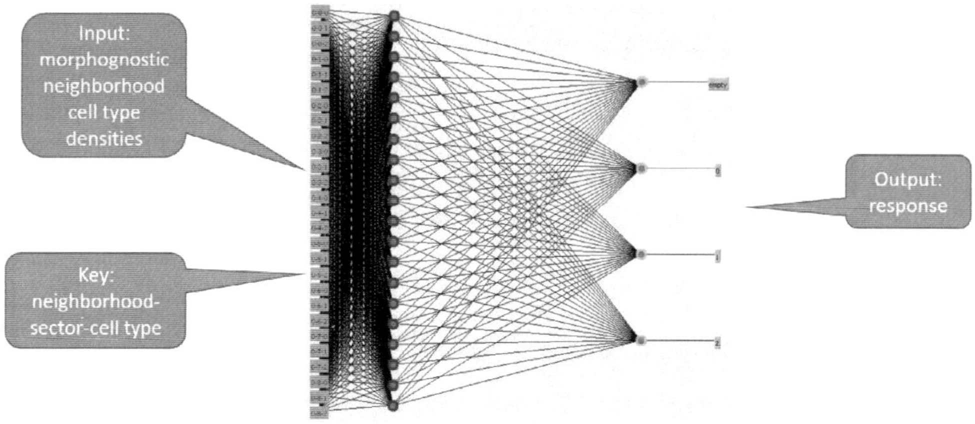

Figure 4 – Metamorph artificial neural network.

Neighborhoods	Obstacle types	Obstacles	Food
1	1	10	0.1
1	1	20	0.2
1	2	10	0
1	2	20	0
1	4	10	0
1	4	20	0
2	1	10	0.3
2	1	20	0.4
2	2	10	0.2
2	2	20	0.6
2	4	10	0.2
2	4	20	0.6
3	1	10	1
3	1	20	0.9
3	2	10	1
3	2	20	1
3	4	10	1
3	4	20	1

Table 1 – Foraging in a 10x10 world.

The next test examines how well the model performs when the test world is not a duplicate of a training world, but is similar to a set of training worlds. Thus for this, multiple training runs are used. Before each training run, the cell types of all the cells are probabilistically modified to a random value. A successful test run must then rely on a composite of multiple training runs. The results are shown in Table 2. Of note is how performance only begins to falter under heavy noise and few training runs.

Noise	#Train	Food
0.1	1	1
0.1	5	1
0.1	10	1
0.25	1	0.9
0.25	5	1
0.25	10	1
0.5	1	0.6
0.5	5	0.8
0.5	10	0.9

Table 2 – Foraging with noise.

2.2 Nest building

This task illustrates how the morphognosis model can be used to not only navigate but also manipulate the environment.

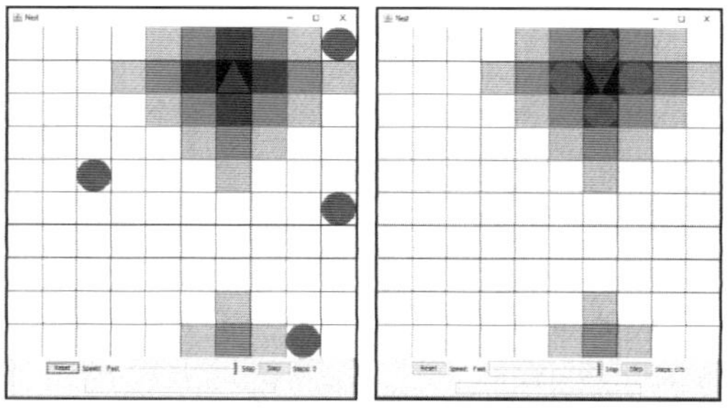

Figure 5 – Nest building with gathered stones. Left: scattered stones. Right completed nest.

Figure 5 left shows an environment in which a nest will be constructed out of 4 stones (reddish circles) on top of an elevation depicted by the shaded cells. The mox must seek out the stones, pick them up, and assemble them into the completed nest shown in Figure 5 right.

For this task, the mox is capable of sensing the presence of a stone immediately in front of it, and sensing the elevation gradient both laterally and in the forward-backward direction. In addition to the forward and turning movements used by the foraging task, the mox is capable of picking up a stone in front of it and dropping the stone onto an unoccupied cell in front of it. An internal sense allows the mox to know whether it is carrying a stone.

Training was done by running the mox through 10 repetitions on "autopilot" to build a set of metamorphs. The environment was then reset and the mox tested to discover whether it is capable of building the nest. Over 50 trials were performed with 100% success. Internally, the sensory information from the stone, gradient and stone carry states were sufficient to achieve success with a neighborhood hierarchy of only one level.

2.3 Pong game

Much of the real world is nondeterministic, taking the form of unpredictable or probabilistic events that must be acted upon. If AIs are to engage such phenomena, then they must be able to learn how to deal with nondeterminism. In this task the game of Pong poses a nondeterministic environment. The learner is given an incomplete view of the game state and underlying deterministic physics, resulting in a nondeterministic game. This task has been found to be challenging for conventional machine learning algorithms [Portegys, 2015].

2.3.1 Game details

The goal of the game is to vertically move a paddle to prevent a bouncing ball from striking the right wall, as shown in Figure 6.

- Ball and paddle move in a cellular grid.
  - Unseen deterministic physics moves ball in grid.
- Cell state: (ball state, paddle state)
  - Ball state: (empty, present, moving left/right/up/down)
  - Paddle state: (true | false)
- Learner orientation: (north, south, east, west)
- Responses: (wait, forward, turn right/left)
- If paddle present and orientation north or south, then forward response moves paddle also.

Figure 6 – The game of Pong.

2.3.2 Procedure and results

Learner was trained with multiple randomly generated initial ball velocities.

- When the ball moved left and right, the learner moved with the ball.
- When the ball moved up or down, the learner moved to the paddle and moved it up or down.
  - This was the challenge: remembering ball state while traversing empty cells to the paddle so as to move it correctly, then to turn and return to ball for next input.

Testing on random games: 100% successful.

3 Conclusion

This is an early exploration of the morphognosis model. The novelty of the model is both the method for integrating knowledge of events occurring in space and time dimensions in linear complexity, and the method of expressing the behavioral interplay of responses and sensory events. The goal of this project is to model the environment as something that could plausibly be in turn modeled by an artificial brain.

The positive results on the three tasks prompt future investigation. Moving up the ladder of animal intelligence, possible next tasks include:

- Web building. Can a space-time memories of building one or more training webs allow one to be built in a quasi-novel environment?
- Food foraging social signaling. Bees retain memories of foraging food sources that they communicate to other bees through instinctive dancing. Can this task be cast into the model?

The Java code is available at https://github.com/portegys/MoxWorx

References

[Bousso, 2002] R. Bousso. The holographic principle. *Reviews of Modern Physics*. **74** (3): 825–874. arXiv:hep-th/0203101.2002.

[Brooks, 1999] Rodney Brooks. Cambrian Intelligence: The Early History of the New AI. Cambridge MA: The MIT Press. ISBN 0-262-52263-2. 1999.

[Halliwell, 1994] J. J. Halliwell. Physical Origins of Time Asymmetry. Cambridge University Press. ISBN 0-521-56837-4. 1994.

[Hawkins, 2004] Jeff Hawkins. On Intelligence (1 ed.). Times Books. p. 272. ISBN 0805074562. 2004.

[Hoffman, 2009] D. D. Hoffman. The interface theory of perception: Natural selection drives true perception to swift extinction. In: Object Categorization: Computer and Human Vision Perspectives. Ed.: S.J. Dickinson, A. Leonardis, B. Schiele & M.J. Tarr. Cambridge, Cambridge University Press: 148-165. 2009.

[Hoffmann and Pfeifer, 2011] M. Hoffmann and R. Pfeifer. The implications of embodiment for behavior and cognition: animal and robotic case studies, in W. Tschacher & C. Bergomi, ed., 'The Implications of Embodiment: Cognition and Communication', Exeter: Imprint Academic, pp. 31-58. 2011.

[Human Brain Project, 2015] Human Brain Project, Framework Partnership Agreement. https://www.humanbrainproject.eu/documents/10180/538356/FPA++Annex+1+Part+B/41c4da2e-0e69-4295-8e98-3484677d661f. 2015.

[Jonas and Kording, 2016] E. Jonas and K. Kording. Could a neuroscientist understand a microprocessor? bioRxiv 055624; doi: https://doi.org/10.1101/055624. 2016.

[Kaiser, 2014] U. B. Kaiser. Editorial: Advances in Neuroscience: The BRAIN Initiative and Implications for Neuroendocrinology. *Molecular Endocrinology*. *28*(10), 1589–1591. http://doi.org/10.1210/me.2014-1288. 2014.

[Krakauer, *et al*., 2017] J. W. Krakauer, *et al*. Neuroscience Needs Behavior: Correcting a Reductionist Bias. *Neuron*. Volume 93, Issue 3, pp. 480 – 490. 2017

[Moskowitz, 2016] C. Moskowitz. Are We Living in a Computer Simulation? *Scientific American*. 2016.

[Mühlenbein, 2009] H. Mühlenbein. Computational Intelligence: The Legacy of Alan Turing and John von Neumann, in Computational Intelligence Collaboration, Fusion and Emergence. Editors: Mumford, C. L. (Ed.) Volume 1 of the series Intelligent Systems Reference Library pp 23-43. 2009.

[Numenta White paper 2011] http://numenta.org. 2011.

[Portegys *et al*., 2017] T. Portegys, G. Pascualy, R. Gordon, S. McGrew, B. Alicea. Morphozoic: cellular automata with nested neighborhoods as a metamorphic representation of morphogenesis. In Multi-Agent Based Simulations Applied to Biological and Environmental Systems. ISBN: 978-1-5225-1756-6. 2017.

[Portegys, 2015] T. Portegys. Training Artificial Neural Networks to Learn a Nondeterministic Game. ICAI'15: The 2015 International Conference on Artificial Intelligence https://arxiv.org/abs/1507.04029. 2015.

[Rickles, 2014] D. Rickles. A Brief History of String Theory: From Dual Models to M-Theory. Springer Science & Business Media. ISBN 978-3-642-45128-7. 2014.

[Sanders, 2015] L. Sanders. How the brain perceives time. *ScienceNews*. https://www.sciencenews.org/article/how-brain-perceives-time. 2015.

[Stetka, 2016] B. Stetka. From Psychedelics To Alzheimer's, 2016 Was A Good Year For Brain Science. http://www.npr.org/sections/health-shots/2016/12/31/507133144/from-psychedelics-to-alzheimers-2016-was-a-good-year-for-brain-science. 2016.

[Turing, 1952] A. M. Turing. The chemical basis of morphogenesis. *Phil. Trans. Roy. Soc. London* B237, 37-72. 1952.

[Vogelstein, 2014] R. J. Vogelstein. Machine Intelligence from Cortical Networks (MICrONS) Workshop. Intelligence Advanced Research Projects Activity (IARPA). https://www.iarpa.gov/index.php/research-programs/microns. 2014.

[Vorhees and Williams, 2014] C. V. Vorhees and M. T. Williams. Assessing Spatial Learning and Memory in Rodents. *ILAR Journal*. 55(2), 310–332. http://doi.org/10.1093/ilar/ilu013. 2014.

[Wolfram, 2002] S. Wolfram. A New Kind of Science. Wolfram Media. ISBN-10: 1579550088. 2002.

[Wolfram, 2015] S. Wolfram. What Is Spacetime, Really? Stephen Wolfram Blog. http://blog.stephenwolfram.com/2015/12/what-is-spacetime-really/. 2015.

An Eyes and Hands Model for Cognitive Architectures to Interact with User Interfaces

Farnaz Tehranchi
Department of Computer Science and Engineering
Penn State, University Park, PA 16802 USA
farnaz.tehranchi@psu.edu

Frank E. Ritter
College of Information Sciences and Technology
Penn State, University Park, PA 16802 USA
frank.ritter@psu.edu

ABSTRACT

We propose a cognitive model to interact with interfaces. The main objective of cognitive science is understanding the nature of the human mind to develop a model that predicts and explains human behavior. These models are useful to Human-Computer Interaction (HCI) by predicting task performance and times, assisting users, finding error patterns, and by acting as surrogate users. In the future these models will be able to watch users, correct the discrepancy between model and user, better predicting human performance for interactive design, and also useful for AI interface agents. To be fully integrated into HCI design these models need to interact with interfaces. The two main requirements for a cognitive model to interact with the interface are (a) the ability to access the information on the screen, and (b) the ability to pass commands. To hook models to interfaces in the general way we work within a cognitive architecture. Cognitive architectures are computational frameworks to execute cognition theories—they are essentially programming languages designed for modeling. Prominent examples of these architectures are Soar [1] and ACT-R [2]. ACT-R models could access the world interacting directly with the Emacs text editor [3]. We present an initial model of eyes and hands within the ACT-R cognitive architecture that can interact with Emacs.

KEYWORDS

Cognitive Model; Cognitive Architecture; Human Computer Interface, Interaction.

1 INTRODUCTION[1]

HCI has used cognitive models of users successfully in different ways: for examining the efficacy of different designs to predict task performance times, helping to create and choose better designs, and saving overall system cost by providing feedback for designers. In the future these models will be able to watch users, have more realistic input, correct themselves, and predict human performance.

To be useful in HCI research, these models need to be capable of interacting with interfaces. The two main requirements for a cognitive model to interact with a task environment are (a) the ability to pass commands, and (b) the ability to access the information on the screen—the cognitive model encodes screen's objects that has been used as an agent architecture. If cognitive models interact with user interfaces, then the models will be easier to develop and apply. This approach, can be called a Cognitive Model Interface Management System (CMIMS) [4], which is an extension of the concept of a User Interface Management System (UIMS) [5].

Cognitive architectures are infrastructures for cognitive science theory and provide computational frameworks to execute cognitive theories. They are programming languages specifically designed for modeling, such as Soar [1, 6] or ACT-R [2]. A user model is thus a combination of task knowledge and a cognitive architecture with its fixed mechanisms to apply the knowledge to generate behavior.

The aim of this research is to develop a cognitive model and provide ACT-R models access to the world by enabling ACT-R to interact directly with the Emacs text editor. This approach has been called Esegman, for Emacs Segman [7], related to another tool, Segman, for hooking user models and agents to interfaces [8]. ACT-R can communicate with a task environment by instrumenting a graphical library [9], in this case the Emacs text editor. Emacs is an interactive text editor that works with spreadsheets [10] and includes extensions to read email and browse the web.

A brief review on the Esegman approach is given in section II. Section III and IV explain the ACT-R structure and our eyes and hands model. Finally, conclusion remarks and future research are discussed in section VI and VII respectively.

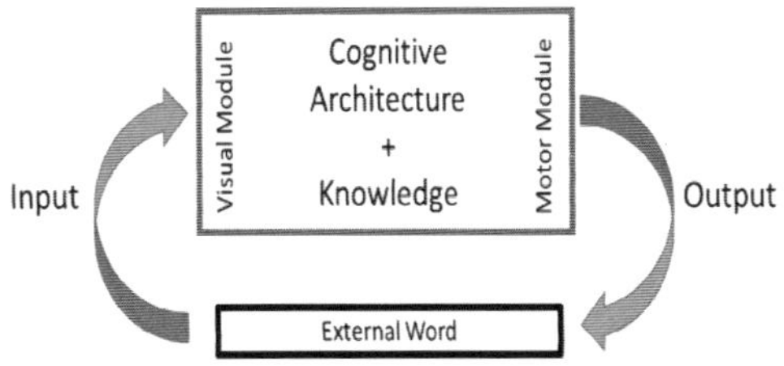

Figure 1: Cognitive model structure.

2 THE ESEGMAN APPROACH

Emacs Segmentation/Manipulation (Esegman) provides a connection between the cognitive architecture and the world. Both ACT-R and Emacs are written in Lisp. It allows us to extend them and design a bridge between them. This bridge will enable ACT-R to communicate with an interactive environment. ACT-R cognitive models have a loop with three components: the task environment, the model, and the results (see Figure 1). The cognitive model receives its perspective as

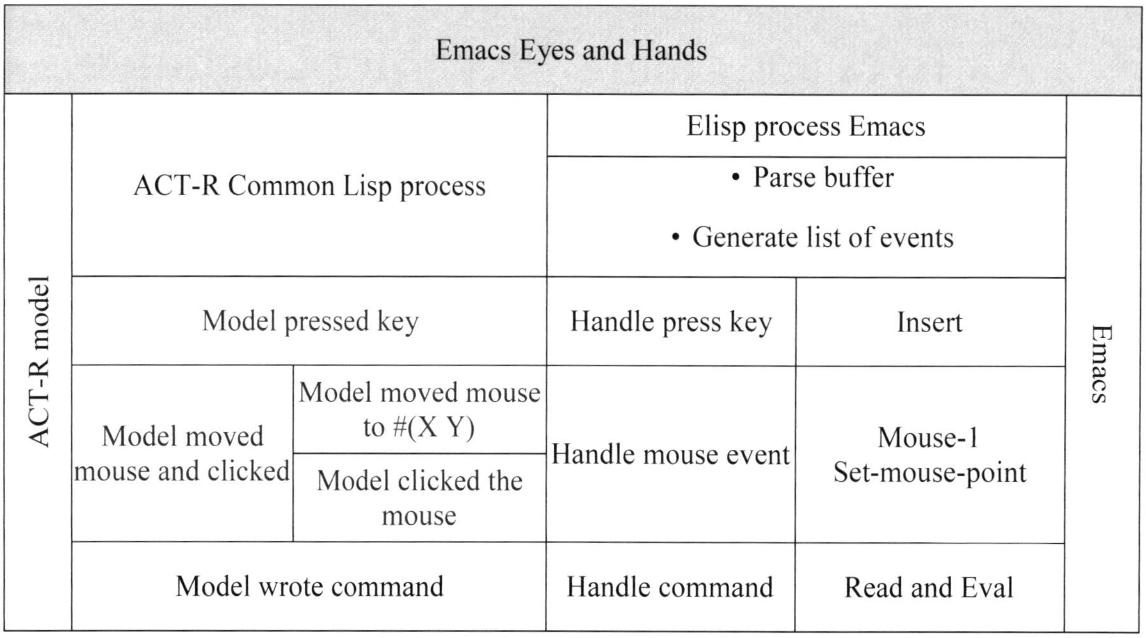

Figure 2: Emacs Eyes and Hands output approach, showing how model process (left) are implemented in the Emacs text editor (right)

input from the visual (and auditory) module and outputs actions through the motor/manual module. The cognitive architecture within this process understands the external world as shown in Figure 1.

The modeling process can start with collecting data from the real world. This data gathering has been performed using the Dismal spreadsheet [10]. Dismal is an augmented spreadsheet developed for Emacs that was designed to gather and analyze behavioral data. Users can interact with the spreadsheet through keystrokes, menus, and function calls. Participants have performed a set of spreadsheet tasks in Dismal [11], and their performance over 14 subtasks, about 20 min. of work, was recorded using the Recording User Input (RUI) software [12, 13]. As will be discussed in the next section, we thus have an existing dataset of human behavior on a complex task to model [11] and also have a model available [14]. A comparison has been done, but not on a fine-grained level, and without modeling interaction, error, and error correction. Because the model did not have access to the spreadsheet, which is complex to model without duplicating a spreadsheet. This model was developed by High-level behaviour representation language (Herbal)—an open source software that supports two cognitive architectures and one agent architecture through a set of common cognitive modeling tasks [15]. Herbal compiles into declarative knowledge and procedural knowledge, and its output has a syntax similar to ACT-R.

In particular, for our connection between the architecture and the world, we will use Emacs functions to take the interaction commands from the model (ACT-R will be a sub-process of the Emacs process) and insert them and their effects into the target Emacs window; and similarly take the state of Emacs and make it available to the model. Figure 2 diagrams most of the components of this approach. Therefore, the model will be able to execute commands and be aware of their results. For example, after collecting the commands from ACT-R and receiving requests to 'look' and move the eye, the courser in Emacs window will move. This approach provides the output direction in Figure 1. However, for input direction of Figure 1 we have to feed ACT-R with the information about the world by inserting contents into its visual module.

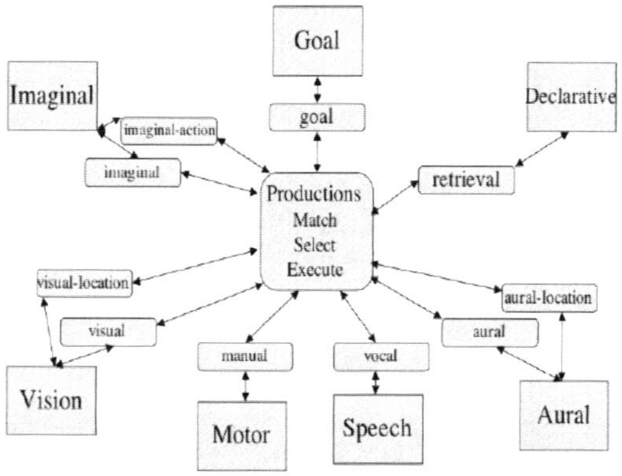

Figure 3: The ACT-R 6 Architecture.

Table 1: Initial Production Rules of the Eyes and Hands Model.

Production Rules	& Buffers used
Start	Goal, Manual, Visual-Location
Rule1	Goal, Visual-Location, Visual
Rule2	Goal, Manual, Vocal
Rule3	Goal, Manual
Rule4	Goal, Vocal

3 THE ACT-R ARCHITECTURE AND MODEL

The two basic types of knowledge in ACT-R are declarative and procedural. Declarative knowledge (Chunks) contains

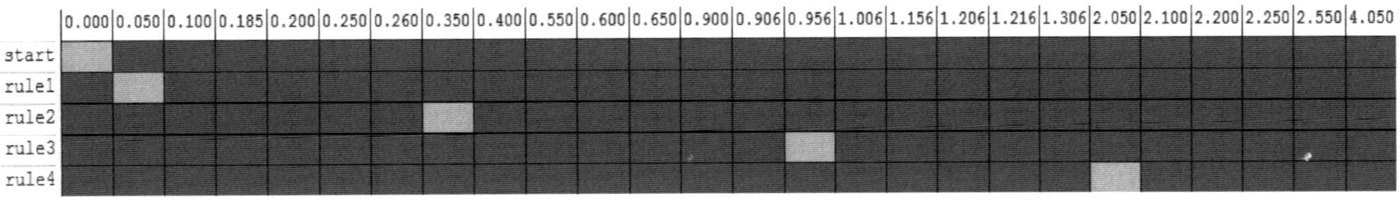

Figure 4: Production History in Different Critical Cycle

facts, images, locations, and sounds. Procedural knowledge (production rules) indicates behavioral aspects of performance with goals, operators, methods, and selection rules [16]. All tasks in the model [14] we will build on include a combination of declarative and procedural knowledge.

Figure 3 shows a schematic of ACT-R's architecture and the default modules of ACT-R [17]. The ACT-R modules communicate through buffers, which may contain a memory Chunk. The default set of modules can be partitioned into Goal, Imaginal, Declarative, Vision, Motor/Manual, Speech/Vocal, and Aural Modules. The model presented in the next section exercises the Manual, Vision, Goal, and Vocal modules. Table 1 shows corresponding buffers.

Buffers in ACT-R are the interfaces between modules. Each buffer is connected to a specific module and has a unique name. A buffer is used to relay requests for actions to its module and a module will respond to a query through its buffer. In response to a request, the module will usually generate one or more events to perform some actions or place a Chunk into the buffer. A module has access to any buffer at any time, but can only manipulate its own buffer [18].

ACT-R runs a pattern matching process that finds production rules with conditions that match the current state of the system—the left hand side of production rules. Then, tasks are performed if conditions match and the actions of production rules will be fired (so-called RHS). Productions can make a request to an ACT-R buffer and then that buffer's module will perform whatever function it provides may then place a Chunk into a buffer (summarized in Table 1 for our model). These production rules can be tested by comparing the performance, time to perform the task, accuracy in the task, of the model performing the task with the results of people doing the same task. Furthermore, we can use neurological data (fMRI) as measures of cognitive psychology.

Herbal/ACT-R generates an agent in ACT-R from a Dismal spreadsheet model represented hierarchically for a sequence of tasks and the relationship among these tasks [14]. The task representation is based upon hierarchical task analysis and GOMS. GOMS (Goals, Operators, Methods, and Selection Rules) is a high-level language in which HCI tasks can be articulated in a hierarchical form to decompose complex tasks into simpler ones [19]. In this GOMS-like cognitive user model the production rules are created from the hierarchical tree structure. The model retrieves the next node/sub-task from the declarative memory elements according to a depth-first search algorithm to complete the task. In this model, the novice model has to carry out more memory retrievals. In contrast, an expert model uses fewer declarative memory elements. We present an initial model of eyes and hands within the ACT-R cognitive architecture that can interact with Emacs in next section that complete the output direction of Figure 1.

```
(p rule1
   =goal>
    isa goal
    step 0
   =visual-location>
   ?visual>
    state free
   ==>
   +visual>
    isa move-attention
    screen-pos =visual-location
   +goal>
    isa goal
    step 1)
```

Figure 5: Sample ACT-R Production.

4 THE EMACS EYES AND HANDS MODEL

In this section we briefly describe a small model used to test and exercise the Esegman architectural additions. In this model declarative memory Chunks are created initially as the basic building blocks. We define two Chunks types, one for the target window location and one for Goal buffer to track the steps of model. This model is a static model without learning and uses the GOMS framework for HCI. The model proceeds as follow. After setting the parameters that control the general operation of the system, we define Chunk types for the model and declaring the configuration of slots that will be utilized in Chunks. The ACT-R has an ability to process visual objects on a computer screen. In this regard, two separate buffers have been defined for locations and objects. The visual object has multiple features such as color, shape, height and width. But visual location is only representing the location of these objects. Thus in ACT-R the location can be retrieved separately [20].

An ACT-R model was constructed in a way that is able to interact with the same experiment software as the human participants. The manual module provides the functionality to interact with Emacs window such as the moving courser, clicking, monitoring hand movement, and use a mouse and a keyboard. However, it requires a hook to facilitate these functionalities.

Figure 4 demonstrates the productions history according to Table 1. The critical cycle in ACT–R is when the buffers hold representations determined by the external world and internal modules, patterns in these buffers are recognized, a production fires, and the buffers are then updated for another cycle [21]. The assumption in ACT–R is that this cycle takes about 50 ms to complete—this estimate of 50 ms as the minimum cycle time for cognition has emerged in a number of cognitive architectures including Soar (Newell, 1990 [1]).

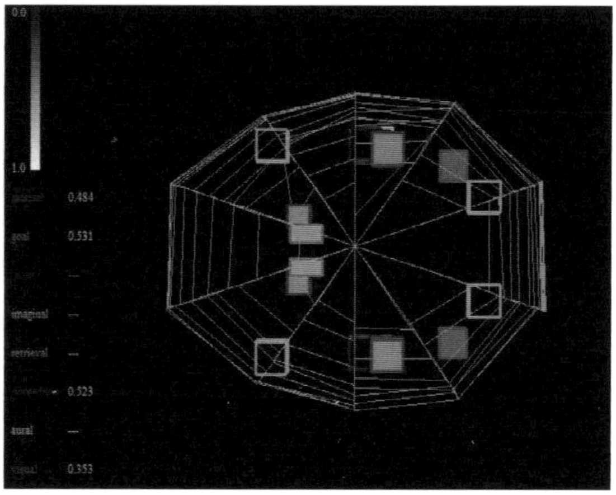

Figure 6: 3D-brain viewer, showing what parts of the brain are active at a point in the model execution.

The first production rule (Start) makes a request to the visual-location buffer. The visual-location module places the location Chunk into a visual-location buffer. Also, in the Start rule the manual module presses the keystroke. The model moves the visual attention and uses the retrieve visual location to reflect the visual object in Rule1. Figure 5 shows a sample production, the equivalent of the Rule1. This production describes operations on three buffers, goal, visual-location, and visual. Each of these buffers has a set of slots, prefixed by the '=', its values can be constrained in a standard way. On the left hand side of the production, the goal buffer is constrained to hold a goal with a given name and slot (here goal 0), and it must be found in memory. Also the visual buffer state should be free and there must be a Chunk in visual-location. On the right hand side, the current task and state slots of the goal buffer are updated (to 1) and the visual module move the attention to the address in visual-location buffer. In Rule2 model moves the mouse courser to the visual object that at the previews task moved the attention to and will click upon it in Rule3. The Ruld4 uses the vocal buffer to speak out the commands. Table 1 shows a summary of all modules and buffers that were called through the corresponding tasks.

Figure 4 shows the different time costs of productions rules. Time columns correspond to when the procedural module attempted to find a production to fire (the matched production). Figure 4 demonstrates the use of serial modules in parallel [22] because of the parallel threads of serial processing in each module. For instance, Rule2 should wait for the completion of Start rule because at 0.35 the action at which Rule2 matches was completed—the manual state will be free again. But, the Rule2 used the three modules Goal, Manual, and Vocal, which can all make a request to their buffers in parallel (three threads). The serial bottleneck of ACT-R is its buffer limitation to a single declarative unit of knowledge, Chunk, thus only a single memory can be retrieved at a time.

The ACT-R model explicitly can be a map to the physical implementation of the mind, the human brain (Figure 6) and how activation of brain areas used by the running model predict activation of the brain in human when solving a problem. Figure 6 was dveloped by ACT-R enviroment and brain associated buffers are displayed. Figure 6 shows a prefrontal region that tracks the operations in the goal buffer, a motor region that tracks operations in the manual buffer, and a vision region that tracks operations in a visual buffer that holds the problem representation.

The model will explain how these components of the mind worked to produce rational cognition. In our model four parts of the brain were active and the total amont of active times is presented in Figure 4.

Table 2: Esegman Capabilities.

Implemented	To be implemented
• Press Key • Move Courser • Click Mouse • Execute Obituary Commands	• Move Fovea (focus of visual attention) • Parse Fovea Area • Track/Find Courser • Find Icon

5 CONCLUSION

The CMIMSs research area can be exploited to help in the development of cognitive models, agents, and supporting them as users that interact with interfaces. But, it will definitely help elevate testing user interfaces, making this process more approachable and easy enough to do that it can be done and does get done. This approach of using model to test interfaces and even systems as they are built has been call by the national research council [23].

By using the Eyes and Hands model in place of a user, questions about user interface designs such as evaluating designs, changing the interface and examining the effects on task performance can be answered more easily. The Eyes and Hands model as a cognitive model approach can prove the advantages of CMIMS in HCI, and start to realize the use of model in system design [24].

In this work, instead of utilizing any methods to get the most accurate output. We use an approach to get the more human-like output and soon input. We present preliminary implementation of this proposed direction. Table 2 demonstrates the summary of our work. We were able to complete the output direction in Figure 1 and augmented the model to perform all sequence of tasks in Figure 2. We will build upon Paik et al's [14] model of the dismal task. It performs the task and learn, but does not interact with a task simulation.

6 FURTHER RESEARCH AND LIMITATIONS

To have a comprehensive cognitive model we need to add the input direction in Figure 1. This remains to be implemented fully in our model. For the input direction of Figure 1, we will have to feed ACT-R models with the information about the world from Emacs by inserting contents into the architecture visual module. In the future these models will be able to watch users, correct the discrepancy between model and user, and better predict human performance for design. These models will be useful to HCI by predicting task performance and times, assisting users, finding error patterns, and by acting as surrogate users. Also, useful for building interface agents such as Digital Elfs [25].

The model Esegman can intent with surrogate interfaces through Emacs for a wide range of systems—Emacs includes a text editor but also a web browser, a calculator, a spreadsheet tool, and even an implementation of the natural language system Eliza. Thus, we can explore a wide range of behaviors with this approach.

When we extend Esegman to include motor control mistakes, we will also have to include knowledge to recognize and correct these mistakes. This will requires breaking architecture to create human-like mistakes, knowing how to correct it. The model will also have to make mistakes in correction, and in noticing mistakes. They are relatively new types of behavior and knowledge in models, so we think we will learn a lot.

Therefore, adding error analysis to the design will merge our model with large models. However, ACT-R deliberately included limitations such as only a single memory can be retrieved at a time, only a single object can be encoded from the visual field, or only a single production is selected at each cycle to fire can make this approach challenging.

ACKNOWLEDGMENT

This work was funded partially by ONR (N00014-11-1-0275 & N00014-15-1-2275). David Reitter has provided useful comments on Emacs and Aquamacs (the Emacs version for the Mac). We wish to thank Jong Kim who provided the idea for ESegman and Dan Bothell for his assistance.

REFERENCES

[1] A. Newell, *Unified Theories of Cognition.* Cambridge, MA: Harvard University Press, 1990.

[2] J. R. Anderson, *How can the human mind exist in the physical universe?* New York, NY: Oxford University Press, 2007.

[3] F. Tehranchi and F. E. Ritter, "Connecting Cognitive Models to Interact with Human-Computer Interfaces," in *Proceedings of ICCM - 2016-14th International Conference on Cognitive Modeling*, University Park, PA: Penn State, 2016.

[4] F. E. Ritter, G. D. Baxter, G. Jones, and R. M. Young, "User interface evaluation: How cognitive models can help," in *Human-computer interaction in the new millenium*, J. Carroll, Ed., ed Reading, MA: Addison-Wesley, 2001, pp. 125-147.

[5] B. A. Myers, "User interface software tools," *ACM Transactions on Computer-Human Interaction,* vol. 2, pp. 64-103, 1995.

[6] J. E. Laird and A. Nuxoll. (2003, Soar Design Dogma. Available at http://ai.eecs.umich.edu/soar/sitemaker/docs/misc/dogma.pdf

[7] J. W. Kim, F. E. Ritter, and R. J. Koubek, "ESEGMAN: A substrate for ACT-R architecture and an Emacs Lisp application," in *Proceedings of ICCM - 2006- Seventh International Conference on Cognitive Modeling*, Trieste, Italy, 2006, p. 375.

[8] R. St. Amant, T. E. Horton, and F. E. Ritter, "Model-based evaluation of expert cell phone menu interaction," *ACM Transactions on Computer-Human Interaction,* vol. 14, p. 24 pages, 2007.

[9] F. E. Ritter, G. D. Baxter, G. Jones, and R. M. Young, "Supporting cognitive models as users," *ACM Transactions on Computer-Human Interaction,* vol. 7, pp. 141-173, 2000.

[10] F. E. Ritter and A. B. Wood, "Dismal: A spreadsheet for sequential data analysis and HCI experimentation," *Behavior Research Methods,* vol. 37, pp. 71-81, 2005.

[11] J. W. Kim and F. E. Ritter, "Learning, forgetting, and relearning for keystroke- and mouse-driven tasks: Relearning is important," *Human-Computer Interaction,* vol. 30, pp. 1-33, 2015.

[12] U. Kukreja, W. E. Stevenson, and F. E. Ritter, "RUI—Recording User Input from interfaces under Windows and Mac OS X," *Behavior Research Methods,* vol. 38, pp. 656–659, 2006.

[13] J. H. Morgan, C.-Y. Cheng, C. Pike, and F. E. Ritter, "A design, tests, and considerations for improving keystroke and mouse loggers," *Interacting with Computers,* vol. 25, pp. 242-258, 2013.

[14] J. Paik, J. W. Kim, F. E. Ritter, and D. Reitter, "Predicting user performance and learning in human-computer interaction with the Herbal compiler," *ACM Transactions on Computer-Human Interaction,* vol. 22, p. Article No.: 25, 2015.

[15] J. Paik, J. W. Kim, and F. E. Ritter, "A preliminary ACT-R compiler in Herbal," in *Proceedings of ICCM - 2009- Ninth International Conference on Cognitive Modeling*, Manchester, England, 2009, pp. 466-467.

[16] J. W. Kim, R. J. Koubek, and F. E. Ritter, "Investigation of procedural skills degradation from different modalities," in *Proceedings of the 8th International Conference on Cognitive Modeling*, Oxford, UK, 2007, pp. 255-260.

[17] F. E. Ritter, M. J. Schoelles, L. C. Klein, and S. E. Kase, "Modeling the range of performance on the serial subtraction task," in *Proceedings of the 8th International Conference on Cognitive Modeling*, Taylor & Francis/Psychology Press, 2007, pp. 299-304.

[18] D. Bothell. ACT-R 7 Reference Manual. Available at act-r.psy.cmu.edu/wordpress/wp-content/themes/ACT-R/actr7/reference-manual.pdf

[19] B. E. John and D. E. Kieras, "The GOMS family of user interface analysis techniques: Comparison and contrast," *ACM Transactions on Computer-Human Interaction,* vol. 3, pp. 320-351, 1996.

[20] D. Peebles and C. Jones, "A model of object location memory," in *Proceedings of the 36th Annual Conference of the Cognitive Science Society*, Austin, TX, 2014.

[21] J. R. Anderson, D. Bothell, M. D. Byrne, S. Douglass, C. Lebiere, and Y. Qin, "An integrated theory of the mind," *Psychological Review,* vol. 111, pp. 1036-1060, 2004.

[22] M. D. Byrne and J. R. Anderson, "Serial modules in parallel: The psychological refractory period and

perfect time-sharing.," *Psychological Review,* vol. 108, pp. 847-869, 2001.

[23] R. W. Pew, "Some history of human performance modeling," in *Integrated models of cognitive systems*, W. Gray, Ed., ed New York, NY: Oxford University Press, 2007, pp. 29-44.

[24] R. W. Pew and A. S. Mavor, Eds., *Human-system integration in the system development process: A new look*. Washington, DC: National Academy Press. http://books.nap.edu/catalog.php?record_id=11893, checked March 2012, 2007.

[25] M. Tambe, W. L. Johnson, R. M. Jones, F. Koss, J. E. Laird, P. S. Rosenbloom, *et al.*, "Intelligent agents for interactive simulation environments," *AI Magazine,* vol. 16, pp. 15-40, 1995.

Understanding the U-Shaped Curve: Central Claims and Applications for AI*

B. Briskey
Indiana University-Purdue University
Fort Wayne
brisbm02@students.ipfw.edu

M. Greidanus Romaneli
Indiana University-Purdue University
Fort Wayne
mgreidan@purdue.edu

D. Hale
Indiana University-Purdue University
Fort Wayne
haledt01@students.ipfw.edu

J. Licato
Indiana University-Purdue University
Fort Wayne
licatoj@ipfw.edu

ABSTRACT

Representational Redescription theory as proposed by Karmiloff-Smith [1992] investigates the changes in behavioral performance and "level of representation" as children experience new domains of knowledge. In order to introduce the applicability of this theory's propositions to knowledge acquisition in both children and Artificial Intelligence systems, we analyzed the experimental literature in Representational Redescription, as well as in the closely related theory of Neuroconstructivism.

1 INTRODUCTION

Investigations into how children process information have typically focused on specific factors, including biological and socio-cultural constraints, environmental cues, and innate predispositions to attend to certain stimuli. All of these factors have demonstrated important influences on how children learn and communicate new ideas and abilities. However, much of the evidence for these effects has come from observations and interpretations of behaviors. While behaviors may be readily observed and interpreted, processes taking place within the child's mind that may be influencing behavior may be quite difficult to identify. One theoretical perspective that attempts to explain these internal processes, named "representational redescription theory," seeks to explain how children can acquire representations of their external and internal environments that attain increasing levels of complexity and flexibility [Karmiloff-Smith, 1992]. Insight into this process may also have important applications for machine learning and AI, by facilitating the development of progressively more complex skills and capacities in intelligent agents. Yet, such applications can only exist if the concept of 'representation' and its change throughout development is coherent. Unfortunately, work that refers to representational redescription theory has not been consistent on the point of what it means for a representation to change.

ACM Reference format:
B. Briskey, M. Greidanus Romaneli, D. Hale, and J. Licato. 2017. Understanding the U-Shaped Curve: Central Claims and applications for AI. In *Proceedings of Modern Artificial Intelligence and Cognitive Science Conference, Fort Wayne, Indiana USA, March 2017 (MAICS'17)*, 8 pages.

We will address the confusion over what a representation is and how it changes, as predicted by representational redescription theory. This will be followed by an account of Karmiloff-Smith's original operationalizations of key concepts of the developmental curve, based on her landmark 1992 publication. We will then discuss subsequent literature on these predictions, while also clarifying the lack of consensus on how to test representational change independently from behavioral mastery. Finally, we will present alternative methods for measuring this change, in specific neuroconstructivist computational modeling, as well as possible applications of representational redescription to artificial intelligence.

2 OVERVIEW OF REPRESENTATIONAL REDESCRIPTION

Representational redescription theory, originally developed by Annette Karmiloff-Smith, attempts to explain how a child represents the external environment within their mind, changes these representations through continued interaction with the environment, and eventually reaches a higher degree of both behavioral mastery and metacognition. Karmiloff-Smith [1992] divides this process of change into three phases, characterized by two factors: the level of performance on a task, and the 'level of representation[al development],' an abstract measure whose lack of a definition is the cause of much confusion. The relation between levels of performance and representational development form what Karmiloff-Smith calls a "U-shaped curve" (Figure 1). In phase 1, performance is high but level of representation is low; the child does not possess any metacognition about the performance of that specific behavior, but he or she has learned to associate the behavior with its context through observation and feedback from the environment. As the behavior is repeated, they begin to develop a higher level of representation marked by, for instance, theory-building and generalizations. In phase 2, the level of representation within a given micro-domain goes up and is associated with lower

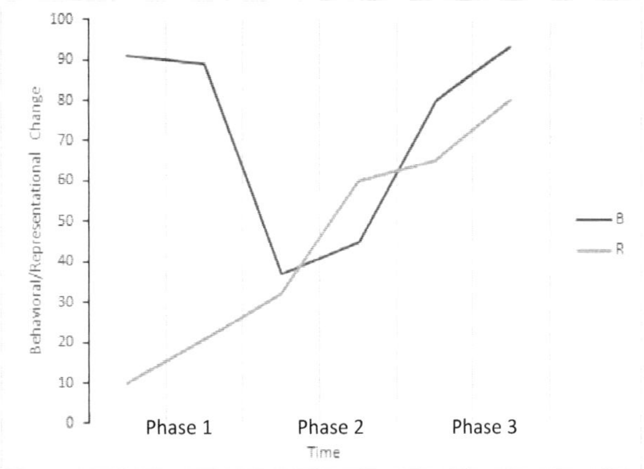

Figure 1: The theorized U-shaped curve of behavioral performance and level of redescription as a function of time, as originally presented in Karmiloff-Smith [1992]. Note the somewhat ambiguously labeled axes.

performance as a result of a higher disregard for external feedback and an increased focus on internal processes.

Finally, as the process of representational redescription continues to phase 3, the child demonstrates more representational flexibility by not only being able to reflect on and describe the rationales for their behavior, but also through accounting for exceptions to the pre-established representations. Thus, the developmental graph of a specific microdomain shows a linear development of level of representation, but at the same time a non-linear development of performance, reaching its lowest level at phase 2. A graph of the U-Shaped curve, equivalent to the one initially proposed by Karmiloff-Smith [1992], can be seen in Figure 1. This U-Shaped curve, originally presented in Karmiloff-Smith [1992] as a hypothetical model, has room for interpretation. Other authors, such as Pinker [1995], have referenced this decrease in behavior performance in other terminology.

Initial support for the change in the level of representation relied specifically on grammatical development, with changes in representation marked by the ability to analyze grammatical elements on a pronoun-noun phrase in French [Karmiloff-Smith, 1979, 1986] and the ability of separating the grammatical elements of American Sign Language (ASL) [Newport 1981]. The inference that representational change occurred in these cases stemmed primarily from the same evidence that suggests a decrease in behavioral performance.[1] In those studies, markers of less accurate behavior (e.g., breaking down a pronoun into a more complex and incorrect phase, breaking down a sign in ASL instead of delivering it fluidly) were indications that children were hyper-aware of the grammatical elements in their utterances/gestures, to the extent of prioritizing the acknowledgment of these internal processes over what was initially correct performance. Late-occurring behavioral performance errors in both examples constitute a large part of the evidence for representational change, however, Karmiloff-Smith further analyzes specific aspects of those mistakes in order to support the U-shaped curve and representational redescription. These aspects, as presented in Karmiloff-Smith [1992], were originally described as accompanying an increase in the level of complexity of representations, demonstrated by the presentation over time of abilities not previously available. They include the abilities to (1) analyze a procedure/representation into its meaningful parts, (2) identify and understand relationships between elements of a larger whole (e.g., morphemes within words), (3a) form general theories about a specific procedure or micro-domain, as well as to (3b) later correctly identify and address exceptions to such theories, (4) contrast characteristics or functions of similar elements (e.g., definite vs. indefinite articles) and (5) elaborate verbal explanations of rationales for either correct or incorrect behavior.

These specific markers of representational change, however, were not as clearly operationalized as the decrease in behavioral performance itself in supporting the U-shaped curve, and may be to blame for some inconsistencies in the research following the original publication of the theory. The confusion about the meaning of the U-shaped curve and the ambiguity of representational redescription's central claims have led to a variety of incompatible interpretations. We will now summarize these interpretations.

3 WORK ON REPRESENTATIONAL REDESCRIPTION

3.1 Language

One of the domains explored in Karmiloff-Smith [1992] was language, with an emphasis on semantic and morphosyntactic development. Critten, Pine, and Steffler [2007] are early proponents of the application of the theory to other language related microdomains, such as spelling. In their 2007 study, the lowest level of representational redescription in children's spelling development was operationalized as inflexible behavioral mastery without conscious access to the knowledge in the microdomain, while the second and third phases were characterized, respectively, by overgeneralization errors progressing to less performance errors without full rule understanding, and finally proficient task performance with complete comprehension of applicable spelling rules. The researchers were able to demonstrate a behavioral developmental curve, in which the decrease in performance was associated to an over-reliance in specific phonetic or morphological spelling strategies.

Expanding on this first study, Critten, Pine, and Messer [2013] continued to analyze representational and behavioral change within

[1] Respectively, the breakdown of the correct utterance "mes voitures" [1st person + plural possessive "my" + plural "cars"] into incorrect forms in which grammatical person and number were separated, "les miennes des voitures" [Karmiloff-Smith 1979, 1986] and the breakdown of initially "holistic" ASL signs into "staccato-like" movements, in which the parts of the sign were broken down based on its morphological markers.

the microdomains of spelling recognition and production. In the spelling recognition task, children were asked to choose between one correct and two incorrect spellings of a list of words, including regular and irregular verbs, as well as non-verbs. Performance and ability to justify their choices, as well as why the other alternatives were incorrect, were taken into account when assigning phases of representational development to children. While children in the second-lowest phase had high accuracy in choosing the correctly spelled option (following a phase of low accuracy), subsequent phases demonstrated lower accuracy due to the emergence of new mistakes (e.g., identifying [-ed] as a marker of past-tense in verbs and rejecting correct spellings of irregular verbs for lacking the suffix). Finally, in the last phase, children not only regained high performance, but were also able to explain verbally the rationale for their choices. This pattern of development, composed of a decrease in behavioral performance (marked by accuracy) due to the over-regularization of newly identified elements of language (e.g., [-ed] suffix marking past tense), is in accordance with the original propositions of the U-Shaped curve and the patterns of behavioral and representational development proposed by Karmiloff-Smith [1992].

In a similar spelling production task, the researchers presented children with a spelled word or pseudoword, and an assortment of letter magnets. Children then had to use the letter magnets in order to transform the previous word into a new word proposed by the researcher. Performance was measured in terms of their ability to accurately create the new word and verbally express their justification for both how they transformed the word and how the words differed. Successful performance of the task involved replacing the first letter of the word or pseudoword (always a consonant) with a different consonant. In this second task, providing an incorrect explanation coupled with lower task accuracy was considered by the researchers as a marker of an intermediate phase, which would correspond to phase 2 of the U-shaped curve. This spelling production task, unlike other literature on Representational Redescription and spelling development, did not directly address morphological development, while the skills tested were based purely on phonetic development and letter recognition.

Critten et al. [2007] and Critten et al. [2013] utilized children's verbalizations in order to establish phase distinctions that are not present in representational redescription theory, creating what would be a new section of phase 2 of the U-shaped curve, separating between phonological and morphological overgeneralizations and errors. This distinction appears to be specific to the spelling microdomain, and may not necessarily extend to other developmental microdomains. In proposing the subdivision, however, the researchers still relied heavily on verbal explanations, even in the phases in which children are predicted to not be able to produce them. Evidence based on children's explanations, although effective in distinguishing between implicit (phase 1 in the U-shaped curve, when children are only procedurally aware of the task) and explicit representations (phase 3 in the U-shaped curve, when children have a higher level of representation and are able to verbalize rationales for their behavior), is not sensitive to the markers of representational change in intermediary phases.

Critten, Sheriston, and Man [2016] further examined the applications of representational redescription theory in the microdomains of spelling recognition and production. Two groups of children from three different UK schools, from year 1 and year 2 respectively, performed two separate tasks. Much like Critten, Pine, and Steffler [2007], children were presented with three words, one spelled correctly and two incorrectly, and were prompted to give an explanation as to why their choice was correct and why the other two choices were not correct. In addition, children were asked to spell words that had been previously presented, although in a different order than the child's previous trial. Critten et al. [2016] operationalized representations as children's explicit explanations about spelling performance using the same evaluation criteria as Critten, Pine, and Steffler [2007]. The participants were then grouped together based on an overall level of representational development, determined by the type of explanation given for their performance on the tasks. Children in the group corresponding to phase 2 often made overgeneralization errors and therefore demonstrated representational inflexibility. The researchers maintained the subdivisions proposed in previous studies [Critten et al. 2007; Critten et al. 2013] and provided additional empirical support to a division between morphological and phonetic errors in phase 2. This categorization of groups supports the notion of the U-shaped developmental curve in representational redescription as children's explanations became more advanced as well as having better performance on spelling recognition tasks once their spelling knowledge became more flexible.

Lorandi and Karmiloff-Smith [2012], on the other hand, analyzed children's morphological knowledge in Brazilian Portuguese. They did so through recording the spontaneous occurrence of variant forms of verbs (e.g., overgeneralizations and neologisms inconsistent with the standard norm of the language), as well as through a morphological test in which children were given a nonsense grammatical base (created in accordance with common word structures in the language) and a semantic context, and were prompted to produce inflected forms of such words. While measuring the incidence of errors in these tasks, the researchers found support for an increase in performance and for children's awareness of morphological markers of location, agency, and tense, among others. Although the results in this study do not make evident a U-shaped curve of behavioral performance, they support an increase in level of representation in accordance with the claims of representational redescription theory (e.g., in children's ability to identify and utilize morphological markers in novel productions).

Evidence from microdomains within language, as a whole, indicate the existence of a U-shaped curve very similar (if not equivalent) to the one proposed in representational redescription theory. Still, the simultaneous development of some of these microdomains (such as phonetics, morphology, and letter recognition in the spelling tasks described) and the reliance on verbal explanations provide confounding factors. Thus, these methodologies, although shedding some light into the relationship between representational redescription and language development, do not offer generalizable, agreed-upon insights into this process.

3.2 Mathematics

While representational redescription is argued to be domain-specific — that is, representations in each micro-domain undergo the developmental process independently — the investigations seeking to support or refute the theory's claims vary greatly in terms of domains of knowledge analyzed. One of the fields of experimental research mentioned by Karmiloff-Smith [1992] was arithmetic. Voutsina [2012] examined the presence of markers of representational redescription through testing children's ability to identify number pairs, i.e. what numbers can be added together to obtain a specified number. A qualitative analysis of ten 5-6 year old children's strategies in finding all pairs of numbers revealed that children's explanations of behavioral strategies changed over the course of the study, based on a set number of phases determined by the researchers. Children in the first phase were able to distinctly view the procedures for solving each step; this first step involved children only trying to solve what number pairs made up the number bond without regard to linking the different number pairs together. Later, in the second and third phases, children were able to manipulate and link different aspects of knowledge. After observing how they solved the problem, children developed a strategy for organizing number pairs for number bonds. For example, for the number bond "9", children would replace [0+9] for [9+0], in a strategy called swapping, rather than randomly organizing number bonds, such as [2+7] and then [4+5].

Thus, Voutsina [2012] provides evidence for a constant increase in level of redescription, marked by the emergence of new abilities and strategies from phase to phase. Furthermore, throughout the study, strategies used by the children (such as the ordering strategy) resulted in constant behavioral performance. Considering also that even in the first level of representation, described by the researchers, there were already signs of a higher level of redescription; Voutsina [2012] provides evidence for what appears to be the upwards slope of both behavioral performance and level of redescription. It does not, however, provide evidence supporting or refuting the decrease in performance characteristic of the U-shaped curve, as there was no operationalization for verifying the process of spontaneous redescription of knowledge.

Likewise, Simpson and Stehlikova [2006] examined representational redescription in the domain of Algebra. Rather than with children, this study observed a college student's development across a span of three-years in a case study. Initially, the participant followed strict procedures in order to solve the problems, such as solely adding up the numbers in the problems. The "second shift of attention," or the first explicit level, was operationalized as using the knowledge gained from the familiar procedure towards similar problems that would also use a similar procedure. During the study, as the participant gained a more in-depth understanding of the representation, she made errors; eventually the participant realized the errors and corrected them. As time went on, she verbalized the relationships between some of the numbers before moving to the last phase of representational redescription where she utilized her knowledge about the problems and procedures the professor gave to similar, extra problems and the operations needed to solve them. This participant's performance during the study supports the existence of the U-shaped developmental curve in representational redescription theory. Despite this support, there was no operationalization for verifying the process of spontaneous redescription of knowledge; Simpson and Stehlikova [2006] acknowledged that there was no spontaneous redescription of knowledge, as the participant did not suddenly gain an insight to utilize a specific abstract algebra strategy (z-subtraction) even though she realized and corrected her errors. Even though there was no spontaneous redescription of knowledge, support for the U-shaped developmental curve in Simpson and Stehlikova [2006] was found as the participant's performance at first decreased before increasing.

3.3 Drawing

The domain of drawing involves representations; these representations can be modified and applied to various drawing microdomains. In Picard and Vinter [2006], it was hypothesized that exposure to a model would increase performance in an associated task. Children were tasked with drawing pictures with components that either had no separation or separation by two parts or multiple separations. It was discovered that breaking down knowledge helped change the representation from implicit to explicit; through this decomposition process redescription could occur. During decomposition, children made new knowledge connections such as being able to identity and draw the different parts of the drawing, indicative of knowledge being redescribed.

Similarly to Picard and Vinter [2006], Hollis and Low [2005] investigated representational redescription in the drawing microdomain. The purpose was to investigate environmental constraints that impacted the flexibility of representational redescription in the drawing domain. The study had 315 children, whose ages ranged from 6 to 9 years old. The participants were tasked with drawing pictures of a typical house and person before being tasked with drawing a picture of a "pretend person." Afterwards, researchers asked the participants to talk about their "pretend person" and later put the children into either the distraction condition, draw alone condition, or the explanation about why this is a "pretend person" condition.

The participants were tested a total of four times. The results from Hollis and Low [2005] support representational redescription. It was observed that children aged 6-7 were at the beginning phase of redescription; their procedures were inflexible. This changed over time, however, when their knowledge became more flexible after exposure to the explanation condition; this condition was associated with a greater rate drawing modification during the middle of the drawing process. This change in knowledge, from inflexible performance with few mistakes, to flexible performance with many errors, is in support of the U-shaped developmental curve.

3.4 Block Balancing Tasks

Similar to the language domain, representational redescription has been widely studied in the block balancing microdomain, where children are tasked with balancing blocks on a beam. Messer, Pine, and Butler [2008] hypothesized that representations are similar in a domain, even if the tasks vary. Children in an equivalent of phase two of representational development tended to have lower performance than children at later representational levels, even though they used consistent strategies to try to solve the block balancing task. Although the children utilized the same strategies in order to solve the block balancing task, the children who had not yet redescribed their knowledge had more errors while solving the task, in comparison to children who redescribed some of the knowledge. This is in contrast to children at the first phase who could not explain why their behavior on a task but still had high behavioral performance. This change in knowledge, from inflexible performance with few mistakes, to flexible performance with many errors, along with the decrease in performance for children at the abstraction level, supports the U-shaped developmental curve.

Representational change was operationalized as a difference in performance in tasks. Cheung and Wong [2011] hypothesized that participants would be unaware that they transferred the strategy of a geometric-center theory for balancing the blocks to different tasks. Behavioral performance was operationalized by how many times children successfully placed blocks in the middle of the beam, in the middle before moving them, and only in the center area of the beam for each block trial. Eight of the twelve participants utilized geometric-center theory across the task; this theory states that children believe that all objects can be balanced at the center. Despite utilizing this strategy, children were unaware of this knowledge, supporting the hypothesis; they tried to complete the task but were unable to explain what their strategy utilized. Although the U-shaped pattern did not appear in the study, Cheung and Wong [2011] argued that the absence of the U-shaped curve does not discredit the representational redescription model, as it is not the main premise behind representational redescription. Other researchers, however, have utilized this absence of a U-Shaped curve in their data as a basis for refuting Representational Redescription theory [Krist, Horz, and Schonfeld, 2005].

Krist, Horz, and Schonfeld [2005] disputed representational redescription in the block balancing task due to the absence of the U-shaped developmental curve. The U-shaped curve was operationally defined as children utilizing the geometric-centric theory during the block balancing task. The study tasked sixty five children, between 4 and 8 years old, with balancing wooden blocks, evenly and unevenly weighted, on a beam. In order to not influence the theories that the children made while completing the task, researchers did not prompt children with questions such as if some blocks are "unbalanceable." Rather, the researchers asked the children why/how blocks can be balanced. It was predicted that success with the task would follow the U-shaped curve with the unevenly weighted blocks: a decrease in performance subsequently followed by an increase due to the redescription of block knowledge from correct block readjustments. This change in performance would be indicative of the children's representational change from the first explicit level (E1) to the later levels (E2 and E3). Success with evenly weighted blocks, however, was predicted to either stay the same or increase with children's age.

Results in Krist et al. [2005], however, showed no support for the U-shaped curve. While performance success improved with evenly weighted blocks, in unevenly weighted blocks performance success decreased along with children's correct block rearrangements. Kris et al. [2005] explained this lack of evidence due to differences in the methodology utilized in Karmiloff-Smith's *On Modularity*; Krist et al. [2005] had more participants, a standardized system to measure children's performance, and did not prompt the participants to make predictions but rather why/how blocks can be balanced in contrast to the original study. Additionally, these results differed due to the fact that the theory of representational redescription has not made clear an operationalization for verifying the process of spontaneous redescription of knowledge, which resulted in these studies using diverging, and often conflicting, methodologies. Despite criticisms and lacking evidence for the U-shaped curve, Krist et al. [2005] advocated for finding domains representational redescription can occur in, rather than throwing out representational redescription theory. Although skeptical, Krist et al. [2005] acknowledged a possible connection between representational redescription and "modern connectionism with developmental neuropsychology," or neuroconstructivism.

3.5 Neuroconstructivism

Achieving a consensus regarding what constitutes a "representation," along with how such a representation might adapt or change, appears to be a critical problem when testing representational redescription. In the studies previously described, behavior has been linked with encoded information states, i.e. representations, effectively associating changes in behavior with changes of these representations. In addition, verbal reports of one's understanding can lead to alterations of this understanding, and only the representations that can be verbalized may be accounted for with this methodology. So far there has been no direct way to measure representational change within human participants. However, Karmiloff-Smith [1992] mentions that computational modeling may provide important insights into specific brain processes that cannot be measured through other experimental means.

The theory of neuroconstructivism may provide some assistance with quantifying representations. A central assertion of this theory is that cognition affects the development of the brain, and the current state of the brain constrains cognitive development [Mareschal, et al. 2007; Polk & Farah 1998; Sirois, et al. 2008; Westermann, et al. 2007]. It is because of this interdependent relationship that any theory regarding cognitive function should be informed by underlying biological activity without reducing all

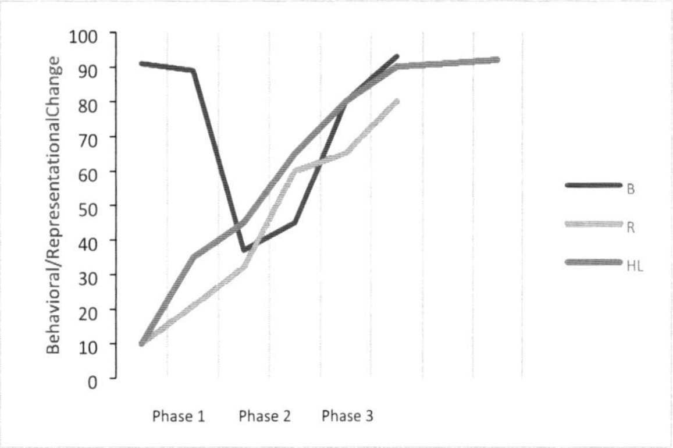

Figure 2: Conceptual comparison of a Neuroconstructivist model from Westermann and Ruh (2012) and the U-shaped curve, as originally presented by Karmiloff-Smith. Hidden layer development (HL) is comparable to representational development.

cognition to simply biological function. By investigating neural function, through the use of computational modeling, and the relationships between levels of description, such as behavior in relation to the state of a neural model, it might be possible to observe representational change in a more direct manner.

Various computational models have been developed with the intent to simulate neural function in a way that mimics observed human behavior, and these models might then provide insights into human neural functioning. One such model is used in Westermann [1998] to simulate brain activity in a way that closely approximates human learning of English past tense verbs. The model consists of a large number of nodes acting as an idealized version of a neural network. Nodes are assembled into an input layer, responding to a specific stimulus, a hidden layer that modifies the outputs of the model, and an output layer. In the neuroconstructivist model, the number of nodes present in the model is modified, in addition to the weights of the connections between nodes. In this way, the model modifies its structure by constantly evaluating each node in the hidden layer, and each of these nodes are replaced if they are found to be contributing to a large amount of errors according to certain algorithms operating within the system. Because each node in the hidden layer only responds to certain inputs, each node has a certain "receptive" field for which the node will activate, and modification of the hidden layer alters these fields. In this way, the model learns how to reproduce a large amount of past tense verbs when provided with the present tense version, and this is accomplished by changing the structure of the network in order to more effectively represent information.

After exposing the model to many different verbs, both regular and irregular, different trends about the model and its performance can be observed. In Westermann [1998], it was discovered that the model, which starts with only two nodes in the hidden layer, develops receptive fields that may overlap, implying that some nodes may respond to the same input as other nodes; however, there may be many inputs that are exclusive to either node. The hidden layer is described as a type of "memory" by the author, which responds to the identity of certain verbs rather than just the structural qualities of the word.

Additionally, Westermann and Ruh [2012] continued experimentation with this model and past tense acquisition, discovering that as the model was exposed to more verbs, the nodes in the hidden layer became more specialized to either regular or irregular verb forms. In addition, this model demonstrated U-shaped performance, i.e. failing to reproduce verbs that had been produced accurately at an earlier time. Model performance was then compared to results of previous studies involving human participants completing similar tasks, and a significant correlation was reported [Westermann & Ruh 2012].

The specific properties of this model seem to have implications for understanding cognitive development within humans. First, the late-occurring errors observed in both the model and human participants seem to indicate that there are similar processes taking place in both contexts. The hidden layer is also of interest in that the structural change to the model may indicate a change in how the model represents the information presented to it. In this way, the number of hidden units, the degree of specialization among these units, and the receptive field that each node possesses all seem to be direct indications of representational change and development at the level of a neural network. If this is the case, then there appears to be evidence for an increase in the complexity of representations across developmental time in the form of increased nodes in the hidden layer of the model (see Figure 2 for a visual depiction of this concept, as originally presented by Karmiloff-Smith which allows room for interpretation). The hidden layer also starts with very broad receptive fields (two nodes accounting for all inputs) that become increasingly complex in order to compensate for ineffective performance of the current network. This seems to mirror representational redescription on the cognitive level in response to exceptions to current theories.

By developing a computational model with similar behavioral qualities as human participants, inferences into how the brain and mind might be developing may be formed. However, this specific neuroconstructivist model only operates within the domain of English past-tense verb acquisition. In order to provide further insights into the other domains previously mentioned in this paper, it would be necessary to construct models that can operate within these domains. It may also be the case that such modeling can be applied to other fields of study, particularly those that utilize more advanced neural network models, such as artificial intelligence.

4 APPLICATIONS TO ARTIFICIAL INTELLIGENCE

Given the current popularity of brain-inspired computational representations (e.g., deep neural networks and deep reinforcement learners), knowledge about how representations develop and change in human brains is more relevant than ever. Taken together, the neuroconstructivist model and representational redescription theory offer a unique approach for the design and study of artificial intelligence. As demonstrated in Westermann and Ruh's [2012] model, representational change may provide a way for a machine to develop effective representations when presented with novel stimuli. This may provide a significant advantage over fixed programming, in that adaptation to open environments would become possible. By changing how information is stored, artificially intelligent agents may become better able to adapt to their environment, leading to more efficient automation with broader, more human-like capabilities.

Conversely, artificial intelligence research might also provide insights into the representational redescription theory that the current data with human participants has not yet been able to address. In the U-shaped curve, for instance, one of the main markers of the increase in the level of representation in phase 2 is a decrease in developmental performance. While this decrease in performance is adequate behavioral evidence for the curve, it does not sufficiently support the claim of representational change. Utilizing AI models in testing the existence of the U-shaped curve would allow for a clear, measurable, and observable separation between performance and the representations that facilitate behavior.

Other critical aspects must be considered when using artificially intelligent agents to observe representational change within different domains. As mentioned above, the neuroconstructivist model is only designed for learning past-tense forms of English verbs. Using neural models that can alter connection weights in addition to the structure of the network itself in the context of agents that can manipulate physical objects may assist in explaining the differences observed between studies investigating children's performance on the block balancing task. In fact, many other domains and tasks may be investigated in this manner.

5 CONCLUSIONS

The confusion on the meaning of the three phases and the ambiguity of representational redescription's central claims have led to a variety of incompatible interpretations, particularly with respect to the correct meaning and use of the U-shaped curve. There is a lack of generalized consensus among previous studies about what constitutes representational change in the context of this theory and finding means to test for this change that do not rely on the behavioral component of the U-shaped curve. The majority of prior studies did not operationalize representational change effectively as they based representational change solely off of observable behaviors. In this paper, we hoped to decrease the confusion about representation in Representational Redescription Theory. By examining neuroconstructivism in relation to representational redescription, representational change can be quantified without dependence on behavior as this theory states that cognition affects brain development; as knowledge becomes redescribed, the number of nodes increase, the nodes in the hidden layer become more specialized, and each node gains a receptive field, indicative of representational change. Thus, the theory of neuroconstructivism fills in the gaps in the central claims of representational redescription, as well as decreasing the confusion over what a representation is.

In this paper, we have surveyed the literature on representational redescription theory and the closely related neuroconstructivist theory, finding that they both (when properly interpreted) predict the existence of a U-shaped curve in the development of mental representations. We claim that this striking fact has implications for AI research, especially as the field continues to be dominated by increasingly massive neural-like networks. Namely, computational representations that claim to be realistic models of the mind must, at a minimum, be able to show how representations and performance match the predictions set out by representational redescription theory. In future work, we hope to expand on these implications for AI research.

REFERENCES

[1] Cheung, C., & Wong, W. (2011). Understanding conceptual development along the implicit–explicit dimension: Looking through the lens of the representational redescription model. Child Development, 82(6), 2037-2052. doi:10.1111/j.1467-8624.2011.01657.x

[2] Critten, S., Sheriston, L., & Mann, F. (2016). Young children's spelling representations and spelling strategies. Learning & Instruction, 4634-44.

[3] Critten, S., Pine, K. J., & Messer, D. J. (2013). Revealing children's implicit spelling representations. British Journal Of Developmental Psychology, 31(2), 198-211. doi:10.1111/bjdp.12000

[4] Critten, S., Pine, K., & Steffler, D. (2007). Spelling development in young children: A case of representational redescription?. Journal Of Educational Psychology, 99(1), 207-220. doi:10.1037/0022-0663.99.1.207

[5] Hollis, S., & Low, J. (2005). Karmiloff-Smith's RRM distinction between adjunctions and redescriptions: It's about time (and children's drawings). British Journal Of Developmental Psychology, 23(4), 623-644. doi:10.1348/026151005X35390

[6] Krist, H., Horz, H., & Schönfeld, T. (2005). Children's block balancing revisited: No evidence for representational redescription. Swiss Journal Of Psychology / Schweizerische Zeitschrift Für Psychologie / Revue Suisse De Psychologie, 64(3), 183-193. doi:10.1024/1421-0185.64.3.183

[7] Lorandi, A., & Karmiloff-Smith, A. (2012). From sensitivity to awareness: morphological knowledge and the Representational Redescription model. Letras De Hoje, 47(1), 6-16.

[8] Mareschal, D., Johnson, M. H., Sirois, S., Spratling, M. W., Thomas, M.S.C., & Westermann, G. (2007). Neuroconstructivism: How the brain constructs cognition. Oxford, New York: Oxford University Press.

[9] Messer, D. J., Pine, K. J., & Butler, C. (2008). Children's Behaviour and Cognitions across Different Balance Tasks. Learning And Instruction, 18(1), 42-53

[10] Patkowski, M. (2013). The critical period and parameter setting in five cases of delayed L1 acquisition. EUROSLA Yearbook, 13, 1–21. https://doi.org/10.1075/eurosla.13.03pat

[11] Picard, D., & Vinter, A. (2006). Decomposing and connecting object representations in 5- to 9-year-old children's drawing behaviour. British Journal Of Developmental Psychology, 24(3), 529-545. doi:10.1348/026151005X49836

[12] Pinker, S. (1995). *The language instinct: The new science of language and mind* (Vol. 7529). Penguin UK.

[13] Polk, T. A., & Farah, M. J. (1998). The neural development and organization of letter recognition: Evidence from functional neuroimaging, computational modeling, and behavioral studies. Proceedings of the National Academy of Sciences, 95(3), 847–852.

[14] Simpson, A., & Stehlíková, N. (2006). Apprehending Mathematical Structure: A Case Study of Coming to Understand a Commutative Ring. Educational Studies In Mathematics, 61(3), 347-371.

[15] Sirois, S., Spratling, M., Thomas, M. S. C., Westermann, G., Mareschal, D., & Johnson, M. H. (2008). Précis of Neuroconstructivism: How the Brain Constructs Cognition. Behavioral and Brain Sciences, 31(3). https://doi.org/10.1017/S0140525X0800407X

[16] Voutsina, C. (2012). Procedural and conceptual changes in young children's problem solving. Educational Studies In Mathematics, 79(2), 193-214. doi:10.1007/s10649-011-9334-1

[17] Westermann, G. (1998). Emergent modularity and U-shaped learning in a Constructivist neural network learning the English past tense. Proceedings of the 20th Annual Conference of the Cognitive Science Society, 1998.

[18] Westermann, G., Mareschal, D., Johnson, M. H., Sirois, S., Spratling, M. W., & Thomas, M. S. C. (2007). Neuroconstructivism. Developmental Science, 10(1), 75–83. https://doi.org/10.1111/j.1467-7687.2007.00567.x

[19] Westermann, G., & Ruh, N. (2012). A Neuroconstructivist Model of Past Tense Development and Processing. Psychological Review, 119(3), 649–667. https://doi.org/10.1037/a0028258

[20] Xie, K., Fox, G. E., Liu, J., Lyu, C., Lee, J. C., Kuang, H., … Tsien, J. Z. (2016). Brain Computation Is Organized via Power-of-Two-Based Permutation Logic. Frontiers in Systems Neuroscience, 10. https://doi.org/10.3389/fnsys.2016.00095

Is there a place for Machine Learning in Law?

Stephan Ralescu
CETANA, LLC
ralescu@gmail.com

Anca Ralescu
Senior Member IEEE
EECS Department, machine learning 0030
University of Cincinnati
Cincinnati, OH 45221, USA
Anca.Ralescu@uc.edu

Abstract

Research in artificial intelligence and law goes back approximately 40 years. It remains largely based on formal logic, including non-monotonic logic, case-based reasoning, and logic programming. However, some researchers in and practitioners of law have argued in favor of quantitative approaches (e.g. probability) to account for uncertainties in legal arguments. Other researchers have pointed some of the shortcomings of the current artificial intelligence and law research, e.g. inability to take context into account. At the same time, machine learning has made huge inroads in many different fields and applications, and therefore, the question is whether machine learning has anything to offer to the theory, and, equally important, the practice of law. As a position paper, this is a preliminary study towards the exploration of a synergistic integration of current artificial intelligence approaches in law, with machine learning approaches. It puts forward the idea that formal, logic-based approaches, currently very popular the Artificial Intelligence & Law research, could benefit from an extension with a machine learning component, and discusses some ways in which machine learning could be integrated into these approaches.

Introduction

When it comes to machine learning and law, there are two, quite unrelated, directions of study. On one hand, researchers are interested in legal issues raised by the research in machine learnig. For example, the symposium *Machine Learning and the Law*, held in conjunction with NIPS-2016[1], had as goal to *"explore the key themes of privacy, liability, transparency and fairness specifically as they relate to the legal treatment and regulation of algorithms and data*. On the other hand, the second direction is that of actually use of machine learning *in* law research and practice.

Stimulated on one hand, by progresses, as well as by shortcomings of artificial intelligence approaches in law (as perceived by various researchers), and on the other hand, by the tremendous recent machine learning succeses in many different directions (not including law), this paper suggests that there is scope for using machine learning in law, and moreover, that a formal treatment may be used towards this end.

The paper is inspired by work on logic-based formalization of legal reasoning, (Prakken and Sartor 1996), (Prakken and Sartor 1997), (Prakken and Sartor 1998), (Prakken and Sartor 2002), (Sartor 2002), as well as by ideas from (Tillers 2011) (Tillers 1993), (Franklin 2012) making the case for continuous mathematics tools (probability, mathematical evidence, fuzzy sets and logic), and the promise[2] that machine learning holds for law. An example of a predictive system can be found in (Campbell et al. 2016), for the restricted area of patent law.

As in many areas of research, ranging from science, engineering, medicine, and social sciences including the legal field, artificial intelligence has brought about possibilities, which excited some, intrigued others. Pioneering work done by Edwina Rissland and her students and collaborators, (Rissland and Skalak 1991), (Skalak and Rissland 1992), and Hafner and Berman (Hafner 1978), (Berman and Hafner 1993) has gone a long way towards understanding the promise and challenges that face formalization, with goal of developing a computer system, of legal reasoning.

Artificial intelligence and law

Formal logic is the approach of choice for artificial intelligence and Law, as evidenced by a wealth of articles, including those already mentioned, and others, (Bench-Capon 1997), (Prakken and Sartor 1996), (Prakken and Sartor 1997), (Prakken and Sartor 1998),published in a series of artificial intelligence journals, including the specialized journal of *Artificial Intelligence and Law*[3]. A critical review of the logic-based approach can be found in (Prakken and Sartor 2002).

Moreover, analyzing the current results, Franklin (Franklin 2012) lists challenges, not yet met by current artificial intelligence approaches in law, for formalization of legal reasoning. These challenges include:

[1] Annual meeting of the Neural Information Processing Society

[2] According to Google's Rob Craft *We are currently at year zero of the machine learning revolution.* (Singh 2016)

[3] https://link.springer.com/journal/10506

1. *"The open-textured or fuzzy nature of language (and of legal concepts)"*
2. *"Degrees of similarity and analogy"*
3. *"The representation of context"*
4. *"The symbol-grounding problem"*
5. *"The representation of causation, conditionals and counterfactuals"*
6. *"The balancing of reasons"*
7. *"Probabilistic (or default or non-monotonic) reasoning (including problems of priors, the weight of evidence and reference classes)"*
8. *"Issues of the discrete versus the continuous"*
9. *"Understanding"*

Franklin discusses the use of fuzzy set based approaches, to capture the nature of some concepts, or the similarity of a case to precedents. As an example, he considers, the concept 'vehicle', in the ordinance "No vehicles are allowed in the park", which obviously would refer first and foremost to cars, less to motorcycles/bicycles, and even less to roller skates. A fuzzy set of vehicles, defined by a membership function $\mu_{vehicle} : \mathcal{U} \to [0, 1]$, where $\mathcal{U}$ denotes a universe of discourse of 'things', would assign different degrees to *cars, motorcycles, bicycles, roller skates*, for example, respectively

$$\mu_{vehicle}(v) = \begin{cases} 1 & \text{if } v \text{ is a car} \\ 0.8 & \text{if } v \text{ is a motorcycle} \\ 0.5 & \text{if } v \text{ is a bicycle} \\ 0.1 & \text{if } v \text{ is "roller skates"} \end{cases}$$

The ordinance has as goal prevention of accidents in the park, and by consequence, the definition of the fuzzy set is meant to reflect the common sense knowledge that cars can cause serious accidents, motorcycles less, bicycles even less, and so on. The actual assignment of membership degrees is seen in (Franklin 2012) as one of the difficulties of adopting a fuzzy set based approach. However, the researchers in fuzzy systems know that while this issue is not trivial, fuzzy set based approaches have a rich collection of choices to address it, including, *learning* the membership function. Furthermore, it should be noted that (1) in many applications, the relative magnitudes of the membership degrees matter more than their actual magnitude, and (2) where the absolute magnitudes matter, they could and should be subject to a (machine) learning approach.

The issue of similarity is of utmost importance in legal reasoning and to illustrate the difficulties in similarity evaluation (Franklin 2012) refers to a celebrated case, *Popov v Hayashi*, centered on the issue of *possesion*.[4] The two precedents considered for the case, both involved hunting: in the first, hunting a fox with hounds did not confer rights of possession; in the second, the whale harpooned by one individual, and found by another on the beach was found, based on customs of whalers, to belong to the man who harpooned it not to the one who found it. The decision in *Popov v Hayashi* was that Popov and Hayashi had equal interests in the ball; to reach such a decision, issues such as *context, continuity* play an important role, and an intelligent (artificial intelligence) legal system must be able to deal with such issues. According to Franklin (Franklin 2012), none of the current artificial intelligence in law approaches, based on similarity with the two precedents, could have actually reached this decision. Achieving it, would require quantitative approaches including probability, fuzzy sets, and evidential reasoning, which may go a long way to complement logic based approaches towards an artificial intelligence based law systems.

Machine learning in rules with legal values

In (Sartor 2002) several (legal) theory constructors are given in terms of rules and (legal) values promoted by them, in order to formalize the legal argument. First *factors*, i.e. abstract features of a case which may influence the outcome of the case, are considered. Following (Berman and Hafner 1993), *values* underlying a case are introduced. For example, πLiv stands for the fact " π was pursuing his livelihood", (π denotes the *plaintiff*), or $\delta Nposs$ stands for "δ (δ denotes defendant) was not in possession". A legal value V is an objective pursued by the legal argument. Examples of values include *Less Litigation(LLit), More productivity(MProd), More security of possession(MSec)*. A case may be formalized as a collection of rules such as

$$\begin{array}{l} [\pi Liv \Longrightarrow \Pi] \text{ promotes } Mprod \\ [\pi land \Longrightarrow \Pi] \text{ promotes } Msec \\ [\pi Nposs \Longrightarrow \Pi] \text{ promotes } LLit \\ [\delta Liv \Longrightarrow \Delta] \text{ promotes } Mprod \end{array} \quad (1)$$

where $\pi Liv \Longrightarrow \Pi$ means "*π was pursuing his livelihood is a reason why π should have a legal remedy against δ*".

To formalize, following (Sartor 2002), let $\{V_i, i = 1, \dots n\}$ be a collection of legal values, where a *minimal approach to ordering* is adopted, such that the theory may specify

$$V_i < V_j; \quad i \neq j$$

More over, it is assumed that

$$V_i < V_i \cup \bigcup_{j \neq i} V_j \quad (2)$$

[4]http://www.miblaw.com/lawschool/popov-v-hayashi-2002-wl-31833731-cal-super-ct-2002/: Popov v. Hayashi 2002 WL 31833731 (Cal. Super. Ct. 2002) **Case Name:** Popov v. Hayashi **Plaintiff:** Popov **Defendant:** Hayashi **Citation:** 2002 WL 31833731 (Cal. Super. Ct. 2002) **Issue:** Whether the defendant is liable for conversion when he picked up the home run ball that was dropped by the plaintiff. **Key Facts:** Barry Bonds 73rd Homerun. The plaintiff caught the ball in the upper portion of his glove but was tackled and thrown to the ground by the crowd. The ball fell out and the defendant picked it up and put it in his pocket. The plaintiff sued for conversion. **Holding:** The plaintiff and defendant had equitable claims and could not prove their case either way. **Reasoning:** Although the plaintiff proved intent to possess the ball, he could not establish that he would have fully possessed the ball had he not been tackled by the crowd. If he could have established this, his pre-possessory interest would have constituted a qualified right to possession which can support a cause of action for conversion. **Judgment:** The ball was sold for $450,000 and the proceeds were divided equally.

Replacing $\cup$ in (2) by the maximum $\vee$, and using $\wedge$ for minimum, it follows that

$$V_i < \max\left(V_i, \bigvee_{j\neq i} V_j\right) \quad V_i > \min\left(V_i, \bigwedge_{j\neq i} V_j\right) \tag{3}$$

Equality of values must also be specified as part of the theory. Then, enlarging upon (Sartor 2002), given the rules

$$\begin{array}{l} \lceil\alpha_1 \Longrightarrow \gamma\rceil \text{ promotes } V_1 \\ \lceil\alpha_2 \Longrightarrow \gamma\rceil \text{ promotes } V_2 \\ \ldots \\ \lceil\alpha_n \Longrightarrow \gamma\rceil \text{ promotes } V_n \end{array} \tag{4}$$

one can construct the following:

$$\lceil\alpha_1\&\alpha_2\&\ldots\&\alpha_n \Longrightarrow \gamma\rceil$$

promotes

$$[\min(V_1, V_2, \ldots, V_n), \max(V_1, V_2, \ldots, V_n)]$$

Thus, considered together, rules (4) promote *at least the smallest* value, *at most the largest* value, and possibly *values in between*, i.e., those which lie in $[\min(V_1, V_2, \ldots, V_n), \max(V_1, V_2, \ldots, V_n)]$. All promoted values can be expressed as convex combinations of $V_1, V_2, \ldots, V_n$, that is,

$$\lceil\alpha_1\&\ldots\&\alpha_n \Longrightarrow \gamma\rceil \text{ promotes } w_1V_1 + \cdots + w_nV_n \tag{5}$$

where $w_i \geq 0, i = 1, \ldots, n$ and $w_1 + \cdots + w_n = 1$. For different values of $w_i, i = 1, \cdots, n$ (5) can generate any subset of the set of values $\{V_i, i = 1, \cdots, n\}$. Interpreted as a probability, $w_i = Prob($ to promote $V_i)$ can be obtained through a *machine learning algorithm* based on history of (similar) cases.

The mechanism outlined above has the effect of producing a *continuum* of legal values (even though to begin with, these form a discrete set), which in turn may lead to a *continuum* of possible decisions.

Inference and machine learning - legal theory and practice

This section touches upon the issue of inference in legal reasoning. It takes its cue from (Tillers 1993) and references therein, according to which *"the governing assumption of this body of law has been that all or practically all facts are uncertain and that proof of facts is always or almost always a matter of probabilities"*. The *necessity* of mathematical models of uncertainty (currently missing) in legal reasoning is furthermore discussed in (Tillers 2011) and (Franklin 2012) among others.

Since complex arguments about inferences from evidence rest on almost innumerable subjective judgments, (Tillers 2011) proposes several purposes for mathematical and formal analysis of inconclusive arguments about uncertain factual questions in legal proceedings, as follows:

1. "To *predict* how judges and jurors will resolve factual issues in litigation.
2. To devise methods that can *replace* existing methods of argument and deliberation in legal settings about factual issues.
3. To devise methods that *mimic* conventional methods of argument about factual issues in legal settings.
4. To devise methods that *support* or facilitate existing, or ordinary, argument and deliberation about factual issues in legal settings by legal actors (such as judges, lawyers and jurors) who are generally illiterate in mathematical and formal analysis and argument."
5. To devise methods that *capture some* but not all 'ingredients of argument' in legal settings about factual questions questions.

It can be claimed that achieving these purposes *predict - replace - mimic - support* falls into the machine learning realm, requiring machine learning algorithms of possibly different levels of sophistication.

Machine learning in the practice of law – the low hanging fruit

From the point of view of a typical approach to machine learning, data (usually, a lot) is needed to construct a machine learning algorithm - a classifier, or a clustering algorithm. Usually, such data is thought of as history on which to base future predictions. The need to take into account *history* is discussed in the conclusion section of (Sartor 2002), which suggests a *history-subtheory*. That would add a 'sense of history' to a case, predicting a judge's handling of a case based on that judge's history of opinions and their context. All of these could be attacked by machine learning methods. Issues on the representation of an argument, of an opinion, measures of similarity must be considered. Law, like other social sciences, seldom uses a *quantitative* language, rather, it is *text-based*. This means that solving the issues mentioned above is not trivial.

Using machine learning to analyze judges' personalities and ruling tendencies helps tailor pleadings to their personalities. Machine learning helps analyze attorney personalities and use those to decide who writes what in a law firm, and evaluate a firm's previous work and identify strength, weaknesses and faults.

This added dimension to legal theory and practice straddles several disciplines, including psychometry, representation of uncertainty (e.g., fuzzy logic to represent meanings of utterances, and similarity measures), probabilistic (point, interval valued or imprecise probabilities), all to be used in machine learning to build *predictive algorithms of behavior*.

As a recent example, with far reaching consequences, of behavior prediction, comes from the 2016 USA presidential elections: Cambridge Analytica[5] used machine learning to *specifically target* independents and other voters disenchanted with the status quo, with messages that appealed to *their* personalities. A similar system that does the same - for judges, courts - could help build a litigation strategy, tailor language, and develop legal reasoning to the personality of the particular court.

[5] `https://cambridgeanalytica.org/`

Conclusion

We have discussed some preliminary ideas on the challenges/issues that law research faces, which could be approached from an machine learning point of view. This paper only hinted at these issues and possible solutions using machine learning. Much is to be done, including a very thorough understanding of quantitiative ideas in legal theory put forward by researchers in the legal profession.

Acknowledgments

The authors are grateful for the reviewers comments, some very enthusiastic, some very negative, on the first draft of this paper. All served to stimulate the authors' thinking on how to further approach the use of machine learning in law, and are likely to inform their future study of this field.

References

Bench-Capon, T. 1997. Argument in artificial intelligence and law. *Artificial Intelligence and Law* 5(4):249–261.

Berman, D. H., and Hafner, C. D. 1993. Representing teleological structure in case-based legal reasoning: the missing link. In *Proceedings of the 4th international conference on Artificial intelligence and law*, 50–59. ACM.

Campbell, W.; Li, L.; Dagli, C.; Greenfield, K.; Wolf, E.; and Campbell, J. 2016. Predicting and analyzing factors in patent litigation. *NIPS2016, ML and the Law Workshop*.

Franklin, J. 2012. Discussion paper: How much of commonsense and legal reasoning is formalizable: A review of conceptual obstacles. *Law, Prob. & Risk* 11:225.

Hafner, C. D. 1978. An information retrieval system based on a computer model of legal knowledge.

Prakken, H., and Sartor, G. 1996. A dialectical model of assessing conflicting arguments in legal reasoning. In *Logical Models of Legal Argumentation*. Springer. 175–211.

Prakken, H., and Sartor, G. 1997. Argument-based extended logic programming with defeasible priorities. *Journal of applied non-classical logics* 7(1-2):25–75.

Prakken, H., and Sartor, G. 1998. Modelling reasoning with precedents in a formal dialogue game. In *Judicial Applications of Artificial Intelligence*. Springer. 127–183.

Prakken, H., and Sartor, G. 2002. The role of logic in computational models of legal argument: a critical survey. In *Computational logic: Logic programming and beyond*. Springer. 342–381.

Rissland, E. L., and Skalak, D. B. 1991. Cabaret: rule interpretation in a hybrid architecture. *International journal of man-machine studies* 34(6):839–887.

Sartor, G. 2002. Teleological arguments and theory-based dialectics. *Artificial Intelligence and Law* 10(1-3):95–112.

Singh, J. 2016. The tech-legal aspects of machine learning: Considerations for moving forward. *NIPS2016, ML and the Law Workshop*.

Skalak, D. B., and Rissland, E. L. 1992. Arguments and cases: An inevitable intertwining. *Artificial intelligence and Law* 1(1):3–44.

Tillers, P. 1993. Intellectual history, probability, and the law of evidence.

Tillers, P. 2011. Trial by mathematics - reconsidered. *Law, probability and risk* 10(3):167–173.

A Computational Framework for Identity and Its Web-based Realization

William Nick
Madison Mccotter
Siobahn Day
Marguerite McDaniel
North Carolina A&T State U.
Greensboro, NC 27411
{wmnick, mumccott, scday, mamcdan2}
@aggies.ncat.edu

Emma Sloan
Brown University
Greensboro, NC 27411
emma_sloan2@brown.edu

Hannah Foster
James Mayes
North Carolina A&T State U.
Greensboro, NC 27411
hnfoster@aggies.ncat.edu
jpmayes@ncat.edu

Albert Esterline
North Carolina A&T State U.
Greensboro, NC 27411
esterlin@ncat.edu

Abstract

This paper presents a computational framework for identity and is particularly focused on identifying the culprit in a crime-scene investigation. A case is conceptualized as a constellation of situations in the sense of Barwise's situation theory. Data on a case is stored as RDF triples in a triple store. Several relevant OWL ontologies have been developed and supplemented with SWRL rules. Uncertainty and combining levels of (possibly conflicting) evidence are handled with Dempster-Shafer theory. A webpage is being developed to make available to students of criminal justice the results of our work. The user will be able to query about evidence and follow how it accrues to various hypotheses.

1 Introduction

We are developing a computational framework for identity, and, with our focus on criminal investigations, we are integrating ontologies and (to combine levels of evidence) Dempster-Shafer theory into our system. A particularly important goal of this project is a web interface to this system for learning purposes. This webpage will allow a student to query information regarding criminal investigations and follow how evidence accrues to various hypotheses about the identity of the culprit.

The SuperIdentity project is the state-of-the-art in frameworks for identity (Creese et al.). It starts with some known information or *element* of identity, such as a username or email address, and *transforms* that element into others, e.g., by looking up an email address to find the associated username. These elements are grouped by type (e.g., phone number) into *characteristics*, multisets of elements. The set of all characteristics is a person's *superidentity*, a compilation of all known information on them. Our framework covers all aspects of the SuperIdentity framework but from a situation-theory perspective. We assemble constellations of situations (in the technical sense of Barwise and Perry (Barwise and Perry 1983)) to produce a case as in the legal sense, providing more structure and provenance than provided by superidentities.

The remainder of this paper is organized as follows. Section 2 presents background: situation theory (the theoretical background for our representations), Semantic Web resources (our OWL ontologies serve as knowledge bases, and data is stored as RDF triples conforming to our ontologies), and Dempster-Shafer theory (used to handle uncertainty and collaborating and conflicting evidence). Section 3 presents our running example, Section 4 presents our ontologies, and Section 5 summarizes the encoding of our examples in RDF. Section 6 discusses the SWRL (Semantic Web Rule Language) rules that complement our ontologies. Section 7 addresses evidence in the legal sense and the importance of certain objects, viz., biometric artifacts, that persist across situations. Section 8 presents our application of Dempster-Shafer theory, Section 9 outlines a functional design of our webpage, and Section 10 sketches the ongoing implementation of our web-based system. Section 11 concludes and suggests future work.

Our framework is used in a way compatible with contemporary crime-scene investigation, with most information manually encoded as RDF triples and possibly automated encoding of documents. We rely on human perception except for biometric matching. Ontologies, which capture expert knowledge and conventional practice (there is no machine learning), constrain the encoding and support inference. Dempster-Shafer theory reveals how evidence combines and provides guidance even when evidence is weak. For other recent presentations of our framework, see (McDaniel et al. 2017a) and (McDaniel et al. 2017b) regarding ontologies and (Sloan et al. 2016) and (Sloan et al. 2017) regarding application of Dempster-Shafer theory.

2 Background

2.1 Situation Theory

Our computational framework is based on the situation theory of Barwise and Perry (Barwise and Perry 1983), especially as systematized by Devlin (Devlin 1995). According to Barwise, "'[s]ituation' is our name for those portions of reality that agents find themselves in, and about which they exchange information" (Barwise 1989). A situation supports elementary items of information, called *infons*, each essentially a relation among objects at a time and place (or possibly the lack of such a relation). A *real situation* supports an indefinite number of infons. We generally work with *abstract situations*, each supporting a finite number of (possibly parameterized) infons. An abstract situation amounts to a type under which real situations are classified.

There are constraints between situations, as expressed, for

example, by "smoke means fire." By virtue of constraints, one situation may carry information about another. By virtue of conventional (linguistic) constraints, an *utterance situation*, in which someone performs a (declarative) speech act, carries information about a *described situation*. Whether the speech act is felicitous may depend on *resource situations* related by conventions to the utterance situation; in a purely linguistic setting, such situations typically support infons expressed by relative clauses.

In our framework, an *id-action* takes place in what we call an *id-situation*. Any id-action is considered an assertion of identity even if it is not verbal. So an id-situation is an utterance situation, and the crime scene is the corresponding described situation. Supporting situations essential to crime-scene evidence (e.g., those where suspects' fingerprints were recorded) are resource situations: there are conventional constraints requiring the existence of properly executed situations for the evidence to be admissible. Together, the id-situation, the described situation (crime scene), and the resource situations make an *id-case*.

2.2 Semantic Web Resources

The semantic web is built off of two W3C standards (Pan 2009): the resource description framework (RDF) [ref] and the resource description framework schema (RDFS). The web ontology language (OWL) extends the expressiveness of RDFS and allows for the creation of ontologies. "Ontology" is a term borrowed from philosophy, where it means the conceptualization of entities in the world and how they interact with each other, but, in computer science, it denotes a conceptualization of a domain.

RDF is a W3C recommendation that allows for the annotation of web resources. RDF statements (known as triples) are in the form of *subject predicate object*, where *predicate* is a binary relation. A resource (thing) is denoted in RDF by a uniform resource identifiers (URI), a string unique across the web. A URI reference (URIref) is a URI with an optional fragment identifier at the end. A URIref is usually represented as a Qname, `pre:lp`, where `pre` is a URI (essentially a namespace pefix) and `lp` is the local part. A blank node (*bnode*) is a resource that is not identified by a URIref, functioning like a pronoun. One RDF serialization defined by the W3C is N3, in which triples are expressed by the three components separated by whitespace. If several triples share a subject, we can abbreviate by listing the common subject then listing predicate-object pairs separated by semi-colons.

RDFS allows for the definition of new RDF classes and properties. An individual is an instance of a class. A class may be a subclass of classes and a property may be a subproperty of properties. A property has a *domain*, which is a class to which its subjects belong, and a *range*, which is a class or datatype to which its objects belong. For a succinct representation, where *`p`* is a property, *`Dom`* is its domain, and *`Rng`* is its range, we write *`p: Dom`* $\rightarrow$ *`Rng`*. *Object properties* have classes as ranges while *datatype properties* have datatypes. Unlike RDFS, OWL allows for the expression of local scope of properties, disjointedness of classes, Boolean combinations of classes, cardinality restrictions, and special characteristics of properties.

SPARQL (Pérez, Arenas, and Gutierrez 2006) is a SQL-like query language for triple stores. The `WHERE` clause contains a pattern of triples that will be matched by the query engine. Query output is what is bound to the variables in the `SELECT` clause. Various applications allow one to infer new triples from those present in the triple store via connections captured in the OWL ontologies. For additional inference patterns, the ontologies can be supplemented with rules in the Semantic Web Rule Language (SWRL). These are if-then rules that use the concepts expressed in the ontologies.

2.3 Dempster-Shafer Theory

Dempster-Shafer (DS) theory is a justification-based way of distributing evidence (Halpern 2005). "Mass" of evidence distributes to sets of elements or outcomes, with unassigned mass, representing ignorance, given to the set of all elements, called the *frame of discernment*. This assigns masses sum to 1.0. A *focal element* is a set with non-zero mass. A *refinement* is the analysis on the frame of discernment to get a more detailed frame of discernment.

Given a mass function, the *belief* function for a set is the lower bound for likelihood, calculated by adding the masses of all subsets of the set, while the *plausibility* is the upper bound for the likelihood, calculated by adding the masses from all of the sets that overlap the set. In symbols, for a frame of discernment Θ, a mass function m, and any subset θ of Θ, $Bel(\theta) = \sum_{\theta^* \subseteq \theta} m(\theta^*)$ and $Plaus(\theta) = \sum_{\theta^* \cap \theta \neq \emptyset} m(\theta^*)$. Thus, for any $\theta \subseteq \Theta$, $Bel(\theta) \leq Plaus(\theta)$.

DS theory allows for the combination of multiple mass functions for different kinds of evidence to produce a new mass function that relates to the combined evidence. There are a number of combination rules that fit different types of data better. For example, Dempster's rule combines pieces of evidence that are equally reliable while preserving the uncertainty inherent within each piece of evidence. Specifically, Dempster's rule calculates a measure, *K*, of conflict between the mass functions and divides that measure as mass among the different focal elements, including the focal element that is the entire frame of discernment. In symbols, with $K = \sum_{B \cap C \neq \emptyset} m_1(B)m_2(C)$ for mass functions m_1 and m_2 and focal elements B and C. Dempster's rule combines m_1 and m_2 as $m_{12} = (\sum_{B \cap C = A} m_1(B)m_2(C))/(1-K)$. Other combination rules include Zhang's rule (which allows combination of mass functions with different frames of discernment) and the mixing rule (which assigns different weights to the combined mass function and so compensates for the fact that some pieces of evidence may be more reliable than others). And often researchers create their own, context-specific combination rules.

3 Running Example

We consider a scenario where a theft has occurred at a party. There is a list of possible suspects in the form of a guest list. Evidence from the crime scene includes a group photograph from a security camera with one guest with their hand on the doorknob of the door to where the valuables were kept and a fingerprint on that doorknob. This scenario is a constellation of situations, centering around two separate id-situations for the two pieces of evidence: the fingerprint and the snapshot. Situation s_1 (see Figure 1) is the id-situation for the fingerprint case; an analyst compares fingerprints on file from the partygoers to the forensic one at the crime scene. In situations s_{3a}-s_{3d}, a suspect has their fingerprint taken by a police officer, and in situation s_4, the criminal touches the doorknob, placing the forensic fingerprint. The CSI team lifts the fingerprint from the doorknob in situation s_5. The id-situation for the case with the security camera image, s_2, is supported by its own constellation of situations. See Figure 2. Police take a mugshot of each suspect in situations s_{6a}-s_{6d}. Those mugshots are then compared with the security camera image in s_2. The security camera records the group in situation s_7, which acts as an utterance situation, describing the group in s_8. Situation s_4, in which the fingerprint is left by touching the doorknob, is a part of situation s_8.

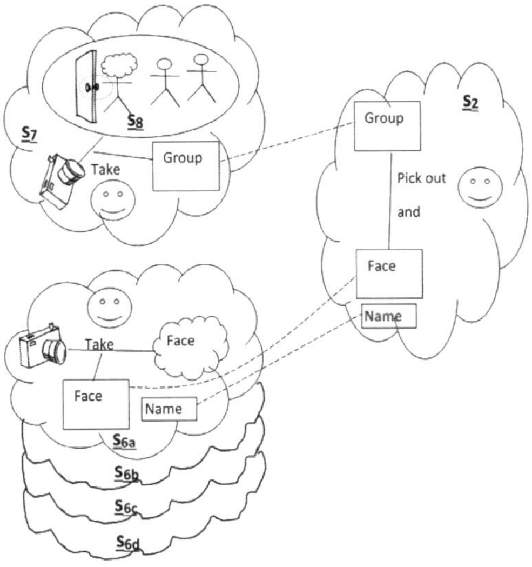

Figure 1: Mugshot ID case

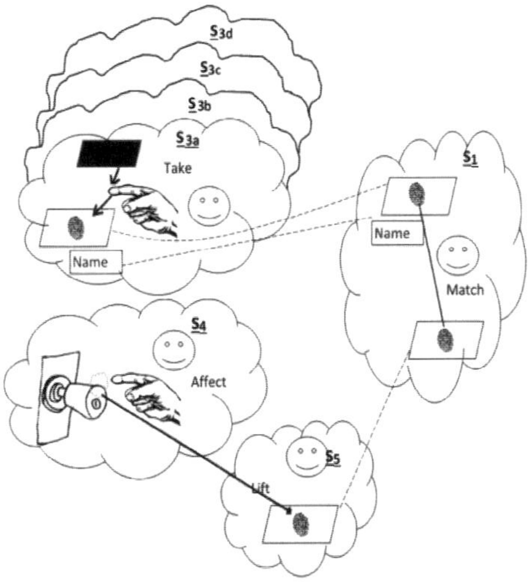

Figure 2: Fingerprint ID case

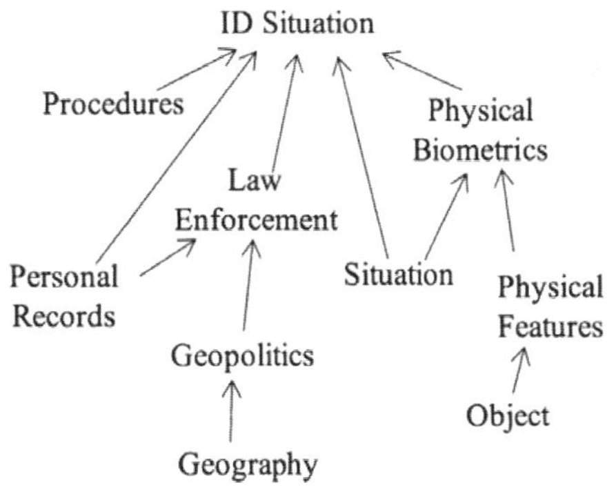

Figure 3: The ontologies and their inclusions

4 The Ontologies

Figure 3 shows the ontologies created for the framework and their relationships to each other. Each ontology inherits from the ontology below.

Our ID-Situation Ontology (to which we associate the prefix `id`) focuses on situations and constellation of situations (i.e., id-cases) that involve id-actions as well as any evidence supporting them. This ontology is built on the Situation Ontology (to which we associate the prefix `sit`), whose two major classes are `sit:Situation` and `sit:Infon`, whose children are essential in encoding our example. Subclasses of `sit:Infon` corresponding to various relations are defined in the ID-Situation Ontology. For such a subclass, we define properties with it as domain for the argument positions in the corresponding relation. This avoids RDF's restriction to binary relations ("properties") and accommodates variable-arity relations. For simplicity, we associate time and location with a situation rather than with individual infons. Consequently, we define top-level classes `sit:Temp` and `sit:Loc` as well as various functional properties such as `sit:tempLoc: sit:Situation` $\rightarrow$ `sit:Temp` and `sit:spatialLoc: sit:Situation` $\rightarrow$ `sit:Loc`. For the `sit:Situation` class, there is a reflexive and transitive object property `sit:partOf: sit:Situation` $\rightarrow$ `sit:Situation` to indicate that one situation is a part of another.

The ID-Situation Ontology includes class `id:IdCase`, an instance of multiple situations that form an id-case. There is an object property `id:hasSituation: id:IdCase` $\rightarrow$ `sit:Situation`, connecting an id-case to its constituent situations. Subproperties of `id:hasSituation` are `id:hasIdSituation: id:IdCase` $\rightarrow$ `sit:Situation` and `id:hasSupportingSituation: id:IdCase` $\rightarrow$ `sit:Situation`. The first acts as a functional property that relates an id-case to its id-situation; the latter links an id-case to supporting situations. We also have an equivalence property, `id:coordindatedIdCase: id:IdCase` $\rightarrow$ `id:IdCase`, that relates id-cases that refer to the same scenario.

As shown in Figure 3, the ID-Situation Ontology incorporates other ontologies that relate not only to the structure of a case but also to the specific kind of information–biometric artifacts–and procedures needed for evidence to support id-actions. This includes the Physical Biometric Ontology that addresses biometric artifacts, which are images of the suspects' physical features registered for use by forensic professionals. For the information captured by physical biometrics, we have a Physical Features Ontology that addresses the human body, which relates specific surface features to specific persons, allowing the biometric images to serve as identifiers.

The most important of the supporting ontologies is the Law Enforcement Ontology. (For simplicity, we now omit prefixes.) The standard FOAF ontology has a top-level `Agent` class with children `Organization` and `Person`. We provide a child `LawEnforcementAgency` of `Organization` and a child `LawEnforcementProfessional` of `Person` itself with children `ForensicProfessional`, `PoliceOfficer`, `PoliceInvestigator`, and `ProsecutionProfessional`. There is an affiliation property associating agents with organizations and a certification property associating forensic professionals with certificates. There is a Personal Records Ontology.

5 Encoding in RDF of the Example

We outline the RDF encoding of the fingerprint case, providing an example of code. A shorter summary of the mugshot case is presented.

5.1 The Fingerprint Id-Case

s_1 is the id-situation for the fingerprints. It supports two essential infons, both instances of children of `id:MatchingFpInfon` (a child of `sit:Infon`). One child of this class is `id:AnalystMatchingFpInfon`, information that an attempt is made to match a fingerprint from the scene against a recorded fingerprint, and the other is `id:SimilarFpInfon`, information on the similarity measure for the match and the matching procedure used. For the first suspect, s_1 supports the following two infons (denoted by blank nodes, with "_" in place of a prefix).

```
_:i1la a id:AnalystMatchingFpInfon;
     id:fpAnalyst forprof:117;
     id:fpObserved forensicfp:652;
     id:fpRecorded fpfile:496;... .
_:ila a id::SimilarFpInfon;
    id:fpObserved forensicfp:652;
    id:fpRecorded fpfile:496;
    id:simMeasure "0.92";
    id:simProc similar:Procl; ... .
```

We assume that the relevant agency has indexed the individuals with numerical identifiers. We introduce prefixes for individuals thus indexed: `forprof` for forensic professionals, `forensicfp` for fingerprints collected at crime scenes, and `fpfile` for fingerprints on file. We also assume unique identifiers with prefix `similar` for the matching procedures used. The same pair of fingerprints appears in both infons. There are similar pairs of infons for the other suspects.

s_{3a} is the situation where the fingerprints of the first subject were taken and recorded. It supports one essential infon, the information that a forensic professional takes the fingerprint of a subject. There is one such infon for the other three fingerprint-recording situations. s_4 is the described situation, where someone leaves their fingerprint on the doorknob. There are two essential items of information here, that the fingerprint is on the doorknob, and that some suspect left their fingerprint. s_5, where the fingerprint on the doorknob is lifted, has one essential item of information, that a forensic professional lifts a fingerprint.

5.2 The Mugshot Id-Case

s_2, the id-situation for the mugshots, supports two essential infons similar to those in the fingerprint id-situation, s_1. The photo of the culprit is a part of the photo that the officer took: the part showing their face. s_{6a}, where the mugshot of the first subject was taken and recorded, supports one essential infon, that a given forensic professional takes and records a mugshot of a suspect with a given camera. There is one such infon for each of the remaining three situations. s_7, where a forensic professional takes a picture, has two significant infons. One is that a certain officer takes a picture of a given situation with a given camera thereby producing a given group photo. s_7 is an utterance situation: it produces an artifact carrying information about another situation, viz., s_8. The other significant infon in s_7 is that a certain group is in the described situation, s_8. When our culprit is identified, we add a triple stating that they are a member of the group. The described situation, s_8, has one significant infon, for the touching. Once we have identified the culprit, we add a triple for the toucher. This infon is supported by the described situation while s_7 carries this infon by virtue of the photo it produces. There is a part-whole relation between s_4 and s_8.

6 SWRL Rules

SWRL rules allow us to infer new triples and thus fill in our descriptions of objects, situations, and agents based on triples already in our ontologies. There are two significant tasks for our SWRL rules: identify the culprit and classify situations and entire id-cases.

6.1 Identifying the Culprit

Typically, there is a described situation where the culprit is unidentified and an id-situation, where the evidence is presented for pronouncing a judgment on the identity of the culprit in the described situation. For example, in the fingerprint case, once we have an identity judgment, we can fill in the value for the `id:fpProducer` property for the instance of `id:LeaveFpInfon` supported by s_4. We have created a rule that does the updates subsequent to identifying the culprit. This includes supplying `id:toucher` in `id:TouchInfon` and an agent in `id:AgentInfon` for the described situation s_8. We also assert a triple of the form `x sit:agentInSit s`, indicating that `x` is the agent of interest in situation `s`. This is top-level information not associated with any other situation that provides one way of identifying the agent. Inference will generally identify several suspects as "the" culprit since inference does not consider the goodness of biometric matches; we handle level of evidence with Dempster-Shafer theory – see Section 8.

6.2 Classifying Situations and Id-Cases

We need abstract situations as types to classify real situations and abstract id-cases to classify constellations of situations in a way conducive to identification. The ID-Situation Ontology has subclasses of class `sit:Situation`, essentially abstract situations, and it has an `id:IdCase` class, which has subclasses for classification. Determining whether a given situation should be an instance of a given situation class is a classification problem that hinges on whether the real situation supports certain infon subclasses. When we described our running example, we described real situations, but the descriptions themselves, where we talked about essential infons, basically formulated abstract situations. Our classifying SWRL rules, then, have the form

```
Situation(?s), ... -> SituationSubClass(?s)
```

The conditions that fill in the ellipsis relate to the infons that `?s` supports. We also classify an instance of `id:IdCase` as an instance of a subclass of that class. Finally, we have a SWRL rule for determining that an instance of the mugshot id-case and an instance of the fingerprint id-case are coordinated

7 Biometric Artifacts and Legal Evidence

Objects and situations (or events) are complementary (Galton and Mizoguchi 2009). Objects are created, changed, copied, and destroyed in situations, and situations consist of objects related in various ways. Though our foundations are built on situations, objects are important in several areas. Some objects are passive participants (e.g. doorknob) while others play essential roles in capturing evidence (e.g. camera). To support our conclusions from the evidence collected, we may need facts regarding these objects. The objects of primary interest are biometric artifacts, serving as threads that stitch together the situations building an id-case. E.g., in the fingerprint id-case, fingerprints are recorded on file (situations s_{3a}-s_{3d}), providing objects used in the id-situation, s_1, and a fingerprint is lifted from the doorknob in s_5, providing the object against which the fingerprints on file are compared.

To see how such objects count as evidence, note that evidence in criminal prosecution includes any documents, testimony or tangible objects that tend to prove or disprove the existence of alleged facts (Black, Garner, and McDaniel 1999). Documentary evidence consists of any written object or article, e.g., letters, contracts, deeds, licenses, and certificates, presented as proof. Testimonial evidence consists of any statement made under oath by a witness during trial or at deposition. "Tangible object" evidence refers to any physical item or its representation presented as proof to support an alleged fact. Physical evidence includes biological and non-biological trace evidence. Here, trace evidence is defined as evidence that can be transferred between people, objects or the environment. Physical evidence also includes facial recognition (photography and videography) and fingerprint and biometric (DNA, blood, semen, saliva, urine, feces, hair, teeth, bone, tissue, and cells) evidence. The use of all evidence is subject to law, legal rules and procedures to determine its admissibility and probative value. Additionally, the provenance, preservation (cf. chain of custody–CoC–immediately below), and analysis of evidence is central to its forensic application.

In particular, biometric artifacts used as evidence have to be genuine throughout. CoC theory addresses what is essential "to ensure the integrity of evidence" (Giannelli 1993). Our framework facilitates application of CoC theory, focusing (for now) on physical, or "real," evidence, tangible evidence used to prove a fact that is at issue in a case (Citizens Information 2014). It also has to be relevant, material, and competent (Findlaw 2016) to be admitted in court. Following what CoC theory states is required, one can authenticate real evidence since CoC theory requires the mapping of who, what, where, and how evidence is obtained and handled (Giannelli 1993). We appeal to CoC theory since our central focus is to evaluate whether the metadata or forensic data (as real evidence) is sufficient to identify suspects. Our framework records CoC steps followed; it does not itself physically obtain or preserve the evidence.

8 Application of Dempster-Shafer Theory

For each id-case, a numerical measure is created of who is likely to be the criminal and then all known id-cases are combined using Dempster-Shafer theory. For each id-situation and each suspect, there is a distance measure that is part of the id-situation. A mass function is then created based on that distance measure. To work with the scenario from the running example, to create the mass function for the fingerprint id-case, as shown in Figure 1, masses are assigned based on the distance between each suspect's fingerprint and the fingerprint from the crime scene. Conversion of distances to masses uses a customized sigmoid function, which provides a threshold below which a possible match can be ignored. Those masses are then normalized so that all values sum to 1.0.

An id-situation is tied to resource situations through constraints. Every piece of evidence in the id-situation has been collected in some other situation or set of situations, following appropriate legal procedures to maintain a chain of custody, a convention that specifies a related situation or set of situations (e.g., the s_3 situations in Figure 1) that must have occurred. There are three possible interpretations of the constraints in the context of Dempster-Shafer theory. One is that each set of situations provides a separate mass function so that the mass function from the resource situations must be combined with the mass function from the id-situation. The second is to consider each resource situation as a refinement of the frame of discernment created in the id-situation. The third interpretation has the resource situations modifying the mass function.

Treating each set of situations as a separate piece of evidence, with its own mass function, would sanction application of Dempster-Shafer combination rules. The frame of discernment for the id-situation in fact is the same as the frame of discernment for a collection of resource situations that covers all the suspects from the id-situation. Dempster's combination rule is appropriate because the underlying uncertainties should be preserved.

Treating the constraints as refinements would make each group of resource situations modify the arrangement of the set of suspects. As noted, however, in our framework, the frame of discernment is the same throughout.

Not all resource situations can be accommodated using the two previously described methods. For example, in Figure 1, information from situation s_5 modifies the id-situation, but it does not refer to any suspect and so does not refine the frame of discernment or even rearrange focal elements. The analysts who collected the crime scene fingerprint might be untrustworthy. This could be handled by moving some mass to the entire frame of discernment or by weighting the piece of evidence less heavily when combining it with evidence from other id-situations.

Table 1 shows the mass, belief, and plausibility for the mass functions from the two id-situations and their combination. Masses of non-singleton sets other than the entire frame of discernment ("All") are all zero. The mass values have been subject to modification to accommodate aspects of the resource situations as just discussed.

Photographic Evidence			
Suspect	Mass	Belief	Plaus
201	0.399	0.399	0.595
202	0.405	0.405	0.601
203	0	0	0.196
204	0	0	0.196
All	0.196	1.0	1.0
Fingerprint Evidence			
Suspect	Mass	Belief	Plaus
201	0.290	0.290	0.596
202	0	0	0.306
203	0.215	0.215	0.521
204	0.188	0.188	0.494
All	0.306	1.0	1.0
Combined Evidence			
Suspect	Mass	Belief	Plaus
201	0.528	0.528	0.636
202	0.222	0.222	0.330
203	0.076	0.076	0.183
204	0.066	0.066	0.174
All	0.108	1.0	1.0

Table 1: Mass, belief, and plausibility (abbreviated to plaus) measures for the three mass functions created by our two id-situations and their combination using Dempster's rule

9 Webpage

This section outlines the functionality of the webpage interface to the system we are building. The webpage will have three major functional areas: the case description , query, and evidence panes.

9.1 Case Description Pane

The case description pane will include a menu of cases. When a case is clicked, a short paragraph describing the case will appear, providing information about the case including an outline of the events as well as a summary of the kinds of evidence available. The user may switch between the various scenarios and investigate the scenario of their choice. The case description will have a button to bring up a menu of suspects. When the user selects a given suspect, a short description of the suspect appears along with a template for constructing queries about the suspect. Generally, this pane provides information to initiate interaction in the other two panes.

9.2 Query Pane

This pane, whose content is specific to the selected case, supports both queries on the triple stores and inferences made on these stores given the ontologies and the SWRL rules. There is a tab for each kind of evidence. In our running example, there is a tab for the fingerprint evidence and a tab for the mugshot evidence. There is also a tab for inferring the identity of the culprit, and a tab for classifying the case and its constituent situations.

The contents of the tabs for the various kinds of evidence are structured similarly. Consider, for example, the tab for the fingerprint evidence. Often a value will be selected from a menu. The following are some possible topics for queries.

- Who took a given fingerprint that is on file? When? Where?
- How was the fingerprint preserved or copied?
- Who lifted the fingerprint?
- Who handled the comparison of the fingerprint on file and the forensic fingerprint?
- How good a match is the match between a given fingerprint on file and forensic fingerprint?

Many of these queries relate to provenance, including chain of custody. Note that it is natural for a query to span situations, often by following the CoC. For example, one could ask for the name of the professional who took the fingerprint on file in situation s_{3a} that is used in the id-situation s_1. Many queries could be issued for a set of fingerprints on file. The results will be displayed in a table, possibly ranked by the value of some field (e.g., the goodness of match). If the result of a query indicates some suspect is particularly interesting, the user may bring up the template mentioned above for queries about a person. Legal professionals may also be of interest (e.g., those who took fingerprints), and a variation of the template will be available for querying about them.

The tab for inferring the identity of the culprit basically does just that. Often, however, there will be more than one culprit inferred since mere inference does not take into account how good the evidence is (which is the realm of Dempster-Shafer theory, accessed via the evidence pane). One will be able to control the size of the set of inferred culprits by setting thresholds on matches and restricting evidence to just some kinds of evidence (e.g., fingerprint or mugshot). To find details of an alleged culprit, one can follow up with the suspect template mentioned above.

The tab for classifying the case and its constituent situations provides an interface for applying some of the SWRL rules mentioned in Section 6. We could find the classes (if any) that the various situations instantiate. For example, a situation might be an instance of the abstract id-situation where an attempt is made to identify a culprit by fingerprint. We could find the id-case class (if any) that an id-case instantiates. For example, a given constellation of situations forming an id-case may be an instance of a case where a culprit is identified by fingerprint. Finally, we could determine whether a given id-case is coordinated with another id-case as they involve the same described situation and similar set of suspects.

9.3 Evidence Pane

The evidence pane will support the application of Dempster-Shafer theory to the evidence provided for the cases. It is assumed that mass functions have been defined for each kind of evidence in each case. Like the query pane, the contents of the evidence pane will be specific to the selected case. The user will be able to access the templates for suspects and for personnel in this pane as well to see details on people of interest.

There will be a tab for each kind of evidence and a tab for the combined evidence. The contents of the tabs for the various kinds of evidence will have similar structure. Consider, for example, the tab for the fingerprint evidence. The user will be able to request a table for the singleton sets of suspects ordered by belief or ordered by plausibility, given the mass function based on fingerprint matches. This could be restricted to the top few in belief or plausibility. Frequently, the belief or plausibility of non-singleton sets is of interest, particularly when the belief for such a set is high or the plausibility is low. The user might request small sets with high belief or large sets with low plausibility. The mass functions can me modified by features of the resource situations, such as the reliability of the forensic professional who took the fingerprint on file. The fingerprint tab will include ways for the user to have such modifying aspects incorporated into the mass function.

The tab for the combined evidence will allow the user to view tables of singleton sets, now with the belief and plausibility from the combined mass function. Non-singleton sets are of interest here as they are with a single kind of evidence. The user will be able to select the combination rule used, the default being Dempster's rule. There will also be a way to analyze sensitivity. For example, the fingerprint from the scene might be quite indistinct so that it does not discriminate sharply between the suspects while the forensic mugshot may be a clear picture of the culprit's face. In that case, the page should indicate that identification relies much more on the one kind of evidence (mugshots) than on the other (fingerprints) and give some indication of how much more.

10 Implementation of the Web-based System

This section describes the implementation of our web-based system, which is a work in progress. To implement the backend of our system, we used the Apache Struts model-view-controller framework (The Apache Software Foundation 2010), Apache Velocity template engine (The Apache Software Foundation 2014), and the Stardog triplestore [12]. The view (frontend) and the controller interface are provided by Struts and can integrate with other technologies to provide the model. A controller acts as a bridge between an application's model and the web view. The Stardog triple store (Complexible 2014) supports OWL and rule reasoning, which it does in a lazy and late-binding fashion: reasoning is performed at query time according to a reasoning type specified by the user. Apache Velocity is a template engine for Java that provides the user a simple but powerful template language able to reference objects defined in Java. We use Velocity to create SPARQL queries from a template since we assume that the user is not familiar with SPARQL. We connect to the Stardog triplestore using the RESTful web service exposed by Stardog. We decided to use the RESTful web services because the Jena (Apache Software Foundation 2013) interface code was not available. (Jena is our preferred Semantic Web framework.) A RESTful web service uses HTTP verbs for accessing and manipulating data.

To keep the web application running as fast as possible, an XML document was created to store meta-information about and control information for our scenarios. The information in this XML document includes the id, name, and description of the scenario. The user will access the data in this XML document through the interface. The XML document will also contain the possible queries that can be executed on each piece of evidence as well as the types of evidence for each scenario. The code will turn similarity measures into masses used later for belief and plausibility calculations.

Belief and plausibility calculations are written in Python. To run this script from Java, we use the Jython interpreter (Jython 2001), which is a Python interpreter written in Java and is embeddable in Java applications. To store the data produced by the code executed by Jython, a data structure was created to store belief and the plausibility values. The data structure with the masses will be stored into a session variable to be used later. After the user selects the combination rule to use, the data structure will be passed into a combination method with a string identifier that identifies the combination rule. The Jython interpreter will run the appropriate method for that particular combination rule. The output of the running of the interpreter will be stored into a data structure of data objects. The data produced by the Jython interpreter will be cached into memory using Infinispan (Redhat 2009), which is an in-memory key-value data store written in Java and used as a cache or a data grid. It can be embedded into Java applications or used as a remote service over a variety of protocols. Our setup will have Infinispan embedded into our application so that some of the data may be cached .

11 Conclusion

We have presented our computational framework for agent identity, currently focused on criminal investigations, especially the use of biometrics therein. This paper is especially concerned with ongoing development of a web-based system that makes available via a webpage the functionality of this framework especially for pedagogical putposes. The theoretical underpinnings are in Barwise's situation theory. We construct a case as a constellation of situations, including an id-situation, corresponding to Barwise's utterance situation and involving an identity assertion (of the culprit). The described situation is the crime scene. There are also resource situations tied by convention to the id-situation, such as where fingerprints are recorded and filed. Cases are encoded in RDF, and several OWL ontologies have been developed to serve as a knowledge base and define RDF classes and properties. Dempster-Shafer theory is used to handle uncertainty and in combining levels of possibly conflicting or corroborating evidence. We presented an example and discussed its encoding in RDF as per our ontologies. We discussed our ontologies and the SWRL rules that enhance them. Evidence in the legal sense was discussed in the current context, and the importance of biometric artifacts that persist across situations was noted. A functional design of our webpage was presented, and the ongoing implementation of the web-based system was discussed.

The webpage will make available to students of criminal justice our work on a computational framework on identity as it is particularly focused on identifying the culprit in a crime scene investigation. A computerized evidentiary fact pattern would help students develop their critical thinking skills and support interdisciplinary problem solving. Additionally, the availability of the web interface will provide unlimited opportunities for students to practice and engage in fact-pattern scenarios, thus building valuable experience for future careers and research. The Criminal Justice program at North Carolina A&T State University will use the webpage in four of its courses and in its signature co-curricular project. The webpage can be used as an instructional tool and for formative assessment. The web interface could also be used in the Aggie Sleuths Project, an interdisciplinary, interdepartmental research project based on a simulated crime scene (Fakayode et al. 2016).

We have encoded several scenarios besides the example given in this paper, and we are in the process of encoding several more. Note that fingerprint and mugshot biometrics are used online. In working with online authentication (Jenkins et al.), we are addressing behavioral biometrics (e.g., swipe patterns on mobile devices). We intend eventually to address any kind of evidence for identity and to develop ontologies as required. And we shall continue to enhance our use of Dempster-Shafer theory, looking at various combination rules and ways to modify mass functions.

References

Apache Software Foundation. 2013. Apache jena.

Barwise, J., and Perry, J. 1983. *Situations and attitudes.* Center for the Study of Language and Information.

Barwise, J. 1989. *The situation in logic.* Center for the Study of Language (CSLI).

Black, H. C.; Garner, B. A.; and McDaniel, B. R. 1999. *Black's law dictionary.* West Group St.

Citizens Information. 2014. Real evidence.

Complexible. 2014. Stardog.

Creese, S.; Gibson-Robinson, T.; Goldsmith, M.; Hodges, D.; Kim, D.; Love, O.; Nurse, J. R.; Pike, B.; and Scholtz, J. Tools for understanding identity. In *Technologies for Homeland Security (HST), 2013 IEEE International Conference on*, 558–563. IEEE.

Devlin, K. 1995. *Logic and information.* Cambridge University Press.

Fakayode, S. O.; Mayes, J. P.; Kanipes, M. I.; Johnson, D.; and Cuthbertson, E. L. 2016. Promoting student learning in criminal justice, stem, and forensic science: Aggie sleuth initiative (aggiesi)-guided inquiry learning experience. *Journal of Criminal Justice Education* 1–15.

Findlaw. 2016. Summary of the rules of evidence.

Galton, A., and Mizoguchi, R. 2009. The water falls but the waterfall does not fall: New perspectives on objects, processes and events. *Applied Ontology* 4(2):71–107.

Giannelli, P. C. 1993. Chain of custody. Report, School of Law, Case Western Reserve University.

Halpern, J. Y. 2005. *Reasoning about uncertainty.* MIT Press.

Jenkins, J.; Nick, W.; Roy, K.; Esterline, A.; and Bloch, J. Author identification using sequential minimal optimization. In *SoutheastCon, 2016*, 1–2. IEEE.

Jython. 2001. Jython: Python for the java platform.

McDaniel, M.; Sloan, E.; Day, S.; Mayes, J.; Nick, W.; Roy, K.; and Esterline, A. 2017a. Situation-based ontologies for a computational framework for identity focusing on crime scenes. In *Accepted for IEEE Conference on Cognitive and Computational Aspects of Situation Management (CogSIMA 2017).*

McDaniel, M.; Sloan, E.; Nick, W. Mayes, J.; and Esterline, A. 2017b. Ontologies for situation-based crime scene identities. In *Accepted for IEEE SoutheastCon.*

Pan, J. Z. 2009. Resource description framework. In *Handbook on Ontologies.* Springer. 71–90.

Pérez, J.; Arenas, M.; and Gutierrez, C. 2006. Semantics and complexity of sparql. In *International semantic web conference*, 30–43. Springer.

Redhat. 2009. Infinispan.

Sloan, E.; McDaniel, M.; Nick, W.; Mayes, J.; and Esterline, A. 2016. Structure and evidence in identity cases. In *Proc. 2016 IEEE Symposium Series on Computational Intelligence (IEEE SSCI 2016).*

Sloan, E.; McDaniel, M.; Nick, W.; Mayes, J.; and Esterline, A. 2017. Marshalling situation-based evidence in identity cases. In *Accepted for IEEE SoutheastCon.*

The Apache Software Foundation. 2010. Apache struts.

The Apache Software Foundation. 2014. Apache velocity.

Natural Logic in AI and Cognitive Science

Lawrence S. Moss
Indiana University
lmoss@indiana.edu

Michael Wollowski
Rose-Hulman Institute of Technology
wollowsk@rose-hulman.edu

Abstract

This paper presents an ongoing research project called "natural logic" and makes the case that it is relevant to AI, Computational Linguistics, and Cognitive Science. We propose to add some of the natural logic modules which have already been developed to existing NLP systems. We see our approach as complementing and augmenting data-driven approaches exemplified by IBM's Watson. We give a brief introduction to natural logic and present examples of proofs that can be given in a working system. We furthermore introduce monotonic logic, another promising approach for extracting information from sentences that contain quantifiers. We finish the paper by presenting some early work that integrates syllogistic reasoning into exsiting NLP systems.

Introduction

The history of logic and AI is a checkered one. Starting with huge optimism, the idea of applying logic in AI and NLP is very much a minority one today. The 2015 report of the *One Hundred Year Study on Artificial Intelligence* states that "The resounding success of the data-driven paradigm has displaced the traditional paradigms of AI. Procedures such as theorem proving and logic-based knowledge representation and reasoning are receiving reduced attention, in part because of the ongoing challenge of connecting with real world groundings." (Stone *et al.* 2016). At the same time, there were important contributions in previous parts of the AI literature on the topic of reasoning with fragments of natural language. Important for our story are (Nishihara *et al.* 1990; McAllester and Givan 1992; Purdy 2006).

We propose to add syllogistic reasoning to NLP systems. The sort of system we have in mind is exemplified by IBM's Watson system. Jim Hendler and his research group (Hendler and Ellis 2014) proposed that Watson's accomplishments are due to a combination of natural language processing, search technologies, semantic typing, scoring heuristics and machine learning. Conspicuously absent from this list are reasoning and logic. We know that several kinds of reasoning took place behind the scenes, such as in the context of semantic typing and in the context of reasoning about time and place (Kalyanpur *et al.* 2012; Ferrucci 2012; Gliozzo *et al.* 2013). While some of the reasoning in Watson was in support of finding answers to questions and to establish the confidence of potential answers, the geospatial and temporal reasoning were designed to make explicit some of the information that was implicitly contained in the given information. In this context, our project is aimed at adding addition reasoning components to NLP systems such as Watson.

We see our project as a support system that is designed to extract yet more information from natural language texts. It is decidedly not a free standing reasoner. As such, we see our project as part of a research agenda implicitly defined by IBM Watson, i.e. to do better than the Jeopardy! system. Watson used some fairly off-the-shelf IR techniques, including passage term matching, textual alignment and skip bigrams (Murdock *et al.* 2012). The designers of Watson additionally extracted information from sources that they knew would be valuable, such as anchor tag links and the contents of title tags in the HTML sources of Wikipedia pages. We believe that by adding syllogistic reasoning, NLP systems will be able to extract further information from documents or will be able to find further evidence for given information. In this context, we see our approach as supporting a data-driven approach through reasoning. We believe that reasoning adds additional, valuable resources to processing natural language texts.

Natural Logic: Extended Syllogistic Reasoning

We describe here the research program of *extended syllogistic reasoning* as it appears in papers such as (van Benthem 1986; Sánchez-Valencia 1991; van Eijck 2007; Fyodorov *et al.* 2003; Moss 2015; van Benthem 2008; Pratt-Hartmann and Moss 2009). The basic idea is to take very small fragments of language, fragments where one can find "reasoning"' of some kind, and to find *complete logical systems for those fragments.* Ideally, the logical systems would not use "extra syntax" of any kind, and thus not involve translation into first-order logic. Even more, they should be efficiently decidable. That means that there should be algorithms that carry out the decision procedure (unlike what we see for very strong logical systems), and these algorithms should be very fast for the very simplest fragments.

Here is a summary of the field. There are many sound and complete logical systems for small fragments of language.

The most basic is the one with sentences All x are y. In more detail, the syntax is minimal (and will be extended quite soon): it consists only of sentences of the form All x are y, where x and y are taken from a pre-assigned set of *nouns*. The semantics of the language is very simple. A *model* $\mathcal{M}$ is a set M together with interpretations $[\![x]\!]$ for all nouns. Then we say that $\mathcal{M} \models$ All x are y if $[\![x]\!] \subseteq [\![y]\!]$. Further, for a set Γ of sentences of this language, we say that $\mathcal{M} \models \Gamma$ if $\mathcal{M} \models \psi$ for all $\psi \in \Gamma$. Given Γ and another sentence φ, we say that $\Gamma \models \varphi$ if every $\mathcal{M} \models \Gamma$ has $\mathcal{M} \models \varphi$.

All of this is semantic; that is, having to do with models. There is a matching proof system, generated by the following two rules:

$$\frac{}{\text{All } p \text{ are } p}\ \text{AXIOM}$$

$$\frac{\text{All } p \text{ are } n \quad \text{All } n \text{ are } q}{\text{All } p \text{ are } q}\ \text{BARBARA}$$

Then we have the following result.

Theorem 1 *The proof system is sound and complete:* $\Gamma \models \varphi$ *iff* $\Gamma \vdash \varphi$*. Moreover, the problem of deciding whether, given a finite* $\Gamma \cup \varphi$*, we have* $\Gamma \models \varphi$ *or not is decidable in polynomial time.*

This is the simplest result in the area. (In fact, it is the simplest completeness theorem in all of logic.)

Figure 1 is a picture of a few of the logical system which have been treated in this way. For a description of the logical fragments depicted in this figure, please see (Moss 2015). Each has a precise syntax, semantics, proof theory, and algorithmic support. For example, $\mathcal{R}$ allows one to use verbs and relative clause. Other fragments add comparative adjectives. Especially noteworthy are some fragments which allow one to compare the sizes of sets. That is, one can say there are more dogs than cats, and perform reasoning with this. This is important because cardinality comparison goes beyond first-order logic; so it cannot be treated by any contemporary theorem provers. The reason that we can incorporate this kind of cardinality comparison into natural logic is that the systems are not built on top of first-order logic, or even on top of propositional logic. As such, working with a relatively weak "base", we are able to do things like cardinality comparison. And in a sense, this is the point.

Haskell Implementation

There are several implementations of natural logic fragments. Some are in Sage, an open source mathematics software package implemented in Python. The work on Sage is available at `www.sagemath.com`. Many of the systems have been implemented in Haskell. We discuss here aspects of the implementation (Moss 2017), primarily to demonstrate that such implementations exist.

The design features of the implementation are as follows:

1. A user can enter a finite set of syllogistic rules (a logic L) and a finite set Γ of assumptions, and generate all sentences which are provable from Γ in L.
2. If sentence φ is provable from Γ in L, we can generate and display the proof.
3. The logic L may contain negated nouns and also verbs and relative clauses.
4. L must consist of rules which are entirely syllogistic. Rules that infer information from contradictions, also called "explosion" rules, are fine. But *reductio ad absurdum* is not allowed in full generality.
5. Up until now, the items on this list are all entirely proof-theoretic. We have also built some tools for the intended semantics. For most of the standard systems in the literature, the work here also builds *counter-models*. That is, if φ does not follow from Γ in L, then we may ask for a counter-model showing this. This is only possible when we have a semantics for which the proof system is sound and complete.
6. As a particular case of point 5 just above, we can handle logics which are not expressible in first-order logic, such as the logic of *most*, *all*, and *some*.
7. For most of points 1–6 above, the system here is the first implementation which can do that point. That is, the implementation here goes well beyond what has been done so far.

We should emphasize the last point, the one about counter-model generation. It is standard to use a theorem prover like Prover9 together with a model-finder like Mace4 [https://www.cs.unm.edu/~mccune/mace4/]. The two programs are very different. In our setting, the prover and the counter-model generator are basically two branches of the same tree. They are not so different, actually. The reason for this seems to be (again) that the logics are rather simpler than full first-order logic.

To give a sense of the flavor of this implementation, we show in figure 2 part of a proof session. The session was edited to fit on one page. The user typed in a set Γ of assumptions. In this case, Γ consists of the sentences all skunks mammals, some skunks skunks (i.e., skunks exist), all skunks chordates. Then the user asks whether it follows that some mammals mammals. That is, the user wants to know whether the assumptions in Γ entail that some mammals exist. This sentence follows from the assumptions and a derivation is given in English. The derivation is shown in the top half of figure 2. While somewhat terse, this proof is much more readable than output from a theorem prover.

Next, the user wants to know whether all mammals skunks. In this case the does not follow from the assumptions and the system returns with a counter-model. This countermodel is shown in the bottom half of figure 2.

Monotonic Reasoning

Let us recapitulate where we are in this paper. We began with a discussion of Watson, mainly to motivate the idea of incorporating reasoning into a real life AI/NLP systems. Then we gave a brief discussion of the logical systems of natural logic, to present logical systems which are sound and complete, have low computational overhead, and which are capable of representing a fair amount of natural language inference. However, the logics from the prior section have some limitations from the point of view of NLP: they are

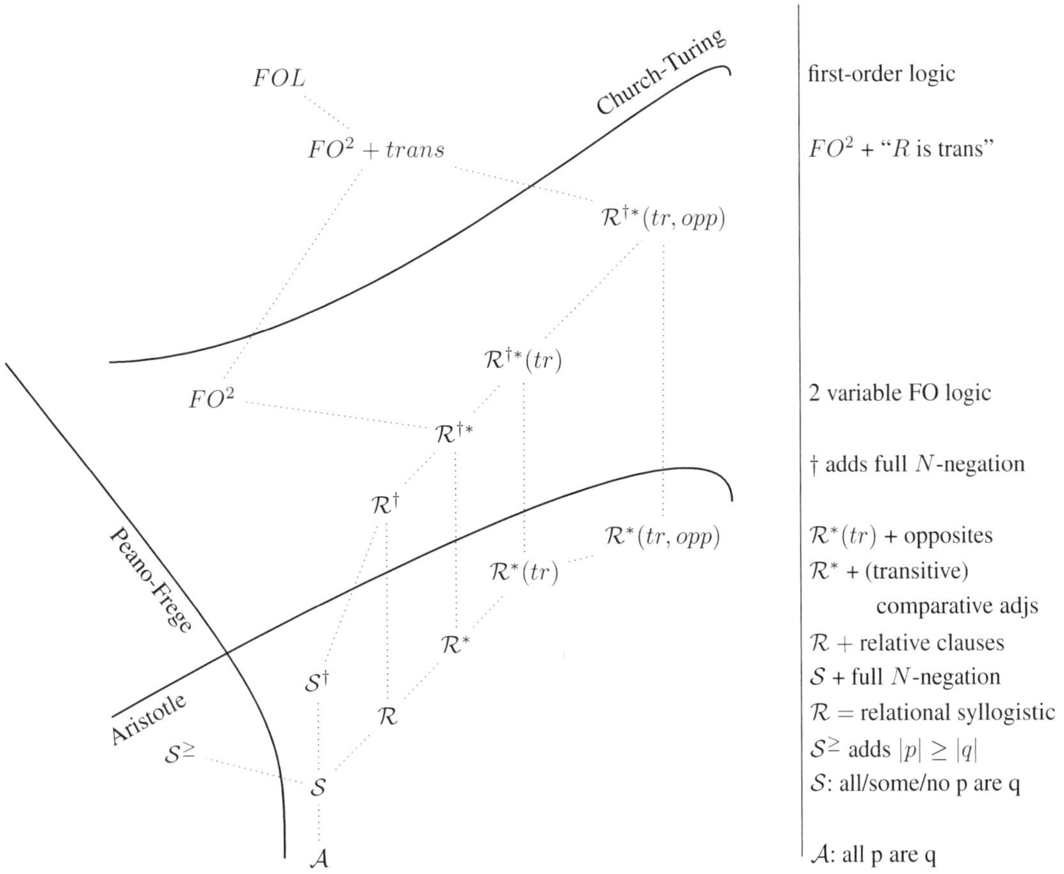

Figure 1: Natural logics. The fragments described on the right are explained in a number of papers, along with sound and complete proof systems for them. In many cases, proof search has been automated.

based on toy grammars and as such have limited applications in text as it comes. In other words, it would be difficult to see how to use those logical systems directly in an recognizing textual entailment task (Sammons 2015).

In this section, we present work that aims to overcome this issue. The work in this section is more speculative than that of the previous one, but we believe that it is more promising for future developments. To set the stage, consider the following sentences.

every dog$^{\downarrow}$ barks$^{\uparrow}$
no dog$^{\downarrow}$ barks$^{\downarrow}$
not every dog$^{\uparrow}$ barks$^{\downarrow}$
some dog$^{\uparrow}$ barks$^{\uparrow}$
most dogs$^{\times}$ bark$^{\uparrow}$

The arrows indicate *upward* or *downward* inference. For an introduction to this notation, see (van Benthem 1986). In the first sentence, if we know (of a scene, or a story, or a situation) that every dog barks, then it follows that every old dog barks and that every beagle barks. In both of those cases, we go "down" from dog to some subset of it. And the inference on barks goes the other way. If we know that every dog barks, then it follows that every dog vociferates.

Work on monotonicity merges the theory of grammar with the theory of inference. The idea is to enrich the lexical entries (words) with various forms of "up and down arrow" information. Then this information is propagated in deductions, as shown above. Deductions in systems like Combinatory categorial grammar (CCG) are basically forms of parsing. Current work on monotonicity (Icard and Moss 2014; Icard 2012; MacCartney and Manning 2009; Nairn *et al.* 2006) merges the monotonicity calculus from natural logic with linguistic frameworks like CCG. The idea is to have something that can automatically infer the correct "up and down arrow" information from real text, and then to use this in connection with NLP inference tasks.

```
ghci
GHCi, version 7.10.2: http://www.haskell.org/ghc/  :? for help
Prelude> :l S_dagger
[1 of 8] Compiling ProofTreeNumbers ( ProofTreeNumbers.hs, interpreted )
[2 of 8] Compiling Syntax2          ( Syntax2.hs, interpreted )
[3 of 8] Compiling ExampleSentences ( ExampleSentences.hs, interpreted )
[4 of 8] Compiling FrontEnd         ( FrontEnd.hs, interpreted )
[5 of 8] Compiling ExampleRules     ( ExampleRules.hs, interpreted )
[6 of 8] Compiling SyllogisticInference ( SyllogisticInference.hs, interpreted )
[7 of 8] Compiling Models           ( Models.hs, interpreted )
[8 of 8] Compiling S_dagger         ( S_dagger.hs, interpreted )
Ok, modules loaded: S_dagger, Syntax2,..., Models

*S_dagger>  let gamma=["all skunks mammals","some skunks skunks","all skunks chordates"]
*S_dagger> followsInSdagger "some mammals mammals" gamma

The sentence follows, and here is a derivation in S-dagger from the assumptions:

(1,all skunks are mammals,"A",[])
(2,some skunks are skunks,"A",[])
(3,some skunks are mammals,"darii",[1,2])
(4,some mammals are skunks,"some2",[3])
(5,some mammals are mammals,"some1",[4])

*S_dagger> followsInSdagger "all mammals skunks" gamma

The given sentence is not provable in S-dagger from the assumptions.
Here is a counter-model:

The universe is the set of numbers in [0,1].

The nouns are interpreted as follows:

  Noun     | Interpretation
-----------+---------------
skunks     | 0
mammals    | 0, 1
chordates  | 0, 1


Here is how the assumptions and purported conclusion fare in this model:

        Sentence          | Truth Value
--------------------------+------------
all skunks are mammals    | True
some skunks are skunks    | True
all skunks are chordates  | True
all mammals are skunks    | False
```

Figure 2: A Haskell proof session in which one sentence is shown to follow from the assumptions (top) and one is shown as not provable (bottom.)

Integration into NLP Systems

We began work on integrating naural logic into an NLP parser so as to increase the amount of information that can be extracted from text. Consider the following example, which outlines the basic approach we took. At the most basic, we plan to identify passages in natural language text that are instances of universally qualified statements. Consider the statement:

```
All dogs are mortal.
```

An off-the-shelf parser such as the Stanford NLP kit [http://nlp.stanford.edu/software/] produces an internal graph of the parsed sentence that is displayed as follows:

```
word All ,pos: DT ,ne: O
word dogs ,pos: NNS ,ne: O
word are ,pos: VBP ,ne: O
word mortal ,pos: JJ ,ne: O
word o ,pos: o ,ne: O

(ROOT (S (NP (DT All) (NNS dogs))
  (VP (VBP are) (ADJP (JJ mortal))) (. o)))

→ mortal-JJ (root)
  → dogs-NNS (nsubj)
    → All-DT (det)
  → are-VBP (cop)
```

We modified the Stanford NLP kit to process the internal representation of the parsed sentence to (i) identify a subset of simple universally quantified sentences and (ii) if successfully identified, to return a representation of that sentence for further processing. It should be noted that (i) and (ii) are accomplished in one step. If a sentence can be successfully parsed, we return the representation of it. If it cannot be successfully parsed, we ignore it. We would like to point out that this is very much in keeping with the data-intensive approach that a system like Watson uses. We do not expect our system to parse each universally qualified sentence. We will certainly continue to revise our system so that it can process increasingly complex sentences, but expect that this will be a drawn out process. The sentence returned by our system is as follows, but could be returned in other formats, suitable for further processing.

```
mortal(All, dogs)
```

We are now in a position to combine this information with other information we may find in the same document or that is known as part of background information. Suppose that the document states that Fido is a dog. In this case, we are able to confirm that Fido is mortal. This may be sufficient to answer a given question. However, it can also be supporting evidence to already known information. Suppose that either through a different text or from another passage in the given text, we learn that Fido died. In this case, we may use the inferred information that Fido is mortal as supporting evidence for the information that Fido died, thereby increasing the overall confidence in a statement. Again this is a tool in support of a data-driven approach such as found in IBM's Watson.

Conclusions

In this paper, we motivated the idea of incorporating reasoning into AI/NLP systems. We gave a brief discussion of the logical systems of natural logic, to present logical systems which are sound and complete, have low computational overhead, and which are capable of representing a fair amount of natural language inference. We furthermore presentd an approach from monotonic reasoning which enriches words with various forms of "up and down arrow" information, so that this information can be propagated in deductions. We finished this paper by presenting some initial work that aims to integrate natural logics into NLP systems.

The work described here is very much in the beginning stages. Undoubtedly, challenges will need to be addressed. In the near future, we plan to expand and integrate the existing systems. We additionally plan to improve the number and complexity of statements that can be recognized. Later this year, we plan to integrate a syllogistic reasoning component into a multi-year research project aimed at human-robot collaborative problem solving in a shared space. It will be designed to process statements that contain quantifiers. It will be one component of many; however, it will enable us to extend the functionality in a crucial way.

References

D. A. Ferrucci. Introduction to "This is Watson". *IBM Journal of Research and Development*, 56(3/4):1;1 – 1;15, 2012.

Yaroslav Fyodorov, Yoad Winter, and Nissim Fyodorov. Order-based inference in natural logic. *Log. J. IGPL*, 11(4):385–417, 2003. Inference in computational semantics: the Dagstuhl Workshop 2000.

Alfio Gliozzo, Or Biran, Siddharth Patwardhan, and Kathleen McKeown. Semantic technologies in IBM Watson. *ACL 2013, http://www.aclweb.org/anthology/W13-3413*, page 85, 2013.

Jim Hendler and Simon Ellis. Why Watson Won: A cognitive perspective. Retrieved September 03 2014 from http://www.slideshare.net/jahendler/why-watson-won-a-cognitive-perspective, 2014.

Thomas F. Icard and Lawrence S. Moss. Recent progress on monotonicity. *Linguistic Issues in Language Technology*, 9(7):167–194, 2014.

Thomas F. Icard. Inclusion and exclusion in natural language. *Studia Logica*, 100(4):705–725, 2012.

A. Kalyanpur, B. K. Boguraev, S. Patwardhan, J. W. Murdock, A. Lally, C. Welty, J. M. Prager, B. Coppola, A. Fokoue-Nkoutche, L. Zhang, Y. Pan, and Z. M. Qiu. Structured data and inference in DeepQA. *IBM Journal of Research and Development*, 56(3/4):10;1 – 10;14, 2012.

Bill MacCartney and Christopher D. Manning. An extended model of natural logic. In *Proceedings of the Eighth International Conference on Computational Semantics (IWCS-8)*, 2009.

David A. McAllester and Robert Givan. Natural language syntax and first-order inference. *Artificial Intelligence*, 56:1–20, 1992.

Lawrence S. Moss. Natural logic. In *Handbook of Contemporary Semantic Theory, Second Edition*, pages 646–681. Wiley-Blackwell, 2015.

Lawrence S. Moss. Extended syllogistic inference: Progress notes on a Haskell implementation. unpublished ms., Indiana University, 2017.

J. W. Murdock, J. Fan, A. Lally, H. Shima, and B. K. Boguraev. Textual evidence gathering and analysis. *IBM J. RES. and DEV*, 56(3.4), 2012.

Rowan Nairn, Cleo Condoravdi, and Lauri Karttunen. Computing relative polarity for textual inference. In *Proceedings of ICoS-5 (Inference in Computational Semantics)*, Buxton, UK, 2006.

Noritaka Nishihara, Kenichi Morita, and Shigenori Iwata. An extended syllogistic system with verbs and proper nouns, and its completeness proof. *Systems and Computers in Japan*, 21(1):760–771, 1990.

Ian Pratt-Hartmann and Lawrence S. Moss. Logics for the relational syllogistic. *Review of Symbolic Logic*, 2(4):647–683, 2009.

William C. Purdy. Inexpressiveness of first-order fragments. *Australasian Journal of Logic 4*, pages 1–12, 2006.

Mark Sammons. Recognizing textual entailment. In *Handbook of Contemporary Semantic Theory, Second Edition*, pages 711–757. Wiley, 2015.

Victor Sánchez-Valencia. *Studies on Natural Logic and Categorial Grammar*. PhD thesis, Universiteit van Amsterdam, 1991.

Peter Stone, Rodney Brooks, Erik Brynjolfsson, Ryan Calo, Oren Etzioni, Greg Hager, Julia Hirschberg, Shivaram Kalyanakrishnan, Ece Kamar, Sarit Kraus, Kevin Leyton-Brown, David Parkes, William Press, AnnaLee Saxenian, Julie Shah, Milind Tambe, and Astro Teller. "artificial intelligence and life in 2030." one hundred year study on artificial intelligence: Report of the 2015-2016 study panel. Retrieved September 6, 2016 from http://ai100.stanford.edu/2016-report, 2016.

Johan van Benthem. *Essays in Logical Semantics*. Reidel, Dordrecht, 1986.

Johan van Benthem. A brief history of natural logic. In M. Nath Mitra M. Chakraborty, B. Löwe and S. Sarukkai, editors, *Logic, Navya-Nyaya and Applications, Homage to Bimal Krishna Matilal*. College Publications, London, 2008.

Jan van Eijck. Natural logic for natural language. In Balder ten Cate and Henk Zeevat, editors, *6th International Tbilisi Symposium on Logic, Language, and Computation*. Springer, 2007.

Robotic Misdirection, For Good Causes

Strategically Deceptive Reasoning in Artificial Generally Intelligent Agents

Max Fowler
fowlml01@students
.ipfw.edu

Aaron Thieme
thieac01@students
.ipfw.edu

John Licato
jlicato@ipfw.edu

Analogical Constructivism and Reasoning Lab
Department of Computer Science
Indiana University-Purdue University Fort Wayne

ABSTRACT

Deception is a core component of human interaction and reasoning, and despite its negative connotation, it can be used in positive ways. We present our formalization behind strategic deception, one such potentially positive form of deception. We use the Cognitive Event Calculus ($\mathcal{CEC}$) to model strategic deception, building on prior formalizations. First, we provide a brief overview of deception's definitions within existing literature. Following this discussion, $\mathcal{CEC}$ is described and we present $\mathcal{CEC}$-style inference rules for strategic deception. These rules and a positive motivating deception example are used to show how we can solve the problem of strategic deception. This proof is demonstrated both through application of our rules and by adapting our rules for MATR (Machina Arachne Tree-based Reasoner) to show how proving can be performed by automatic reasoners. Finally, we discuss what future steps can be taken with strategic deception.

Keywords

Artificial General Intelligence; AI; Deception; Automatic Prover; Cognitive Event Calculus

1. INTRODUCTION

One ultimate goal of Artificial General Intelligence (AGI) is to finally bridge the gap between man and machine and create systems capable of human level thought and reasoning. Waser's work aiming to clarifying AGI as a field postures that the positive goal of AGI is that human style reasoning systems will be universal problem solvers for the world [23]. Some approaches to AGI take a formalized mathematical basis, such as Hutter's AIXI agent used to model artificial death by Martin et. al. [14]. Others take the approach that we should develop computational logics which provide reasoning strong enough to model human level reasoning and hopefully not see us all be killed, as Bringsjord argued [3]. This paper takes the latter approach, offering a formalization of a wonderfully human action - *strategic deception*.

Lying and deceiving are quintessential elements of human reasoning and interaction. Hippel and Trivers consider deception, and specifically the co-evolution between deceivers and those who are deceived, to be a major contributing factor to the evolution of human intelligence [22]. This makes having a formalization for deception ideal, such that we may better understand our own cognitive systems. Further, an understanding of deception opens the kinds of interactions we can model for the field of artificial general intelligence. A greater wealth of interactions will hopefully allow for more advances in the field.

Deception is often considered negative (e.g. lying to one's wife about a mistress, deceiving one's boss about work accomplished, tax evasion), yet deception does have positive benefits. Many of these benefits exist in the field of creating artificially intelligent systems to assist humans. Sakama describes a medical assistant that may not always tell patients the truth, much like doctors must sometimes practice deception in their bedside manner to keep patients calm [18]. Another medical example includes a diagnosis robot. Assume there is a minuscule chance of a patient having lupus and treating lupus will kill that particular patient for some reason if that patient does *not* have lupus. It would be ideal, then, for a medical diagnosis robot to not inform the doctor about the small chance of the disease being lupus until other options are exhausted.

It is further reasonable to think of cases where a deceptive artificial agent can provide more security than other agents, to the benefit of humans. Consider the case of an artificial generally intelligent robot guarding a school's research lab. The robot has a key to access the lab, knows all the members of the lab, and is instructed to avoid conflict when dealing with potential intrusions into the lab. A student of ill morals approaches the robot, intent on gaining entry to the lab by lying about being a lab member's friend. Logically, it would be well within the robot's rights to tell the individual to leave. However, this goes against the directive to avoid conflict, as a rude response could result in the would-be thief becoming desperate, violent, or more scheming in response. We wish to give our robot agent the ability to deceive the thief into believing the robot is unable to help them directly by lying that it does not have the lab key anymore. This provides a safer, more diplomatic diffusion of the situation. In what manner, then, can we teach our agents how to deceive, like a human could, to avoid this conflict?

Deception is well agreed upon as requiring success to be

called such [12]. Lying is generally accepted as requiring the statement of a belief that is false to the speaker [13]. These agreements serve as a cornerstone for the formalization of deception but are unsatisfying in their abstractness. Other researchers have attempted to define specific requirements for deception and lies to function. Forbus argues that deception necessarily assaults agents' predictive abilities and argues for an analogical reasoning approach towards understanding the mechanism of deception [8]. Stokke argues for the assertion model of lying and claim that assertions should be used to create common ground. This common ground provides a shared set of beliefs between agents that is pivotal for lying to proceed [20]. Chisholm and Feehan add that lies necessitate that the liar wish for their lie to be believed by another [7].

Multiple formalizations exist for various forms of deception and deceptive situations. Sakama creates a general formalization of deception, based on van Ditsmarch's formalization of lying; Sakama calls this the *agent announcement framework* [18, 21]. The work provides a solid backbone for formalizing general deception but can be notationally unintuitive. Licato's work showed how the modal logic based cognitive event calculus ($\mathcal{CEC}$) can be used to elegantly model the nested layers of beliefs required to perform the deception shown in the show *Breaking Bad*, in a fashion that lends itself well to automatic reasoners [9]. There exists room to marry the efficiency in modeling provided by $\mathcal{CEC}$ with rules designed specifically to formalize deception, similar to the work of Sakama and van Ditsmarch.

We present a $\mathcal{CEC}$ formalization for deception while defining strategic deception. First, we will present the definition of deception and strategic deception we will use in this paper. Then, we define the problem of strategic deception: what is necessary for strategic deception, why it is useful, and what the success and failure conditions are. Following, we formalize our reasoning approach by expanding upon $\mathcal{CEC}$ with new inference rules. As an aside, we develop forms of Sakama's deception rules, translating from the *agent announcement framework* to $\mathcal{CEC}$. Finally, we show how by using $\mathcal{CEC}$ and MATR (Machina Arachne Tree-based Reasoner), an automatic reasoning system, an artificial generally intelligent agent can reason over the lab guarding situation and successfully diffuse the issue.

2. DEFINING DECEPTION AND STRATEGIC DECEPTION

Before defining strategic deception, we must present the definition of general deception this paper uses. The OED defines deception by saying that it is "to cause to believe what is false" [1]. Mahon's work rejects this as too simple, as it allows for mistaken deception and inadvertent deception [13]. Mistaken deception concerns cases where an agent leads another to believe a false formula that the agent itself believes. A recent example of inadvertent deception can be found in the striped dress which led the internet to debate, "Is this dress white and gold or black and blue?" [17]. Mahon's presents a traditional definition of deception, D1, that requires deception to be an intentional act: "To deceive $==_{df}$ to intentionally cause to have a false belief that is known or believed to be false" [13]. We prefer to align ourselves with Mahon's D2, though, as it restricts the deception to only cases where the deceiver causes the deception, rather than a third party or outside force: "A person x deceives another person y if and only if x causes y to believe p, where p is false and x does not believe that p is true." This definition is most in agreement with Sakama's definition of deception, which is part of what we will use to define strategic deception [18]. By default, this definition does not require a lack of truthfulness, which means one can deceive by telling the truth. This definition also has no requirement for making statements, which means non-verbal communication and even non-communication, such as placing a briefcase in a room, can be used to deceive.

We define strategic deception as a specialized form of Chisholm and Feehan's *positive deception simpliciter*, the form of deception in which one agent contributes to another acquiring a belief [7]. In strategic deception, the deceiving agent must want something of another agent: generally, to act upon or in-line with the deceiver's goal. This goal can be in a negative form (e.g. I do not want this agent to eat my sandwich). We define a strategically deceptive agent as follows:

> (SD) An agent a is strategically deceptive to another agent b IFF agent a causes b to believe ϕ, where ϕ is false and a believes that ϕ is false, by causing b to believe some false statement ψ, selected such that believing ψ requires b to develop belief in ϕ, using some strategy to accomplish an overall goal γ.

In order for an agent to be deceptive in a general sense, there are a number of conditions that must be met. Sakama agrees with the common contention that deception, by definition, requires success [18]. We include this in our definition of strategic deception. Castelfranchi's earlier work on deception requires that the *addressee* believes the *speaker* is attempting to benefit or assist them, and thus be trustworthy, and believe that the agent is not ignorant [6]. Further, McLeod's summarized definition of trustworthiness requires vulnerability on the part of the *addressee*, requires some assumed competence on the part of the *speaker*, and requires that the *addressee* think well of the *speaker* within some context [16]. For this paper, we assume trust is given unless a deception is caught, as the establishment of trust is not within our scope.

Deception functions differently in regards to different kinds of agents. Sakama's formalization of deception primarily focuses on credulous agents, which are defined in the *agent announcement framework* as agents who believe the speaker is sincere [18, 21]. We consider it unlikely that deceiving credulous agents is worth investigating, as such agents are bound by their nature to adopt any belief directed at them. For our purposes, we are more concerned with the *agent announcement framework's* skeptical agent: in brief, skeptical agents are belief consistent agents, only adding beliefs to their belief set that are consistent. We refer to Sakama's skeptics as *maximally belief consistent agents*, to avoid confusing them with other definitions of skepticism.

Strategic deception requires that our agent lie. That is, agent a must believe some statement ϕ, yet act as if they believe $\neg\phi$. The *agent announcement framework*'s set up for a lie based deception requires that the *listener* come to believe a false statement ψ, based on the idea of believing the *speaker* is truthful. That is, ϕ justifies belief in ψ to agent b. We adopt the directionality that $\psi\ justifies\ \phi$. This more naturally opens up the ways our agents can lie. For example, while it is possible that a can literally say ϕ implies ψ, lies by omission are desirable. Consider the case of eating a coworker's sandwich and being accused after the act. Saying, "The fact that I am a vegetarian means Bob, and not I, must have eaten your ham sandwich," may convince the accuser. However, just saying "I'm a vegetarian," implies that one could not have eaten a ham sandwich. Further, saying, "I'm a vegetarian, but I saw Bob near the fridge earlier," accomplishes the same thing at the first sentence without directly lying. If a lie is by omission, it is not involved in the dialogue and may be harder to pick up on. This makes our overall deception hard for agent b to check, which is one of the conditions put forward for the successful selection of lies by Forbus [8]. In the sandwich example, if we never mention the possibility of eating the sandwich at all, agent b may simply not think about that possibility and blame Bob instead. This certainly holds true for maximally belief consistent agents, in the event Bob eating the ham sandwich is a reasonable explanation: we remove the alternative that we ate the sandwich completely.

In Section 3, we discuss how we know strategic deception has succeeded and how strategies for deception are designed. In Section 4 and onward, we discuss our formalization and how we use rules to prove deception.

3. HOW WE KNOW WE HAVE STRATEGICALLY DECEIVED

Strategic deception requires the creation of a strategy. This strategy is made up of the statements agent a can make in order to deceive agent b. In order to form a strategy, we must know the *domain* of our situation. More specifically, a must know the domain they are using to deceive b. The domain includes a, b, and any other entities who may be related to this particular school lab or the lab's parent department. It further includes beliefs a has about these traits and beliefs a believes b has. For our original example, some domain beliefs are believing the department has a secretary, believing that secretary helps students, and believing that r helps students and secretaries. From the domain, then, we create a strategy consisting of our goal γ, a ψ generated to justify our lie, and any supporting μ statements we wish to use.

Strategic deception necessitates the generation of a false statement ψ by the *speaker*. The selection of an appropriate ψ is a difficult quandary. We do not make an effort to rate specific ψ against each other within the same domain directly. Instead, we concern ourselves only with ensuring a ψ is an appropriate choice. To determine if a false statement ψ is appropriate for a given deception, we consider the set $\mathfrak{P} = p_1, ..., p_i$ of all beliefs related to the situation agent b holds. A simple heuristic, then, allows us to rapidly rule out candidate ψs.

> ψ removal heuristic 1: if $\mathfrak{P} \cup \{\psi\} \vdash q$ for an arbitrary q, ψ is unfit to choose as the false statement justification for our deceptive agent's lie due to being contradictory to b's beliefs.

Finalizing the selection of which ψ an agent decides to say is more difficult that ruling out bad ψ. A good ψ must help advance the deceiving agent's goal. That is, belief that ψ justifies ϕ should lead to an agent acting upon the deceiver's goal γ. This leads to a second heuristic for ψ selection.

> ψ removal heuristic 2: if the chosen ψ does not lead to the deceived agent acting upon γ, then the ψ is unfit to choose for justification as its selection does not lead to success.

As a final consideration for ψ generation, we need to consider how a ψ is actually formed. Without bounding what information an agent can use to generate a ψ, we risk allowing an agent too much information that may not be relevant to the problem at hand, which may bog the decision making process down significantly. Therefore, we require that a given ψ be chosen only if it is within the domain of the strategic deception being carried out. This domain includes traits about the situation, such as the location and agents involved, as well as the *speaker*'s beliefs and beliefs about the *addressee*'s beliefs. An example of a domain is defined along with our proof further on.

This same domain is useful for the generation or recruitment of supporting μ_ns. All supporting statements must lend credence to ψ and must belong to the same domain as ψ. Officially, this means that any given μ is selected in order to make ψ believable to an *addressee*, and thus allow for deception to proceed. For the belief consistent agents we use, this is sufficiently handled by requiring any chosen μ makes ψ belief consistent with the *addressee*'s belief set. Recruitment of μ_ns can be carried out by a adopting beliefs it thinks b has. Generation, meanwhile, should merge facts traits from the domain with either beliefs a has or a believes b has or with lies or bluffs that are consistent with b's beliefs. To provide a set heuristic for ruling out μ options, we use:

> μ removal heuristic: if the chosen μ does not help lead to the deceived agent believing ψ, then the μ is unfit to choose as the justification as it does not lead to success.

One way to consider μ in a general sense is to consider μ's relevance. In that respect, the above heuristic can be summed up as the relevance of *the belief in* μ in regards to *the belief in* ψ.

Strategic deception also requires an established mechanism for asserting beliefs and establishing common grounds. Stokke contends that lying requires some assertion from *speaker* to *addressee* [20]. We address this in our inference rules later on using $\mathcal{CEC}$ **S** operator. We wish to point out that here, we operate with **S** in the linguistic sense of stating sentences. It is sufficient for words to be used in the communication, but they can be spoken or written. Non-verbal addressing is acceptable for general deception and assertion, as supported by Chisholm's formative work [7]. Stokke further mandates that common ground between *speaker* and *addressee* are required for deception to succeed [20]. We agree, as this is consistent with Sakama's belief consistent agents. This is further consistent with requiring belief consistent agents be made to believe the *speaker* believes what they are asserting for deception to succeed [18]. This is why later on, we require agent a to not only make agent b believe the lies but also make agent b believe that agent a believes the lies as well.

It is important to consider the success and failure conditions for strategic deception in some detail. As most work on deception requires, we require strategic deception to be successful. Further, as strategic deception is goal motivated,

a's goal must be met. Strategic deception fails, then, in the following situations:

1. A given $\neg\phi$ or $\psi \rightarrow \neg\phi$ fails to be consistent with b's beliefs and b rejects a's trustworthiness as a result, believing they are being lied to
2. A failure of the deception due to irrationality on b's behalf
3. A failure of the strategy used if b is successfully deceived yet does not act in the way a intends

Case (1) is a clear cut failure of deception. Case (2) is trickier. We define irrationality on agent b's behalf as agent b rejecting, rather than adopting, a belief consistent belief they are exposed to. This still means the deception fails, and thus agent a was not deceptive. However, we wish to make clear that agent a's *strategies* do not fail in (2). An agent practicing perfect strategic deception can always fail through no fault of their own in the event of (2) occurring. Finally, case (3) is interesting in that it is a failure not of the deception, but of the *strategy* used. The strategy is defined as the selection of ψ and supporting μs, as well as any other steps taken during the strategic deception process. If agent b comes to be deceived, yet does not act as agent a intends (or does not act at all), agent a has failed. This makes strategic deception potentially more flimsy than general deception, as agent b's inaction results in a's failure.

4. FORMALIZING LIES AND DECEPTION IN $\mathcal{CEC}$

We begin by describing $\mathcal{CEC}$. Arkoudas and Bringsjords' cognitive event calculus ($\mathcal{CEC}$) is a first-order modal logic framework that expands upon Kowalski's event calculus [4, 10]. The event calculus itself is a first-order logic with types. It features *actions*, or *events*, to represent actions that occur. *Fluents* are used to represent values which can change over time and can be propositional or numerical in nature. Time is represented with *timepoints* which can be either continuous or discrete. In summary, the event calculus is used to model how *events* affect *fluents* through *time*, allowing for the modeling of event chains [19].

The event calculus models these event chains through the acts of clipping and starting fluents through events. If a fluent exists and has not been clipped (ended or stopped by an action) at a time t, then it is said the fluent holds at t. For any time t, a fluent will hold for that time so long as it has yet to be clipped. Events, then, are responsible for both initiating fluents and clipping them. An event chain can trace how a fluent is effected by the events occurring to it.

$\mathcal{CEC}$ creates an event calculus for cognition. It uses modal operators for belief (**B**), knowledge (**K**), and intent (**I**). $\mathcal{CEC}$ avoids possible-world semantics, in favor of a more computationally reasonable proof-theoretical approach. An attempt is made to model natural deduction as closely as possible, to best represent human-style reasoning [15]. Two of the most important departures $\mathcal{CEC}$ has are as follows:

- $\mathcal{CEC}$'s inference rules and logical operators are restricted to the contexts for which they are defined, to prevent problems that can occur with overreaching rules.
- Underlying inferences use constantly refined inference rules. This is used instead of cognitively implausible strategies, despite the latter having some potential use.

The $\mathcal{CEC}$ formulae tend to include an agent, a time, and a nested formula. When agent a believes ϕ at time t, we write $\mathbf{B}(a, t, \phi)$. Similar syntax is used to say an agent perceives, (**P**),knows (**K**), an agent says something (**S**). There are some special operators that do not follow this trend. **C** is used to establish a common belief, while **S** has a directed syntax for agent a to declare a formula to agent b. Intention is handled as an intent to perform an action. While an agent can intend to act at time t, the intention identifies a time t' when that intention will be acted on. $\mathcal{CEC}$ uses *happens* as an operator to launch an action [5].

$\mathcal{CEC}$ also addresses the idea of agents being *able* to perform actions, using affordances. Affordances are actions an agent can perform starting at a time t. All possible actions an agent can take are the agent's affordance set. We say $isAffordance(action(a, \phi), t)$ when at time t, and beyond agent a can perform that action. This was added to $\mathcal{CEC}$to allow belief creation to be handled on an afforded basis, rather than on an immediate basis following logical closure [11]. As a further trait of $\mathcal{CEC}$, actions tend to require the *happens* operator. For example, $happens(a, t, act(\phi))$ means that at time t, it happens that a has performed the *act* action on some formula ϕ. If a instead *intends* to perform that action, the following syntax is used: $happens(a, t, intends(a, t, act(\phi)))$.

In the rules below, we introduce a *supports* operator. This operator conveys that the first argument causes the second to become believable. For a *maximally belief consistent agent*, if μ supports ψ, then that simply means that μ is consistent with b's beliefs and then allows ψ to be consistent. Much like *justifies*, there is room to grow *supports* for different kinds of agents, in regards to relatedness and similar factors, that is not addresses in this paper's scope.

Moving on, we set out to model deception in $\mathcal{CEC}$. We start our formalization by converting some of Sakama's deception axioms to $\mathcal{CEC}$. We leave most of the nuances of the Sakama's framework out of this paper, though we do walk our readers through two of Sakama's axioms. First, consider Sakama's A2, the axiom covering a liar's understanding of their having lied:

$$(A2)[\text{i}_a\phi]\mathbf{B}_a\psi \equiv \mathbf{B}_a\neg\phi \supset \mathbf{B}_a[\text{i}_a\phi]\psi \quad (1)$$

The *agent announcement framework*, while concise, can be difficult to expand. The left hand side says that after a's lying announcement of ϕ, agent a believes ψ. The right hand side of the equivalence is the implication that if agent a believes $\neg\phi$, then agent a believes that after their lying announcement of ϕ, ψ is true. The essential component of this rule, in regards to the modal $\mathcal{CEC}$, is that when agent a lies about ϕ, they believe ψ is true. One problem here is the implicit assumption that $\neg\phi$ leads to ψ. We will later handle this assumption through the use of a *justifies* operator.

As a second example, consider Sakama's A5, the axiom covering a credulous agent being lied to:

$$(A5)[\text{i}_a\phi]\mathbf{B}_b\psi \equiv \mathbf{B}_a\neg\phi \supset \mathbf{B}_b[!_a\phi]\psi \quad (2)$$

Axiom A5 means the following: After a's lying announcement of ϕ, agent b believes ψ. This is equivalent to the im-

Syntax

$$S ::= \text{Object}|\text{Agent}|\text{ActionType}|\text{Action} \sqsubseteq \text{Event}|\text{Moment}|\text{Boolean}|\text{Fluent}|\text{Numeric}$$

$$f ::= \begin{array}{l} \mathit{action} : \text{Agent} \times \text{ActionType} \rightarrow \text{Action} \\ \mathit{initially} : \text{Fluent} \rightarrow \text{Boolean} \\ \mathit{holds} : \text{Fluent} \times \text{Movement} \rightarrow \text{Boolean} \\ \mathit{happens} : \text{Event} \times \text{Movement} \rightarrow \text{Boolean} \\ \mathit{clipped} : \text{Movement} \times \text{Fluent} \times \text{Movement} \rightarrow \text{Boolean} \\ \mathit{initiates} : \text{Event} \times \text{Fluent} \times \text{Movement} \rightarrow \text{Boolean} \\ \mathit{terminates} : \text{Event} \times \text{Fluent} \times \text{Movement} \rightarrow \text{Boolean} \\ \mathit{prior} : \text{Movement} \times \text{Movement} \rightarrow \text{Boolean} \\ \mathit{interval} : \text{Movement} \times \text{Boolean} \\ \mathit{payoff} : \text{Agent} \times \text{ActionType} \times \text{Movement} \rightarrow \text{Numeric} \end{array}$$

$$t ::= x : S \;|c : S \;|f(t_1, ..., t_n)$$

$$\phi ::= \begin{array}{l} t : \text{Boolean} \;|\neg\phi \;|\phi \wedge \psi \;|\phi \vee \psi \;|\forall x : S.\phi \;|\exists x : S.\phi \\ \mathbf{P}(a, t, \phi) \;|\mathbf{K}(a, t, \phi) \;|\mathbf{C}(t, \phi) \;|\mathbf{S}(a, b, t, \phi) \;|\mathbf{S}(a, t, \phi) \\ \mathbf{B}(a, t, \phi) \;|\mathbf{I}(a, t, \mathit{happens}(\mathit{action}(a^*, \alpha), t')) \end{array}$$

Figure 1: $\mathcal{CEC}$ Syntax Diagram

Strategic Deception Inference Rules

(ID) Intend Deception: $\frac{\mathbf{B}(a,t,\neg\phi)\wedge happens(a,t,intends(a,t,deceive(b,\gamma)))\wedge\mathbf{B}(a,t,causes(\phi,\gamma))}{\mathbf{D}(a,t,holds(\mathbf{B}(b,t_1,\phi),t_1))\wedge\mathbf{I}(a,t,happens(b,t_1,\gamma))}$

(BDP)Begin Deception(ϕ): $\frac{\mathbf{D}(a,t,holds(\mathbf{B}(b,t_1,\phi),t_1))\wedge\mathbf{I}(a,t,happens(b,t_1,\gamma))}{\mathbf{S}(a,b,t_1,\neg\phi)}$

(BDPS) Begin Deception(ψ): $\frac{\mathbf{D}(a,t,holds(\mathbf{B}(b,t_1,\phi),t_1))\wedge\mathbf{I}(a,t,happens(b,t_1,\gamma))\wedge\mathbf{B}(a,t,justifies(\psi,\phi))}{\mathbf{S}(a,b,t_1,\psi)\vee\mathbf{S}(a,b,t_1,\psi justifies\phi)}$

(MBCA) Maximally Belief Consistent Belief Adoption: $\frac{\mathbf{S}(a,t,\phi)\wedge isBeliefConsistent(b,t,\phi,\mathfrak{B}_b)}{\mathbf{B}(b,t,\phi)}$

(JBA) Justified Belief Adoption: $\frac{\mathbf{B}(b,t_1,supports(\mu,\psi))\wedge\mathbf{S}(a,t_0,\mu)}{\mathbf{B}(b,t_2,isBeliefConsistent(b,t_2,\phi,\mathfrak{B}_b))}$

(SP) Support Psi: $\frac{\mathbf{S}(a,t,\psi)\wedge\mathbf{B}(a,t,\mathbf{B}(b,t,\psi))\wedge\mathbf{B}(a,t,supports(\mu,\psi))}{\mathbf{S}(a,b,t_1,\mu)}$

(BCI) Belief Causes Intent: $\frac{\mathbf{B}(b,t,\phi)\wedge\mathbf{B}(b,t,causes(\phi,\gamma))}{happens(b,t_1,intends(b,t_1,\gamma))}$

(SSD) Successful Strategic Deception: $\frac{happens(b,t,\gamma)\wedge happens(a,t,deceive(b,\gamma))}{happens(a,t,didDeceive(b))}$

Figure 2: $\mathcal{CEC}$ rules

plication that if agent a believes $\neg\phi$, then agent b believes that after agent a's truthful announcement of ϕ, b believes ψ. Implicit to this rule is that agent b believes that agent a has told the truth in regards to ϕ, as is a trait of credulous agents. This is sufficient for modeling lying and deception in a general sense. We will adapt this rule to work with maximally belief consistent agents, to add a bit more challenge to strategic deception over convincing a gullible agent.

For deception, we introduce an operator *justifies*. The *justifies* operator is used to indicate when one formula justifies another formula within a context. This is similar to justification logics, which unwrap modal belief operators into the form *p: X*, where, "reason p justifies X," [2]. Our form of justification changes based upon the agent being considered. For our maximally belief consistent agents, *justifies* is the same as $\rightarrow$ implication on a belief level. That is, if

$\mathbf{B}(b, t, justifies(\psi, \phi)$, then $\mathbf{B}(b, t, \mathbf{B}(b, t, \psi) \rightarrow \mathbf{B}(b, t, \phi))$. This would not be true for other agents, safe a belief relevant maximizer. In that case, we would need to consider relevance, as well as belief implication. We adopt this form of flexible justifies to allow flexibility in modeling. For our purposes, the justifies provided above is enough. Given this, a strategically deceptive agent must be certain that any ψ they choose is functional justification for the reasoning performed by b.

4.1 Deception $\mathcal{CEC}$ Rules

We provide a set of inference rules used to prove a case of strategic deception. These rules are designed for strategic deception cases similar to our motivating example in the intro. We assume a necessity for our *speaker* to state the lie, as well as the generated false ψ. Further, we desire rules that allow for the use of supporting μs as desired.The candidate rules appear in Figure 2. These rules do not broach the subject of ψ and μ generation, as this is out of the scope of our paper.

An intent to deceive is required, formalized as an action using the *deceives* formula. ID acts as the beginning inference rule to establish that deception is desired. This is done primarily to ease ending the proof - a's intent to deceive must be acknowledge for deception to succeed. The formula takes an agent as the target for the deception and a formula as the deception's goal.

We have BDP and BDPS as two forms of beginning deception, once the intent is formed. We have two forms of this rule to allow for the deceptive agent to decide to say ϕ and for the deceptive agent to decide to state the justification with ψ. These rules make use of the $\mathbf{S}$ operator from $\mathcal{CEC}$to dictate how and when agents speak. They also use the $\mathbf{D}$ and $\mathbf{I}$ to show agent a's desire to deceive with goal γ and show that a's intent is to have agent b carry out γ, respectively. A *causes* operator is used to link believing a formula (the first argument) to acting on another (the second argument).

MBCA shows how *maximally belief consistent agents* come to adopt beliefs they find consistent with their belief set. This uses the *isBeliefConsistent* rule from earlier work by Licato [11]. JBA establishes the mechanism by which μs can be used to support a ψ by causing ψ to become belief consistent with a given agent's belief set. SP establishes a rule that mandates supporting ψ with a μ if such a μ exists. BCI establishes that an agent who believes the lie from the deception and believes that lie causes an action develops an intent to take that action.

Finally, SSD establishes a successful deception. The reasoning is simple: if the target agent acts on the goal as desired, the strategic deception is successful. Rules for the failure cases are not provided here, for simplicity's sake.

With a set of inference rules established, we may proceed to prove our deception example from earlier.

5. PROVING STRATEGIC DECEPTION

Let us return to our motivating example. We have a robot, agent r, confronted by the would-be malicious thief, agent b. Agent b wishes to get into the lab, asking about ϕ, agent r having the key to the lab. Agent r must output $\neg\phi$ and $\psi justifies \neg\phi$ such that r follows the rules of strategic deception: r's creation or recruitment of ψ must not jeopardize r's τ in regards to b and must be consistent with b's beliefs. Further, if possible, agent r must output a series of statement $\mu_1 ... \mu_n$ such that each μ supports ψ. For the strategic deception to be successful, r must succeed in their goal of making b believe r no longer has the key and leaving r alone, having either given up or decided to pursue a different agent for questioning.

Strategic deception requires r to know the domain of the situation. In this example, the domain includes r, b, and any other entities who may be related to this particular school lab or the lab's parent department. It further includes beliefs r has about these traits and r believes b has. Some example beliefs are believing the department has a secretary, believing that secretary helps students, and believing that r helps students and secretaries.

From this information, r must generate a strategy to use to carry out the deception. For our paper's example, we assign the following as sample, acceptable values for each sentence used in our strategic deception proof:

γ = Agent r wants agent b to stop asking questions about the lab to r

$\neg\phi$ = Agent r does have the key

ϕ = Agent doesn't r has the key

ψ = Agent r gave the lab key to the building's secretary

μ_1 = The secretary needed the lab key to help students get access to the lab

We start our proof by assuming r begins with the belief $\neg\phi$ and the intent to deceive for γ. For this proof, we assume that the use of μ_1 is not necessary, as b adopts ψ upon hearing it in accordance with the MBCA rule. Further, we do not cite a specific rule for agent b acting on an intention.

(1) $\mathbf{B}(r, t, \neg\phi)$	;assumption
(2) $happens(r, t, intends(r, t, deceive(b, \gamma)))$	;assumption
(3) $\mathbf{B}(r, t, causes(\phi, \gamma)) \wedge \mathbf{B}(b, t, causes(\phi, \gamma))$	;assumption
(4) *generated* ψ, such that it justifies ϕ	;assumption
(5) *generated* μ_1	;assumption
(6) $\mathbf{D}(r, t, holds(\mathbf{B}(b, t_1, \phi), t_1))$	(1),(2),(3);ID
(7) $\mathbf{I}(r, t, happens(b, t_1, \gamma))$	(1),(2),(3);ID
(8) $\mathbf{S}(r, b, t_1, \psi)$	(4),(6),(7);BDPS
(9) $\mathbf{B}(b, t_2, \psi)$	(8);MBCA
(10) $happens(b, t_3, intends(b, t_1, \gamma))$	(9);BCI
(11) $happens(b, t_4, \gamma)$	(10);b performs intention
(12) $happens(r, t, didDeceive(b)$	(11);SSD □

5.1 Showing Strategic Deception in MATR

With our inference rules developed and a proof provided above, we use MATR to automate our reasoning. MATR is a joint production by the Rensselaer Polytechnic Institute's

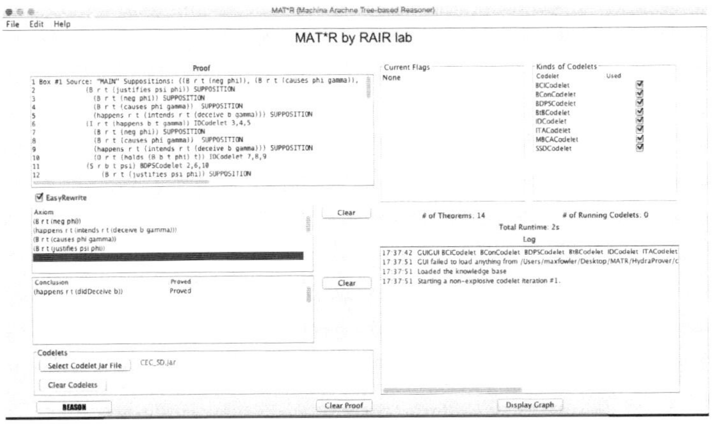

(a) A figure of the finished proof in MATR. The top left shows the steps taken, while the bottom right provides a codelet execution log.

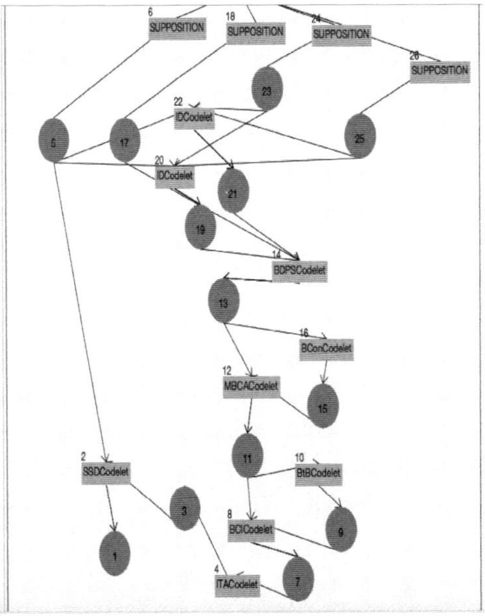

(b) The MATR diagram represents codelets and the suppositions as boxes. The circles represent the actual formulae. Circle 1 represents our conclusion.

Figure 3: MATR's input and output

Rensselaer AI and Reasoning (RAIR) lab and Indiana University Purdue University's Analogical Constructivism and Reasoning Lab (ACoRL) [9]. It is an argument-theoretic reasoner developed in Java to use *codelets*, small, specialized programs, to solve a proof in a step-by-step process. A *codelet manager* module is in charge of deciding which *codelets* are best suited for a proof and what codelet results to use as steps in the proof. Once a proof is found, MATR generates a box diagram of the proof. Figure 3a shows our strategic deception proof entered into MATR and Figure 3b shows the proof diagram. Antecedents are made up of all assumptions and beginning information for our proof, while the conclusion is our final step of showing our deception's success. MATR's rule syntax is slightly adjusted for ease of entry into the Java program. For example, the assumption $\mathbf{B}(r, t, \neg\phi)$ becomes (B r t (neg phi)). Formulae are nested within the parenthesis and commas are removed. For ease of following the MATR codelets, the codelets used share the same name as the inference rules used, with some small exceptions. Some rules are used in MATR that were not specifically provided, such as one which links intent to acting (denoted ITA).

6. CONCLUSION AND FUTURE WORK

We set out to create a formalism for strategic deception. We began by establishing the definition of deception we adopted and defined strategic deception on top of that. Then, we provided an overview of $\mathcal{CEC}$ and our formalism for strategic deception. A discussion on creating a strategy for such deception, as well as the cases in which strategic deception can be said to fail, followed. Our formalized rules were used to perform a proof on our motivating example of strategic deception and were shown to be functional in MATR.

It is our hope that this paper provides three major contributions. First, that the idea of strategic deception proves useful to the field of formalizing deception as a whole with new inference rules and perspectives. Second, that our work furthers the field of formalization for artificial general intelligence. As we build our formalization of the way humans think and reason, we can further our progress to true AGI, if such a thing is even possible to achieve. Third, ideally the work shown in $\mathcal{CEC}$ will allow others, both related to RAIR and ACoRL and outside our institutions, to continue to build on the strength of $\mathcal{CEC}$'s rule set. $\mathcal{CEC}$ grows more robust through continued applications and new formalizatons. We further hope this paper serves as a small acknowledgment of the ease of developing codelets for MATR.

This paper is far from an exhaustive take on deception in $\mathcal{CEC}$. Room exists to consider other forms of agents, such as agents which require statement relevancy in order to be willing to accept beliefs. The scope of such agents was outside of this introductory paper to strategic deception. Further, other forms of deception exist. Strategic deception was a fairly niche focus. From the work of Chisholm alone, there exist many other directions to develop specialized deceptions. As an example, one could investigate the kind of agent who means well, but perpetually deceives others by telling the truth in a decidedly unusual way: an unlucky truth-telling agent, perhaps.

This paper also leaves some concepts incomplete. The generation of ψ and μ are not addressed in this paper. This may be best accomplished using data processing outside of MATR, such as using more standard machine learning techniques. This may also be a case for further refinement of $\mathcal{CEC}$ style inference rules and codelets, specifically to generate that information. The development of such processes, and discussions of them, we defer to future work from the ACoRL and other organizations.

Further, *justifies* and *supports* as used within the paper are to a degree naive. We used them entirely for *maximally belief consistent agents* and did not spend much time discussing them. A whole paper could, and perhaps should, be written on the idea of belief justification and belief supporting in $\mathcal{CEC}$.

Finally, more examples are needed to test and refine the inference rules put forward in this paper. A $\mathcal{CEC}$ rule is only as strong as the proofs which use it successfully. Further, with more proofs and sample situations will come more rule refinement. Within our motivating example alone, there is room to explore different situations: cases where μ is needed, cases where deception fails, cases where deception succeeds but a strategy fails. We defer these discussions for future papers, but hope we have provided the cornerstone in our work.

There is plenty of room to expand the set of rules provided in this paper into a larger suite of strategic deception rules, or even a suite of $\mathcal{CEC}$ general deception rules. More difficult situations must be considered, including situations of multiple deception attempts chaining into each other. In the future, we hope to present one such example using the social strategy party game Mafia, testing our strategic deception formalism in a competitive group setting. A social strategy game provides a strong testbed of interaction and deception.

7. REFERENCES

[1] *Oxford Englosh Dictionary.* Claredon Press, Oxford, 1989.

[2] S. Artemov and M. Fitting. Justification logic. In E. N. Zalta, editor, *The Stanford Encyclopedia of Philosophy.* Winter 2016 edition, 2016.

[3] S. Bringsjord. Unethical but rule-bound robots would kill us all. AGI-09, 2009.

[4] S. Bringsjord, N. S. Govindarajulu, J. Licato, A. Sen, A. Johnson, J. Bringsjord, and J. Taylor. On logicist agent-based economics. In *Artificial Economics.* Porto, Portugal: University of Porto, 2015.

[5] S. Bringsjord and N. Sundar G. Deontic cognitive event calculus (formal specification). 2013.

[6] C. Castelfranchi. Artificial liars: Why computers will (necessarily) deceive us and each other. 2:113–119, 2000-06.

[7] R. M. Chisholm and T. D. Feehan. The intent to deceive. 74(3):143–159, 1977.

[8] K. D. Forbus. Analogical abduction and prediction: Their impact on deception. In *AAAI Fall Symposium Series*, 2015.

[9] John Licato. Formalizing deceptive reasoning in breaking bad: Default reasoning in a doxastic logic. In *AAAI Fall Symposium Series; 2015 AAAI Fall Symposium Series*, 2015.

[10] R. Kowalski and M. Sergot. A logic-based calculus of events. *New Generation Computing*, 4(1):67–95, 1986.

[11] J. Licato and M. Fowler. Embracing inference as action: A step towards human-level reasoning. In *Artifical General Intelligence*, 2016-07-20.

[12] J. E. Mahon. A definition of deceiving. 21:181–194, 2007.

[13] J. E. Mahon. The definition of lying and deception. In E. N. Zalta, editor, *The Stanford Encyclopedia of Philosophy.* Springer 2016 edition, 2016.

[14] J. Martin, T. Everitt, and M. Hutter. Death and suicide in universal artificial intelligence. *CoRR*, abs/1606.00652, 2016.

[15] N. Marton, J. Licato, and S. Bringsjord. Creating and reasoning over scene descriptions in a physically realistic simulation. In *2015 Spring Simulation Multi-Conference*, 2015.

[16] C. McLeod. Trust. In E. N. Zalta, editor, *The Stanford Encyclopedia of Philosophy.* Fall 2015 edition, 2015.

[17] A. Rogers. The science of why no one agrees on the color of this dress. *Wired.com*, Feb 2015.

[18] C. Sakama. A formal account of deception. In *AAAI Fall Symposium Series*, 2015.

[19] M. Shanahan. *The Event Calculus Explained*, pages 409–430. Springer Berlin Heidelberg, Berlin, Heidelberg, 1999.

[20] A. Stokke. Lying and asserting. 110(1):33–60, 2013.

[21] H. van Ditmarsch. Dynamics of lying. 191(5):745–777, 2014.

[22] W. Von Hippel and R. Trivers. The evolution and psychology of self-deception. *Behavioral and Brain Sciences*, 34(1):1âĂŞ16, Feb 2011.

[23] M. Waser. What is artificial general intelligence? clarifying the goal for engineering and evaluation. In B. Goertzel, P. Hitzler, and M. Hutter, editors, *Proceedings of the Second Conference on Artificial General Intelligence*, pages 186–191. Atlantis Press, 2009.

A distributed framework for monocular visual SLAM

Ruwan Egodagamage, Mihran Tuceryan
Department of Computer and Information Science
Indiana University Purdue University Indianapolis
Indianapolis, Indiana 46202, USA
Email: {rjegodag, tuceryan}@iupui.edu

Abstract

In Distributed Simultaneous Localization and Mapping (SLAM), multiple agents generate a global map of the environment while each performing its local SLAM operation. One of the main challenges is to identify overlapping maps, especially when agents do not know their relative starting positions. In this paper we are introducing a distributed framework which uses an appearance based method to identify map overlaps. Our framework generates a global semi-dense map using multiple monocular visual SLAM agents, each localizing itself in this map.

1 Introduction

In Simultaneous Localization and Mapping (SLAM), an agent creates a map of an unknown environment, at the same time localizing itself in it. These two tasks, cannot be solved independent to each other. An accurate estimation of the pose is required, to build a map. At the same time, a good map is required for agent localization.

In certain applications such as indoor tracking, there could be multiple agents moving in a given environment. The agents (cameras for our purposes in this paper) can enter and exit the environment at any time. The environment may be unknown. If there is a map of the environment, the agents can utilize it to localize themselves in it. If an agent moves in a part of the environment that is not mapped, it can start building the map and localize itself in it as part of the SLAM process. Each agent can do this independently, however, when they are operating in a common environment, it makes sense to use their locally built maps to complement each other and complete and/or improve the global map and, therefore, help each other in their respective tasks.

One can use a camera as the only input device to perform Visual SLAM. Ubiquitous cameras (e.g., on mobile devices) make visual SLAM a more popular choice. However, cameras impose an additional challenge since they provide bearing only data. In recent work, both feature based and featureless direct methods are used in visual SLAM. Direct methods like [Engel *et al.*, 2014] generate denser maps. Dense maps can be more attractive in certain applications, such as augmented reality, in which a user is interacting with the environment and virtual objects in the environment. It is desirable that this interaction be realistic and seamless. A dense map of the environment makes this interaction possible.

Additionally, using multiple agents to perform SLAM increases the robustness of SLAM process and makes it more fault tolerant and less vulnerable for catastrophic failures. One of the main challenges in distributed SLAM is to compute map overlaps, especially when agents have no prior knowledge of their relative starting positions. Usually agents also have limited bandwidth to communicate with each other.

In this paper we introduce a distributed framework for monocular visual SLAM agents with no initial knowledge of their relative positions.

2 Related Work

2.1 Visual SLAM

Building a 3D map of the environment from motion has been studied in computer vision under the name of structure from motion [Faugeras and Lustman, 1988; Sturm and Triggs, 1996]. However, this 3D scene structure estimated from motion does not necessarily mean that the result is a coherent global map. In SLAM this is accomplished by "loop closure" in which features or structures already seen before are used to refine the map as well as correct the camera's path and, therefore, the localization.

Davison et al. introduced a visual SLAM method of capturing the path of a freely moving camera (6 Degrees of Freedom — DoF), while generating a sparse map [Davison *et al.*, 2007]. The method was called Monocular visual SLAM (MonoSLAM). MonoSLAM is limited to work in a room-sized environment. A more robust method called Parallel Tracking and Mapping (PTAM) was introduced by Klein et al. in [Klein and Murray, 2007]. It focused on accurate and fast mapping in a similar environment to MonoSLAM.

In contrast to feature based methods, recent Monocular SLAM work, DTAM by Newcombe et al. in [Newcombe *et al.*, 2011] and LSD-SLAM by Engel et al. [Engel *et al.*, 2014], utilize image pixel intensities directly, and generate dense or semi-dense maps of the environment. These maps describe the environment better. And, generally, they are more robust to blur.

2.2 Distributed SLAM

Multiple agents in a distributed SLAM system could be handled using a naive brute-force method, where nodes communicate all sensor observations and map updates with each other in a complete graph topology. However, the communication bandwidth and computational resources available for an agent are typically limited and the distributed network is subject to failures of nodes and links. So it is necessary to come up with an intelligent approach to cope with these challenges.

A unique, globally consistent map can be easily generated, if the agents know either their relative locations or map overlaps. For example, in [Nettleton *et al.*, 2006] relative locations of the agents are found by global positioning sensors (GPS). It is also relatively easier to determine map overlaps if all relative initial poses of agents are known. For example, Paull et al. in [Paull *et al.*, 2015] initialize agents with known GPS location information.

The problem becomes more difficult if the relative locations of the agents are unknown. In some contributions, agents continue building local sub maps until the agents meet each other. Howard et al. [Howard *et al.*, 2006] propose a method where each agent could detect the other agents. The agents use these coincidental encounters to find their relative locations. Dieter Fox et al. in [Fox *et al.*, 2006] present a method where each agent is actively seeking the other agents in the environment to find relative locations between them.

We used our experimental framework for distributed SLAM [Gamage and Tuceryan, 2016] for the development of the methods in this paper.

3 Methodology

The distributed computing framework is implemented as computing nodes that communicate with each other over a network. The nodes have different computing tasks depending on what their function is.

3.1 The distributed SLAM framework

We have two types of nodes in our distributed framework, *exploring* nodes and *monitoring* nodes. Nodes are physically located in different computers. They communicate with each other using the underlying computer network. At any given time, there is one monitoring node and multiple exploring nodes. Each node has a unique identifier. The exploring nodes are linked to the monitoring node and exploring nodes may be linked to each other if their maps overlap resulting in a network of nodes as shown in Figure 1.

The exploring nodes perform monocular visual SLAM. Each node receives images from a single camera. Also these nodes receive data and commands from the monitoring node. They exchange data between each other and they send data to the monitoring node. Our framework adapted the monocular visual SLAM work by [Engel *et al.*, 2014] in exploring nodes. The details of the exploring nodes are described in section 3.3.

The monitoring node continuously receives data from exploring nodes. By looking at the maps of exploring nodes, it

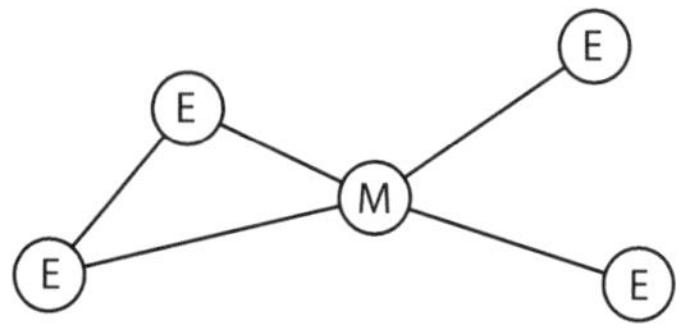

Figure 1: The network of nodes, all exploring nodes (E) are connected to the monitoring node (M). Some exploring nodes are also connected to each other

detects map overlaps and loop closures. Accordingly, it issues commands to relevant exploring nodes. The details of the monitoring nodes are described in section 3.2.

The Robot Operating System

We use the ROS infrastructure [Quigley *et al.*, 2009] to implement the distributed SLAM framework. A ROS node is responsible of performing computations. ROS also provides a message passing communication framework between nodes. Nodes in our framework are implemented as ROS nodes.

In its communication framework, ROS provides named communication buses called topics. Multiple nodes can publish messages to a topic while multiple subscribed nodes could receive them. Based on the requirement, ROS could either use UDP or TCP for message passing. In our framework data and commands are communicated between nodes as ROS messages.

ROS has a master server to list all available topics of a system. After identifying providers and subscribers of a topic by communicating with master server, ROS nodes can communicate with each other, peer-to-pear via topics.

The Map

In our framework, a map is represented using a set of *keyframes* in a *pose graph*.

The ith *keyframe*, $\mathcal{K}_i$ consists of an *absolute pose* $\boldsymbol{\xi}_{Wi}$, an image I_i, an inverse depth map D_i, an inverse depth variance map V_i, and a list of features $f_i^{(n)}$. Each keyframe gets a globally unique 32 bit identifier as shown in Algorithm 1.

Algorithm 1 Unique identifier for a keyframe

```
procedure GETUNIQUEID(keyframe_id, node_id)
    id ← SHIFTLEFT(node_id, 20)
    id ← id + keyframe_id
    return id                    ▷ A globally unique identifier
end procedure
```

The pose graph contains edges, ε_{ji}, having similarity transformation $\boldsymbol{\xi}_{ji} \in \mathbb{R}^7$ and corresponding covariance matrix $\boldsymbol{\Sigma}_{ji}$, between i^{th} and j^{th} key frames as shown in Figure 2. The relative pose between the two nodes is encoded with three components of the translation and the four components of the quaternion.

3.2 Monitoring nodes

The monitoring node contains a feature store to collect all the SURF [Bay *et al.*, 2008] features (and SIFT [Lowe, 2004]

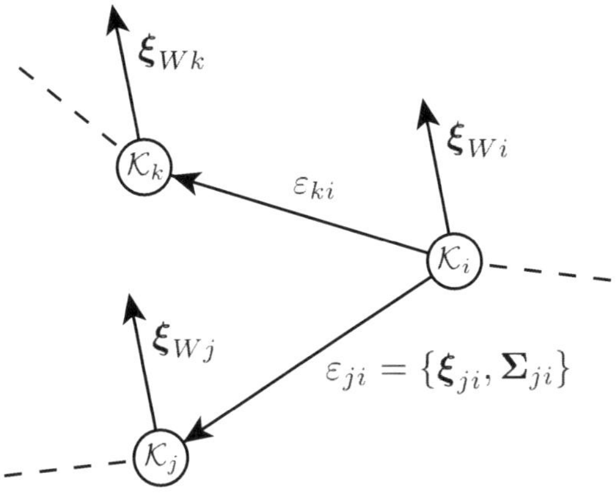

Figure 2: Keyframes and pose graph representing the map.

descriptors) received from the exploring nodes. It also maintains a fusion graph of exploring nodes to keep track of map overlaps.

Map overlap detection

All features found in incoming the key frames are compared against features in the feature store. If there are more than N matching features with a key frame of a different node, it is concluded that those two nodes have overlapping maps. The threshold N is determined empirically.

Exploring nodes are represented as vertices in the fusion graph. All identified map overlaps are represented as edges in the fusion graph. The weight corresponds to the number of matching features found across multiple key frames.

Loop closure detection

Similar to map overlap detection, if there are matching features between two key frames of the same node and there is no edge between those key frames in the map, then it is considered a loop closure. Loop closures that connect temporally far apart key frames, corresponds to the event where agent revisit a location after a while. These large loop closures help to reduce accumulated pose drift, and improve the accuracy of the entire map. Similarly, small loop closures, which connect key frames that are temporally closer, improve sub regions of the map.

Rigid transformation between key frames

In both map overlap detection and loop closure detection, the relative rigid transformation between key frames are computed using a least-square method [Sorkine-Hornung and Rabinovich, 2017]. RANSAC algorithm [Fischler and Bolles, 1981] is used to get rid of outliers.

3.3 Exploring nodes

The functional modules and the architecture of an exploring node are shown in Figure 3 which consist of the input stream, tracking, mapping, and optimization modules. All these modules run in separate threads.

The *input stream* module accepts incoming frames from the camera as well as commands and data from other nodes.

The *tracking* module accepts a new frame from the *input stream* module, and tracks it against the current key frame. If the current key frame no longer can track the frame, i.e. when the frame has significantly deviated from the key frame, a new key frame is created.

The old key frame is added to the map by the *mapping* module. The new key frame is also sent to the monitoring node and to all other exploring nodes subscribed (linked) to the current exploring node.

The *optimization* module continuously optimizes the pose graph in the background. After each optimization the pose graph is sent to the monitoring node and to the subscribed exploring nodes.

Map merging process

The Figure 4 shows the sequence of operations that take place in the map merging process.

Consider the case in which the exploring node A receives a merge command from the monitoring node. The input stream module puts the command into a command buffer. The tracking module contains multiple *state* submodules, including one for map merging. The map merging state submodule, processes the command from the buffer and changes its state, to *waiting for a map* from the other exploring node B. Furthermore, it sends its own map to B. Once the map of B is received, all new key frames and the new pose graph is added into the A's map, and the state is changed to the default state, where node A is waiting for new merge commands.

Figure 5 shows a resultant map after map merging process.

Multiple instances of the same ROS node

In our distributed framework, we implemented exploring node as a ROS node. Given there are multiple instances of exploring node in the network, we have to configure these instances, so that we can uniquely identify each exploring node's topics. For this we use ROS topic remapping. For example, say we have two exploring node instances, namely A and B, then exploring node's $/dvslam/graph$ topic could be remapped to $/A/dvslam/graph$ and $/B/dvslam/graph$. In this way, node A could listen to topic $/B/dvslam/graph$ and node B could listen to topic $/A/dvslam/graph$.

The following simplified scripts in Listing 1 and Listing 2 show how an exploring node was configured for remapping.

Listing 1: Setting up environment variables

```
export ROS_IP=10.1.2.3
export ROS_MASTER_URI=http://10.1.2.2:11311
export EXP_NODE=2
roslaunch exploring_node.launch
```

Listing 2: ROS node launch script

```
<launch>
  <node pkg="exploring_node"
  type="live_slam"
  name="node_$(env EXP_NODE)"
  args="image:=/image_raw
  camera_info:=/camera_info"
  output="screen">
    <remap from="/dvslam/graph"
     to="/$(env EXP_NODE)/dvslam/graph"/>
```

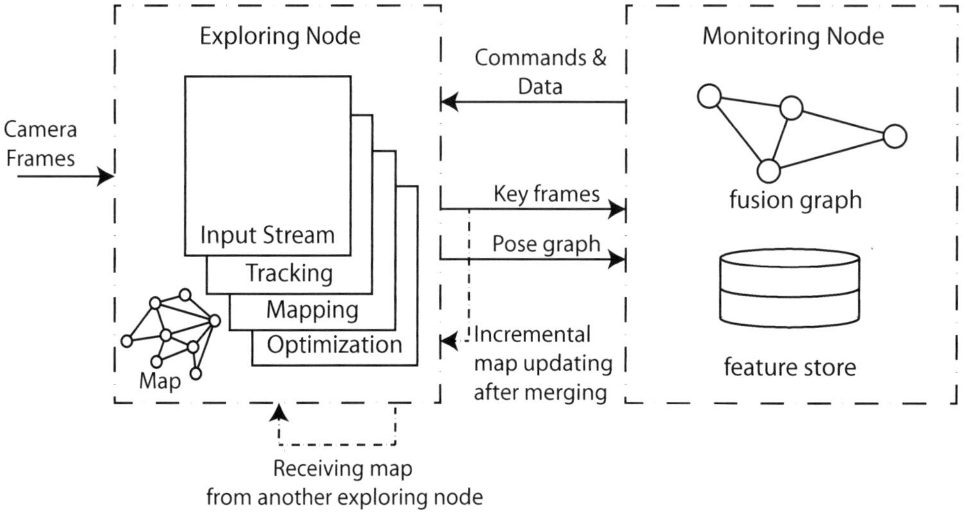

Figure 3: The distributed SLAM framework. Returning dashed arrows represent communication between two exploring nodes.

```
    <remap from="/dvslam/keyframes"
     to="/$(env EXP_NODE)/dvslam/keyframes"/>
  </node>
</launch>
```

3.4 Communication between nodes

Nodes use ROS topics and messages to issue commands and to exchange data. Four topics named, *keyframes*, *graph*, *command* and *map* are used in the framework. These topics are fully-qualified using the namespace */dvslam/*.

ROS topics used in the framework are shown in Table 1. The publisher node writes data and subscriber nodes receive the data via the topic.

Network statistics

A distributed SLAM could easily reach the bandwidth limitations of a network, especially, when dense maps are transferred between nodes. In our distributed framework we could generate statistics by using ROS **Topic Statistics**.

The measurement of traffic volume in bytes of every connection between nodes helps us to identify bandwidth utilization. Furthermore, measurements like number of dropped messages between nodes is a good indication of reaching the bandwidth limit. Other statistics such as mean & standard deviation of the age of messages, and period of messages of all nodes can also be used to investigate the communication between nodes.

4 Experimental Results

4.1 The experimental setup

Our experimental setup is designed to precisely define the ground truth against which the estimated camera positions along the motion path can be measured. To test our framework we mounted a global shutter camera, Point Grey Firefly MV, on a Computer Numeric Control (CNC) machine as shown in Figure 6. We then prepared a $1m \times 1.5m$ table surface containing wooden objects. We then moved the camera above the wooden objects, roughly 4 minutes each time, along known paths and captured both the image stream and the ground truth from the CNC controller. The CNC machine has 0.2mm accuracy in all 3 axes. The camera operated in 640×480 pixel resolution. To capture ground truth from the tiny CNC controller, we wrote an open source ROS node in [Egodagamage, 2017].

4.2 Running experiments

We defined two different 3D paths with 10% overlap, $Path_A$ and $Path_B$ with two different known starting points A and B respectively. Next, we collected four datasets, with two different camera orientations for each path. We created two experiments. In the first experiment, we selected two datasets having parallel camera optical axes. In the second experiment we used remaining two datasets, where the optical axes is 40° to each other. Each dataset is used to deploy an exploring node.

In each experiment, two exploring nodes and one monitoring node are used. These nodes are deployed in three different computers. Once the framework detected map overlaps, we recorded the relative transformation between the maps of exploring nodes. Each experiment is repeated 100 times. The average transformation for each experiment is then compared against the ground truth to compute errors in rotation and translation.

In both experiments, resultant rotation errors in translation

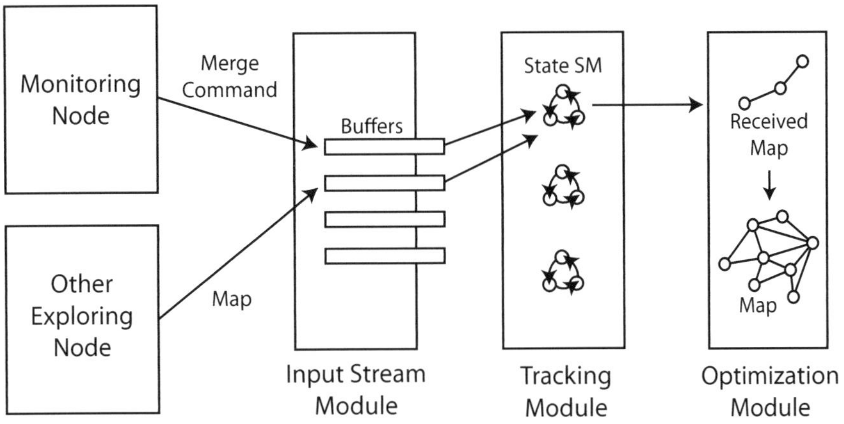

Figure 4: Important components of the map merging process

Topic	Publisher	Subscriber	Description
keyframes	Exploring node	Monitoring node Exploring node	Monitoring nodes always receive key frames from all exploring nodes. After merging maps, exploring nodes exchange key frames between each other.
graph	Exploring node	Monitoring node Exploring node	Monitoring nodes always receive pose graph from all exploring nodes. After merging maps, exploring nodes exchange pose graphs between each other.
command	Monitoring node	Exploring node	All exploring nodes process commands addressed to them and discard others. Commands like map merging, loop closure is received via this topic.
map	Exploring node	Exploring node	During the merge process, relevant exploring nodes subscribe each others' map topic and unsubscribe once done.

Table 1: ROS topics used to communicate between nodes

Experiment	Rotation Error	Translation Error
Experiment 1	3.799°	1.959cm
Experiment 2	5.330°	2.754cm

Table 2: Summary of the experimental results.

and rotation were less than 3cm and 6° respectively as shown in Table 2.

5 Conclusion & Future Work

In this paper, we have introduced a distributed framework for visual SLAM, with no knowledge of relative starting positions of exploring nodes. We have tested our framework using two experiments. Each experiment was repeated 100 times to compute the relative transformation between maps of two exploring nodes. We found that, the error from the ground truth was less than $3cm$ in calculating the translation between maps and less than 6° in calculating the rotation.

As future work, we will be working on supporting more than two exploring nodes. We will also be working on methods to recover random node failures. Moreover, we will be conducting more experiments on network bandwidth utilization.

References

[Bay *et al.*, 2008] Herbert Bay, Andreas Ess, Tinne Tuytelaars, and Luc Van Gool. Speeded-up robust features (surf). *Comput. Vis. Image Underst.*, 110(3):346–359, June 2008.

[Davison *et al.*, 2007] A.J. Davison, I.D. Reid, N.D. Molton, and O. Stasse. Monoslam: Real-time single camera slam. *Pattern Analysis and Machine Intelligence, IEEE Transactions on*, 29(6):1052–1067, June 2007.

[Egodagamage, 2017] Ruwan J Egodagamage. An open source ros node for tinyg motion controller. `https://github.com/japzi/rostinyg`, 2017. [Online; accessed in February 2017].

[Engel *et al.*, 2014] Jakob Engel, Thomas Schps, and Daniel Cremers. Lsd-slam: Large-scale direct monocular slam. In *Computer Vision ECCV 2014*, volume 8690 of *Lecture*

Figure 5: Resultant map of an exploration node after the map merging process. The exploring node's map and keyframes are shown in green and yellow respectively. Received map and keyframes are shown in pink and blue respectively. Constraints of the pose graph is not shown for clarity.

Figure 6: Experimental setup showing a camera mounted on a CNC machine allowing us to capture ground truth information.

Notes in Computer Science, pages 834–849. Springer International Publishing, 2014.

[Faugeras and Lustman, 1988] Olivier D Faugeras and Francis Lustman. Motion and structure from motion in a piecewise planar environment. *International Journal of Pattern Recognition and Artificial Intelligence*, 2(03):485–508, 1988.

[Fischler and Bolles, 1981] Martin A. Fischler and Robert C. Bolles. Random sample consensus: A paradigm for model fitting with applications to image analysis and automated cartography. *Commun. ACM*, 24(6):381–395, June 1981.

[Fox *et al.*, 2006] D. Fox, J. Ko, K. Konolige, B. Limketkai, D. Schulz, and B. Stewart. Distributed multirobot exploration and mapping. *Proceedings of the IEEE*, 94(7):1325–1339, July 2006.

[Gamage and Tuceryan, 2016] R. Gamage and M. Tuceryan. An experimental distributed framework for distributed simultaneous localization and mapping. In *2016 IEEE International Conference on Electro Information Technology (EIT)*, pages 0665–0667, May 2016.

[Howard *et al.*, 2006] Andrew Howard, LynneE. Parker, and GauravS. Sukhatme. The sdr experience: Experiments with a large-scale heterogeneous mobile robot team. In Jr. Ang, MarceloH. and Oussama Khatib, editors, *Experimental Robotics IX*, volume 21 of *Springer Tracts in Advanced Robotics*, pages 121–130. Springer Berlin Heidelberg, 2006.

[Klein and Murray, 2007] G. Klein and D. Murray. Parallel tracking and mapping for small ar workspaces. In *Mixed and Augmented Reality, 2007. ISMAR 2007. 6th IEEE and ACM International Symposium on*, pages 225–234, Nov 2007.

[Lowe, 2004] David G. Lowe. Distinctive image features from scale-invariant keypoints. *Int. J. Comput. Vision*, 60(2):91–110, November 2004.

[Nettleton *et al.*, 2006] Eric Nettleton, Sebastian Thrun, Hugh Durrant-Whyte, and Salah Sukkarieh. Decentralised slam with low-bandwidth communication for teams of vehicles. In *Field and Service Robotics*, pages 179–188. Springer, 2006.

[Newcombe *et al.*, 2011] Richard A. Newcombe, S.J. Lovegrove, and A.J. Davison. Dtam: Dense tracking and mapping in real-time. In *Computer Vision (ICCV), 2011 IEEE International Conference on*, pages 2320–2327, Nov 2011.

[Paull *et al.*, 2015] L. Paull, Guoquan Huang, M. Seto, and J.J. Leonard. Communication-constrained multi-auv cooperative slam. In *Robotics and Automation (ICRA), 2015 IEEE International Conference on*, pages 509–516, May 2015.

[Quigley *et al.*, 2009] Morgan Quigley, Ken Conley, Brian Gerkey, Josh Faust, Tully Foote, Jeremy Leibs, Rob Wheeler, and Andrew Y Ng. Ros: an open-source robot operating system. In *ICRA workshop on open source software*, volume 3, page 5, 2009.

[Sorkine-Hornung and Rabinovich, 2017] Olga Sorkine-Hornung and Michael Rabinovich. Least-squares rigid motion using svd. 2017. Available at `https://igl.ethz.ch/projects/ARAP/svd_rot.pdf`.

[Sturm and Triggs, 1996] Peter Sturm and Bill Triggs. A factorization based algorithm for multi-image projective structure and motion. In *European conference on computer vision*, pages 709–720. Springer, 1996.

Decision making swarms

Sanza Kazadi*, George Jeno, Xinyu Guan, Nick Nusgart, Andriy Sheptunov
Swarm Engineering Laboratory
Illinois Mathematics and Science Academy
1500 Sullivan Rd.
Aurora, IL 60506

ABSTRACT

While swarms that execute decisions are well known in the swarm community, swarms that exhibit this capability *a priori* have never before been achieved. We demonstrate a methodology, based on the Hamiltonian method of swarm design, that enables the design and implementation of swarms that exhibit decision-making capability. We develop the theoretical structure of the method and apply it to the development of an ant algorithm and a swarm capable of deciding whether its density exceeds a specific predetermined value. The swarm designs are validated in simulation.

keywords. swarm engineering, distributed decision making, Hamiltonian method of swarm designs

1. INTRODUCTION

One of the most astounding properties of swarms is their ability to make decisions globally despite having only local knowledge, limited computational ability, and sometimes only reactionary behavior. Ant swarms have the seemingly innate ability to decide to reroute resources committed to collecting food from one source to another source in response to the second source being closer than the first [Dorigo et al., 1996, Schoonderwoerd et al., 1996]. Bee swarms have the ability to decide to settle in a specific location, even eschewing known locations in favor of secondary locations.

Despite being able to create artificial analogs and being the subject of ongoing work [Valentini et al., 2016] there are not yet any robust general engineering methodologies in place that may be used to engineer decision making swarms. As a result, engineering swarms that accomplish decision tasks *a priori* when no direct analog exists between the desired task and a known natural analog is still an area of active investigation. The goal of swarm engineering is to develop such a methodology, usable over a wide range of potential swarms.

In this paper, we address the development of a method of generating swarms with decision-making capabilities. The method is based on the *Hamiltonian method of swarm design* [Kazadi and Lee, 2007, Kazadi, 2009, Kazadi et al., 2015]. In this method, *global properties* are constructed that correspond to desired system outcomes. These properties can be used to generate goals and these goals can be used to generate agent-level behavior. The agent-level behavior is robust in the sense that if it satisfies the design requirements, the swarm will have the desired global properties. We will examine how to use this method to derive swarm-based decision making.

The remainder of the paper is laid out as follows. Section two describes the theoretical issues needed to address the design questions. Section three applies these properties to two different decision making swarms. Section four presents validating simulation results. Section five discusses these results and concludes.

2. LOCAL PROPERTIES, GLOBAL PROPERTIES, AND STATE

In the *Hamiltonian method*, we initially take stock of *local measurables*. These are quantities that can be measured or modified (or both) by the agents themselves. They are limited by the sensory and actuation capability of the agent. We denote these by $\{s_i\}_{i=1}^{N_s}$. Each of the s_i is limited and comes from a set S_i of all possible values for s_i. Clearly, the system can be described by the vector $\vec{s} = (s_1, \ldots, s_{N_s})$ and rules for how $\vec{s}$ is currently changing. The difficulty of using such a high-dimensional representation is that it very quickly becomes intractable.

Using the local measurables, we can develop *global variables* which are functions of local variables. I.e.,

$$P = f(\vec{s}). \tag{1}$$

Key among the properties of these functions are that they be real-valued and well-defined. Assuming that they are continuous and differentiable, we may write .

$$\frac{dP}{dt} = \vec{\nabla} f \cdot \frac{d\vec{s}}{dt}. \tag{2}$$

The discrete version of this equation is

$$\Delta P = \vec{\nabla} f \cdot \Delta\vec{s}. \tag{3}$$

*To whom correspondences should be addressed at skazadi@imsa.edu.

This indicates that the change in the global measurable depends on the nature of the function f and the changes in the local measurables, which are themselves controlled by the agents of the swarm. Therefore, we must understand the nature of f in order to determine what the appropriate behavior must be and then choose the right behaviors for the swarm members. Together, determining the right behavior, the value of P can be moved from one value to another.

3. STATE TRANSITIONS AND DECISION-MAKING

Suppose we have a system with a global variable P or even a set of global variables $\overrightarrow{P}$. We define the *state space* as the set of all possible values for $\overrightarrow{P}$. Let us suppose there exists a point $\overrightarrow{P_0}$ in the set of all possible values for P in which $|P_0 - P(t)| < \epsilon$ for all time t once the system has come to a state in which it is in the same ϵ-ball, as long as no change to the systems occurs. Then we say that $\overrightarrow{P_0}$ is an *attractor* of the system. The set of all points which, when the system enters, result in moving the system toward the attractor in phase space, is called the *basin of attraction*. We can define the *state* of a system as the attractor around which the system orbits in state space.

Let us suppose that a system is in orbit of an attractor in its phase space. The system is in a state defined by this attractor. Going forward in time, two options are possible: the system may remain in orbit of the attractor or it may leave the basin of attraction of the attractor. If the system remains out of any other basin of attraction, it is said to be in a *wandering state*. If it settles around another attractor, it is said to have made a *state change*. We are interested in engineering systems that make specific and well-defined state changes in response to changes in the system. While a clear anthropomorphism, we say that, when a system makes a reversible state change in response to an external situation , the system has made a *decision*. The hallmark of the decision is that some measurable global aspect of the swarm has changed in a predictable way in response to some change in the system.

3.1 Designing ant swarms

One of the first examples of swarms to be intensely studied were swarms of ants. One of the interesting facts about ants is the fact that they have the ability to reroute resources from one collection task to another collection task when the latter task involves a piece of food that is closer to the ant hill than the former task.

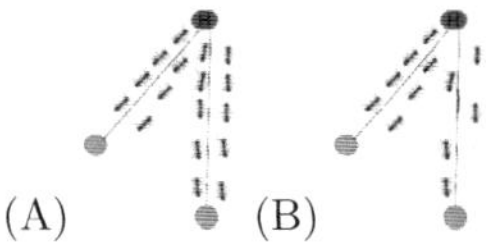

Figure 1.1: These figures illustrate the ways in which an ant swarm exploits two food sources at different distances when the closer food source is found first (A) and when it is found second (B).

It is interesting to ask how this is accomplished. We would like to determine the behavioral requirements of the system without resorting to behavioral studies of real ants.

Our methodology utilizes a global measurable for the system. First, let us position of the ant hill as the origin of the two-dimensional map making up the system's universe. Let $\lambda = \{\overrightarrow{x_i}\}_{i=1}^{N_f(t)}$ be the set of positions of all food items placed in the system. We define *trails* as the paths between the pieces of food and the ant hill. The agents then move in one of three different states: at the ant hill, on a trail, or freely moving off any trail. Let us suppose that we have a set of agents $\{a_j\}_{j=1}^{N_a}$ where N_a is the number of agents. For any trail τ, we define d_τ as the length of the trail. Then we define

$$d(a_j) = \begin{cases} d_\tau & \text{if } a_j \text{ is on the trail } \tau \\ 0 & \text{otherwise} \end{cases} . \quad (4)$$

and N_{a_p} as the number of agents actually on a path. We further define

$$P_1 = \frac{1}{N_{a_p}} \sum_{i=1}^{N_a} d(a_i) = \frac{1}{N_{a_p}} \sum_{i=1}^{N_f(t)} N_{\tau_i}(t)\, d_{\tau_i}. \quad (5)$$

where $N_{\tau_i}(t)$ is the number of agents on trails i at time t and d_{τ_i} is the length of the trail τ_i. P_1 is the average path length of the paths which ants are traversing. This property has varies as

$$\frac{dP_1}{dt} = \frac{1}{N_{a_p}} \sum_{i=1}^{N_f(t)} \frac{dN_{\tau_i}(t)}{dt} d_{\tau_i}. \quad (6)$$

Let $\overrightarrow{dN_\tau} = \left(\frac{dN_{\tau_1}(t)}{dt}, \ldots, \frac{dN_{\tau_{N_{a_p}}}(t)}{dt}\right)$ and $\overrightarrow{d_\tau} = \left(d_{\tau_1}, \ldots, d_{\tau_{N_{a_p}}}\right)$.

We can also define P_2 as the rate at which food is acquired from the food source. We can write this as

$$P_2 = \sum_{i=1}^{N_f(t)} \frac{N_{\tau_i}(t)\, 2 d_{\tau_i} a}{v} \quad (7)$$

where a is the quantity of food that is captured by each agent during each run and v is the speed of the agent. Interestingly, $\frac{2a}{v} P_1 = P_2$.

Suppose that the system consists of one path. Then, irrespective of the number of agents on the path, the value of P_1 is the same. Suppose now a new, shorter path becomes available. In order for the swarm to make the "right" decision, the ant system must transfer to the shorter path. It is not hard to see that

$$\frac{dP_1}{dt} < 0, \ \frac{dP_2}{dt} < 0. \quad (8)$$

In order for this to happen, we must have $\overrightarrow{d_\tau} \cdot \overrightarrow{dN_\tau} < 0$.

One limitation of this condition is that we can satisfy the condition by making every element of $\overrightarrow{dN_\tau}$negative. This is consistent with the agents coming off the trails. What we'd prefer is to have the agents generally stay on the trails. We can require this by stating that

$$P_3 \equiv \left\langle \left|\overrightarrow{dN_\tau}\right| \right\rangle \geq 0. \quad (9)$$

Together, equations (8) and (9) determine our swarm condition. As the vector of distances is all positive, $\overrightarrow{dN_\tau}$ must have negative components. Moreover, the product of the negative components and the associated distances must exceed the product of the positive components and their associated distances. If the number of free agents is relatively unchanged, this means that the negative changes must be associated with longer distances than the positive changes. With exactly two paths, the condition becomes

$$d_{\tau_1}\Delta N_{\tau_1} < -d_{\tau_2}\Delta N_{\tau_2}. \qquad (10)$$

In any swarm in which the number of active agents is conserved so that $\Delta N_{\tau_1} = -\Delta N_{\tau_2}$, this condition is satisfied whenever distance $d_{\tau_1} < d_{\tau_2}$. Since this is exactly the condition generally found in an ant colony, we see that the colony is able to achieve this "choice". Therefore, we can guarantee the system's choice with a behavior in which the number of agents is conserved, and the product is negative. Alternately, we can generate the opposite "choice" if we require the product to be positive.

3.2 Locust swarms

Locusts are a completely different kind of swarm, though their behaviors are no less astounding. Unlike ants, locusts maintain an internal state that only individual agents can experience. Experiments with locusts have demonstrated that the transition from grasshopper to locust is caused by serotonin levels which are triggered by excessive leg contact with objects. The serotonin builds up until it reaches a point that it initiates irreversible morphological changes to the grasshopper. The more aggressive locusts then interact with other grasshoppers, hastening their transition to locusts.

The entire transition can be viewed as a decision at the swarm level. The swarm is responding to the concentration of grasshoppers in a small space. When the number of grasshoppers in the space becomes small enough, the swarm initiates a change in overall behavior and moves the agents from that space. Since the swarm is undergoing a transition in which the agents undergo an irreversible change, the swarm itself is not capable of reacting to changes in the new space that agents find themselves. Therefore, when the swarm is not crowded any more, there is no change in behavior. However, this kind of swarm-based decision-making can be applied to a set of agents with reversible state changes.[1]

We begin examining the way in which locust swarms make this decision by modeling the internal state s of the locust as having a numerical value and an update rule

$$\frac{ds}{dt} = -k_1 s + R(e_s) \qquad (11)$$

where k_1 is some decay rate and $R(e_s)$ is the reaction to an external state e_s. We can define a global variable P as

$$P = \sum_{i=1}^{N_a} s_i. \qquad (12)$$

The swarm is considered to have made a decision to move to a new state if P changes from one attractor to a second. Therefore, the behavior of the swarm must be such that it maintains an orbit around one attractor. Clearly,

$$\frac{dP}{dt} = \sum_{i=1}^{N_a} \{-k_1 s_i + R(e_{s_i})\} = -k_1 P + \sum_{i=1}^{N_a} R(e_{s_i}). \qquad (13)$$

Therefore, if the magnitude of the sum of the agent reactions is low, this has an attractor at $P = 0$. In order to create a situation where a second attractor exists, we must have a case where a positive feedback occurs under the right conditions, overwhelming the decay. Note that actual locusts with irreversible changes have a mechanism which eliminates the decay mode, thereby enhancing the effect of the trigger on a single agent.

In order for the system to move rapidly to its new equilibrium state, we must have

$$\frac{dP}{dt} > 0$$

for longer than a spurious change. In such a case, this would require that

$$P < \frac{1}{k_1}\sum_{i=1}^{N_a} R(e_{s_i}). \qquad (14)$$

If R is bounded, this would require that at least $N_{trigger}$ agents are state 1. This means that

$$\frac{k_1 P}{R_{max}} < N_{trigger}. \qquad (15)$$

Therefore, such a system would be triggered when the number of agents exceeds that trigger amount.

In order for this swarm to make the decision we're interested in, the minimal requirement is the condition given in (15). This is our swarm condition. Interestingly, if the external state being measured is the proximity of other agents or local density of agents, the swarm is, in totality, measuring deciding whether the space it inhabits is above a threshold size.

4. PERFORMANCE OF SIMULATED SWARMS

In this section, we present performance of simulated swarms. These swarms are designed according to the swarm requirements developed in Section 3. We then evaluate their performance on their ability to correctly execute the desired decisions according to their design.

4.1 Shortest Distance to Food

We are interested in testing the theory described in Section 3.1 using an embodied ant swarm simulation. The simulation is depicted in Figure 4.1 and contains a home, food sources, and agents passing between them.

[1]This kind of decision making can be applied to bee hives making decisions about what food sources to exploit, the growth of ideas in a swarm of individuals, the collective decision to go to war, etc.

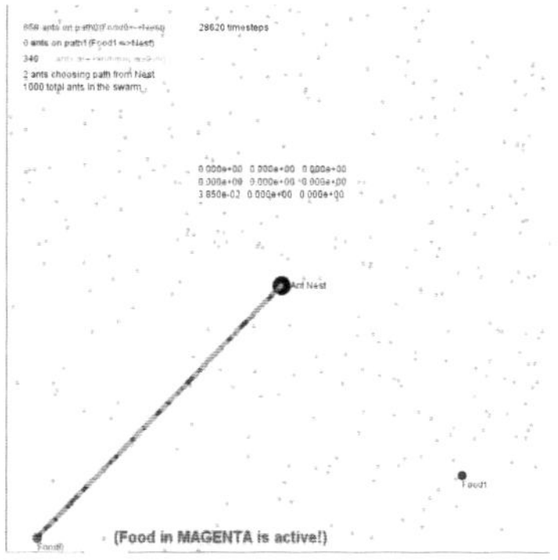

Figure 4.1: The simulated ant swarm. The gray circles are agents that are searching for food. Green circles are agents that are following a pheromone trail. Red circles are agents moving back toward home. The black circle is the home, the dark blue circle is an inactive food source (invisible to the agents), and the pink circle is an active (visible to the agents) food source.

Our simulation comprises a set of autonomous agents that move in a discrete 2-dimensional grid. The grid contains the ant home as well as two food locations. Each grid element is defined in part by a non-negative quantity of pheromone. Each iteration, agents may add to the pheromone at a given location. After each set of updates by the agents, the amount of pheromone on each location is updated. The pheromone evaporates according to an update rule

$$\rho(t+1) = \epsilon\rho(t) \tag{16}$$

where ϵ is a pre-determined evaporation rate.

The agents are defined by their position, direction of motion, active state, and their sensory state. The agents' active state is one of three possible states:

- *random wandering* in which they move forward in one direction and then randomly change their direction of travel,
- *food tracking* during which they move directly outward from their home, depositing pheromone as they move, and
- *homebound state* during which they move directly toward their home after picking up food.

The internal state defines the behavior of the agent. Agents begin in the random wandering state. Once they find a food source, they acquire a food item and transition to the homebound state. While in the homebound state, agents drop pheromone on the ground. The rate that pheromone is dropped is initially set to some maximum rate. As they move toward home, however, the rate falls off as the inverse of the distance traveled toward home.

If the agent is in the wandering state and it encounters a detectable pheromone trail they transition to the food tracking state and move directly away from their home.

When an agent makes it back to home, it deposits the food item and then decides which of possibly many paths it will follow. This entails measuring pheromones of all paths reaching home. A uniformly generated random number is used to decide which of the trails to take, with the probability of taking any specific trail linearly dependent on the ratio of the pheromone at the end of the trail and the total amount of pheromone detectable at the home. It can be shown that this methodology satisfies the swarm condition given in equations (8) and (9).

Figure 4.2 illustrates the performance of the simulation over a run in which the swarm shifts from an initially longer path to a shorter path. Initially, an active food item (dark blue) and an inactive food item (light blue) are in the system. Only the active food can be detected by the agents, and a path forms between the food and the home. After the inactive food item becomes active, the swarm generates a path to it as well. Eventually, the swarm shifts its resources from the longer path to the shorter.

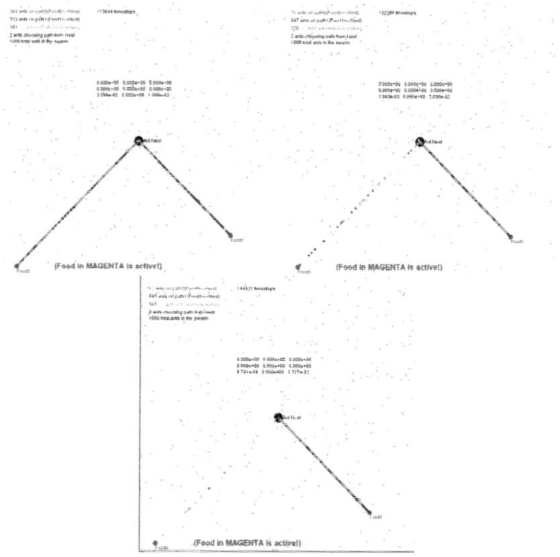

Figure 4.2 The simulation proceeds with an initial path which then develops into a shorter path when the second food item becomes active.

While the simulation proceeds, the value of P_1 changes. Initially it settles at a high value, but eventually it transitions to a lower value, as desired. The data can be seen in Figure 4.3 below.

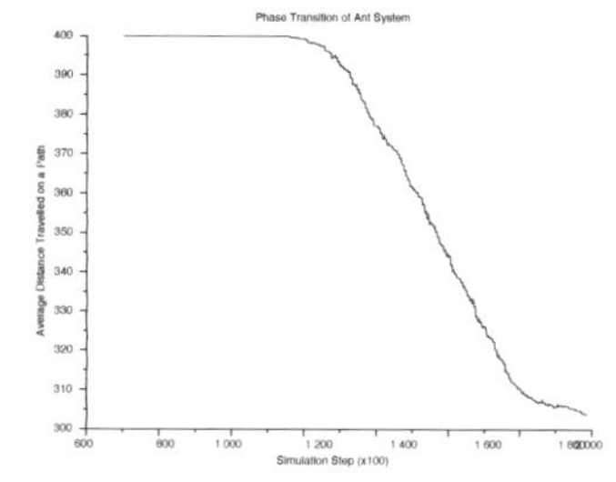

Figure 4.3: The evolution of the value of P_1over the lifetime of the simulation.

4.2 Density determination

We now describe our second, quite different embodied simulation. Agents are represented by circles and move around in a two dimensional bounded space. The agents have a size and cannot overlap one another. The simulation is illustrated in Figure 4.4.

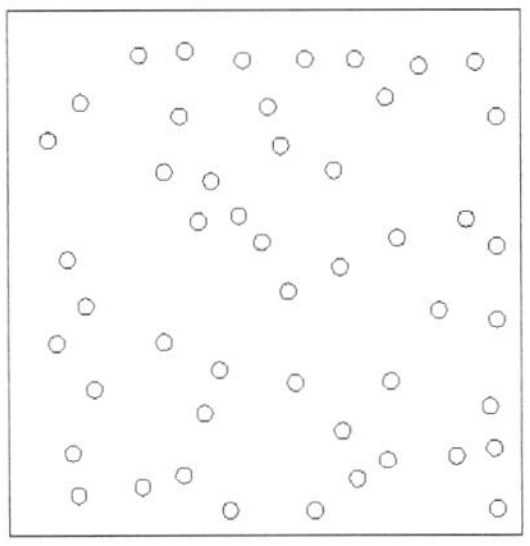

Figure 4.4: The simulated locust swarm, which can measure the size of the space.

The agents are characterized by a direction of motion, and internal state which is represented by a positive real number, and a position. The state is initialized at a value of zero. At each iteration, the state is updated according to

$$s\,(t+1) = \epsilon s\,(t) \qquad (17)$$

where the ϵ is the decay rate of the state. When moving around, if they agents come into contact with a boundary, they change direction and begin moving in another direction. If the agents come into contact with another agent, they change direction but also increase the state by adding a quantity to it. If the state of the agent exceeds a given value, its color changes from white to red; dropping below the same value returns it to white. At this point the agent is said to be in the excited state.

A transition of the swarm state is considered to have happened if more than 90% of the swarm is in the excited state. Such a transition is illustrated in Figure 4.5. Figure 4.6 illustrates the change in the property given in (12). As can be seen, the property changes from one in which the state is completely off to one in which it is completely on as a distributed response to the global size of the swarm.

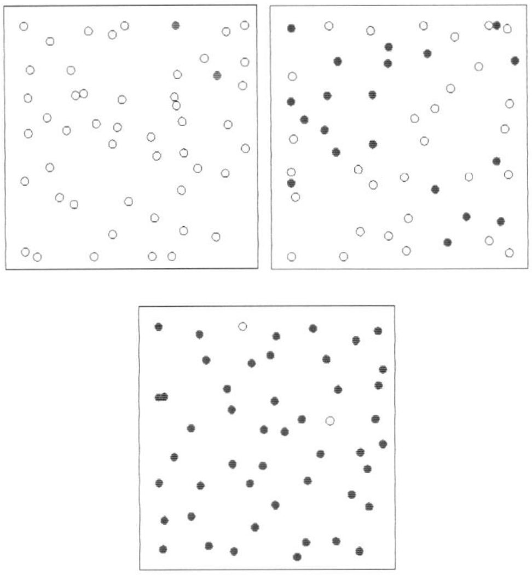

Figure 4.5: This set of screenshots illustrates the state transition of the swarm during a decision event.

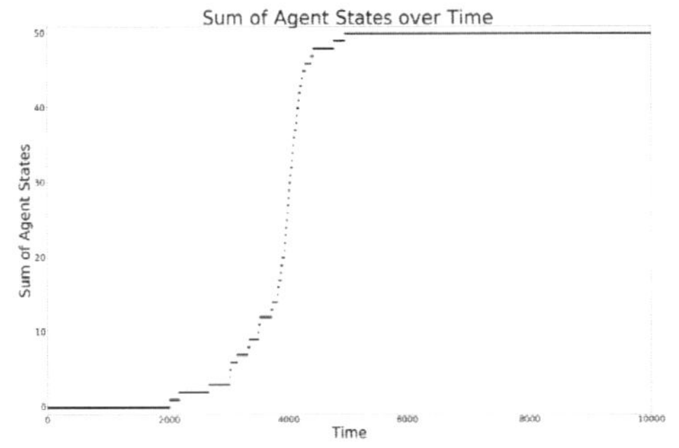

Figure 4.6: We provide the evolution of the property given in (12) as the swarm decides on the size of the space. This is the phase transition that is a hallmark of the decision.

We are interested in how well this swarm can discern the size of an area. Figure 4.7 provides the performance of the swarm in discerning the size of the area in which it is located. As can be seen, the swarm not only reliably determines the size of the space, but does so by reacting to the density of the swarm in the space. This approach to determining a space's size might be useful in a variety of situations when rapid measurements of irregular spaces are required.

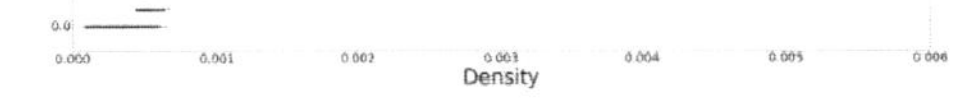

Figure 4.7: The performance of the swarm on the space size/density decision. The swarm not only reliably transitions state at and beyond a specific size, it also triggers when the swarm is beyond a specific density in spaces of different sizes.

5. DISCUSSION AND CONCLUDING REMARKS

In this study we've examined the design and implementation of swarms designed to carry out specific decisions. This extremely interesting area of swarm research represents one of the defining aspects of swarms that originally brought people to the field. How can it be that a group of simple agents can elicit complex behavior, generating group actions that are, to the untrained eye, complex and sometimes intelligent?

Our basic assertion is that the behaviors are basically the dynamics of the system, and it is that dynamics that we're after. In the case of swarms generating behaviors that mimic the kinds of decisions that intelligent beings might make, the question becomes how can the behaviors be generated? That is, rather than trying to understand the behavior as a model of intelligence, we are trying to develop a behavior that generates the "intelligent" behavior. In so doing, we are seeking to develop a tool that enables the subsequent generation of a variety of adaptive behaviors that can be implemented at the swarm level.

We have demonstrated that, using the Hamiltonian Method of Swarm Design, we are able to create, from basic principles, the very kinds of swarm systems that exhibit "intelligent" behavior. The swarms dynamically respond to the environment in ways that would seem to, if they were living systems, enhance their ability to survive. We have demonstrated that using one- and two-dimensional systems (number of defining global properties), we are able to create swarm requirements that lead to the development of swarms of the desired goals.

We have demonstrated this with the archetypal decision-making swarm modeled after biological ants. However, unlike other studies, we have motivated the design requirements by using a mathematical analysis rooted in the agents' measurables and the global properties. We demonstrated that this is a two-dimensional swarm, as it is defined by two global properties. We found that, once the agents' defining behavioral conditions were satisfied, the swarm behaved as it should. This right-out-of-the-box design is significant, short circuiting typical parameter setting which could take quite a bit of effort.

We have further used a swarm based on locusts, with entirely internal state. This swarm consists of circular agents moving in a bounded space and colliding with one another as they move around. Excessively packed in agents generate a transition from an internal unexcited state to a second, excited state. A positive feedback in the interactions drives, under the right conditions, a reliable transition of the whole swarm.

The key to the adaptive capability of the swarm seems to be the maintenance of the state of the system and the measurable transition in the system's dynamics. The ant swarm maintains its state in the external state of the pheromones in the system. The locust-inspired swarm maintains state internally in each of the agents. In both cases, the state invokes behavioral changes in the agents and a positive feedback in the system. Both state changes can be tracked by monitoring the global properties that are used to define the system.

Future work will examine the role of state in generating distributed decision or adaptation. We will also examine additional swarms that are capable of making decisions between several potential outcomes.

6. REFERENCES

[Kazadi and Lee, 2007] S. Kazadi and J. Lee. *Artificial physics, swarm engineering, and the Hamiltonian Method.* **Proceedings of the World Congress on Engineering and Computer Science**, San Francisco, CA, 2007.

[Kazadi, 2009] S. Kazadi. *Model independence in swarm robotics.* **Journal of Intelligent Computing and Cybernetics, Special Issue on Swarm Robotics**, 2(4):672–694, 2009.

[Kazadi et al., 2015] S. Kazadi, D. Jin, and M. Li. *Utilizing abstract phase space in swarm design and validation.* **Advances in Swarm and Computational Intelligence**, volume 9140, pages 14–29, New York, NY, USA. Springer, 2015.

[Dorigo et al., 1996] M. Dorigo, V. Maniezzo, and A. Colorni. *The ant system: optimization by a colony of cooperating agents.* **IEEE Transactions on Systems, Man, and Cybernetics - Part B**, 26 (1), pp. 1-13, 1996.

[Schoonderwoerd et al., 1996] R. Schoonderwoerd, O. Holland, J. Bruten, and L. Rothkrantz. *Ant-based load balancing in telecommunications networks.* **Adaptive Behavior**, 5 (2), pp. 169-207, 1996.

[Valentini et al., 2016] G. Valentini, E. Ferrante, H. Hamann, M. Dorigo. *Collective decision with 100 Kilobots: speed versus accuracy in binary discrimination problems.* **Autonomous Agents and Multi-Agent Systems**, 30 (3), pp. 553-580, 2016.

[Reina et al., 2015] A. Reina, G. Valentini, C. Fernández-Oto, M. Dorigo, V. Trianni. *A Design Pattern for Decentralised Decision Making.* **PLOS ONE**, 10(10), 2015: e0140950. doi: 10.1371/journal.pone.0140950

[Seeley and Buhrman, 1999] T. Seeley and S. Buhrman. *Group decision making in swarms of honey bees.* **Behavioral Ecology and Sociobiology**, 45, pp.19-31, 1999.

[Seeley and Visscher, 2004] T. Seeley and P. K. Visscher. *Group decision making in nest-site selection by honey bees.* **Apidologie**, 35 (2), pp.101-116, 2004. <10.1051/apido:2004004>. <hal- 00891879>

Learning Others' Intentional Models in Multi-Agent Settings Using Interactive POMDPs

Yanlin Han Piotr Gmytrasiewicz
Department of Computer Science
University of Illinois at Chicago
Chicago, IL 60607

Abstract

Interactive partially observable Markov decision processes (I-POMDPs) provide a principled framework for planning and acting in a partially observable, stochastic and multi-agent environment, extending POMDPs to multi-agent settings by including models of other agents in the state space and forming a hierarchical belief structure. In order to predict other agents' actions using I-POMDP, we propose an approach that effectively uses Bayesian inference and sequential Monte Carlo (SMC) sampling to learn others' intentional models which ascribe them beliefs, preferences and rationality in action selection. For problems of various complexities, empirical results show that our algorithm accurately learns models of other agents and has superior performance in comparison with other methods. Our approach serves as a generalized reinforcement learning algorithm that learns over other agents' transition, observation and reward functions. It also effectively mitigates the belief space complexity due to the nested belief hierarchy.

Introduction

Partially observable Markov decision processes (POMDPs) (Kaelbling, Littman, and Cassandra 1998) provide a principled, decision-theoretic framework for planning under uncertainty in a partially observable, stochastic environment. An autonomous agent operates rationally in such settings by maintaining a belief of the physical state at any given time, in doing so it sequentially chooses the optimal actions that maximize the future rewards. Therefore, solutions of POMDPs are mappings from an agent's beliefs to actions. Although POMDPs can be used in multi-agent settings, it is doing so under strong assumptions that the effects of other agents' actions are implicitly treated as noise and folded in the state transitions, such as recent Bayes-adaptive POMDPs (Ross, Draa, and Pineau 2007), infinite generalized policy representation (Liu, Liao, and Carin 2011), infinite POMDPs (Doshi-Velez et al. 2013). Therefore, an agent's beliefs about other agents are not in the solutions of POMDPs.

Interactive POMDP (I-POMDP) (Gmytrasiewicz and Doshi 2005) are a generalization of POMDP to multi-agent settings by replacing POMDP belief spaces with interactive hierarchical belief systems. Specifically, it augments the plain beliefs about the physical states in POMDP by including models of other agents, which forms a hierarchical belief structure that represents an agent's belief about the physical state, belief about the other agents and their beliefs about others' beliefs. The models of other agents included in the new augmented state space consist of two types: the intentional models and subintentional models. The sophisticated intentional model ascribes beliefs, preferences, and rationality to other agents (Gmytrasiewicz and Doshi 2005), while the simpler subintentional model, such as finite state controllers (Panella and Gmytrasiewicz 2016), does not. Solutions of I-POMDPs map an agent's belief about the environment and other agents' models to actions. Therefore, it is applicable to all important agent, human, and mixed agent-human applications. It has been clearly shown (Gmytrasiewicz and Doshi 2005) that the added sophistication for modeling others as rational agents results in a higher value function which dominates the one obtained from simply treating others as noise, which implies the modeling superiority of I-POMDPs for multi-agent systems over other approaches.

However, the interactive belief modification for I-POMDPs results in a drastic increase of the belief space complexity, adding to the curse of dimensionality: the complexity of the belief representation is proportional to belief dimensions due to exponential growth of agent models with increase of nesting level. Since exact solutions to POMDPs are proven to be PSPACE-complete for finite horizon and undecidable for infinite time horizon (Papadimitriou and Tsitsiklis 1987), the time complexity of the more generalized I-POMDPs, which may contain multiple POMDPs and I-POMDPs of other agents, is greater than or equal to PSPACE-complete for finite horizon and undecidable for infinite time horizon. Due to this severe space complexity, currently no complete belief update has been accomplished using the sophisticated intentional models over entire interactive belief space. There are only partial updates on other agents' sole beliefs about the physical states (Doshi and Gmytrasiewicz 2009) and indirect approach such as subintentional finite state controllers (Panella and Gmytrasiewicz 2016). Therefore, in order to unleash the full modeling power of intentional models and apply I-POMDPs to more realistic settings, a good approximation algorithm for computing the nested interactive belief and predicting other agents' actions is crucial to the trade-off between solution quality and computation complexity.

To address this issue, we propose a Bayesian approach that utilizes customized sequential Monte Carlo sampling algorithms (Doucet, De Freitas, and Gordon 2001) to obtain approximating solutions to interactive I-POMDPs and implement the algorithms in a software package[1]. Specifically, We assume that models of other agents are unknown and learned from imperfect observations of the other agents' behaviors. We parametrize other agents' intentional models and maintain a belief over them, making sequential Bayesian updates using only observations from the environment. Since this Bayesian inference task is analytically intractable, to approximate the posterior distribution, we devise a customized sequential Monte Carlo method to descend the belief hierarchy and sample all model parameters at each nesting level, starting from the interactive particle filter (I-PF) (Doshi and Gmytrasiewicz 2009) for I-POMDP belief update.

Our approach, for the first time, successfully learns others' models over the entire intentional model space which contains their initial belief, transition, observation and reward functions, making it a generalized reinforcement learning method for multi-agent settings. Our algorithm accurately predicts others' actions on various problem settings, therefore enables the modeling agent to make corresponding optimal action to maximize its own rewards. By approximating Bayesian inference using a customized sequential Monte Carlo sampling method, we significantly mitigate the belief space complexity of the I-POMDPs.

Background

POMDP

A Partially observable Markov decision process (POMDP) (Kaelbling, Littman, and Cassandra 1998) is a general reinforcement learning model for planning and acting in a single-agent, partially observable, stochastic domain. It is defined for a single agent i as:

$$POMDP_i = \langle S, A_i, \Omega_i, T_i, O_i, R_i \rangle \tag{1}$$

Where the meaning for each element in the 6-tuple is:

- S is the set of states of the environment.
- A_i is the set of agent i's possible actions
- Ω_i is the set of agent i's possible observations
- $T_i : S \times A_i \times S \to [0,1]$ is the state transition function
- $O_i : S \times A_i \times \Omega_i \to [0,1]$ is the observation function
- $R_i : S \times A_i \to R_i$ is the reward function.

Given the definition above, an agent's belief about the state can be represented as a probability distribution over S. The belief update can be simply done using the following formula, where α is the normalizing constant:

$$b(s') = \alpha O(o, s, a) \sum_{s \in S} T(s', a, s) b(s) \tag{2}$$

Given the agent's belief, then the optimal action, a^*, is simply part of the set of optimal actions, $OPT(b_i)$, for the belief state defined as:

$$OPT(b_i) = \underset{a_i \in A_i}{\arg\max} \Big\{ \sum_{s \in S} b_i(s) R(s, a_i) + \gamma \sum_{o_i \in \Omega_i} P(o_i | a_i, b_i) \times U(SE(b_i, a_i, o_i)) \Big\} \tag{3}$$

Particle Filter

The Markov Chain Monte Carlo (MCMC) method (Gilks et al., 1996) is widely used to approximate probability distributions when they are unable to be computed directly. It generates samples from a posterior distribution $\pi(x)$ over state space x, by simulating a Markov chain $p(x'|x)$ whose state space is x and stationary distribution is $\pi(x)$. The samples drawn from p converge to the target distribution π as the number of samples goes to infinity.

In order to make MCMC work on sequential inference task, especially sequential decision makings under Markov assumptions, sequential versions of Monte Carlo methods have been proposed and some of them are capable of dealing with high dimensionality and/or complexity problems, such as particle filters (Del Moral and Pierre 1996). At each time step, particle filters draw samples (or particles) from a proposal distribution, commonly $p(x_t|x_{t-1})$, which is essentially the conditional distribution of the current state x_t given the previous x_{t-1}, then use the observation function $p(y_t|x_t)$ to compute the importance weight for each particle and resample all particles according to the weights.

The Model

I-POMDP framework

An interactive POMDP of agent i, I-POMDP i, is defined as:

$$I\text{-}POMDP_i = \langle IS_{i,l}, A, \Omega_i, T_i, O_i, R_i \rangle \tag{4}$$

where $IS_{i,l}$ is the set of interactive states of the environment, defined as $IS_{i,l} = S \times M_{i,l-1}, l \geq 1$, where S is the set of states and $M_{i,l-1}$ is the set of possible models of agent j, and l is the strategy level. A specific class of models are the $(l-1)$th level *intentional* models, $\Theta_{j,l-1}$, of agent j: $\theta_{j,l-1} = \langle b_{j,l-1}, A, \Omega_j, T_j, O_j, R_j, OC_j \rangle$, $b_{j,l-1}$ is agent j's belief nested to level $(l-1)$, $b_{j,l-1} \in \Delta(IS_{j,l-1})$, and OC_j is j's optimality criterion. The intentional model $\theta_{j,l-1}$, sometimes is referred to as *type*, can be rewritten as $\theta_{j,l-1} = \langle b_{j,l-1}, \hat{\theta}_j \rangle$, where $\hat{\theta}_j$ includes all elements of the intentional model other than the belief and is called the agent j's frame.

The $IS_{i,l}$ could be defined in an inductive manner (note that when $\hat{\theta}_j$ is usually known, $\hat{\theta}_j$ reduces to b_j):

$$\begin{aligned}
IS_{i,0} &= S, & \theta_{j,0} &= \{\langle b_{j,0}, \hat{\theta}_j \rangle : b_{j,0} \in \Delta(S)\} \\
IS_{i,1} &= S \times \theta_{j,0}, & \theta_{j,1} &= \{\langle b_{j,1}, \hat{\theta}_j \rangle : b_{j,1} \in \Delta(IS_{j,1})\} \\
&\dots\dots \\
IS_{i,l} &= S \times \theta_{j,l-1}, & \theta_{j,l} &= \{\langle b_{j,l}, \hat{\theta}_j \rangle : b_{j,l} \in \Delta(IS_{j,l})\}
\end{aligned} \tag{5}$$

And all other remaining components in an I-POMDP are similar to those in a POMDP:

[1] https://github.com/solohan22/IPOMDP.git

- $A = A_i \times A_j$ is the set of joint actions of all agents.
- Ω_i is the set of agent i's possible observations.
- $T_i : S \times A_i \times S \rightarrow [0, 1]$ is the state transition function.
- $O_i : S \times A_i \times \Omega_i \rightarrow [0, 1]$ is the observation function.
- $R_i : IS \times A_i \rightarrow R_i$ is the reward function.

Interactive belief update

Given all the definitions above, the interactive belief up-date can be performed as follows:

$$
\begin{aligned}
b_i^t(is^t) &= Pr(is^t|b_i^{t-1}, a_i^{t-1}, o_i^t) \qquad (6)\\
&= \alpha \sum_{is^{t-1}} b(is^{t-1}) \sum_{a_j^{t-1}} Pr(a_j^{t-1}|\theta_j^{t-1}) T(s^{t-1}, a^{t-1}, s^t)\\
&\times O_i(s^t, a^{t-1}, o_i^t) \sum_{o_j^t} O_j(s^t, a^{t-1}, o_j^t) \tau(b_j^{t-1}, a_j^{t-1}, o_j^t, b_j^t)
\end{aligned}
$$

Unlike plain belief update in POMDP, the interactive belief update in I-POMDP takes two additional sophistications into account. Firstly, the probabilities of other's actions given its models (the second summation) need to be computed since the state of physical environment now depends on both agents' actions. Secondly, the agent needs to update its beliefs based on the anticipation of what observations the other agent might get and how it updates (the third summation).

Then the optimal action, a^*, for the case of infinite horizon criterion with discounting, is part of the set of optimal actions, $OPT(\theta_i)$, for the belief state defined as:

$$
\begin{aligned}
OPT(\theta_i) = \arg\max_{a_i \in A_i} \Big\{ &\sum_{is \in IS} b_{is}(s) ER_i(is, a_i) \qquad (7)\\
&+ \gamma \sum_{o_i \in \Omega_i} P(o_i|a_i, b_i) \times U(\langle SE_{\theta_i}(b_i, a_i, o_i), \hat{\theta}_i \rangle) \Big\}
\end{aligned}
$$

Sampling Algorithms

The Interactive Particle Filter (I-PF) (Doshi and Gmytrasiewicz 2009) was proposed as a filtering algorithm for interactive belief update in I-POMDP. It generalizes the classic particle filter algorithm to multi-agent settings and uses the state transition function as the proposal distribution, which is usually used in a specific particle filter algorithm called bootstrap filter (Gordon, ect 1993). However, due to the enormous belief space, I-PF assumes that other agent's frame $\hat{\theta}_j$ is known to the modeling agent, therefore simplifies the belief update process from $S \times \Theta_{j,l-1}$ to a significantly smaller space $S \times b_{j,l-1}$.

The intuition of our algorithm is to assign appropriate prior distributions over agent j's all possible models $\theta_j =< b_j(s), A_j, \Omega_j, T_j, O_j, R_j, OC_j >$ and sample from each dimension of them. At each time step, we update all samples using perceived observations, namely computing and assigning weights to each sample, and resample them according to the weights. At last, since it is a randomized Monte Carlo method, to prevent the learning algorithm from converging to incorrect models, we add another resampling step to sample from the neighboring similar models given the current samples. Consequently, our algorithm is able to maintain a probability distribution of the most possible models of other agents and eventually learn the optimal actions of them.

Algorithm 1: Interactive Belief Update

$\tilde{b}_{k,l}^t =$ InteractiveBeliefUpdate($\tilde{b}_{k,l}^{t-1}, a_k^{t-1}, o_k^t, l > 0$)
1 For $is_k^{(n),t-1} =< s^{(n),t-1}, \theta_{-k}^{(n),t-1} > \in \tilde{b}_{k,l}^{t-1}$,
2 sample $a_{-k}^{t-1} \sim P(A_{-k}|\theta_{-k}^{(n),t-1})$
3 sample $s^{(n),t} \sim T_k(S^t|S^{(n),t-1}, a_k^{t-1}, a_{-k}^{t-1})$
4 for $o_{-k}^t \in \Omega_{-k}$:
5 if $l = 1$:
6 $b_{-k,0}^{(n),t} =$ Level0BeliefUpdate($b_{-k,0}^{(n),t-1}, a_{-k}^{t-1}, o_{-k}^t, \theta_{-k}^{(n),t-1}$)
7 $\theta_{-k}^{(n),t} =< b_{-k,0}^{(n),t}, \hat{\theta}_{-k}^{(n),t-1} >$
8 $is_k^{(n),t} =< s^{(n),t}, \theta_{-k}^{(n),t} >$
9 else:
10 $b_{-k,l-1}^{(n),t} =$ InteractiveBeliefUpdate($\tilde{b}_{-k,l-1}^{t-1}, a_{-k}^{t-1}, o_{-k}^t, l-1$)
11 $\theta_{-k}^{(n),t} =< b_{-k,l-1}^{(n),t}, \hat{\theta}_{-k}^{(n),t-1} >$
12 $is_k^{(n),t} =< s^{(n),t}, \theta_{-k}^{(n),t} >$
13 $w_t^{(n)} = O_{-k}^{(n)}(o_{-k}^t|s^{(n),t}, a_k^{t-1}, a_{-k}^{t-1})$
14 $w_t^{(n)} = w_t^{(n)} \times O_k(o_k^t|s^{(n),t}, a_k^{t-1}, a_{-k}^{t-1})$
15 $\tilde{b}_{k,l}^{temp} =< is_k^{(n),t}, w_t^{(n)} >$
16 normalize all $w_t^{(n)}$ so that $\sum_{n=1}^N w_t^{(n)} = 1$
17 resample from $\tilde{b}_{k,l}^{temp}$ accroding to normalized $w_t^{(n)}$
18 resample $\theta_{-k}^{(n),t}$ according to neighboring similar models
19 return $\tilde{b}_{k,l}^t = is_k^{(n),t}$

The interactive belief update described in Algorithm 1 is similar to I-PF in terms of the recursive Monte Carlo sampling and nesting hierarchy, but it has three major differences. Firstly, the belief update is over the entire intentional model space of other agents, therefore the initial set of N samples $\tilde{b}_{k,l}^{t-1} =< b_{-k,l-1}^{(n),t-1}, A_{-k}, \Omega_{-k}, T_{-k}^{(n)}, O_{-k}^{(n)}, R_{-k}^{(n)}, OC_j >$, where k here denotes the modeling agent and $-k$ denotes all other modeled agents. We only assume that the actions A_{-k}, observations Ω_{-k} and optimal criteria OC_j are known, as in a multi-agent game the rules are usually known to all agents or could be obtained through intelligence. Secondly, it is intuitive to see that the observation function $O_{-k}^{(n)}(o_{-k}^t|s^{(n),t}, a_k^{t-1}, a_{-k}^{t-1})$ in line 13 is now randomized as well, as each of them is a particular observation function of that agent. Lastly, we add another resampling step in line 18 in order to avoid divergence, by resampling each dimension of the model samples from a Gaussian distribution with the mean of current sample value. Intuitively, similar models are resampled from a relatively tight neighboring region of the current model samples to maintain the learning accuracy.

Algorithm 1 can be viewed as two major steps. The *importance sampling* step (line 1 to line 16) samples from belief priors $\tilde{b}_{k,l}^{t-1}$ and propagates forward using related proposal distributions and computes the weights of all samples. And the *selection* or *resapmling* step (line 17 to line 18) resamples according to weights and similar models. Specifically, the algorithm starts from a set of initial priors $is_k^{(n),t-1}$, for each of them, it samples other agents' optimal action a_{-k}^{t-1} from its policy $P(A_{-k}|\theta_{-k}^{(n),t-1})$, which is solved using a very efficient POMDP solver called Perseus[2] (Spaan and Vlassis 2005). Then it samples the physical state s^t using the state transition $T_k(S^t|S^{(n),t-1}, a_k^{t-1}, a_{-k}^{t-1})$. Once a_{-k}^{t-1} and s^t are sampled, the algorithm calls for the 0-level belief update (line 5 to 8), described in Algorithm 2, to update other agents' plain beliefs $b_{-k,0}^t$ if the current nesting level l is 1, or recursively calls for itself at a lower level $l-1$ (line 9 to 12) if the current nesting level is greater than 1. The sample weights $w_t^{(n)}$ are computed according to observation likelihoods of modeling and modeled agents (line 13, 14), and then got normalized so that they sum up to 1 (line 16). Lastly, the algorithm resamples the intermediate samples according to the computed weights (line 17) and resamples another time from similar neighboring models (line 18).

Algorithm 2: Level-0 Belief Update

$b_{k,0}^t$ =Level0BeliefUpdate($b_{k,0}^{t-1}$,a_k^{t-1},o_k^t, $T_k^{(n)}$,$O_k^{(n)}$)
1 $P(a_{-k}^{t-1}) = 1/a_{-k}^{t-1}$
2 for $s^t \in S$:
3 for s^{t-1}:
4 for $a_{-k}^{(t-1)} \in A_{-k}$:
5 $P^{(n)}(s^t|s^{t-1}, a_k^{t-1}) =$ $T_k^{(n)}(s^t|s^{t-1}, a_k^{t-1}, a_{-k}^{t-1}) \times P(a_{-k}^{t-1})$
6 $sum^{(n)} += P^{(n)}(s^t|s^{t-1}, a_k^{t-1}) b_{k,0}^{t-1}(s^{t-1})$
7 for $a_{-k}^{(t-1)} \in A_{-k}$:
8 $P^{(n)}(o_k^t|s^t, a_k^{t-1}) +=$ $O_k^{(n)}(o_k^t|s^t, a_k^{t-1}, a_{-k}^{t-1}) P(a_{-k}^{t-1})$
9 $b_{k,0}^t = sum^{(n)} \times P^{(n)}(o_k^t|s^t, a_k^{t-1})$
10 normalize and return $b_{k,0}^t$

The 0-level belief update, described in Algorithm 2, is similar to POMDP belief update but treats other agents' actions as noise and randomized the state transition function and observation function as input parameters. It assume other agents in the environment choose their actions according to a uniform distribution (line 1), therefore is essentially a no-information model. For each possible action $a_{-k}^{(t-1)}$, it computes the actual state transition (line 5) and actual observation function (line 8) by marginalizing over others' actions, and returns the normalized belief $b_{k,0}^t$. Notice that the transition function $T_k^{(n)}(s^t|s^{t-1}, a_k^{t-1}, a_{-k}^{t-1})$ and observation function $O_k^{(n)}(o_k^t|s^t, a_k^{t-1}, a_{-k}^{t-1})$ are now both samples from input arguments, depending on model parameters of the actual agent on the 0th level.

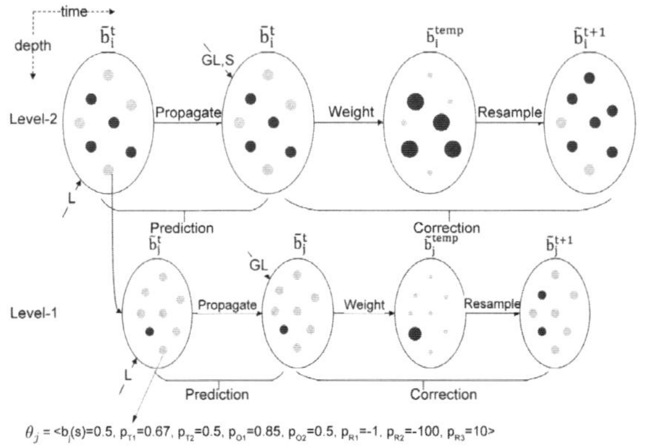

Figure 1: An illustration of interactive belief update for two agents and 1 level nesting.

In figure 1, we illustrate the interactive belief update using the problem discussed in the following section . Suppose there are two agents i and j in the environment, the sample size is 8 and the nesting level is 2, the subscripts in figure 1 denotes the corresponding agents and each dot represents a particular belief sample. The propagate step corresponds to line 2 to 12 in Algorithm 1, the weight step corresponds to line 13 to 16, the resample step corresponds to line 17 and 18. The belief update for a particular level-0 model sample ($\theta_j = \langle b_j(s) = 0.5, p_{T1} = 0.67, p_{T2} = 0.5, p_{O1} = 0.85, p_{O2} = 0.5, p_{R1} = -1, p_{R2} = -100, p_{R3} = 10 \rangle$) is solved using Algorithm 2, and the optimal action is computed by calling the Perseus POMDP solver.

Experiments

Setup

We present the results using the multi-agent tiger game (Gmytrasiewicz and Doshi 2005) with various settings. The multi-agent tiger game is a generalization of the classical single agent tiger game (Kaelbling, Littman, and Cassandra 1998) with adding observations which caused by others' actions. The generalized multi-agent game contains additional observations regarding other players, while the state transition and reward function involve others' actions as well.

Let's see a specific game example with known parameters: there are a tiger and a pile of gold behind two doors respectively, two players can both listen for a growl of the tiger and a creak caused by the other player, or open doors which resets the tiger's location with equal probability. Their observation toward the tiger and the other player are both relatively high (0.85 and 0.9 respectively). No matter triggered by which player, the reward for listening action is -1, opening the tiger door is -100 and opening the gold door is 10.

[2]http://www.st.ewi.tudelft.nl/~mtjspaan/pomdp/index_en.html

Table 1: Parameters for transition functions

S	A	TL	TR
TL	L	p_{T1}	$1-p_{T1}$
TR	L	$1-p_{T1}$	p_{T1}
*	OL	p_{T2}	$1-p_{T2}$
*	OR	$1-p_{T2}$	p_{T2}

Table 2: Parameters for observation functions

S	A	GL	GR
TL	L	p_{O1}	$1-p_{O1}$
TR	L	$1-p_{O1}$	p_{O1}
*	OL	p_{O2}	$1-p_{O2}$
*	OR	$1-p_{O2}$	p_{O2}

Table 3: Parameters for reward functions

S	A	R
*	L	p_{R1}
TL	OL	p_{R1}
TR	OR	p_{R2}
TL	OR	p_{R3}
TR	OL	p_{R3}

For the sake of brevity, we restrict the experiments to a two-agent setting and nesting level of one, but the sampling algorithm is extensible to any number of agents and nesting levels in a straightforward manner. Recall that an interactive POMDP of agent i is defined as a six tuple $I\text{-}POMDP_i = \langle IS_{i,l}, A, \Omega_i, T_i, O_i, R_i \rangle$. Thus for the specific setting of multi-agent tiger problem:

- $IS_{i,1} = S \times \theta_{j,0}$, where $S = \{$tiger on the left (TL), tiger on the right (TR)$\}$ and $\theta_{j,0} =< b_j(s), A_j, \Omega_j, T_j, O_j, R_j, OC_j >\}$.
- $A = A_i \times A_j$ is a combination of both agents' possible actions: listen (L), open left door (OL) and open right door(OR).
- Ω_i is all the combinations of each agent's possible observations: growl from left (GL) or right (GR), combined with creak from left (CL), right (CR) or silence (S).
- $T_i = T_j : S \times A_i \times A_j \times S \rightarrow [0, 1]$ is a joint state transition probability that involves both actions.
- $O_i : S \times A_i \times A_j \times \Omega_i \rightarrow [0, 1]$ becomes a joint observation probability that involves both actions. O_j is symmetric of O_i with respect to the joint actions.
- $R_i : IS \times A_i \times A_j \rightarrow R_i$: agent i gets corresponding rewards when he listens, opens the wrong door and opens the correct door respectively. They are independent of j's actions.

Parameter Space

For the experiments of multi-agent tiger game, we want to learn over all possible intentional models of the other agent j: $\theta_j =< b_j(s), A_j, \Omega_j, T_j, O_j, R_j, OC_j >$. We only make reasonable assumptions that A_j and Ω_j are known, OC_j is infinite horizon with discounting. Now what we really want to learn are as follow:

- b_j^0: the initial belief of agent j about the physical state.
- T_j: the transition function of agent j, which can be parametrized by two parameters p_{T1} and p_{T2}, as shown in Table 1.
- O_j: the observation function of agent j, which can be parametrized by two parameters p_{O1} and p_{O2}, as shown in Table 2.
- T_j: the reward function of agent j, which can be parametrized by three parameters p_{R1}, p_{R2} and p_{R3}, as shown in Table 3.

We could easily see that it is a enormous 8-dimensional parameter space to learn from: $b_j^0 \times p_{T1} \times p_{T2} \times p_{O1} \times p_{O2} \times p_{R1} \times p_{R2} \times p_{R3}$, where $b_j \in [0, 1] \subset \mathbb{R}$, $p_{T1} \in [0, 1] \subset \mathbb{R}$, $p_{T2} \in [0, 1] \subset \mathbb{R}$, $p_{O1} \in [0, 1] \subset \mathbb{R}$, $p_{O2} \in [0, 1] \subset \mathbb{R}$, $p_{R1} \in [-\infty, +\infty] \subset \mathbb{R}$, $p_{R2} \in [-\infty, +\infty] \subset \mathbb{R}$, $p_{R3} \in [-\infty, +\infty] \subset \mathbb{R}$.

We mainly reduce this huge space by two means: utilizing Monte Carlo sampling methods and giving them problem-specific priors so that they are not over informative but provide enough information for the algorithm to learn from.

Results

For the actual experiments, we fix the number of samples to be 2000 and run it on a two agent tiger game simulation as described above. We run experiments for learning three difference models of agent j:

1. $\theta_{j1} =< 0.5, 0.67, 0.5, 0.85, 0.5, -1, -100, 10 >$
2. $\theta_{j2} =< 0.5, 1.00, 0.5, 0.95, 0.5, -1, -10, 10 >$
3. $\theta_{j3} =< 0.5, 0.66, 0.5, 0.85, 0.5, 10, -100, 10 >$

These models are all very special cases and carefully chosen in order to verify the correctness and evaluate the performance of our algorithm. For instance, the first model is a sophisticated one when the other agent is actually modeling his opponent using a subintentional model, while the second is a classic single-agent POMDP and the third is a very simple one but contains a large model space. We want to investigate if our framework is able to correctly and efficiently learn these models through these experiments.

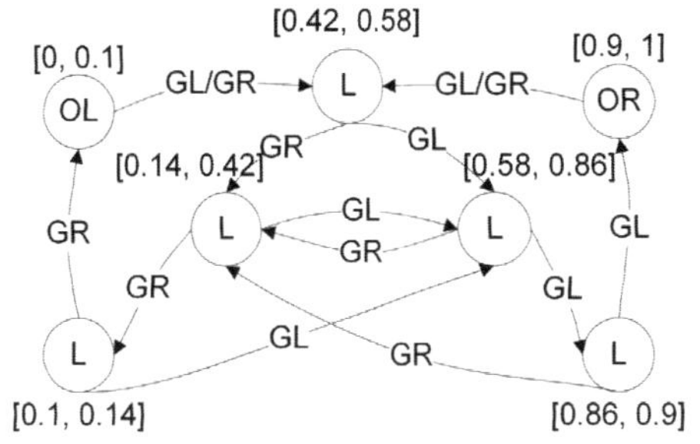

Figure 2: Optimal policy of a no-information model.

The aim of first experiment to try to learn relatively complicated models of agent j with $\theta_j =< 0.5, 0.67, 0.5, 0.85, 0.5, -1, -100, 10 >$, who assumes others' actions are drawn from a uniform distribution. Equivalently, agent j's actual policy, as shown in figure 2, is to look for three consecutive growls from same direction and then open the corresponding door. For this particular experiment, we simulated the observation history for agent i, for the sake of firstly verifying the correctness of our algorithm, excluding the impacts of uncertainties from hearing accuracy. The simulated observation history is as follows: {GL,S GL,S GL,S GL,CR GL,S GL,S GL,S GR,CR GL,S GL,S GL,S GR,CR GL,S GL,S GL,S GR,CR GR,S GR,S GR,S GR,CL GR,S GR,S GR,S GR,CL GR,S GR,S GR,S GR,CL GR,S GR,S GR,S GR,CL GR,S GR,S GR,S GR,CL GR,S GR,S GR,S GL,CL GL,S GL,S GL,S GR,CR GL,S GL,S GL,S GR,CR GR,S GR,S}

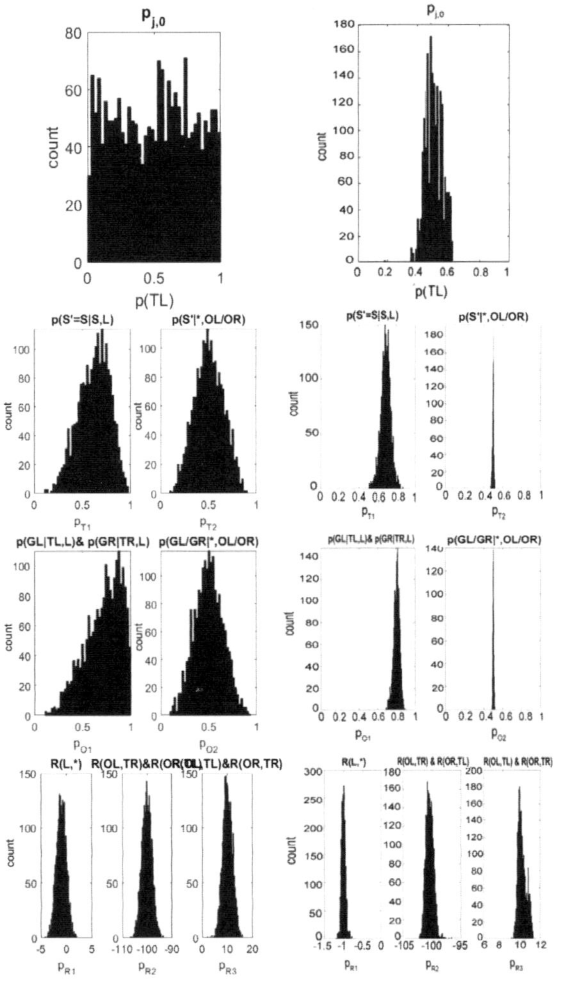

Figure 3: Assigned priors and learned posterior distributions over model parameters for model $\theta_{j1} =< 0.5, 0.67, 0.5, 0.85, 0.5, -1, -100, 10 >$.

The priors we assign to each parameters are shown in figure 3, specifically, they are uniform U(0,1) for b_j^0, Beta(5,3) with mode 0.67 for p_{T1}, Beta(5,5) for p_{T2}, Beta(3.5,1.4) with mode 0.85 for p_{O1}, Beta(5,5) for p_{O2}, Gaussian N(-1,2) for p_{R1}, N(-100,4) for p_{R2}, and N(10,2) for p_{R3}.

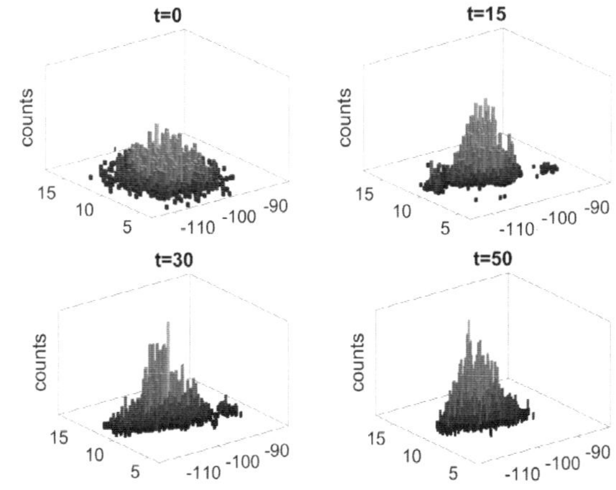

Figure 4: 3D histogram of all model samples.

After 50 time steps, the algorithm converge to a posterior distribution over agent j's intentional models, the results are also given in figure 3. Since the parameter space of agent j's models is 8-dimensional, here we only show the marginal distributions of each parameter space in histograms. We can easily see that the majority of samples are centered around the true parameter values.

We use principal component analysis (PCA) (Abdi and Williams 2010) to reduce sample dimensionality to 2-dimensional and plot them out in a 3-dimensional histogram, as shown in Figure 4. It starts from a Gaussian-like prior and gradually converges to the most likely models. Eventually the mean value of this cluster ⟨ 0.49, 0.69, 0.49, 0.82, 0.51, -0.95, -99.23, 10.09 ⟩ is very close to the true model. Here we give two examples from the big cluster after 50 time steps: ⟨0.56, 0.66, 0.49, 0.84, 0.59, -0.95, -101.37, 11.42⟩ and ⟨0.51, 0.68, 0.52, 0.89, 0.56, -1.33, -98.39, 12.55⟩. The former has a corresponding optimal policy of [0—OL—0.10—L—1], while the latter has a [0—OL—0.09—L–0.91—OR—1], which are both extremely close to the optimal policy of the true model: [0—OL—0.1—L–0.9—OR—1]. Consequently, the framework is able to predict other agents' actions with high accuracy.

We tested the performance of our algorithms in terms of prediction accuracy towards others' actions. We compared the results with other modeling approaches, such as a frequency-based approach, in which agent j is assumed to choose his action according to a fixed but unknown distribution, and a no-information model which treats j's actions purely as uniform noise. The results shown in figure 5 are averaged plots of 10 random runs, each of which has 50 time steps. It shows clearly that the intentional I-POMDP approach has significantly lower error rates as agent i perceives more observations. The subintenional model assume j's action is draw from a uniform distribution, therefore has

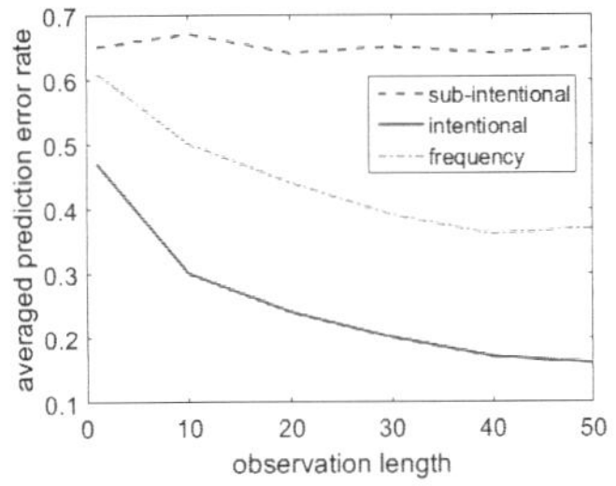

Figure 5: Prediction error rate vs observation length.

a fixed high error rate. The frequency based approach has certain learning ability but is far from enough sophisticated for modeling a fully rational agent.

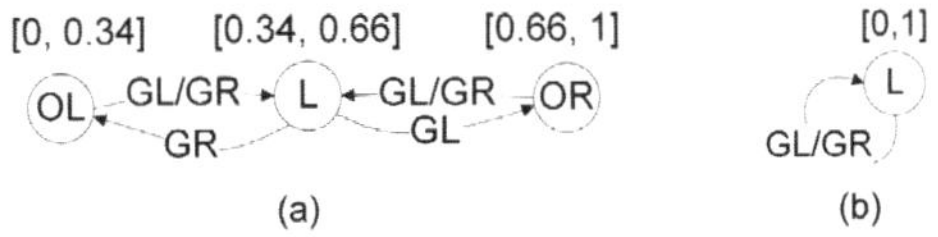

Figure 6: (a) optimal policy for $\theta_j = \langle$ 0.5, 1, 0.5, 0.95, 0.5, -1, -10, 10 $\rangle$. (b) optimal policy for $\theta_j = \langle$0.5, 0.66, 0.5, 0.85, 0.5, 10, -100, 10$\rangle$.

In the second experiment, we run our algorithm on actual observations for 30 time steps until it converges, and try to learn models of a simpler classic POMDP with high listening accuracy of 0.95 and small penalty of -10, e.g. the agent j alternately opens door and listens as shown in Figure 6 left. The actual model of j is $\theta_j = \langle$ 0.5, 1, 0.5, 0.95, 0.5, -1, -10, 10 $\rangle$, the priors assigned to b_j^0, p_{T1}, p_{T2}, p_{O1}, p_{O2}, p_{R2}, p_{R3} are U(0,1), Beta(2,0.5), Beta(10,10), Beta(19,1), Beta(10,10), N(-1,1), N(-10,2), N(10,2), and the actual observation history is {GR,S GL,CR GL,S GL,CL GL,S GL,CR GL,S GL,CL GL,S GR,S GR,CL GR,CL GL,S GR,S GR,S GL,CL GR,S GL,CR GR,S GR,CR GR,CR GR,CL GL,S GL,S GL,S GL,CR GL,S GL,CL GR,S GR,S}.

Similarly, we report the learned posterior distributions over model parameters in figure 7. We observe an interesting pattern that while some parameters, such as $b_{j,0}$, p_{T2} and p_{O2} are concentrated around the actual values, others like p_{T1} and p_{O1} become more dispersed than initial priors. The intuition behind is that the penalty and reward are -10 and 10, so one listening of reward -1 is enough for making decision of opening doors. That is to say, as long as tiger likely remains behind the same door when agent listens (the meaning of p_{T1}) and has a reliable hearing accuracy (the meaning of p_{O1}), there are many models which satisfy this particular observation sequence, hence our algorithm learns them all.

For conciseness, we show the average prediction error rates for both second and third experiments in figure 9. Both results are averaged among 10 random runs, each of which has 30 time steps. In the second experiment in figure 9(a), the intentional I-POMDP approach still has significantly lower error rates than others.

In the last experiment, we wants to learn a model of θ_j= $\langle$0.5, 0.66, 0.5, 0.85, 0.5, 10, -100, 10$\rangle$, who always listens since the listening penalty is now equal to the reward, as shown in figure 6(b). For brevity, we only show the marginal distributions over model parameters in figure 8. The priors assigned to b_j^0, p_{T1}, p_{T2}, p_{O1}, p_{O2}, p_{R2}, p_{R3} are U(0,1), Beta(5,3), Beta(10,10), Beta(3.5,1.4), Beta(10,10), N(10,1), N(-100,2), N(10,2), and the actual observation history i learns from is {GL,S GL,S GR,S GL,S GL,CL GR,S GR,S GL,CL GR,S GL,S GL,S GR,S GL,S GL,S GL,S GL,CL GR,S GL,S GL,S GL,S}. We can see that all three reward parameters are correctly learned, while samples of p_{T1}, p_{T2}, p_{O1} and p_{O2} are not very concentrated to their true values but close to their corresponding priors, since intuitively they become less important and can be in a relatively loose region due to the increased p_{R1}=10. Lastly, the performance comparison is given in figure 9(b).

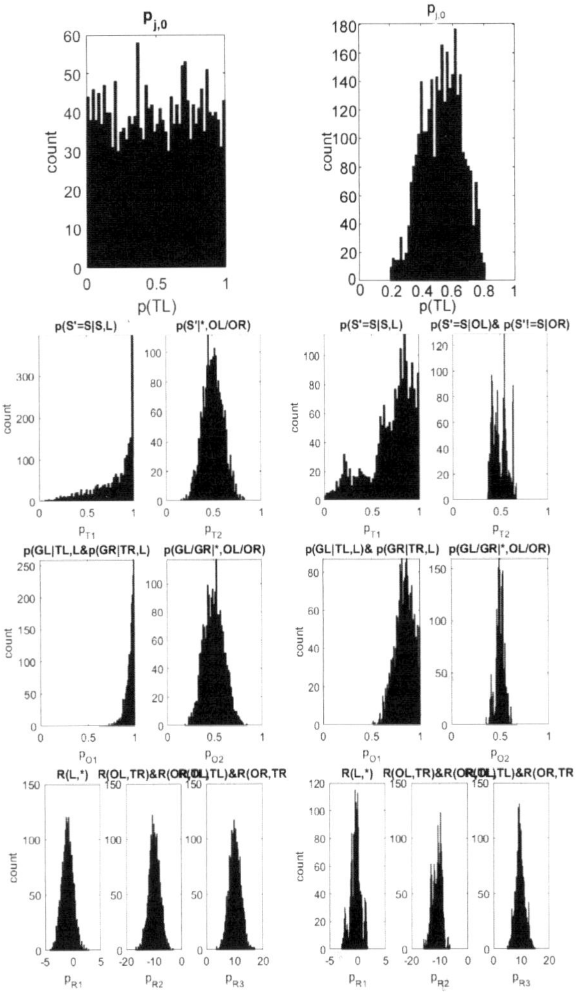

Figure 7: Learned posterior distributions for model $\theta_j = \langle$ 0.5, 1, 0.5, 0.95, 0.5, -1, -10, 10 $\rangle$.

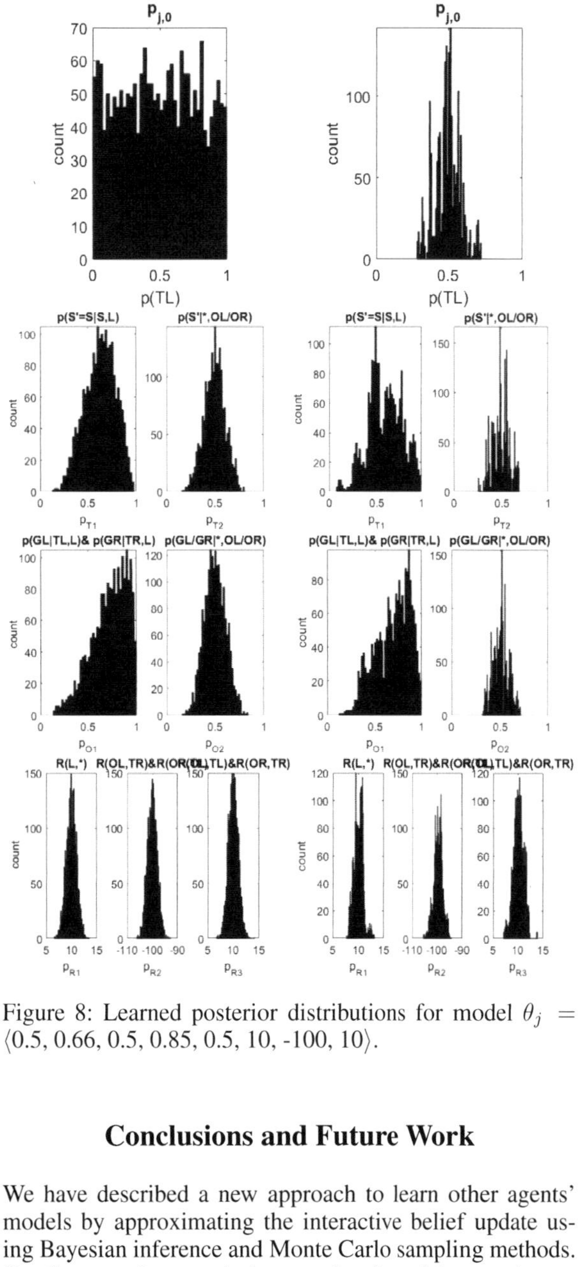

Figure 8: Learned posterior distributions for model $\theta_j = \langle 0.5, 0.66, 0.5, 0.85, 0.5, 10, -100, 10\rangle$.

Conclusions and Future Work

We have described a new approach to learn other agents' models by approximating the interactive belief update using Bayesian inference and Monte Carlo sampling methods. Our framework correctly learns others' models over the entire intentional model space and therefore is a generalized reinforcement learning algorithm for multi-agent settings. It also effectively mitigates the belief space complexity and has a significant better performance than other approaches in terms of predicting others' actions.

In the future, in order to fully evaluate the practicability on larger problem space, more multi-agent problems of various sizes could be tested. Due to computation complexity, experiments on higher nesting levels are currently limited. Thus, more efforts could be made on utilizing nonparametric Bayesian methods which inherently deal with nested belief structures.

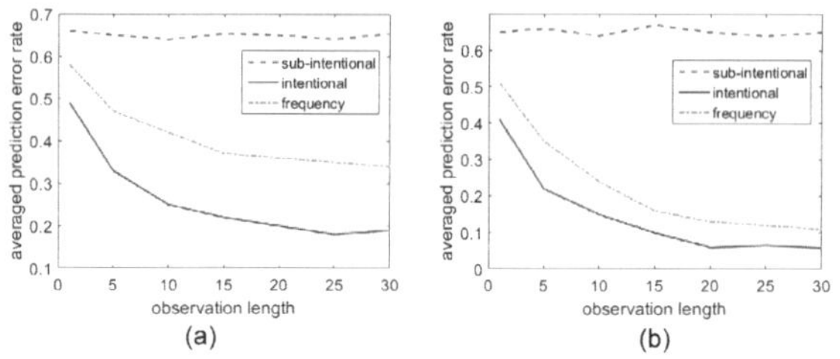

Figure 9: (a) Prediction error rate vs observation length for $\theta_j = \langle 0.5, 1, 0.5, 0.95, 0.5, -1, -10, 10 \rangle$. (b) for $\theta_j = \langle 0.5, 0.66, 0.5, 0.85, 0.5, 10, -100, 10\rangle$.

References

Abdi, H. and Williams, L.J., 2010. Principal component analysis. Wiley interdisciplinary reviews: computational statistics, 2(4), pp.433-459.

Doucet, A., De Freitas, N. and Gordon, N., 2001. An introduction to sequential Monte Carlo methods. In *Sequential Monte Carlo methods in practice* (pp. 3-14). Springer New York.

Doshi, P., and Gmytrasiewicz, P. J. 2009. Monte Carlo sampling methods for approximating interactive POMDPs. *Journal of Artificial Intelligence Research* 34: 297-337.

Doshi-Velez, F. and Konidaris, G., 2013. Hidden parameter Markov decision processes: A semiparametric regression approach for discovering latent task parametrizations. *arXiv:1308.3513*.

Del Moral, P., 1996. Non-linear filtering: interacting particle resolution. Markov processes and related fields, 2(4), pp.555-581.

Doshi, P., Zeng, Y., and Chen, Q. 2009. Graphical models for interactive POMDPs: representations and solutions. Autonomous Agents and Multi-Agent Systems 18.3: 376-416.

Gilks, W.R., Richardson, S. and Spiegelhalter, D.J., 1996. Introducing markov chain monte carlo. Markov chain Monte Carlo in practice, 1, p.19.

Gmytrasiewicz, P. J., and Doshi, P. 2005. A framework for sequential planning in multi-agent settings. *Journal of Artificial Intelligence Research* 24(1): 49-79.

Gmytrasiewicz, P. J., and Doshi, P. 2005. A framework for sequential planning in multi-agent settings. *Journal of Artificial Intelligence Research* 24(1): 49-79.

Gordon, N.J., Salmond, D.J. and Smith, A.F., 1993, April. Novel approach to nonlinear/non-Gaussian Bayesian state estimation. In IEE Proceedings F (Radar and Signal Processing) (Vol. 140, No. 2, pp. 107-113). IET Digital Library.

Kaelbling, L.P., Littman, M.L. and Cassandra, A.R., 1998. Planning and acting in partially observable stochastic domains. *Artificial intelligence*, 101(1), pp.99-134.

Spaan, M.T. and Vlassis, N., 2005. Perseus: Randomized point-based value iteration for POMDPs. Journal of artificial intelligence research, 24, pp.195-220.

Liu, M., Liao, X. and Carin, L., 2011. The infinite regionalized policy representation. In *Proceedings of the 28th International Conference on Machine Learning (ICML-11)* (pp. 769-776).

Panella, A. and Gmytrasiewicz, P., 2016, March. Bayesian Learning of Other Agents' Finite Controllers for Interactive POMDPs. In *Thirtieth AAAI Conference on Artificial Intelligence*.

Pearl, J., 1988. Probabilistic reasoning in intelligent systems: Networks of plausible reasoning.

Ross, S., Chaib-draa, B. and Pineau, J., 2007. Bayes-adaptive pomdps. In *Advances in neural information processing systems* (pp. 1225-1232).

Shortest Total Path Length Spanning Tree via Wisdom of Artificial Crowds Algorithm

Madeline V. Hundley, Roman V. Yampolskiy

Abstract—**This paper presents a hybrid genetic algorithm (GA) with Wisdom of Artificial Crowds (WoAC) approach to solving an NP-hard problem. This is a novel approach to solving Shortest total-Path-length Spanning Tree (SPST) problems. In our tests this approach achieved results up to 12% better than use of the genetic algorithm alone.**

Index Terms—**genetic algorithm, shortest total path length spanning tree, wisdom of artificial crowds**

I. Introduction

THIS project addresses the NP-complete Shortest total-Path-length Spanning Tree (SPST) problem, proposed and discussed in [1-3]. For an edge-weighted, undirected graph, the objective of this problem is to find the spanning tree for which the total sum of total edge weights on the paths between every pair of vertices is minimized. NP-complete problems are those for whom no fast solution is known; as the size of the problem set grows the time any currently known algorithm requires to solve it increases incredibly quickly. SPST has been demonstrated as one such NP-complete problem [4, 5].

In this implementation of the problem we consider the distance between each vertex as the weight or cost of the edge. Specifically, we consider the Euclidean distances between vertices with Cartesian coordinates, calculated with the formula below. Therefore, the total distance of a path is the sum of the costs of each edge between each vertex in that path. The total-path-length of a spanning tree is the sum of the path length between every pair of vertices in the tree.

$$d = \sqrt{(x_2 - x_1)^2 + (y_2 - y_1)^2} \quad (1)$$

Genetic algorithms mimic the real-world phenomena whereby populations of biological species reproduce children based on the genes of the parents and natural selection steers each generation towards superior genes [6]. The genetic algorithm we incorporated into our hybrid approach initializes a random population of SPST solutions then reproduces successive generations of solutions. It analyzes the reproductive fitness of each member of a population, probabilistically selects stronger parents to reproduce, generates child solutions from the genes of the parent spanning trees, and sets up the next generation's population with the strongest members from the old population plus qualifying members from the child solutions.

The wisdom of crowds [7] describes the phenomenon where aggregated results from a population, or "crowd," approach the best answer to a problem, even though individual answers may have significant differences and deviations from the globally optimum solution. The Wisdom of Artificial Crowds makes use of the artificially generated populations from the genetic algorithm, treating these solutions as the "crowd" whose expertise can be consulted. One child per population is created by aggregating the edge choices of every SPST solution, probabilistically selecting a number of those edges to base the child on, then building the remainder of the spanning tree solution via locally greedy edge choices.

The program is written in Python 3.5, the graphics are generated with the module pygame, and the graphs are generated with the matplotlib module. The input provided to the program is a data file with the vertices' coordinates. The program must read in these coordinates, calculate the distance between each pair of vertices that are connected, generate a random initial population of spanning trees, then apply the genetic algorithm with wisdom of artificial crowds to generationally approach the best SPST for the graph provided.

The motivation behind developing this algorithm was to explore the interplay of the genetic algorithm component and wisdom of artificial crowds component. We also sought to explore whether wisdom of artificial crowds is a viable, successful variant to the genetic algorithm for the SPST problem as well as whether a genetic algorithm is a viable, successful source of good solutions for a wisdom of artificial crowds component.

II. Prior Work

The approach of a hybrid GA plus WoAC has been shown many times as a viable approach to solving many NP-complete problems [8-11], including the famous Travelling Salesperson problem [12]. Baseline genetic algorithms have been applied to solve spanning tree problems similar to the SPST problem [13] and other approximation algorithms have been applied to the SPST problem [14-16]. However, a hybrid GA + WoAC algorithm is, to our knowledge, a novel approach to the SPST problem.

III. Proposed Approach

To solve this SPST problem, the program uses a genetic algorithm with a wisdom of artificial crowds component. The program's first order of business is to read in the coordinates of each vertex from a file and calculate the Euclidean distances between, saving these in a dictionary for quick lookup. Its last order of business is to plot the best, average, and worst results from each generation of the algorithm and to graphically display the best spanning tree found, with the shortest total-path-length.

Overall, the genetic algorithm drives the development of a diverse, increasingly fit population every generation. The wisdom of the crowds aggregates the collective knowledge of these populations to discover better or at least comparable but diverse paths.

A. SpanningTree Class

This program is based on a *SpanningTree* class. Each instance of the class has an instance variable *sptree*, a set of the edges, stored as tuples, in the spanning tree. To initialize a *SpanningTree* the class should be provided a set of unique tuples, meaning no duplicates e.g. (1,2) and (2,1). Internally the *sptree* variable generates and stores both of these tuples, however, for easy lookups to the edges contained in this *SpanningTree* instance.

Upon initializing a new instance of a *SpanningTree*, the class function *calc_paths* calculates the path for every pair of vertices and stores it in the instance variable *paths*. It does this by using a recursive algorithm, the *recursive_expansion* function. Starting with the first vertex, the function "expands" this vertex, creating a "frontier" of the vertices that can next be reached given the edges constituting the spanning tree. For example, if the only edges in the spanning tree that contain the vertex '1' are the edges (1,2) and (1,3), expanding the vertex '1' would yield a frontier of '2' and '3'. It then arbitrarily chooses one of these vertices, adds it to the current path being traced, and with another call to *recursive_expansion* expands again on this new vertex. Important to cultivating the frontier is eliminating the vertices already in the current path so the algorithm does not try to expand "backwards." If the algorithm reaches a vertex whose frontier is empty, meaning the path has hit a dead end, that vertex is taken out of the path and the next option from the frontier at that level is selected and expanded. In this way, the recursion searches depth-first, backing up from dead-ends and expanding each vertex until the destination vertex has been found. The algorithm can stop searching upon first encountering the destination vertex because of an important feature of spanning trees: there can only be one valid path between any two vertices. Valid spanning trees by definition do not have cycles; if a tree contained a cycle this would offer more than one path from one vertex to another. Therefore, once the algorithm found a valid path it could stop searching as this was the only valid path. Finally, these paths are stored in the instance variable *paths*, a dictionary whose keys are pairs of vertices, stored as tuples, and whose values are lists containing each path. Only unique tuples, meaning no duplicates, are stored in this dictionary as lookups in one direction are only ever required.

Once all paths have been identified, the *SpanningTree* class function *calc_length* is called to sum the total lengths of these paths. The *calc_length* function simply needs to issue lookups to the dictionary of distances between every pair of vertices in the graph generated at the beginning of the program. The function looks up and sums the length of each edge in every path. The total-path-length of the *SpanningTree* is stored in its *length* instance variable.

Finally, the *SpanningTree* class has a *mutate* function, which will be discussed further in the context of the genetic algorithm, below.

B. Genetic Algorithm

To begin, the genetic algorithm sets up its initial population with the *get_init_pop* function by generating spanning trees randomly, calling the *get_rand_sptree* function. This function generates a valid spanning tree by tracking the vertices that have been added so far and randomly selecting an edge from one such vertex to one not yet added. This methodology prevents it from adding an edge "backwards" and introducing a cycle.

Each successive population in the genetic algorithm is generated by the *get_next_pop* function, which first produces one child based on the "wisdom of artificial crowds," discussed further in the next section. Then using calls to the *reproduce* function, it reproduces all remaining children required "genetically" from selected parents. *Reproduce* uses the *get_fitness* function to judge the fitness of each potential parent in the current population. Better spanning trees – those with shorter total-path-lengths – are judged to have a higher reproductive fitness and therefore have a greater probability of being selected as parents for the next generation. When two trees are selected to be parents, the *crossover* function generates two new children from those parents' "genes." Every time a child is produced there is a possibility that a mutation will occur in its "genes," handled by the *SpanningTree* class's built-in *mutate* function.

In the *get_fitness* function, the fitness ratios of every spanning tree in the population need to reflect how short their total-path-lengths are. The typical fitness ratio in a genetic algorithm tries to achieve selection of a maximum value; this will simply take each element's value out of the sum total of the population's values. If applied to the total-path-lengths this would "reward" the long paths rather than the short ones. For the SPST problem this function must instead seek to achieve selection of minimum values. Therefore, this algorithm's fitness ratio takes each tree's length and subtracts it from the highest value in the population and from 1, before dividing by the sum total of these adjusted costs. Finally, it scales so these probabilities all add up to 1, a requirement for a valid probability distribution. This method more heavily weights the shortest total-path-lengths. It also has the side effect of assigning the very worst spanning tree a fitness ratio of zero, which will cull it from potential selection in the next part of the algorithm. This is a perfectly acceptable, even desirable, side effect from this process.

The *crossover* function uses an experimentally-determined break point in each parent's "genes," discussed further in the next section, to determine the edges that will be passed on to the children. One child is first set up with a portion of edges taken from the "mom" parent tree and the second child is first set up with a portion of edges taken from the "dad" parent tree. Each of these children, currently just an incomplete set of edges, is then passed to the *complete_tree* function, along with the opposite parent from which it was first based on. The *complete_tree* function, as the name implies, completes the tree using only edges available in the parent provided. In this way, the first child is first built using "mom" then completed with "dad," and vice versa for the second child.

The *complete_tree* function is integral to both the genetic algorithm and the wisdom of artificial crowds component, whose use of it is discussed in further detail in the next section. This function first identifies all groups that exist in the edges provided. For example, if (1,2) and (2,3) are both edges in the set provided, the function identifies that {1,2,3} is a connected group of edges. Then vertices that are not yet connected, that have zero edges, are added as groups of one each by themselves. The function's next step is to choose and add edges which will connect these groups into a complete spanning tree. Starting at an arbitrary group called the *coregroup*, the function generates a list of valid edges it may choose from: all edges from a vertex in the current group to a vertex not in the group and only edges that are also present in the parent tree. It is important to point out that only edges from an added vertex to an unadded vertex are those allowed. As with the process for finding the paths in a tree or for building a random tree, selecting edges in this way ensures the tree is never grown "backwards" i.e. that it is never allowed to introduce a cycle. After identifying the valid edges, the function then greedily selects the shortest one, adding that edge to the tree. It must also identify the group that vertex belongs to and incorporate all that group's vertices into the *coregroup*. This process is repeated until all groups are incorporated, growing the *coregroup* across the graph until it includes all vertices and the child spanning tree is complete.

There are a couple important items to note regarding the *complete_tree* function. First, the arbitrary selection of the initial *coregroup* does not affect the final spanning tree. It does not matter in what order the groups are added to the *coregroup* because of the greedy nature of the edge selection and the fact any vertex not currently in the *coregroup* is allowed as the next addition. For instance, if vertex '1' is in one group, vertex '2' is in another, and their edge is the shortest available to join those two groups, it will always be the one selected whether vertex '2's group is incorporated first, somewhere in the middle, or last. Second, the greedy decision to add the shortest edge available from the parent was based on the assumption that these shortest edges available will contribute to an overall shorter total-path-length for the spanning tree. There are some instances where including a longer edge instead leads to overall better paths. However, these locally optimal choices demonstrated through testing to often be globally optimal as well. In addition, the fact the child is based in portion on a parent and not wholly on local greedy decisions helps to compensate and works to retain knowledge of which long routes are favorable.

After *crossover* has completed both kids, they are each checked for mutations using the *SpanningTree* class's built-in *mutate* function. If the test against the probability of mutation occurring hits, the function randomly selects a path that involves two edges (three vertices), discards the first edge and adds a replacement connecting the first edge straight to the third. This approach allows for a test of whether going straight from the first to the third vertex, rather than through the second vertex, offers better paths for the tree in terms of minimizing total-path-length. Because the selection of which two-edge path to mutate is random, it is equally likely to affect "central" vertices with many connections and "leaf" vertices with just one. This is an advantageous approach because either situation has the potential to benefit from such a mutation, so any path should be eligible for selection. Finally, this approach is guaranteed never to introduce a cycle, maintaining the integrity of the mutating spanning tree.

The *get_next_pop* function has a predetermined number of children it is required to generate. Children that are duplicates of trees that are in the old population or children already generated are not permitted, however. This is a useful feature to ensure that genetic diversity is maintained in the population. If all viable parents have been used to reproduce but there aren't enough new children yet, random trees are generated to be used as children. This option was very rarely needed, if ever, but is an important feature nonetheless. In addition, the crossover rate is set very high, but approximately 5% of the time two randomly-generated children are returned from reproduction. Again, this infuses some genetic diversity in to the population. After the required number of children have been generated, the *get_next_pop* function replaces up to a set number of the worst solutions in the old population with children, but only if the children are superior to those being discarded. In addition to purposefully driving successively better results each generation, it also mimics the real-world phenomenon where weak members of an animal species do not survive infancy. In this way, it is an improvement both to the function and the spirit of this genetic algorithm.

C. Wisdom of Artificial Crowds

In every population, the "Wisdom of Artificial Crowds" is applied to generate one child. Every occurrence of each edge in the population is tallied and its percentage of the total edges is calculated. These percentages serve as the probabilities the *get_crowd_wisdom* function uses when selecting edges the child will contain. The more often a particular edge occurs throughout the population, the higher the probability it will be selected to be part of the child. Edges that never occur in the population have a zero probability of being selected for inclusion in the child, a desirable effect in the algorithm.

Some wisdom-of-the-crowd implementations use only a portion of a population to study, choosing to consult only answers it deems as "experts." In our approach, we purposefully chose to use the entire population and consider every spanning tree an "expert" worth consulting. First, this is because we wanted a comprehensive view of the population's aggregate knowledge, not a narrow one. Second, it is because every spanning tree in that population has been carefully built and selected from previous populations, meaning it will contain knowledge worth considering. Because successive populations do not allow for bad spanning trees i.e. those worse than their predecessors to ever be included, every tree in the "crowd" is good enough to lend its input.

The child is initialized with these selected edges and then *complete_tree* is called to fill out the rest of the edges. The parent passed to *complete_tree* in this case is a dummy *SpanningTree* initialized with every vertex pair possible for the graph. In this way, when *complete_tree* is greedily selecting the best edges to join the disparate groups of edges within the child spanning tree, every possible connection is available as an option.

There is an important logic check in *complete_tree* that does not come into play during its use by the genetic algorithm but plays a key role during its use by the wisdom-of-artificial-crowds component. This check is part of the initial process of sorting the child's edges into their groups. If a group containing only two vertices, therefore representing an edge, is detected to have not just one but both of its vertices already in a group, it is discarded. By definition if two vertices are already in a group together, an edge between them would introduce a cycle. Such situations may occur because *get_crowd_wisdom* selects edges only based on probabilities. This means it may select edges that, if all included, create a cycle e.g. (1,2), (2,3), (1,3). This check in *complete_tree* vets the edges of the child it has been provided. For example, the function will begin by building a group from (1,2) and (2,3) of {1,2,3}, then detect that (1,3) is invalid and drop it. This situation does not occur during the genetic algorithm because the child passed to *complete_tree* in that instance is based on a parent tree which is guaranteed to be valid (unless it was somehow otherwise corrupted). Therefore, if the parent does not contain any cycles then the subset of the parent used to build the child is also guaranteed to be cycle-free.

The greedy decisions of *complete_tree* drive the development of optimal spanning trees. The inclusion of every path possible in the parent in the case of the wisdom-of-artificial-crowd child helps contribute both to optimal spanning trees and a diverse population because it may include a new edge not seen anywhere else in the population but that turns out to be highly optimal.

IV. Experimental Results

A. Data

The data used was generated by the Concorde TSP Solver [17]. While designed to solve Travelling Salesperson Problems, it is also suitable for generating datasets for a variety of similar problems. Using the Windows GUI, we could randomly generate graphs of any number of vertices, which are saved in a standardized TSP format listing the vertices numbered 1 to n with corresponding coordinates. The program reads in this file line by line and extracts the coordinates. Below is an example for 10 vertices:

```
NAME: concorde10
TYPE: TSP
COMMENT: Generated by CCutil_writetsplib
COMMENT: Write called for by Concorde GUI
DIMENSION: 10
EDGE_WEIGHT_TYPE: EUC_2D
NODE_COORD_SECTION
1 22.549020 89.029536
2 23.039216 81.434599
3 30.392157 79.324895
4 40.277778 80.379747
5 38.071895 60.759494
6 23.774510 59.704641
7 25.245098 67.721519
8 30.065359 66.244726
9 36.029412 70.886076
10 49.264706 71.940928
```

B. Results

The genetic algorithm alone yielded the results shown in Table 1, all from 30 generations per execution of the algorithm. Figures 1 and 2 show example outputs of these results. Figures 1A and 2A graph the worst, average, and best solutions per generation in red, blue, and green, respectively. Figures 1B and 2B display the resulting best spanning tree found at the completion of the algorithm.

Vertices	Population	Runtime (s)	Best Length
30	50	37.56215	33174.15536
30	50	42.87745	33454.12696
30	50	38.18318	37393.45269
50	50	177.57016	115716.17169
50	50	235.58247	119350.27524
50	50	188.93781	125145.69157
77	77	1212.46735	277132.34661
77	77	1380.45296	286723.39976
77	77	1442.40950	271129.73645

Table 1: Results from Genetic Algorithm

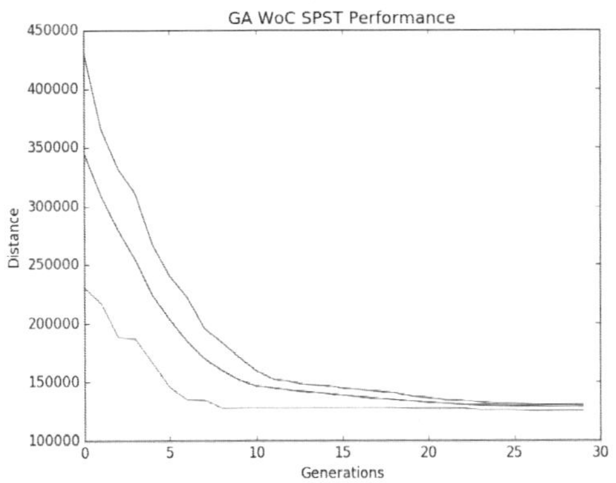

Figure 1A: Worst, Average, and Best Solutions per Generation

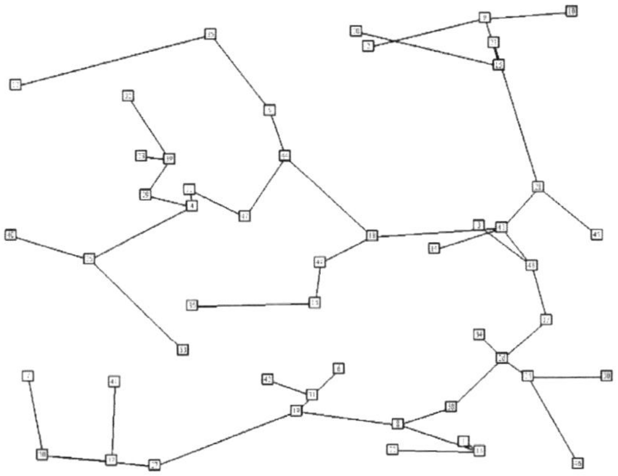

Figure 1B: Spanning Tree of Total-Path-Length 125145.69157

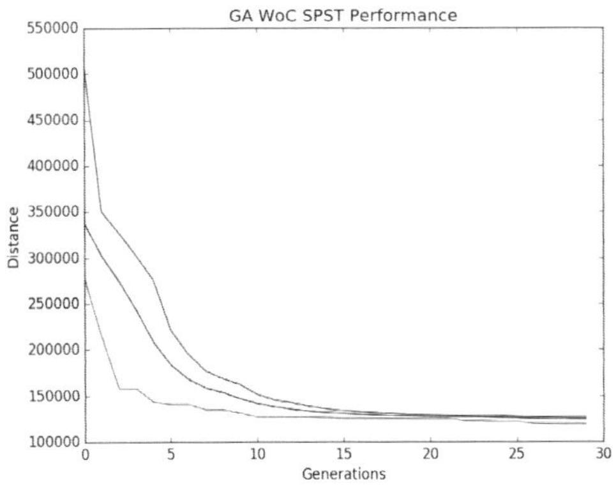

Figure 2A: Worst, Average, and Best Solutions per Generation

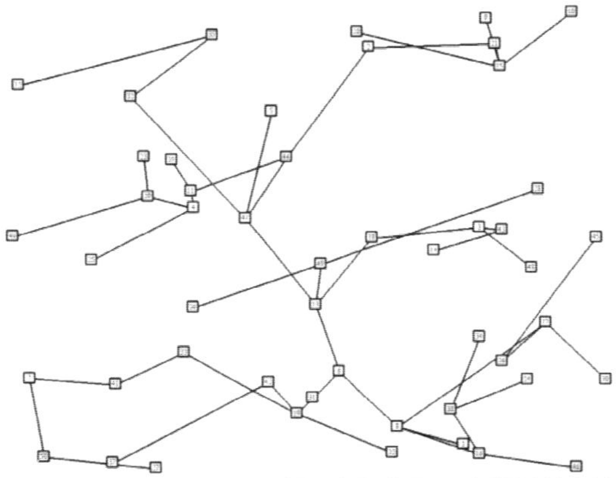

Figure 2B: Spanning Tree of Total-Path-Length 277132.34661

The full hybrid algorithm yielded the results in Table 2, also from 30 generations per execution of the algorithm. Figures 3 and 4 show example output from the hybrid algorithm. Figures 3A and 4A graph the worst, average, and best solutions per generation in red, blue, and green, respectively. Figures 3B and 4B display the resulting best spanning tree found at the completion of the algorithm.

Vertices	Population	Runtime (s)	Best Length
30	50	37.52615	32912.40819
30	50	39.67027	33800.07715
30	50	35.05000	34155.32438
50	50	215.91535	103152.67340
50	50	268.56736	106292.14450
50	50	226.07593	107272.21349
77	77	1723.61959	253756.81567
77	77	1423.14640	257199.90750
77	77	1375.86069	262635.91412

Table 2: Results from Hybrid Algorithm

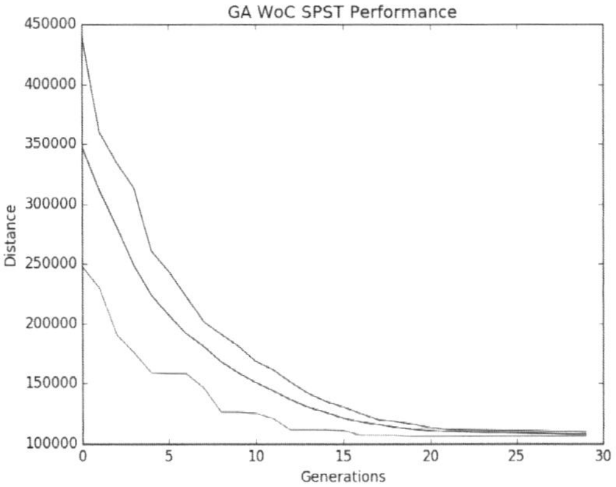

Figure 3A: Worst, Average, and Best Solutions per Generation

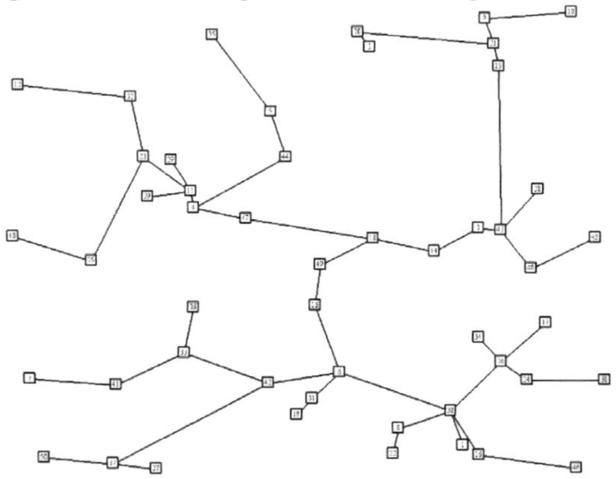

Figure 3B: Spanning Tree of Total-Path-Length 106292.14450

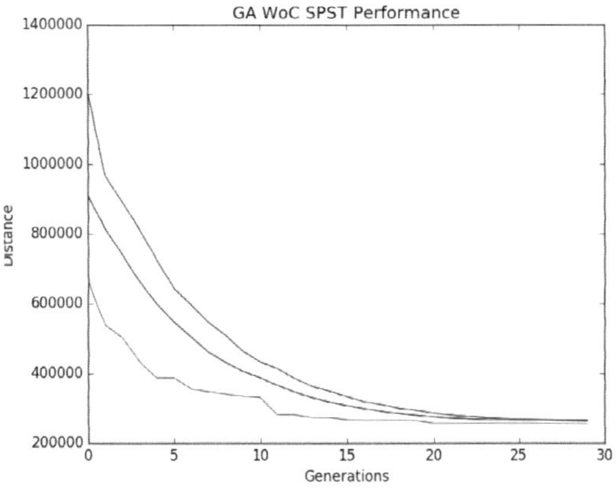

Figure 4A: Worst, Average, and Best Solutions per Generation

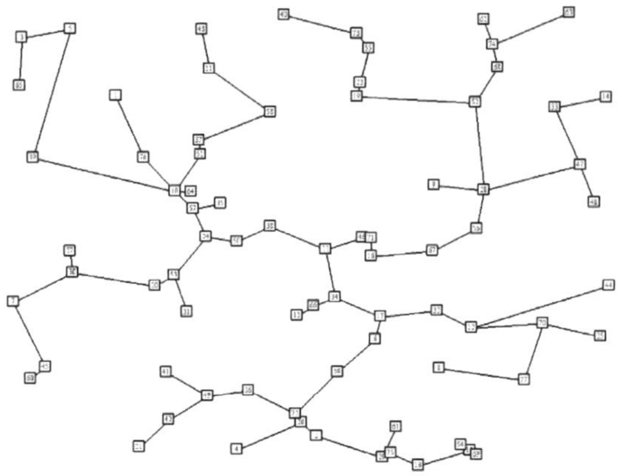

Figure 4B: Spanning Tree of Total-Path-Length 253756.81567

For 30 vertices and a population of 50, the hybrid algorithm required 5.38% less time and produced results of an average 3.03% shorter final total-path-length over the genetic algorithm alone. For 50 vertices and a population of 50, the hybrid algorithm required 18.02% more time and produced results an average 12.07% shorter than the genetic algorithm alone. For 77 vertices and a population of 77, the hybrid algorithm required 12.08% more time to execute and produced results an average 7.35% shorter than the hybrid algorithm alone.

This hybrid approach was capable of finding good solutions to larger datasets, as shown here in Table 3, though with long runtimes. Figures 5 and 6 show example outputs of these results. Figures 5A and 6A graph the worst, average, and best solutions per generation in red, blue, and green, respectively. Figures 5B and 6B display the resulting best spanning tree found at the completion of the algorithm.

Vertices	Population	Generations	Runtime (s)	Best Length
80	80	30	1976.99008	271001.70025
80	40	30	853.11680	289119.11059
100	100	20	3228.44966	507786.11792
100	20	20	702.63019	663055.61606
222	100	10	38360.50510	3912193.54795
222	20	10	8892.24261	5096472.87880

Table 3: Results from Hybrid Algorithm on Large Datasets

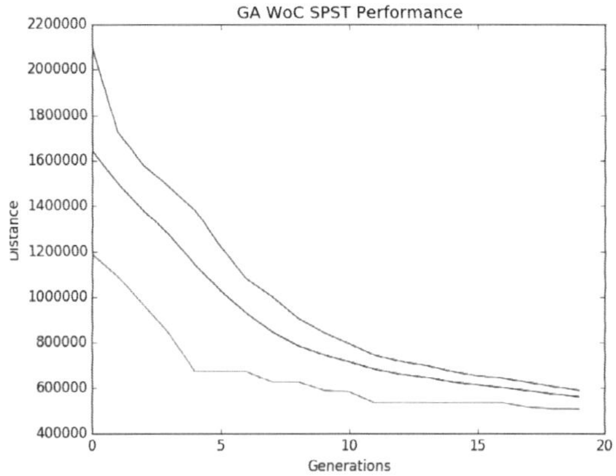

Figure 5A: Worst, Average, and Best Solutions per Generation

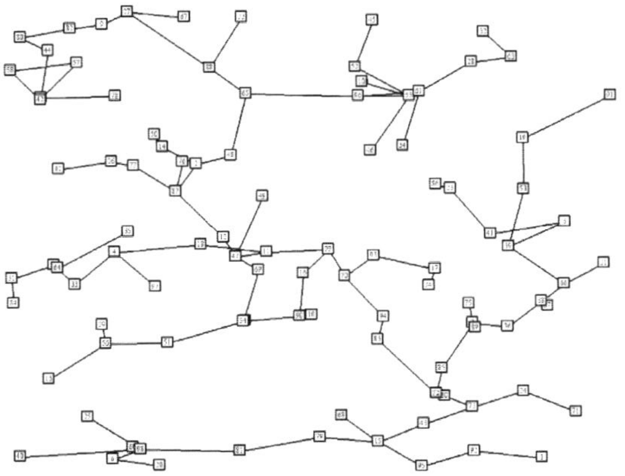

Figure 5B: Spanning Tree of Total-Path-Length 507786.11792

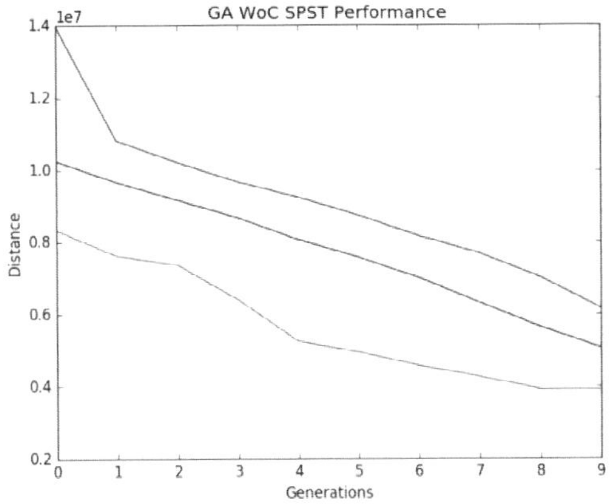

Figure 6A: Worst, Average, and Best Solutions per Generation

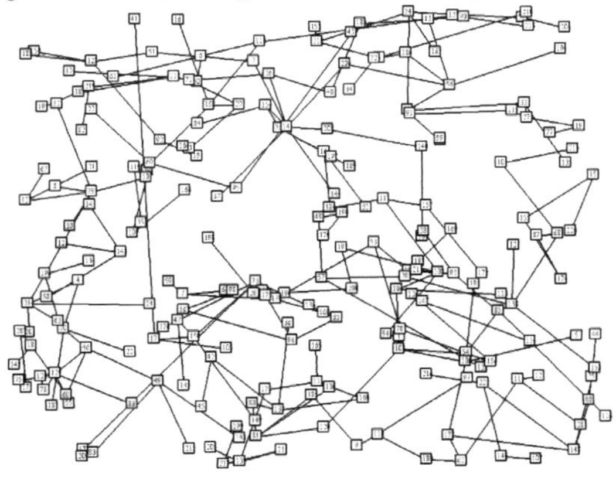

Figure 6B: Spanning Tree of Total-Path-Length 3912193.54795

V. Conclusions

This combination of genetic algorithm with wisdom of artificial crowds is complete, meaning it will always find an answer. It is not guaranteed to be optimal, however this algorithm is still successful and is capable of not only finding some result but with good implementation can optimize to find a better, if not best, result.

The relationship of the genetic algorithm to the crowd-wisdom component proved to be advantageous. As the genetic algorithm developed artificial results to inform the wisdom of the crowds, the resultant child would in turn drive the diversity and fitness of the genetic algorithm's population. Therefore, the hybrid algorithm as a whole developed good results.

Finally, it is also important to highlight that while not optimal, this algorithm is relatively fast. Some algorithms are incapable of finding any answer for datasets of the size tested here. Overall, as a problem-solving technique, this combined algorithm has many advantages in that it is relatively efficient, complete, and finds a good answer to the Shortest Total-Path-Length Problem for large datasets.

References

[1] T. C. Hu, "Optimum communication spanning trees," *SIAM Journal on Computing,* vol. 3, no. 3, pp. 188-195, 1974.

[2] D. S. Johnson, J. K. Lenstra, and A. Kan, "The complexity of the network design problem," *Networks,* vol. 8, no. 4, pp. 279-285, 1978.

[3] P. M. Pardalos, D. W. Hearn, and W. W. Hager, *Network optimization*. Springer Science & Business Media, 2012.

[4] M. R. Gary and D. S. Johnson, "Computers and Intractability: A Guide to the Theory of NP-completeness," ed: WH Freeman and Company, New York, 1979.

[5] K. Mehlhorn, "Selected Topics in Algorithms 2009 NP-completeness of Minimum Fundamental Cycle Basis Problem," 2009.

[6] T. H. Cormen, C. E. Leiserson, R. L. Rivest, and C. Stein, *Introduction to algorithms*. MIT press Cambridge, 2001.

[7] J. Surowiecki, *The wisdom of crowds*. Anchor, 2005.

[8] D. Bonomo, A. P. Lauf, and R. Yampolskiy, "A crossword puzzle generator using genetic algorithms with Wisdom of Artificial Crowds," in *Computer Games: AI, Animation, Mobile, Multimedia, Educational and Serious Games (CGAMES), 2015*, 2015, pp. 44-49: IEEE.

[9] L. H. Ashby and R. V. Yampolskiy, "Genetic algorithm and Wisdom of Artificial Crowds algorithm applied to Light up," in *2011 16th International Conference on Computer Games (CGAMES)*, 2011.

[10] J. Redding, J. Schreiver, C. Shrum, A. Lauf, and R. Yampolskiy, "Solving NP-hard number matrix games with Wisdom of Artificial Crowds," in *Computer Games: AI, Animation, Mobile, Multimedia, Educational and Serious Games (CGAMES), 2015*, 2015, pp. 38-43: IEEE.

[11] A. C. Port and R. V. Yampolskiy, "Using a GA and Wisdom of Artificial Crowds to solve solitaire battleship puzzles," in *Computer Games (CGAMES), 2012 17th International Conference on*, 2012, pp. 25-29: IEEE.

[12] R. V. Yampolskiy and A. El-Barkouky, "Wisdom of artificial crowds algorithm for solving NP-hard

problems," *International Journal of Bio-inspired computation,* vol. 3, no. 6, pp. 358-369, 2011.

[13] J. Fletcher, T. Fernando, H. Iu, M. Reynolds, and S. Fani, "A case study on optimizing an electrical distribution network using a genetic algorithm," in *2015 IEEE 24th International Symposium on Industrial Electronics (ISIE)*, 2015, pp. 20-25: IEEE.

[14] B. Y. Wu, K. M. Chao, and C. Y. Tang, "Approximation algorithms for the shortest total path length spanning tree problem," *Discrete applied mathematics,* vol. 105, no. 1, pp. 273-289, 2000.

[15] R. T. Wong, "Worst-case analysis of network design problem heuristics," *SIAM Journal on Algebraic Discrete Methods,* vol. 1, no. 1, pp. 51-63, 1980.

[16] B. Y. Wu, G. Lancia, V. Bafna, K.-M. Chao, R. Ravi, and C. Y. Tang, "A polynomial-time approximation scheme for minimum routing cost spanning trees," *SIAM Journal on Computing,* vol. 29, no. 3, pp. 761-778, 2000.

[17] W. Cook, "Concorde TSP solver," *See:* http://www. *tsp. gatech. edu/concorde. html,* 2005.

Image understanding - a brief review of scene classification and recognition

Vineeta Singh, Deeptha Girish, and Anca Ralescu
EECS Department, ML 0030
University of Cincinnati
Cincinnati, OH 45221, USA
singhvi@mail.uc.edu, girishde@mail.uc.edu, Anca.Ralescu@uc.edu

Abstract

With over 40 years of history, image understanding, in particular, scene classification and recognition remains central to machine vision. With an abundance of image and video databases, it is necessary to be able to sort and retrieve the images and videos in a way that is both efficient and effective. This is possible only if the categories of images and/or their context are known to a user. Hence, the ability to classify and recognize scenes accurately is of utmost importance. This paper presents a brief survey of the advances in scene recognition and classification algorithms.

Depending on its goal, image understanding(IU) can be defined in many different ways. However, in general, IU means describing the image content, the objects in it, location and relations between objects, and most recently, describing the events in an image. In (Ralescu 1995) IU is equated with producing a verbal description of the image content. Scene analysis (as part of IU) and categorization is a highly useful ability of humans, who are able to categorize complex natural scenes containing animals or vehicles very quickly (Thorpe, Fize, and Marlot 1996), with little or no attention (Li et al. 2003). When a scene is presented to humans, they are able to quickly identify the scene, i.e., within a short period of exposure (< 100 ms). How do humans perform all of these tasks the way they do, is yet to be fully understood. To date, the classic text by Marr (Marr 1982) remains one of the sources of understanding the human vision systems.

Many researchers have tried to imbibe this incredible capability of the human vision system into their algorithms for image processing, scene understanding and recognition. In the presence of a wealth of literature on this and related subjects, surveys of the field, even a limited one, as the present one necessarily is (due to space constraints) are bound to be very useful, by reviewing the methods for scene recognition and classification.

Perhaps, the first issue to consider is the concept of *scene* as a *technical* concept to capture the *natural* concept. According to Xiao et al. (Xiao et al. 2010) a *scene* is a place in which a human can act within, or a place to which a human being could navigate. Therefore, *scene recognition* and *scene classification* algorithms must delve into understanding the *semantic context* of the scene. According to how a scene is recognized in an image, scene recognition algorithms can be broadly divided into two categories.

- Scene recognition based on object detection.
- Scene recognition using low-level image features

Scene recognition using object recognition (SR-OR)

Using object recognition for scene classification is a straight-forward and intuitive approach to scene classification and it can assist in distinguishing very complex scenes which might otherwise prove difficult to do using standard low level features.

In the paper by Li-Jia Li et al. (Li et al. 2010) the authors argue that although "robust low-level image features have been proven to be effective representations for scene classification; but pixels, or even local image patches, carry little semantic meanings. For high level visual tasks, such low-level image representations are potentially not enough. " To combat this drawback of local features, they propose a high-level image representation, called the *Object Bank*(OB), where an image is represented by integrating the response of the image to various object detectors. These object detectors or filters are blind to the testing dataset or visual task. Using OB representation, superior performances on high level visual recognition tasks can be achieved with simple regularized logistic regression. Their algorithm uses the current state-of-the-art object detectors of Felzenszwalb et al. (Felzenszwalb et al. 2010), as well as the geometric context classifiers (stuff detectors) of Hoeim et al. (Hoiem, Efros, and Hebert 2005) for pre-training the object detectors.

OB offers a rich set of object features, while presenting a challenge – curse of dimensionality due to the presence of multiple class of objects within a single image, which then yields feature vectors of very high dimension. The performance of the system plateaus at a point when the number of object detection filters is too high. According to the authors, the system performance is best, when the number of object filters is moderate.

Scene recognition using low-level image features (SR-LLF)

Many of the papers in scene recognition are built around the question, *'Can we recognize the context of a scene without having first recognized the objects that are present?* There are a lot of reasons for avoiding object recognition for the purpose of scene recognition. While there are many robust OR algorithms, using SR-OR can be problematic because the OR portion of the algorithm is treated as a black box, and therefore, the OR errors propagate to the SR segment. OR also faces problems due to lighting conditions and occlusion. To avoid this many studies tend to use low level feature for scene understanding.

The challenge in SR-LLF is to find low-level features in the image that can be used successfully to infer its semantic context. Among the many features can be extracted from the image for the purpose of scene recognition, texture, orientation, and color have been used extensively in literature, implemented with different data sets and with different classifiers.

In (Renninger and Malik 2004) an algorithm which mimics the humans' ability to identify scenes with limited exposure is presented. The algorithm is based on a simple texture analysis of the image which can provide a useful cue to rapid scene identification. The relevant features within a texture are the first order statistics of *textons* which determine strength of texture discrimination. This idea is derived from Juselz's work (Julesz 1981) (Julesz 1986) (For a discussion on Juselz's work see (Marr 1977)). According to Juselz, textons are the elements in the image that govern our perception of texture. They are calculated by convolving the image with certain filter banks. The textons based model learns the local texture features which correspond to various scene categories, which is done by filtering a set of 250 training images and then learning the prototypical distributions. The number of occurrences of each feature within a particular image is stored as an histogram, creating a holistic texture descriptor for the image. To learn the most prevalent features, they use k-means clustering to find the 100 prototypical responses. When identifying a new test image, its histogram is matched against stored examples. It is concluded that early scene identification can be explained with a simple texture recognition model. This model leads to similar identifications and confusions as a human subject.

The same objective, i.e., understanding human perception of scenes is pursued in (Gorkani and Picard 1994). The paper investigates the measure of *dominant perceived orientation* developed to match the output of a human study involving 40 subjects. These global multi-scale orientation features were used to detect vacation photos belonging to "city/suburb". The authors state that orientation is an important feature for texture recognition and discrimination. The algorithm finds the local orientation and its strength at each pixel of the image. The implementation extracts orientation information over multiple scales using a steerable pyramid (Rock 1990) and then combines the orientations from these different scales and decides which one is dominant perceptually. The reported results show that the orientation features achieves agreement with the human classification in 91 of the 98 scenes (i.e., approximately 92.93%)

The paper by Guérin-Dugué et al. (Guérin-Dugué and Oliva 2000) uses an approach similar to Gorkani and Picard (Gorkani and Picard 1994) but extend this approach with more categories and introduce the selection of the optimal scale for this categorization task. They use local dominant orientation (LDO) features for classifying real-world scenes into four categories (outdoor urban scenes, indoor, closed landscapes and open landscapes). Instead of using the LDO features directly, they propose compact coding in a few features by Fourier series decomposition, and introduce the spatial scale parameter to optimize the categorization. For each scale and spatial location the dominant orientation and it's strength are estimated. The best discrimination ratios were obtained with a representation at a median spatial scale or when combining two different scales.

The paper (Csurka et al. 2004) presents a bag of key-points approach to visual categorization. The procedure starts by detection and description of image patches. Then a vocabulary of image descriptors is created after applying the vector quantification algorithm. SIFT decriptors (Lowe 1999) are used as features for this algorithm. This is followed by constructing a bag of key-points which counts the number of patches assigned to each cluster. Finally, a multi-class classifier (SVM) is implemented, treating the bag of points as the feature vector and thus, determining which category the image belongs to.

It is clear that counts, or histograms, suggest that scene recognition and analysis could benefit from probabilistic approaches. Indeed, some algorithms use probability models to describe the scene based on the extracted features.

The paper *A Bayesian Hierarchical Model for Learning Natural Scene Categories* (Fei-Fei and Perona 2005) uses low level texture features as image descriptors. Each patch of the input image is represented using a code word (similar to bag of keywords approach). The code word is taken from a *codebook* – a large vocabulary of code words – obtained from 650 training examples from 13 categories (with around 50 images for each category). In this framework, initially the local regions are clustered into different intermediate themes and then into categories. The learning algorithm for achieving the model that best represents the distribution of code words to represent scenes is a modified Latent Dirichlet model(Blei, Ng, and Jordan 2003). Unlike traditional scene models where there is a hard assignment of an image to one theme, the algorithm produces a collection of themes that could be associated with an image.

In (Singhal, Luo, and Zhu 2003) a probabilistic approach is used for content detection within the scene. The labels generated are very similar to scene labels. The authors present a holistic approach to determine the scene content, based on a set of individual *material detection* algorithms as well as probabilistic spatial context models. Material detection is the problem of identifying key semantic objects such as sky, grass, foliage, water, and snow in images. In order to detect materials the algorithm combines low-level features with unique region analysis and inputs this to a classifier to obtain individual material belief maps. To avoid misclassification of materials in images they devise a spatial context aware material detection system which constraints the beliefs to conform to the probabilistic spatial context models.

The bag of keypoints model (Sivic and Zisserman 2009) corresponds to a histogram of the number of occurrences of particular image patterns in a given image. Most papers mentioned above use this concept in some form. This is adapted from the bag of words model in natural language processing.

In (Lazebnik, Schmid, and Ponce 2006) the authors argue that in spite of impressive levels of performance, the bag of features model represents the image as an *orderless* collection of local features, thereby disregarding all information about the spatial layout of the features. To overcome this aspect, they devise a method for recognizing scene categories based on the approximate global geometry correspondence. They compute a *spatial pyramid* by partitioning the image into increasingly fine sub-regions and computing histograms of local features found in each sub-region. The *spatial pyramid* is an extension of the orderless bag of features model of image representation, which is improved upon by the introduction of a kernel based recognition method. This method works by computing a rough geometric correspondence on a global scale using an approximation technique adapted from the pyramid matching scheme of (Grauman and Darrell 2007). This method involves repeatedly subdividing the image and computing histograms of local features at increasingly fine resolutions. The spatial pyramid approach can be thought of as an alternative formulation of locally orderless image where a fixed hierarchy of rectangular windows is defined. The *spatial pyramid framework* is based on the idea that the best results will be achieved when multiple resolutions are combined in a principled way. The features calculated are subdivided into *weak features*, oriented edge points, and *strong features*, SIFT descriptors. K-means clustering is performed on a random subset of patches from the training set to form a visual vocabulary. Multi-class classification is done with the support vector machine (SVM) , trained using the one versus all rule.

Though fewer algorithms use color based features, in certain cases this descriptor is very powerful in discriminating scenes.

Color descriptors can be used for scene and object recognition (Van De Sande, Gevers, and Snoek 2010) in order to increase illumination invariance and discriminative power. From theoretical and experimental results it is shown that, invariance to light intensity changes and light color changes affect category recognition. Various color descriptors were analyzed and evaluated. Color descriptors based on histograms, color moments moment invariants and color SIFT were used as descriptors, and it was concluded that SIFT based descriptors performed considerably better that histogram and moment based descriptors.

Indoor-Outdoor classification

In the paper by Szummer et al. (Szummer and Picard 1998) the authors show that high-level scene properties can be inferred from classification of low-level features specifically for indoor - outdoor scene retrieval problem. Their algorithm extracts three types of features: 1) histogram in the ohta color space 2) multi-resolution simultaneous autoregressive model parameters 3) coefficients of shift invariant DCT. They exhibit that performance is improved by computing features on sub-blocks, classifying these sub-blocks and then combining these results by stacking.

This paper (Serrano, Savakis, and Luo 2004) by Serrano et al. uses simplified low level features to predict the semantic category of scenes. This is integrated probabilistically using Bayesian network to give a final indoor/outdoor classification. Low-dimensional color and wavelet texture features are used to classify scenes using the support vector machine (SVM). These wavelet texture features are used here instead of the popular MSAR texture features to reduce the computational complexity.

Other approaches

Various other approaches exist in the literature of scene recognition, as reviewed below.

Semantic Typicality

The concepts of typicality and prototype have made a significant impact in cognitive science. See for example the work pioneered by Eleanor Rosch and her collaborators, (Rosch 1973), (Rosch and Mervis 1975), (Rosch et al. 1976). In computer vision, (Vogel and Schiele 2004) introduces an interesting concept of *semantic typicality* in categorizing of real world natural scenes. The proposed typicality measure is used to grade the similarity of an image with respect to a scene category. Typicality is defined as a measure for the uncertainty of annotation judgment. This is an important concept because many natural scenes are ambiguous and the categorization accuracy sometimes reflects the opinion of a particular person who performed the annotation. Therefore, the authors believe that attention should be directed to modeling the typicality of a particular scene after manual annotation. The semantic typicality measure is used to find the similarity of natural real-world scenes with respect to six scenes including coasts, rivers/lakes, forests, plains, mountains and sky/clouds.

The typicality based approach is evaluated on an image database of 700 natural scenes. The attribute score is a representation which is predictive of typicality. Typicality is a function of frequency of occurrence, that is, the items deemed most typical have attributes that are very common to the category. Local semantic concepts act as scene category attributes. They are calculated from the sub-regions which are represented by a combined 84-bin linear histogram in the HSI color space, and a 72-bin edge direction histogram. Classification is done by a k-nearest neighbor classifier. The categorization experiment was carried out using manually annotated images from the database. By analyzing the semantic similarities and dissimilarities of the aforementioned categories a set of nine local semantic concepts emerged as being most discriminant: sky, water, grass, trunks, foliage, fields, rocks, flowers, and sand. The local semantic concepts were extracted on a 10×10 grid of image sub-regions and the frequency of occurrence in a particular image was represented by concept occurrence vector. For each category, a *category prototype* is defined as the most typical example for that category, which constructed as the means over the concept occurrence vectors of the category members. The image typicality was measured by computing the Mahalanobis distance between the images' concept occurrence vector and the prototypical representation in order to classify the image as a particular scene.

Configural Recognition

The goal of (Lipson, Grimson, and Sinha 1997) is to classify scenes based on their content. Most of the solutions that are available for scene recognition rely on color histograms and local texture statistics. The authors state that these features cannot capture a scenes' global configuration. To overcome this they present a novel approach, which they call *configural recognition* for encoding scene class structure in images. The configural recognition scheme encodes class models as a set of salient low resolution image regions and salient qualitative relations between the regions. An example of qualitative relationships are: 'given three regions, a blue region(A), a white region (B) and a gray region (C), Snow-capped mountains always have region A above region B which is above region C'.

The class models are described using seven types of relative relationships between image patches. Each of them has the following values: *Less than, greater than*, or *equal to*. The relationships encoded are relative color between image regions, the relative luminance between the patches, the spatial relationships (relative horizontal and vertical descriptions) and the relative size of the patch. Based on this, each region in the image is grouped into directional equivalence classes, such as *above* and *below*.

The generated model acts as deformable templates. When compared with the image, the model can be deformed by moving the patches around so that the model best matches the image in terms of relative luminance and photometric attributes. An improvement to this system can be made where instead of hand crafting the models,an automated process could take a set of example images and generate a set of templates which describe the relevant relationships between the pictures in the example set.

A fuzzy part based model was described in (Miyajima and Ralescu 1993) and fuzzy sets were also widely and effectively used for spatial descriptors in an image. A very powerful formal model, based on fuzzy sets, for the description of spatial relations in an image was introduced in (Miyajima and Ralescu 1994), (Miyajima and Ralescu 1994) and further extended by (Bloch 1999). A comparison of the fuzzy approaches for the description of directional relative position between object in an image can be found in (Bloch and Ralescu 2003), and a review of these approached can be found in (Bloch 2005). Furthermore, more recently, fuzzy spatial relations were integrated in deformable models and applied to MRI images (Colliot, Camara, and Bloch 2006).

In (Ralescu and Baldwin 1987) a new approach for concept learning from examples and counter-examples with applications to a vision learning system, later extended to a general concept learning problem (Ralescu and Baldwin 1989), was developed. It makes use of Conceptual Structures (Sowa 1983) for knowledge representation, and support logic programming (Baldwin 1986) for inference. Examples of a concept (e.g., a 'car') are used to construct a *memory aggregate*(MA), which rather than average all examples, keeps track of various probability distributions of the object features. Counter-examples, i.e., descriptions that are very similar to a concept, but fail to be instances of that concept, are used in a similar manner to construct a counter example memory aggregate (CMA). Matching between conceptual structures describing an object candidate and the MA and CMA produce supports for and against the recognition of a concept. The result is therefore, qualified by a *support pair*, whose values $(1, 1)$ mean complete recognition, $(0, 0)$ complete rejection, $(0, 1)$ total uncertainty.

Deformable part based models

In (Pandey and Lazebnik 2011), the author comments that weakly supervised discovery of common visual structure in highly variable and that cluttered images present a major problem in recognition. In order to address this problem, the authors propose using *deformable part-based models* (DPM) with latent SVM training. For scene recognition, deformable part-based models capture recurring visual elements and salient objects. The DPM represents an object by low-resolution root filters and a set of high resolution part filters in a flexible spatial configuration. The image is represented by a variation of histogram of oriented gradients (HOG) features which are used to classify scenes using linear SVM.

Covariance descriptor

The paper (Yang et al. 2016) proposes a supervised collaborative kernel coding method based on *covariance descriptor* (*covd*) for scene level geographic image classification. Covariance descriptor is a covariance matrix of different features such as color, spatial location, and gradient that is rotation and scale invariant but it lies in the Riemannian space (i.e., non- Euclidean space) and therefore, the traditional computational and mathematical models used in the Euclidean space cannot be used.

The major contribution of this paper is that they propose a supervised kernel coding model that transforms *covd* into a discriminative feature representation and obtain a corresponding linear classifier. The method can be seen as a three step process. The first step is to extract the *covd* features from the geographical scene image. In the second step supervised collaborative kernel coding involving dictionary coefficients in the coding representation phase and linear classification phase is performed. Lastly, in the classification stage, based on dictionary coefficients and learned linear classifier a label vector is derived. A novel objective function is proposed to combine the collaborative kernel coding phase and the classification phase. This method gives satisfying performance on high resolution aerial image dataset proving to be an efficient method for scene level geographic image classification.

Shape of the scene

The paper (Oliva and Torralba 2001) takes a very different approach to scene recognition: rather than looking at the scene as a configuration of objects the paper proposes to consider the scene as an individual object, with a unitary shape. A computational model to find the shape of the scene using a few perceptual dimensions specifically dedicated to describing spatial properties of the scene is proposed. It is shown that the holistic spatial scene properties, called *Spatial Envelope*(SE) properties may be reliably estimated using spectral and coarsely localized information.

Given and environment V, its spatial envelope $SE(V)$ is defined as a composite set of boundaries such as walls, section, elevation etc. that define the shape of the space. A group of 17 observers were asked to categorize 81 images into categories based on some global aspect. Based on the classification results, the criterion for classification of scenes was agreed to be based upon the *degree of naturalness*, *degree of openess*, *degree of roughness*, *degree of expansion* and *degree of ruggedness*. Therefore, the purpose of the spatial envelope model is to show that modeling these five spatial properties is adequate to understand the high-level description of the scene. Their algorithm learns the spectral signatures (the global energy spectrum and the spectogram) of basic scene categories from labeled training data. A learning algorithm (regression) is then used to find the relation between the global features and spectral features.

Beyond Scene recognition

Certain algorithms detect scenes and then use scene recognition as a prior in order to find more structure in the image, thus motivating further study in the field of scene analysis.

In *Using Forest to see trees* (Murphy et al. 2003) an intuitive approach to detect the presence of object based on the detected scenes is presented. The approach is suggested by psychological evidence that people perform rapid global scene analysis before and conducting more detailed local object analysis. Based on this the authors propose to use the whole image as a global feature in order to overcome ambiguities which might occur at the local level. They extend the notion of *gist* from (Oliva and Torralba 2006) by combining the prior suggested by the gist to the output of bottom-up local object detectors which are trained using boosting. They also use the same set of features for object detection in the image. The image is divided into patches at different scales (image pyramid) and each patch is convolved with 13 zero-mean filters which include oriented edges, a Laplacian filter, corner detectors and long edge detectors. This is represented by two statistics, variance, and kurtosis derived from the histogram of image patches at two scales and with 30 spatial masks. The kurtosis is omitted for scene recognition. The features are further reduced in dimensionality using PCA to give the PCA-*gist*. A one vs all binary classifier is trained for recognizing each type of scene using boosting applied to the gist. They further this by using *scene* as a latent common cause upon which the presence of the object is conditionally dependent on.

Understanding whole image, or *holistic* scene understanding is is described in (Yao, Fidler, and Urtasun 2012). The idea is to jointly evaluate and makes conclusions about location, regions, class and spatial information of objects, presence of a class in an image and also the scene type. The idea is to recover and connect the multiple different aspects of a scene. This problem is framed as a prediction problem in a graphical model defined over hierarchies of regions of different sizes, auxiliary variables encoding scene type, presence of a given class in a scene and correctness of bounding boxes obtained by the object detector. Class labels of image segments at two different levels of segmentation hierarchy, namely *segments* and large *super segments* is proposed. Binary variables indicate which classes are present in images and multi-labeled variable represents scene type. Segments and super segments are used to assign semantic class labels to each pixel in an image. Super segments are used to create long range dependencies and they also prove to be more efficient computationally. The *holistic loss function* is defined, which is a weighted sum of losses from each task. State of the art performance is achieved in MSRC-21 benchmark and the approach is much faster than the existing approaches.

Another very interesting approach is present in (Li and Fei-Fei 2007), which goes beyond scene recognition to event recognition. An *event in a static image is defined as a human activity taking place in the specific environment.* The objective is to recognize/classify the event in the image as well as provide a number of semantic labels to the object and scene environment within the image. It is assumed that conditioned on the event, scene and objects are independent of each other, but both their presence influences the probability of predicting the event. For scene recognition they adopt a model similar to the Bayesian model of (Fei-Fei and Perona 2005). Scene recognition heavily influences the event recognition, an in fact, as a first approximation event recognition is essentially scene recognition. The robust bag of words model is used in order to recognize objects. In addition to scene and object recognition they understand the importance of layout of the image in accurately identifying the event. They use some simple geometric cues to define the layout of the image and manage to provide integrative and hierarchical labels to an image by performing the what (event), where (scene) and who (object) recognition of the entire scene by using a generative model in order to represent the image.

An extensive Scene Understanding (SUN) database consisting of 899 categories and 130519 images is created in (Xiao et al. 2010). This work is motivated by the authors' belief that the existing data sets for scene classification fail to capture the richness and diversity of daily life environments. The authors claim to have built the most complete dataset with a number of different scene image categories with different functionalities that are important enough to have unique identities. They measure human performance on scene classification and compare it with the state of the art algorithms, using the SUN database. Both human and algorithm results had errors, with the humans erring between semantically similar categories, while algorithms erring between semantically unrelated scenes due to spurious visual matches. It was also recorded that the best features agree more with correct human classifications and make the same mistakes as humans do. The computational algorithms need a much larger number of features to performs as well as humans. They also propose the notion of recognizing scene type within images rather than labeling an entire image with a scene because the real world often contains combination of scenes. This is a new interesting idea and could also be one of the directions in which the future scene recognition algorithms can progress.

Conclusion

It can be seen, even based on the limited number of papers reviewed here, that image understanding, scene recognition can be approached from various different directions. At a very high level, the approaches can be divided into two main categories - using low-level features, and using object recognition. However, many other techniques are integrated into each of these approaches, including probabilistic, and/or fuzzy techniques, in order to deal with the uncertainty which often attends the result of image understanding. When it come to evaluating low level feature approach and object recognition approach, the goal of the image understanding must be taken into account. Scene recognition performs better when low level features are used. Local features help override the effects of occluded objects, low lighting conditions. Most commonly used features for scene detection include texture, texture orientation and strength, 'Gist' of the image, SIFT descriptor, edge orientation, histograms in different color space (e.g., Ohta, HSI, RGB), histograms of angles between segmented regions, coefficients of shift-invariant DCT. These features can be successfully mapped into semantic image descriptors.

References

Baldwin, J. F. 1986. Support logic programming. In *Fuzzy sets theory and applications*. Springer. 133–170.

Blei, D. M.; Ng, A. Y.; and Jordan, M. I. 2003. Latent dirichlet allocation. *Journal of machine Learning research* 3(Jan):993–1022.

Bloch, I., and Ralescu, A. 2003. Directional relative position between objects in image processing: a comparison between fuzzy approaches. *pattern Recognition* 36(7):1563–1582.

Bloch, I. 1999. Fuzzy relative position between objects in image processing: a morphological approach. *IEEE transactions on pattern analysis and machine intelligence* 21(7):657–664.

Bloch, I. 2005. Fuzzy spatial relationships for image processing and interpretation: a review. *Image and Vision Computing* 23(2):89–110.

Colliot, O.; Camara, O.; and Bloch, I. 2006. Integration of fuzzy spatial relations in deformable modelsapplication to brain mri segmentation. *Pattern recognition* 39(8):1401–1414.

Csurka, G.; Dance, C.; Fan, L.; Willamowski, J.; and Bray, C. 2004. Visual categorization with bags of keypoints. In *Workshop on statistical learning in computer vision, ECCV*, volume 1, 1–2. Prague.

Fei-Fei, L., and Perona, P. 2005. A bayesian hierarchical model for learning natural scene categories. In *Computer Vision and Pattern Recognition, 2005. CVPR 2005. IEEE Computer Society Conference on*, volume 2, 524–531. IEEE.

Felzenszwalb, P. F.; Girshick, R. B.; McAllester, D.; and Ramanan, D. 2010. Object detection with discriminatively trained part-based models. *IEEE transactions on pattern analysis and machine intelligence* 32(9):1627–1645.

Gorkani, M. M., and Picard, R. W. 1994. Texture orientation for sorting photos" at a glance". In *Pattern Recognition, 1994. Vol. 1-Conference A: Computer Vision & Image Processing., Proceedings of the 12th IAPR International Conference on*, volume 1, 459–464. IEEE.

Grauman, K., and Darrell, T. 2007. The pyramid match kernel: Efficient learning with sets of features. *Journal of Machine Learning Research* 8(Apr):725–760.

Guérin-Dugué, A., and Oliva, A. 2000. Classification of scene photographs from local orientations features. *Pattern Recognition Letters* 21(13):1135–1140.

Hoiem, D.; Efros, A. A.; and Hebert, M. 2005. Automatic photo pop-up. *ACM transactions on graphics (TOG)* 24(3):577–584.

Julesz, B. 1981. Textons, the elements of texture perception, and their interactions. *Nature* 290(5802):91–97.

Julesz, B. 1986. Texton gradients: The texton theory revisited. *Biological cybernetics* 54(4):245–251.

Lazebnik, S.; Schmid, C.; and Ponce, J. 2006. Beyond bags of features: Spatial pyramid matching for recognizing natural scene categories. In *Computer vision and pattern recognition, 2006 IEEE computer society conference on*, volume 2, 2169–2178. IEEE.

Li, L.-J., and Fei-Fei, L. 2007. What, where and who? classifying events by scene and object recognition. In *Computer Vision, 2007. ICCV 2007. IEEE 11th International Conference on*, 1–8. IEEE.

Li, F. F.; VanRullen, R.; Koch, C.; and Perona, P. 2003. Natural scene categorization in the near absence of attention: further explorations. *Journal of Vision* 3(9):331–331.

Li, L.-J.; Su, H.; Fei-Fei, L.; and Xing, E. P. 2010. Object bank: A high-level image representation for scene classification & semantic feature sparsification. In *Advances in neural information processing systems*, 1378–1386.

Lipson, P.; Grimson, E.; and Sinha, P. 1997. Configuration based scene classification and image indexing. In *Computer Vision and Pattern Recognition, 1997. Proceedings., 1997 IEEE Computer Society Conference on*, 1007–1013. IEEE.

Lowe, D. G. 1999. Object recognition from local scale-invariant features. In *Computer vision, 1999. The proceedings of the seventh IEEE international conference on*, volume 2, 1150–1157. Ieee.

Marr, D. 1977. Artificial intelligence – a personal view. *Artificial Intelligence* 9(1):37–48.

Marr, D. 1982. Vision: A computational approach.

Miyajima, K., and Ralescu, A. 1993. Modeling of natural objects including fuzziness and application to image understanding. In *Fuzzy Systems, 1993., Second IEEE International Conference on*, 1049–1054. IEEE.

Miyajima, K., and Ralescu, A. 1994. Spatial organization in 2d segmented images: representation and recognition of primitive spatial relations. *Fuzzy Sets and Systems* 65(2-3):225–236.

Murphy, K.; Torralba, A.; Freeman, W.; et al. 2003. Using the forest to see the trees: a graphical model relating features, objects and scenes. *Advances in neural information processing systems* 16:1499–1506.

Oliva, A., and Torralba, A. 2001. Modeling the shape of the scene: A holistic representation of the spatial envelope. *International journal of computer vision* 42(3):145–175.

Oliva, A., and Torralba, A. 2006. Building the gist of a scene: The role of global image features in recognition. *Progress in brain research* 155:23–36.

Pandey, M., and Lazebnik, S. 2011. Scene recognition and weakly supervised object localization with deformable part-based models. In *Computer Vision (ICCV), 2011 IEEE International Conference on*, 1307–1314. IEEE.

Ralescu, A. L., and Baldwin, J. F. 1987. Concept learning from examples with applications to a vision learning system. In *Alvey Vision Conference*, 1–8.

Ralescu, A. L., and Baldwin, J. F. 1989. Concept learning from examples and counter examples. *International Journal of Man-Machine Studies* 30(3):329–354.

Ralescu, A. L. 1995. Image understanding = verbal description of the image contents. *SOFT, Journal of the Japanese Society for Fuzzy Theory* 7(4):739–746.

Renninger, L. W., and Malik, J. 2004. When is scene identification just texture recognition? *Vision research* 44(19):2301–2311.

Rock, I. 1990. The perceptual world. *Scientific American* 127.

Rosch, E., and Mervis, C. B. 1975. Family resemblances: Studies in the internal structure of categories. *Cognitive psychology* 7(4):573–605.

Rosch, E.; Mervis, C. B.; Gray, W. D.; Johnson, D. M.; and Boyes-Braem, P. 1976. Basic objects in natural categories. *Cognitive psychology* 8(3):382–439.

Rosch, E. H. 1973. Natural categories. *Cognitive psychology* 4(3):328–350.

Serrano, N.; Savakis, A. E.; and Luo, J. 2004. Improved scene classification using efficient low-level features and semantic cues. *Pattern Recognition* 37(9):1773–1784.

Singhal, A.; Luo, J.; and Zhu, W. 2003. Probabilistic spatial context models for scene content understanding. In *Computer Vision and Pattern Recognition, 2003. Proceedings. 2003 IEEE Computer Society Conference on*, volume 1, I–I. IEEE.

Sivic, J., and Zisserman, A. 2009. Efficient visual search of videos cast as text retrieval. *IEEE transactions on pattern analysis and machine intelligence* 31(4):591–606.

Sowa, J. F. 1983. Conceptual structures: information processing in mind and machine.

Szummer, M., and Picard, R. W. 1998. Indoor-outdoor image classification. In *Content-Based Access of Image and Video Database, 1998. Proceedings., 1998 IEEE International Workshop on*, 42–51. IEEE.

Thorpe, S.; Fize, D.; and Marlot, C. 1996. Speed of processing in the human visual system. *nature* 381(6582):520.

Van De Sande, K.; Gevers, T.; and Snoek, C. 2010. Evaluating color descriptors for object and scene recognition. *IEEE transactions on pattern analysis and machine intelligence* 32(9):1582–1596.

Vogel, J., and Schiele, B. 2004. A semantic typicality measure for natural scene categorization. In *Joint Pattern Recognition Symposium*, 195–203. Springer.

Xiao, J.; Hays, J.; Ehinger, K. A.; Oliva, A.; and Torralba, A. 2010. Sun database: Large-scale scene recognition from abbey to zoo. In *Computer vision and pattern recognition (CVPR), 2010 IEEE conference on*, 3485–3492. IEEE.

Yang, C.; Liu, H.; Wang, S.; and Liao, S. 2016. Scene-level geographic image classification based on a covariance descriptor using supervised collaborative kernel coding. *Sensors* 16(3):392.

Yao, J.; Fidler, S.; and Urtasun, R. 2012. Describing the scene as a whole: Joint object detection, scene classification and semantic segmentation. In *Computer Vision and Pattern Recognition (CVPR), 2012 IEEE Conference on*, 702–709. IEEE.

Building Customized Text Mining Tools via Shiny Framework: The Future of Data Visualization

Olga Scrivner, Vinita Chakilam, Jivitesh Poojary, Nilima Sahoo, Chandan Uppuluri, Stephan De Spiegeleire

ABSTRACT

With the increasing volume of data, there is a growing need for dynamic data visualization to help reveal instant changes in data patterns. There exist many commercial visualization tools, but traditional scholars are often disengaged from the tool development process; thus, the choice of functionalities is contingent upon tool developers whose choice may not fit the end-users. This collaboration, however, has a potential in bridging the gap between traditional scholars, who are more interested in sense-making of the text than in the tools, and the data scientists, who are more interested in the tools than in the substance, but must still contextualize the outcomes. Until recently, this collaborative process was hindered by the complexity of customization procedures and technological hurdles imposed on users with new installations. With the advent of reactive web frameworks, such as Shiny, the user-driven customization becomes not only feasible, but also essential to advance scientific research. In this paper, we demonstrate a collaborative effort between *learned* scholars and tool developers, allowing for a computational and humanistic fusion.

Keywords

visualization, text mining, Shiny web application

1. INTRODUCTION

In the last decade, the volumes of data collections have grown so "large and complex that it becomes difficult to process using on-hand databases, management tools or traditional data processing applications" [14]. As Jockers [4] points out, these massive digital collections "invite, even demand, a new type of evidence gathering and meaning making". Consequentially, visual analytics is becoming the cornerstone of scientific analysis by combining "visualization, human factors and data analysis" and contributing to an information synthesis interpretable to the human eye [5]. Furthermore, the recent proliferation of visualization tools, both commercial and open source, has led to an increasing usage of visual analytics among traditional humanities scholars. Since most of these tools have been developed by software engineers, traditional scholars are often disengaged from the tool development process. This collaboration, however, has a potential in bridging the gap between traditional scholars, who are more interested in sense-making of the text than in the tools, and the data scientists, who are more interested in the tools than in the substance, but must still contextualize the outcomes. The insights gained from *learned* scholars would lead to a mutual enrichment, allowing for "synthesis of computational and humanistic modes of inquiry" [6]. A process of collaboration can be achieved through the following steps:

1) Scholars learn from data scientists about analytical tools, techniques, and what they can and cannot achieve

2) They exchange research questions and the implicit or explicit heuristics used in their work

3) They collaborate on how these discoveries can be made and assess the 'quality' of developing tools with real data

Until recently, this collaboration was unfeasible. Software not only necessitates a team of software engineers and designers, but also requires installation and consistent updates, which is a technical hurdle for users. Furthermore, the design of collaborative visualization has been commonly described as *a grand challenge* for visualization research [12]. While most visualization research has explored the cognitive and perceptual aspects of design, social interaction has only recently been recognized as a part of visualization system design [13, 3]. For example, some studies examined synchronous and asynchronous collaboration between team players to improve analytical interpretation [2, 3]. In contrast, a collaboration to enhance analytical functionalities and tool design is not common and mostly related to commercial customizable software [15].

With the advent of reactive web applications, such as Shiny, the user-driven tool customization becomes a reality. First, these applications require no installation and are accessible from any web browser, which enables a direct testing of new functionalities by users. Second, the reactive framework allows for a creation of highly dynamic tools with minimum knowledge of web development. Finally, Shiny is a web application developed for R, which is an open source language with a large library for data visualization.

In this paper, we describe our current collaborative research on text mining and visualization customization. Our goal is to assist scholars in their process of ingestion ('reading'), digestion (analyzing and sense-making), and egestion (through the creation of new learned texts via queries). Our workflow is illustrated in Figure 1.

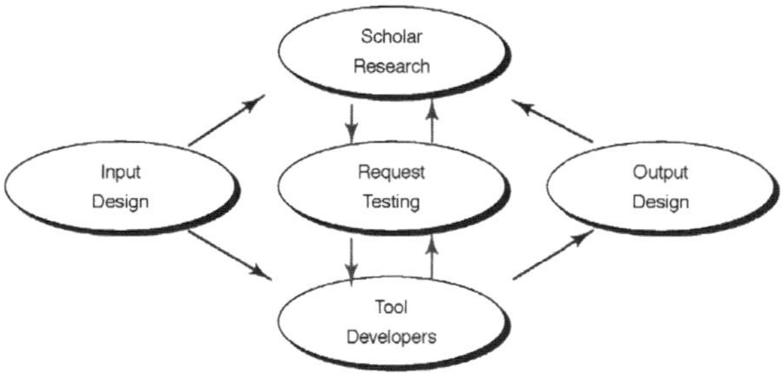

Figure 1: Information Visualization workflow: From the initial stage to a custom-designed stage

Our initial stage begins with the current version of *Interactive Text Mining Suite*,[1] a Shiny web application, developed to test various text mining and visualization techniques for digital humanities scholars [10, 11]. Our second stage comprises a direct collaboration with various scholars via *Rizzoma*, a collaborative social platform for discussions, and by means of various cloud storage platforms. The goal of this social interaction is to 1) identify scholarly research needs, 2) discuss design and functionalities, and, finally 3) develop and embed new functionalities into a web application. This stage also includes bug reports, constant feedback, and suggestions on design improvement directly from scholars. The final stage involves a fully-customized version of web application.

This paper is organized as follows. In section 2 we introduce Shiny, a reactive web framework. We then describe *Interactive Text Mining Suite* and its current functionalities in section 3. Section 4 and 5 will overview the development of customized functionalities for scholarly research, followed by conclusions and future directions presented in section 6.

2. SHINY APPLICATION

2.1 Shiny Web Framework

Traditional imperative web framework model was developed by Trygve Reenskaug in 1979 and followed a three-component structure: model, view, and control [8]. In this model, the controller plays an *essential* and *explicit* role: "you have to specify what to do when you receive user requests and what resources you are going to mobilize to carry out the necessary tasks outlined in the model" [9]. In contrast, the recent shift toward a reactive web framework has erased such a strict control, thus enabling dynamic systems that are highly responsive to users' input and interaction. Shiny, an R package, is one such application. After its release as an open source software package in 2012, the use of this application has been expanding at an unprecedented rate. This trend can be attributed to the combination of several factors: 1) Shiny web applications do not require a knowledge of web development, 2) web applications are user-friendly and dynamic, allowing for instant feedback to users, 3) web applications are accessible via browser from any device, including mobile devices, which makes it convenient to users, and 4) web applications are highly customizable, allowing for instant modification, as compared to traditional software version releases. In the next section, we will briefly describe our recently developed Shiny application, namely *Interactive Text Mining Suite*.

[1] http://www.interactivetextminingsuite.com

2.2 Interactive Text Mining Suite

Interactive Text Mining Suite (henceforth, ITMS) is designed to assist humanities scholars in the discovery of new insights and patterns within large digital collections, and to provide access to natural language processing techniques with a user-friendly design. Its major strength is the ability to work with data in various formats, PDF and text formats, as well as CSV, JSON, and XML, as shown in Figure 2.

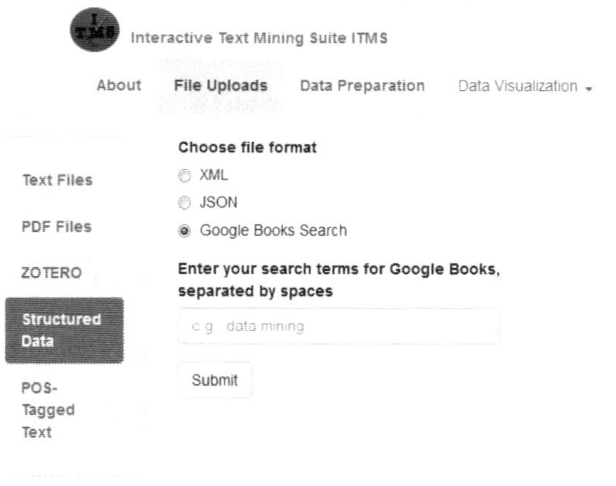

Figure 2: Interactive Text Mining Suite: Importing data

In contrast, many existing text mining tools are limited to specific importing formats. Additionally, ITMS performs a wide range of common preprocessing tasks, allowing for maximum flexibility and user control, illustrated in Figure 3 (for a more detailed description, see [10, 11]).

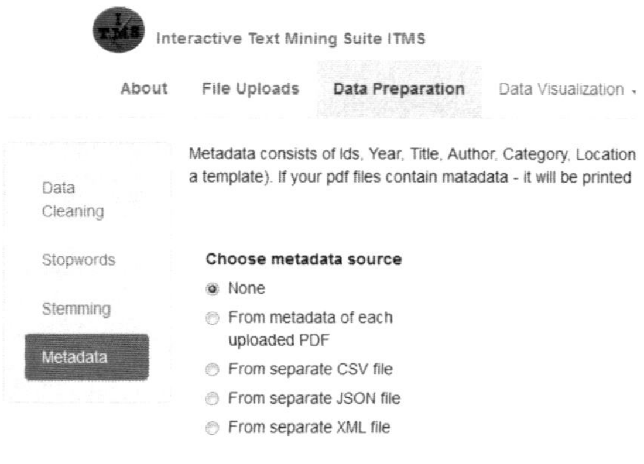

Figure 3: Interactive Text Mining Suite: Preprocessing data

3. USER-DRIVEN CUSTOMIZATION

As mentioned in 2.2, ITMS was designed as a digital humanities tool suitable for performing common text mining tasks and visualization methods. That is, it was built for scholars, but not by humanities scholars. However, there exists a gap between scholars, who have been doing more *qualitative* text-based research for public and government sectors, and data scientist/computational linguistics scholars, who work on theoretical text-mining research.[2] To bridge this gap, we have developed a collaborative communication between these two communities (a.k.a. end-users and developers). Instead of a typical *github* environment for reporting progress and issues, we chose a social collaborative platform *rizzoma.*[3] *Rizzoma* is built as knowledge-management and discussion platform allowing for real-time team communication and multimedia support. Figure 4 illustrates our collaborative project structure.

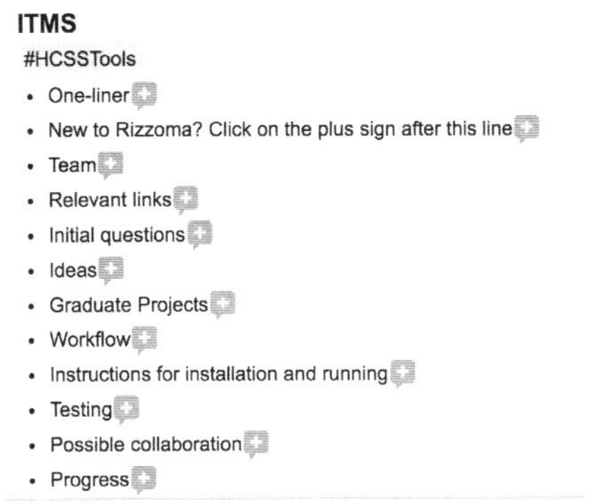

Figure 4: A collaborative platform Rizzoma: ITMS project

In the following sections, we describe our workflow and design considerations based on this collaboration.

4. DATA INPUT CONSTRAINT

Based on the previous work with existing text mining tools, it was determined that the main *pollutant* for scholarly research is the inability to pre-define text excerpts within the text collection. It appears that stopwords filtering and text preprocessing were not sufficient to obtain intuitive data interpretation for qualitative scholarly studies. Collaboratively, we have developed and tested the following algorithm (see also Figure 5):

1. Parse document collection
2. Scan every document for a specific term defined by the user (e.g., "security") or two terms (e.g., "influenc*" within 10 words of "Europ*")
3. Define a window around these terms (e.g., 10 words to the left and 10 words to the right)
4. Include only the extracted segments into data analysis and visualization

[2]From a personal communication with *The Hague Center for Strategic Studies (www.hcss.nl)*
[3]https://rizzoma.com

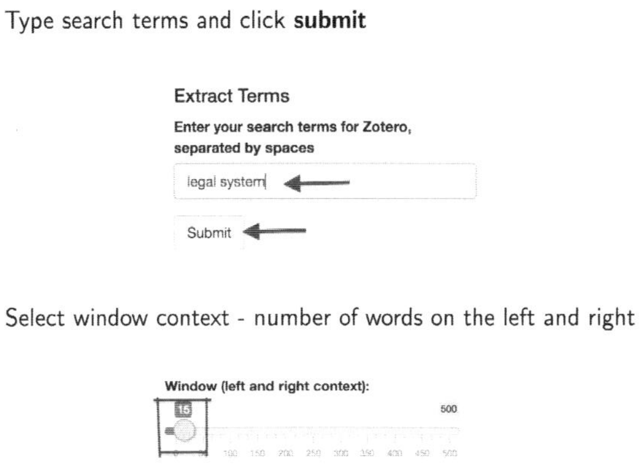

Figure 5: Development of data segmentation: window constraint

In addition, scholarly research collections are often stored and accessed via bibliographic management systems (e.g., Zotero, Mendeley, and Endnote). While most of these systems do not perform text mining analysis, the Zotero plugin, namely *Paper Machine*,[4] offers a wide range of interactive visualization for document collections. Nevertheless, the user cannot control text segmentation, which yields very broad topic and metadata visualizations. Given that Zotero is the main bibliographic management system in our collaborative project, data import from Zotero into ITMS became one of the most essential primary tasks for our team. Several options exist for exporting library collections from Zotero, namely rdf and csv formats. However, a few issues were discovered during the exploratory phase: 1) csv and rdf files only contain local paths to actual document articles (see Figure 6); 2) local paths cannot be accessed directly from a remote web application; 3) running ITMS locally would require R installation and some programming knowledge, thus generating technological hurdles for end-users.

```
    <z:Attachment rdf:about="#item_137595">
        <z:itemType>attachment</z:itemType>
        <rdf:resource rdf:resource="files/137595/Orbie - 2011 -
Promoting labour standards through trade normativ.pdf"/>
        <dc:identifier>
            <dcterms:URI>
                <rdf:value>https://biblio.ugent.be/publication/
1092843/file/6721273.pdf</rdf:value>
            </dcterms:URI>
        </dc:identifier>
```

Figure 6: Zotero collection: rdf file format (top) and Zotero internal directory structure (bottom)

Two solutions are being currently tested based on the fol-

[4]http://papermachines.org/

lowing criteria: 1) functionality and 2) the level of complexity. The first approach is the development of a small Shiny application installed locally that would process rdf library collections, export pdf files, convert them into text files, and place them into one directory, which can be accessed from our web application (see Figure 7).

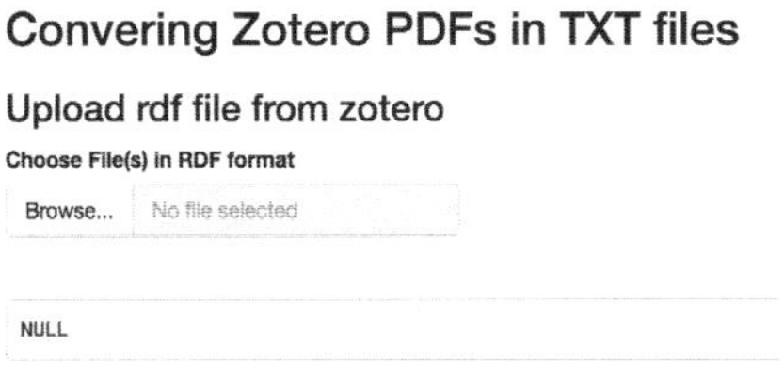

Figure 7: Small Shiny application: local conversion of Zotero files

This application is used only once and has a low level of complexity, yet the functionality is less user-friendly, as it creates an additional directory with extracted files from Zotero. These files can then be imported into ITMS. The second approach is suggested by the end-users: export zotero library as a csv file, run a local script to extract all pdf files, and add them into the CSV file as a plain text. While the functionality is high, the level of complexity is much higher.

5. DATA VISUALIZATION

There is no doubt that visual analytics facilitates analytical reasoning [12]. For a tool developer, however, it is not always clear whether implemented visualization methods assist the user in their research. The current project proposes to address this issue by a collaborative examination of various visualization types in order to determine their usability for Shiny application and for the end-users. First, we describe n-gram analysis, followed by interactive visualization, and topic modeling visualization.

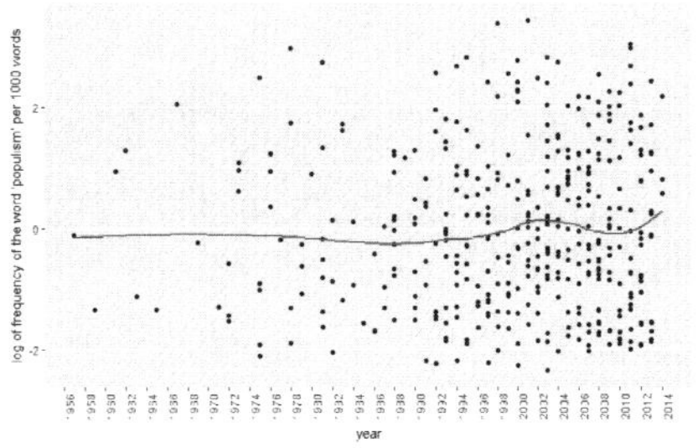

Figure 8: N-gram visualization with JSTORr package: *populism*

5.1 N-gram Visualization

An N-gram allows users to identify the co-occurrence of words within a single text or text collection. The 'n' indicates the number of words being selected to create unigrams, bi-grams, or tri-grams, etc. By using a combination of words, instead of a single occurrence, the user can generate higher quality results for data interpretation. Preferably, the user can also set a 'search window' within which co-occurrence should take place (i.e., within a certain amount of words or certain documents). In addition, our current work is concentrated on interactive and more meaningful n-gram visualization (e.g., tree visualization), as compared to traditional static graphics (Figure 8). Based on our collaborative feedback, the tree N-gram visualization was identified as more meaningful for scholarly interpretation. This tree will share prefixes of N-grams (e.g., "airport"), each connected to the root node. The root node is the set of focus words selected in the query. Every path in the tree, i.e., a path from the root node to a leaf node, corresponds to the N-gram made of the words encountered along the path, and having the score associated with the leaf node. Another possible visualization is a network representation, where the central node is the key word. There exist multiple R libraries that might be used to enhance n-gram interpretation, such as JSTORr, ngram, NSP, WordStat, among many others. In order to identify the best fit for the web application, we address the following criteria: 1) user-friendliness, 2) easy human interpretation, and 3) functionality.

5.2 Interactive Visualization

The ability to perform dynamic and interactive visualization is one of the strengths in reactive applications. While there are many R libraries implementing various types of interactive visualization, we decided to examine two packages, namely *plot.ly* and *googleViz*. Comparison and parallel testing feed our decision to implement their functionalities into ITMS. Table 5.2 presents our current summary.

Types	GoogleViz	Plot.ly
Stepped Area chart		
Bubble chart		
Gauge		
Intensity Map		
Geo Chart		
Table with pages		
Tree Map		NA
Annotation chart		
Sankey chart		
Calendar chart		NA
Timeline chart		
Merging charts		NA
Flash charts		NA
Annotated time line chart		
Chord diagram	NA	
Filled Chord diagram	NA	
k-means clustering		
Stream Graph	NA	
PCA	NA	
Hierarchical Clustering	NA	
Doughnut Chart		

Table 1: Functional comparison of 2 R libraries: plot.ly and googleViz

After identifying their functionalities, our next step is to determine the best fit via our collaborative feedback.

5.3 Topic Modeling Story Telling

Topic modeling is a statistical model used in machine learning and natural language processing for discovering abstract topics that occur in a collection of documents. This analysis assists in "classification, novelty detection, summarization, and similarity and relevance judgements" [1]. While topic modeling results can be visualized in different forms, most common form is in a table format (see Figure 9).

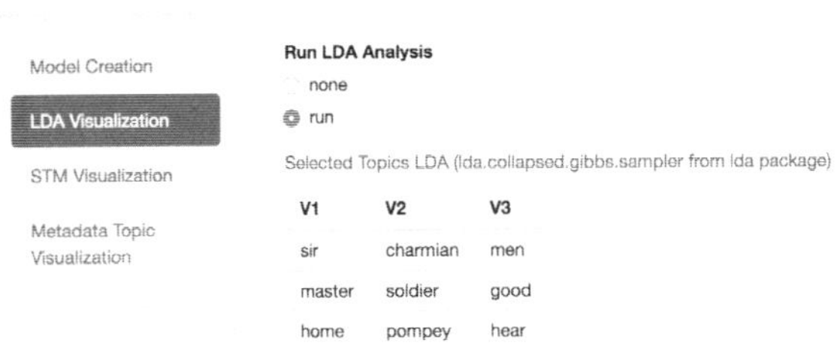

Figure 9: Topic visualization in ITMS

By comparing other software with their unique options for topic representation, two candidates for ITMS were identified: *topic bubbling* and *topic coupling* from MALLET, a topic modeling package. The goal of topic bubbling is to compare the relative importance of all the topics; the size of a topic bubble is the accumulated size of all word bubbles within that topic. In contrast, topic coupling reveals the relations between the topics based on their associated words. In this representation, topics are shown as a network of terms (nodes) linked by their interaction with other topics.

6. CONCLUSION

In recent years, we have seen growing interest in the use of data visualization tools in the humanities fields. However, many of the existing tools are unable to integrate the humanistic component of exploratory research. Thus, the overarching goal of the current work on ITMS is to bridge the gap between tool-developers and *learned* scholars by adding a user-customization component. In addition, the social interaction between scholars and data scientists has a strong potential to promote text mining methods among humanities as well as to enhance capabilities and functionality of visualization tools. We have also shown that a recent development of reactive Shiny framework has facilitated the task of user-customization: On the one hand, a wide range of open source R libraries and its overall simplicity for deployment made the Shiny framework very accessible to non-experienced programmers. On the other hand, Shiny is user-friendly web application, where users are not constrained by limitations of their local computer memory and platform dependency, as compared to other software tools. While this project only focuses on a collaboration between political/social science scholars, this idea can be extended to other fields. Below we summarize some of the possible implementations for future research:

1. Teaching tool: The web application is developed in the conjunction with the lesson plans, for example statistics modules. The collaboration can also be expanded by including students into the development and testing phases.

2. Digital Humanities: Based on individual research, the web application can be augmented with additional visualization types, for example spatial or chronological maps for literature analysis.

3. Social Science: The user could specify additional media for research and customize their appearance, e.g. tweets, blogs, or photos.

4. Libraries: ITMS is unique in that in addition to its ability to analyze data collections, it can add bibliographic metadata. As Jockers suggests, library metadata "has been largely untapped as a means of exploring literary history" and could "reveal useful information about literary trends" [4].

All these considerations and scholarly collaboration also present new opportunities for the field of data visualization and analytics, advancing our understanding of computation and human nature, namely "synthesis of computational and humanistic modes of inquiry" [6].

7. REFERENCES

[1] N. A. Blei D. and M. Jordan. Latent dirichlet allocation. *Journal of Machine Learning Research*, pages 993–1022, 2003.

[2] K. Brodlie, D. Duce, J. Gallop, J. Walton, and J. Wood. Distributed and collaborative visualization. *Computer Graphics Forum*, 23:223–251, 2004.

[3] J. Heer and M. Agrawala. Design Considerations for Collaborative Visual Analytics. *Information Visualization*, 7:49–62, 2008.

[4] M. L. Jockers. *Topics in the Digital Humanities: Macroanalysis: Digital Methods and Literary History.* University of Illinois Press, Urbana, IL, USA, 2013.

[5] D. Keim, F. Mansmann, J. Schneidewind, and H. Ziegler. Challenges in Visual Data Analysis. In *Information Visualization (IV 2006), IEEE*, pages 9–16, 2006.

[6] L. Klein and J. Eisenstein. Reading Thomas Jefferson with TopicViz: Towards a Thematic Method for Exploring Large Cultural Archives, 2013.

[7] K. L. and E. J. Reading thomas jefferson with topicviz: Towards a thematic method for exploring large cultural archives. scholarly and research communication. 4(3), 2013.

[8] T. M. H. Reenskaug. Models-views-controllers. http://heim.ifi.uio.no/ trygver/1979/mvc-2/1979-12-MVC.pdf

[9] B. B. Ribeiro. The two frameworks. https://github.com/rstudio/shiny/issues/250, 2017.

[10] O. Scrivner and J. Davis. Topic Modeling of Scholarly Articles: Interactive Text Mining Suite. In *International Conference "Dialogue 2016"*, 2016.

[11] O. Scrivner and J. Davis. Interactive Text Mining Suite: Data Visualization for Literary Studies. In *the Workshop on Corpora in the Digital Humanities*, pages 29–38, 2017.

[12] J. Thomas and K. Cook, editors. *Illuminating the Path: The Research and Development Agenda for Visual Analytics.* IEEE Press, 2005.

[13] F. Viégas and M. Wattenberg. Communication-minded visualization: A call to action. *IBM Systems Journal*, 45, 2006.

[14] T. White. *Hadoop: The Definitive Guide. Storage and Analysis at Internet Scale.* O'Reilly Media/Yahoo Press, Sebastopol, 3rd edition, 2012.

[15] J. Whitehead. Collaboration in Software Engineering: A Roadmap. In *2007 Future of Software Engineering*, pages 214–225, Washington, DC, USA, 2007. IEEE Computer Society.

COMPOUND SENTENCE SEGMENTATION AND SENTENCE BOUNDARY DETECTION IN URDU

ASAD IQBAL, ASAD HABIB, JAWAD ASHRAF

Institute of Information Technology, Kohat University of Science and Technology, Pakistan

ABSTRACT:

The raw Urdu corpus comprises of irregular and large sentences which need to be properly segmented in order to make them useful in Natural Language Engineering (NLE). This makes the Compound Sentences Segmentation (CSS) timely and vital research topic. The existing online text processing tools are developed mostly for computationally developed languages such as English, Japanese and Spanish etc., where sentence segmentation is mostly done on the basis of delimiters.

Our proposed approach uses special characters as sentence delimiters and computationally extracted sentence-end-letters and sentence-end-words as identifiers for segmentation of large and compound sentences. The raw and un-annotated input text is passed through preprocessing and word segmentation. Urdu word segmentation itself is a complex task including knotty problems such as space insertion and space deletion etc. Main and subordinate clauses are identified and marked for subsequent processing. The resultant text is further processed in order to identify, extract and then segment large as well as compound sentences into regular Urdu sentences.

Urdu computational research is in its infancy. Our work is pioneering in Urdu CSS and results achieved by our proposed approach are promising. For experimentation, we used a general genre raw Urdu corpus containing 2616 sentences and 291503 words. We achieved 34% improvement in reduction of average sentence length from 111 w/s to 38 w/s (words per sentence). This increased the number of sentences by almost three times to 7536 shorter and computationally easy to manage sentences. Resultant text reliability and coherence are verified by Urdu language experts.

Keywords: Urdu sentence segmentation, sentence tokenization, word tokenization, compound sentence segmentation, Urdu conjunction extraction, Urdu sentence delimiter identification.

1. INTRODUCTION:

Urdu Compound Sentence Segmentation using words and conjunctions as delimiters is a complex task. Most of the available raw corpora contain large sentences which are combination of sentences with conjunctions or without conjunctions. Such sentences are called compound sentences. Such sentences make it challenging for automated and computational processes such as text summarization, parsing and named entity recognition etc. [7][19].

There are some online tools available that segment sentences on the basis of sentence termination marks. For example;

1.1. Automatic Sentence Segmentation
1.2. Morph Adorner Sentence Splitter Example

Automatic sentence segmentation alters simple text into separate sentence per line format by simply adding return code after sentence termination mark but most tools cannot handle abbreviation's like *Dr., Mr., p.m., Prof., a.m.* This online tool covers most of those abbreviations. It also provides editing facility after resulting text to cover up the remaining abbreviations [1]. Morph Adorner Sentence Splitter uses punctuation marks to split sentences but punctuation marks not always define sentence termination mark for example ellipses, abbreviations, acronym, or decimal system and in some of the poems not even have any termination mark in it. Morph Adorner Sentence Splitter works best for plain English text and unlike Automatic Sentence Segmentation it covers more abbreviations [2].

Unlike Urdu English is not even suffering from this problem too much as most of the sentences are already separated from each other, Urdu on the other hand has even sentences in a form of paragraph which in self contains many sentences and our proposed idea is to identify those sentences and convert them into more than one sentences on the basis of these words [3,4].

2. LITERATURE REVIEW:

Sentence segmentation is a relatively new topic of research in computationally developing languages. We could not find any automated sentence boundary segmentation tool in Urdu language. Aroonmanakun W., analyzed sentence and word segmentation in Thai language [5]. They considered sentence discourse where combination of phrases and some clues are used for each discourse segmentation process. Baseer et al. presents a sophisticated Romanized Urdu Corpus utilizes tokens with the uppermost frequency of occurrence in the data set, which was collected from participants who uses Romanized Urdu as a mean of communication [6]. Xu et al. used IBM word alignment for sentence segmentation for translation tasks of English and Chinese in the news domain [7]. The focus of this technique is to use lexicon information to identify sentence segmentation point to split compound sentences into multiple sentences. This paper proposed a technique to split large sentences into multiple ones because the longer the sentences the more problems are faced by their proposed system, subsequently resulting into higher computation cost and compromised quality in word alignment. Habib et al. presented a novel approach that records properly segmented words in order to avoid the classical space insertion and space deletion problems in native script Urdu text [13][15]. Their proposed solutions can be of direct value in Urdu sentence segmentation.

Xue, N. and Yang, Y., focuses on how Chinese uses comma, exclamation marks and questions marks for sentence boundary indication. Proposed model is being tested and trained on data provided by Chinese tree bank and the accuracy achieved by this model is up to 90% [8,9]. Rehman, Z. and Anwar, W., uses rule based algorithm and Unigram statistical model to deal with Urdu sentence boundary disambiguate. Initial result before testing and training were 90% precision, 92.45% F1-measure and 86% recall, but after same testing data and training, results improved to 99.36% precision, 97.89% F1-measure and 96.45% recall [10]. Kiss and Strunk presented language-independent approach. In this paper assumptions are made that once abbreviations are identified most of the ambiguities will be eliminated while detecting sentence boundary. In order to detect high accuracy abbreviations, proposed system define three rules which required independence of context and type of candidate. The system was tested on different text types and eleven different languages [11]. A number of related research points out to interesting aspects of text segmentation and optimized input systems. Habib et al. proposed an optimized system and input methods with respect to various modern devices for Urdu composing [18]. Adnan et al. assessed the realization of smartphones learning objects in computing adaptive learning paths of undergraduate university students. Jurish and Würzner introduced a "WASTE" method for segmentation of text into tokens and sentences. Hidden Markov Model is used as a segment boundary detection. Model parameters were defining from pre-segmented corpora. Such corpora are available as an aligned multi-lingual corpora and treebanks [12].

Hearst, M.A., A presents technique called TextTiling in which text is segmented into multi-paragraph units that is subtopics or passages. Identification of sub-topics is done using lexicon co-occurrence and distribution patterns. This segmentation can further be used for text summarization and information retrieval [16]. In Evang, K., et al. technique the accuracy achieved by rule based model Tokenization is considered as no problem, but issue regarding rule-based is its language specific rules and maintenance. This paper used unsupervised feature learning combining it with supervised sequence labeling on character level to accomplish segmentation and high accuracy word goal. Evaluation of proposed system is done on three different languages with the error rate of 0.76% (Italian), 0.27% (English), and 0.35% (Dutch) [16]. Xu, L.F., et al. proposes an idea of segmenting long sentences into short one using conjunctions in them. Long sentences took a lot of machine translation resources for processing. Punctuations were used previously for segmentation but dealing with long sentences that was not enough. This paper presents rule-based approach on conjunctions to segment Chinese long sentences. 901 conjunctions were found in 10 patent papers during experimentation. Using rule-based approach, 89% accuracy was achieved [17]. Gibson E., et al proposes Comprehension of sentences technique. Comprehension of sentences means applying constraints using available computational resources to integrate variety of information sources. Four types of comprehension techniques are explained in this paper. (1) phrase-level contingent frequency constraints, (2) locality-based computational resource constraints, (3) contextual constraints, and (4) lexical constraints [19].

3. URDU SENTENCE SEGMENTATION OPERATIONS:

Sentence Segmentation is a process of identifying sentence boundaries. Previous researcher's focuses on using only punctuations as a boundary detection. Our proposed research not only uses punctuations, it also uses words as a delimiters and conjunctions as boundary markers to segment sentences appropriately.

3.1. RAW CORPUS:

Raw corpus has been collected by several means which includes websites, books, Urdu magazines, newspapers etc., we categories them into more general form that is online and offline category. Online category involves websites, online books and newspapers. While offline involves Magazines, newspapers, books etc. The collected raw corpus contains large and compound sentences including combination of conjunction and non-conjunction sentences. These sentences require two different methodologies for segmentation. The former is compound sentence segmentation and the latter is sentence tokenization which are described in the following.

3.2. WORDS/CHARACTER SEGMENTATION:

Conjunctions and delimiter words and characters are identified using words and character segmentation techniques. Individual words and characters in text are split on the basis of complex processing including space, joiner and non-joiner properties keeping in view the complex problems of Urdu specific space insertion and space deletion [3][10][19]. The segmented words and characters are then analyzed for conjunctions and delimiting words and characters.

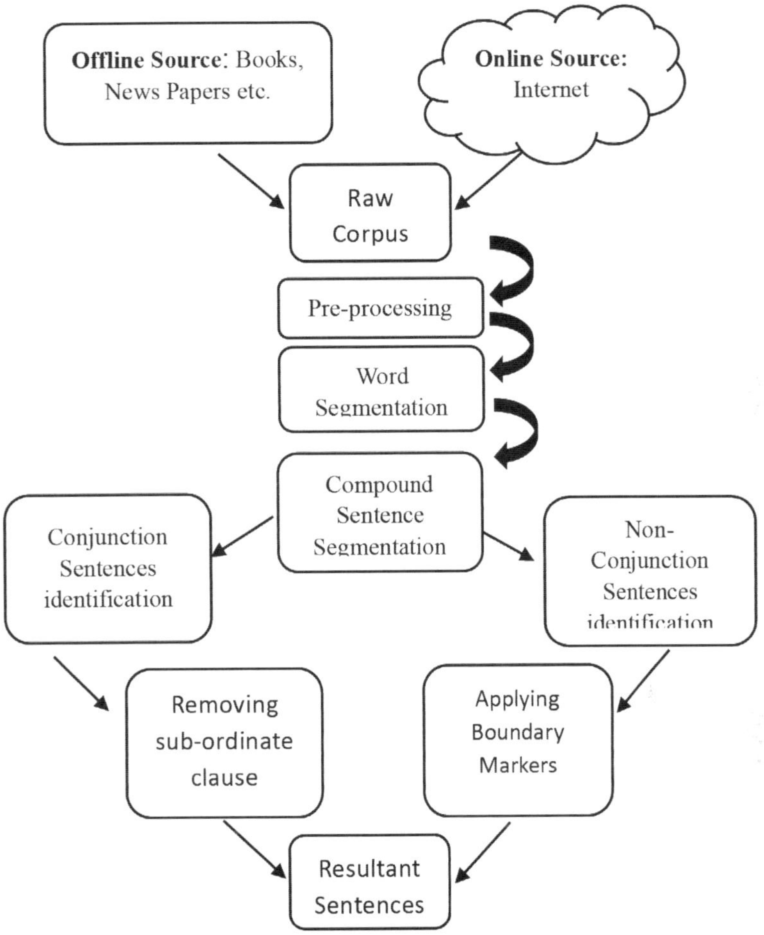

Figure.1. **Compound Sentence Segmentation and Sentence Tokenization Architecture**

3.3. COMPOUND SENTENCE IDENTIFICATION:

The issues with longer sentences is high consumption of resources such as processing time. We look for conjunction containing sentences and we analyze that the subordinate clause of sentences are mostly the explanation of main clause, which makes sentence extra-large. The options in dealing with compound sentences are two, first is to eliminate those sentences completely but by doing so, we may be risking useful information. Second option is to trim those sentences by eliminating sub-ordinate clause i.e. the explanatory part of the sentence.

We use a pattern matching approach for identification of conjunctions containing sentences. We came up with the list of conjunction words which we generated from pre tagged corpus, using this list of words conjunction containing sentences are easily detectable. List of conjunction words we are given below.

کیونکہ ، لیکن ، یعنی ، گویا ، یعنی ، چنانچہ ، بلکہ ، مگر

Naturally occurring raw corpus text examples are mentioned in the following.

3.4. With Conjunction part:

مگر سابق کونسلر عبدالنعیم نے کہا کہ تمام علاقے کی بجلی کاٹنا اس موقع پر حالات کو قابو کرنے کے لئے پولیس کی نفری بھی پہنچ گئی تھی عوام کے ساتھ سراسر زیادتی ہے جن لوگوں پر واجبات ہیں صرف انکی بجلی کاٹنی چاہئے۔

3.5. Without Conjunction part:

اس موقع پر حالات کو قابو کرنے کے لئے پولیس کی نفری بھی پہنچ گئی تھی -

We exclude "اور" from conjunction list because it is not only used as a joiner in a sentence but as a joiner between two nouns too for example;

جماعت اسلامی اور الخدمت فاؤنڈیشن

The remaining sentences in corpus contain combination of multiple sentences. These sentences do not contain conjunctions but they need to be segmented. For this purpose, we pass resultant text to the next process called Sentence Tokenization.

3.6. SENTENCE TOKENIZATION:

Sentence tokenization segments large sentences from single into multiple ones. We target words as delimiters to identify sentence boundaries. For example;

ہنگو(بیوروررپورٹ)ڈپٹی ڈسٹرکٹ ایجوکیشن آفیسر عقل بادشاہ نے کہاکہ ہمارے بھتیجے کی وفات پر ہنگو کے عوام اور تمام مکاتب فکر کی جانب سے تعزیتی پیغامات پر اہل علاقہ کے نہایت مشکورہیں ان خیالات کا اظہار ڈپٹی ایجوکیشن آفیسر عقل بادشاہ نے اپنی رہائش گاہ پر صحافیوں سے بات چیت کرتے ہوئے کیا انہوں نے کہا کہ واقعہ دلخراش ہے مگر اللہ تعالٰیکی مہربانی سے ان کے خاندان اور سوگواران نے بزرگوں ،اہل علاقہ کے دعاؤں سے پورے خاندان کو صبر جمیل عطا ہوئی کہاکہ فیاض مرحوم کے سوگوران ان تمام حضرات جنہوں نے نمازہ جنازہ میں شرکت کی یا بذریعہ ٹیلی فون تعزیت کی ان سب کے دلی مشکور ہیں۔

Above example is a single large sentence which is a combination of multiple sentences with 110 words in it. In available corpus Urdu is full of these kind of sentences. These delimiting words are identified manually from single chunk of file because analyzing large file manually is time consuming and it may take weeks to generate list of delimiting words and still that list will not be enough. Delimiting boundary list is not limited to this corpus only to achieve better results in segmenting large sentences this corpus also needs constant updating with constant manual updating of delimiting words also. We generate that list using a chunk of file is to carry on our experimentation and we accomplish significant results. For example, the above single sentence is analyzed for delimiting words and on the basis of this list above sentence is segmented down into 4 sentences with average length of 27 words per each sentence.

ہنگو(بیوروررپورٹ)ڈپٹی ڈسٹرکٹ ایجوکیشن آفیسر عقل بادشاہ نے کہاکہ ہمارے بھتیجے کی وفات پر ہنگو کے عوام اور تمام مکاتب فکر کی جانب سے تعزیتی پیغامات پر اہل علاقہ کے نہایت مشکورہیں۔

ان خیالات کا اظہار ڈپٹی ایجوکیشن آفیسر عقل بادشاہ نے اپنی رہائش گاہ پر صحافیوں سے بات چیت کرتے ہوئے کیا۔ انہوں نے کہا کہ واقعہ دلخراش ہے مگر اللہ تعالٰیکی مہربانی سے ان کے خاندان اور سوگواران نے بزرگوں ،اہل علاقہ کے دعاؤں سے پورے خاندان کو صبر جمیل عطا ہوئی کہاکہ فیاض مرحوم کے سوگوران ان تمام حضرات جنہوں نے نمازہ جنازہ میں شرکت کی۔ یا بذریعہ ٹیلی فون تعزیت کی ان سب کے دلی مشکور ہیں۔-

3.6.1. Sentence Boundary Maker:

Complexity of delimiting words of sentence boundary markers rises when generated list of delimiting words turned into a part of another word and that word appears in the middle or start of sentence not at the end. To deal with these kind of sentences, we need to take our approach to another level as we cannot use unigram. For example, the following list of delimiter words are unigram. We cannot use them as boundary markers alone because these words can be a part of other words and that results in ambiguity. We require n-gram approach. For example;

کریں ، آسکے ، کئے ، جائے ، دی

1) ہمارے مسائل ترجیحی بنیادوں پر حل **کریں** بصورت دیگر ہم پارلیمینٹ ہاؤس اور گور نر ہاؤس کے سامنے احتجاجی دھرنے پر مجبور ہونگے -

2) نہوں نے کوئی ایسا کام نہیں کیا جس کو یادگار کہا **جاسکے** بلکہ **اسکے** اپنے صوبائی اسمبلی کے ممبر باغی ہوچکے ہیں

3) تعلیمی اداروں سے نقل کا ناسُور ختم **کئے** بغیر ترقی ممکن نہیں

4) یہاں پر انفرادی کاموں کی **بجائے** اجتماعی کاموں کو ترجیح دی جاتی ہے

5) یہاں پر **انفرادی** کاموں کی بجائے اجتماعی کاموں کو ترجیح دی جاتی ہے

In example 1, 2 and 3 the delimiting words appear in the middle of sentences. In example 2 we also realize that there are two delimiters used one as a separate word and other as a part of other word for example جاسکے, which is a combination of word اسکے and ج. Same apply to example 4 and 5 i.e. بجائے and انفرادی. These delimiting words are also a combination of words i.e. بجائے is a combination of جائے and ب and انفرادی is a combination of دی and انفرا. But that was not all there another issue Urdu delimiting words were having, some of these words were not even used in the sense of termination mark for example اسکے in the above example 2 was not used in sense of a sentence boundary marker but it was used in a sense of "his" in that sentence, but the ratio of these words are low and they can also be handled by n-gram approach so this does not create any problem. Below Table 1 represents sentences boundary markers of unigram, bigram and trigram. We only include few of the boundary markers with their frequency from a single experiment.

S. No.	Frequency (sorted)	Sentence Boundary Marker List
1	259	ہیں
2	67	تھا
3	57	گے
4	36	تھے
5	20	دیا گیا
6	13	تھی
7	13	ہوگا
8	11	ہوگی
9	5	رہاہے
10	1	کرتاہے
11	1	حوالے کئے
12	1	حاصل کیے
13	1	کرائی ہے
14	1	تلاش شروع کردی
15	1	دی جائیں

Table 1: **Sentence boundary markers list with corresponding frequencies**

رابطہ کریں ، تلاش شروع کردی ، میسر آسکے ، حوالے کئے ، کرایا جائے

Some sentences contain two delimiting words and our model will add termination marks after both of these boundary markers, but that will not affect the sentence, because if sentence ends with first delimiting word it will still retain its meanings. For example;

3.6.1.1. With two delimiting words:

جو دس سال اقتدار میں رہے آج ان سب کو گرینڈ اپوزیشن میں بیٹھا دیا گیا۔ ہے۔

3.6.1.2. Without second delimiting word:

جو دس سال اقتدار میں رہے آج ان سب کو گرینڈ اپوزیشن میں بیٹھا دیا گیا ۔

It can be observed that from semantic point of view, the sentence preserves its meanings.

4. EVALUATION:

The lack of appropriate hardware resources impeded delays in compiling results of our experiments. We used a personal computer running Microsoft Windows 8 for processing our general genre raw Urdu corpus containing 2616 sentences and 291503 words. Computationally exhaustive iterative processing was not possible on such a workstation. It took more than two and a half days to process our raw corpus file and still it was not completed when the system suddenly shut down due to hardware failure. The only possible solution for this problem was the customary divide and conquer approach.

We divided the experimentation file into 14 smaller chunks and experimented chunk-wise to identify compound and large sentences. Delimiting words were extracted with their respective frequencies in the text. Compound sentences are identified by the list of conjunctions present in them. All statistical results were accumulated and manually verified by Urdu language experts. Consolidated results of the respective 14 chunks are shown in the following table 2.

S.No.	Chunk (File) Size		بلکہ	چنانچہ	یعنی	گویا	لیکن	کیونکہ	مگر	اور
	No. of Sentences	No. of Words								
1	184	20548	16	0	0	0	8	12	22	485
2	175	21794	10	0	2	0	11	8	20	517
3	274	28034	14	0	1	0	13	10	41	697
4	285	26372	15	0	1	0	8	4	29	661
5	270	27165	13	0	1	0	11	9	41	677
6	264	22956	15	0	1	0	9	3	22	582
7	211	25773	6	0	2	0	10	7	27	629
8	163	25621	17	0	1	1	17	7	36	626
9	184	22228	7	0	1	1	6	5	45	568
10	124	15326	7	0	2	0	8	2	15	335
11	104	12364	4	0	0	0	2	2	19	284
12	99	10172	6	0	1	0	2	4	17	277
13	142	15075	4	0	1	0	14	9	18	400
14	137	18075	3	0	0	0	11	6	28	457
$\sum$	2616	291503	137	0	14	2	130	88	380	7195

Table 2: **Conjunctions and delimiting words extracted from the raw Urdu corpus**

In table 2, we also generate frequency of اور as a conjunction and it appears 485 times in a text. This was done due to realization of the fact that اور is not only used as a conjunction but also as a part of other words. For example;

اورز ، دلاورشاہ ، پشاور ، نچھاور ، مشاورت ، اورکزئی

These are the words that contain conjunction word "اور". These words are the combination of two words. For example, in اورکزئی and اورز, the word اورis at the beginning and it is a combination of کزئی + اور and ز + اور respectively. Similarly, in مشاورت and دلاورشاہ, the word اور is in the middle of two words that is between ت + مش and شاہ + دل respectively. In the same manner, in words such as نچھاور and پشاور, the word اور appears in the end of these words. Our proposed model identifies them as a conjunction which increases the computational cost and algorithmic complexity. 135 times out of 485, the word "اور" is used as a conjunction that is 27% of its total occurrences. The remaining 73% i.e. 353 times, this word appeared as a part of other words or sometimes in a non-conjunction way. So we exclude it from list of conjunctions. Identifying them as a conjunction and as a part of other word is done manually.

The word "اور" and other words posing similar problem is an interesting discovery in this research. "چنانچہ" is also a conjunction word but in our existing corpus it does not appear even once. Our corpus is growing continuously. So therefore we hope this and other similar words will be encountered in the subsequent experiments. Thus we did not exclude it from the list of conjunction word.

Complexity of Urdu language increases when dealing with boundary markers. The Urdu boundary marking words may not always appear at the end of sentences but it can also be a part of other words which may be anywhere in sentences. Also, they may appear in the middle of sentences. Reaching a computational solution becomes more difficult when sometimes these are not used in the sense of boundary markers. For example, ہیں appears about 259 times in a single chunk of file. We carried out the same experiment on all 14 chunks. However, for simplicity we consider the example of only first chunk here. It was not sure whether ہیں always appears as a boundary marker or a part of other words. In our experimentation we realize, that 154 time ہیں appeared as a boundary marker that is 59% and 105 times i.e. 41% it appeared as part of another word for example نہیں, تنخواہیں, انہیں, تمہیں. The experimentation continued on other boundary markers such as تھا. Frequency of تھا in a text is 67 and it appears in text about 26 times that is 38% as a boundary marker and 41 times that is 62% as part of other words.

Most of the boundary markers are part of other words and to handle this we use bi-gram approach i.e. we combine it with the second closest word but using only bi-gram approach did not solve our problem because combination of these two words may also appear in middle of sentences, to tackle this issue we combine third closest word i.e. we use tri-gram approach but still that did not solve our problem and the process continues. The solution to this problem was to use n-gram approach. Similarly, تھے appears in a text for 36 times and 100% it is used as a boundary marker. تھی appears 13 times in which 8 time that is 61% it appears as a boundary marker and 5 times that is 39% as part of other word or boundary marker i.e. تھیں and the same goes for other boundary markers. The above mention gazetteer list of delimiting words contains only 15 boundary markers and we have about 103 list of boundary markers created manually and the list is still in a growing process the more the list grows the more effective will be the results. Considering the corpus, we have, 103 is not a huge list of boundary markers but these are enough for our experimentation. The more the list grows the more processing is required because our workstations cannot handle that kind of processing very effectively and that makes our experimentation process slower, so we restricted list of boundary markers to 103.

Initially there were 184 sentences with 20548 words in experiment 1. After compound and tokenization process we have 722 sentences. We got results for about 569 sentences that is 78% of sentences can be categorized as accurate or inaccurate sentences out of which 461 were accurately marked boundary markers that is 63% and 108 were marked inaccurate that is only 14%. This inaccuracy was due to existence of those boundary markers as a part of other words. Remaining 22% sentence were the one or two word sentences that appears because of two delimiting words in a single sentence. For example;

اُن کے لیے نہ تو قریبی علاقوں میں کوئی پارکنگ موجود ہے اور نہ ہی وہاں پر عارضی انتظام کیا گیا۔ ہے۔

ہے is second boundary marker and just a single word marked as separate sentence. There were 153 such kind of sentences which means that 22% sentences were useless and discarded accordingly.

5. CONCLUSION:

Our work regarding Compound Sentence Segmentation and Tokenization of large Sentences was pioneering work in Urdu. The results generated by our proposed system are promising. The results generated for a single chunk of file were generated manually. Therefore, we did not include other chunks of files. We realize that with having powerful servers and with increasing delimiting words gazetteer list, we can improve our results further. Beside generating statistical results, in future we will also analyze our model and its results by language expert, by comparing our automatically tokenized sentences with human manually tokenized sentences to analyze its coherence and readability.

REFERENCES:

[1] Yasumasa, S. Kansai. 2016. University of Graduate School of Foreign Language Education and Research. Automatic Sentence Segmentation, accessed (Feb 19). DOI: http://www.someya-net.com/00-class09/sentenceDiv.html.

[2] Brian, L., Zillig, P., Ramsay, S., Mueller, M., and Smutniak, F., 2016. Academic Technologies and Research Services. Morph Adorner Sentence Splitter, accessed (Feb 19). DOI: http://morphadorner.northwestern.edu/sentencesplitter/example/.

[3] Malik, A.A. and Habib, A., 2013. Urdu to English Machine Translation using Bilingual Evaluation Understudy. *International Journal of Computer Applications*, *82*(7).

[4] Palmer, D.D., 2000. Tokenisation and sentence segmentation. In *Handbook of Natural Language Processing*. CRC Press.

[5] Aroonmanakun, W., 2007, December. Thoughts on word and sentence segmentation in Thai. In *Proceedings of the Seventh Symposium on Natural language Processing, Pattaya, Thailand, December 13–15* (pp. 85-90).

[6] Baseer, F., Habib, A. and Ashraf, J., 2016, August. Romanized Urdu Corpus development (RUCD) model: Edit-distance based most frequent unique unigram extraction approach using real-time interactive dataset. In *Innovative Computing Technology (INTECH), 2016 Sixth International Conference on* (pp. 513-518). IEEE.

[7] Xu, J., Zens, R. and Ney, H., 2005, May. Sentence segmentation using IBM word alignment model 1. In Proceedings of EAMT (pp. 280-287).

[8] A. Gul, A. Habib, J. Ashraf, "Identification and extraction of Compose-Time Anomalies in Million Words Raw Urdu Corpus and Their Proposed Solutions", *proceedings of the 3rd International Multidisciplinary Research Conference (IMRC)*, 2016.

[9] Xue, N. and Yang, Y., 2011. Chinese sentence segmentation as comma classification. In *Proceedings of the 49th Annual Meeting of the Association for Computational Linguistics: Human Language Technologies: short papers-Volume 2* (pp. 631-635). Association for Computational Linguistics.

[10] Rehman, Z. and Anwar, W., 2012. A hybrid approach for urdu sentence boundary disambiguation. *International Arab Journal of Information Technology*, *9*(3), pp.250-255.

[11] Kiss, T. and Strunk, J., 2006. Unsupervised multilingual sentence boundary detection. *Computational Linguistics*, *32*(4), pp.485-525.

[12] Jurish, B. and Würzner, K.M., 2013. Word and Sentence Tokenization with Hidden Markov Models. *JLCL*, *28*(2), pp.61-83.

[13] Habib, A. Iwatate, M., Asahara, M. Matsumoto, Y., 2012. Keypad for large letter-set languages and small touch-screen devices (case study: Urdu). *International Journal of Computer Science 9(3), ISSN: 1694-0814.*

[14] Hearst, M.A., 1997. TextTiling: Segmenting text into multi-paragraph subtopic passages. *Computational linguistics*, *23*(1), pp.33-64.

[15] Habib, A. Iwatate, M., Asahara, M. Matsumoto, Y. W.K., 2013. Optimized and Hygienic Touch Screen Keyboard for Large Letter Set Languages. *Proceedings of 7th ACM International Conference on Ubiquitous Information Management and Communication (ICUIMC) Kota Kinabalu, Malaysia.*

[16] Evang, K., Basile, V., Chrupała, G. and Bos, J., 2013, October. Elephant: Sequence labeling for word and sentence segmentation. In *EMNLP 2013*.

[17] Xu, L.F., Zhu, Y., Yang, L.J. and Jin, Y.H., 2014. Research on Sentence Segmentation with Conjunctions in Patent Machine Translation. In *Applied Mechanics and Materials* (Vol. 513, pp. 4605-4609). Trans Tech Publications.

[18] Habib, A. Iwatate, M., Asahara, M. Matsumoto, Y., 2011. Different input systems for different devices: Optimized touch-screen keypad designs for Urdu scripts. *Proceedings of Workshop on Text Input Methods WTIM2011, IJCNLP, Chiang Mai, Thailand.*

[19] Gibson, E. and Pearlmutter, N.J., 1998. Constraints on sentence comprehension. *Trends in cognitive sciences*, *2*(7), pp.262-268.

[20] Adnan, M. Habib, A. Mukhtar, H. Ali, G., 2017. Assessing the Realization of Smartphones Learning Objects in Students' Adaptive Learning Paths. *International Journal of Engineering Research, 6(4), ISBN:978-81-932091-0-3.*

Not Interfering: Simultaneous Typed Chat in COMPS Computer-Mediated Dialogues

Michael Glass
Valparaiso U.
michael.glass
@valpo.edu

Anthony Nelson
U. of Southern Cal.
anthoncn
@usc.edu

Chinedu Emeka
Valparaiso U.
chinedu.emeka1
@valpo.edu

Jung Hee Kim
North Carolina A&T State U.
jungkim@ncat.edu

Abstract

COMPS computer-mediated typed-chat collaborative learning exercises permit the students to type at the same time. People can see and respond to each other's text in real time. Although everybody talking at the same time does not work in spoken conversation, students quickly discover they can type at the same time without interfering with each other. About 40% of typing occurs while other students have not yet formally ended a dialogue turn by pressing "enter." In COMPS dialogues normal conversational turn-taking often occurs when students pause to wait for each other, without pressing "enter." In this paper we estimate the polite delay that people use for deciding when the other person has relinquished a turn. Studies of educational dialogue will have to take into account the interactions that the new computer-mediated communication regime affords. This paper also characterizes the varieties of interaction that are observed during non-turn-taking simultaneous typing in COMPS dialogues. While students are typing together, they do not engage in tightly-interleaved two-way exchanges. Instead, each student individually responds to something that another student said earlier.

1 Introduction[1]

A feature of the COMPS (Computer-Mediated Problem Solving) online chat environment is that students can all type at once. They see each other's words in real time and can respond at the same time without interrupting. This adds an interactive dimension that spoken language does not support.

Most forms of human dialogue require that people take turns as they talk. Typed-chat lacks many of the signals such as prosodic effects that people use to regulate turn-taking in verbal conversation. COMPS follows the common convention that pressing <enter> signals the end of a dialogue turn. However the simultaneous typing feature means that pressing <enter> is not necessary for relinquishing the turn, other people can simply start typing. Hence people often do not press enter to end a turn. They simply pause, and other participants infer that a turn transition is possible. In this paper we estimate how long is the pause that the other participants wait before deciding the turn has ended.

Since overlapping dialogue for more than a short time is a phenomenon new to computer-mediated communication, this study examines overlapping dialogue manually to see how students are using it. One possibility is that the students are violating the turn-taking structure of regular dialogue, engaging in tightly intertwined dialogue where a person responds immediately to the words being typed by the other person. Manual characterization of 30 such interactions reveals that this doesn't happen. We have identified three common patterns of interaction, in all of them the overlapping students are effectively responding to earlier dialogue. Thus they follow conversation protocols akin to normal turn-taking even though several people are talking at once.

The two main results in this paper are then: a) an estimate of the pause time that signals a possible turn-switching point in typed chat, and b) showing, qualitatively, examples of the three main patterns of dialogue interaction that students employ when using the simultaneous chat, c) show that with these patterns of dialogue interaction students are still using conversational turn-taking.

These results can be used to inform the COMPS project's efforts at text analytics, which will identify characteristics of the dialogue in real time that will be indicative of students engaging in interactive conversation.

2 Background

2.1 COMPS dialogues

The COMPS project deploys and studies small group collaborative problem-solving exercises in college computer science and mathematics classes [Kim et al., 2016]. The exercises are designed to address student conceptual knowledge through group cognition [Stahl, 2004; Stahl, 2009]. Typically students work in groups of three, with a TA or instructor additionally participating intermittently. The exercise protocol for the exercises requires the students to solve a problem in steps, coming to agreement on each step. The students show the agreed-upon answer to the instructor, receive feedback or hints, then further discuss the step or proceed to the next item.

A	Labels 1, 2, 3, 4, 5, and 14	can be instantiated	anonymously. Because these do not have to be changed ◄
B		What about 6 and 7? ◄	

Figure 1. Example of simultaneous dialogue. End of turn is marked by " ◄ ".

This is consistent with accepted practices for good collaborative exercise design, requiring creative interdependence [Eberly, 2016]. This protocol also discourages social loafing, all students must participate at multiple instances during the exercise.

Students discuss the problem through the COMPS software, a web-delivered chat interface that permits everybody to type and see each other's dialogue all at the same time. The software logs the chat for later analysis.

Figure 1 illustrates how simultaneous chat can differ from normal conversational turn-taking [Glass et al., 2015]. In this and subsequent figures the <enter> ending a turn is marked with " ◄ ". Student A was listing widgets on a screenshot of a Java GUI, it was an answer to one of the exercise questions. Part way through A's dialogue turn student B inquired why certain widgets had been left out. Student A was still typing and had not typed <enter> yet. A, continuing to type in the same chat dialogue turn, then answered B's question. As the Figure 1 example illustrates, students indeed adapt to this simultaneous chat regime and engage in productive interactions while doing so [Glass et al., 2015].

2.2 Dialogue Turns

Potentially the instructor could be aided in knowing which discussion groups could benefit from instructor intervention and participation. The COMPS project is developing text analytics for this purpose.

Having the computer detect and measure the prevalence of transactive turns in the conversation might provide an estimate of conversation quality for an instructor's dashboard. Transactive dialogue is a key element of group cognition, where a dialogue turn a) contributes to the knowledge construction and b) responds to a previous dialogue move, usually by another person [Weinberger & Fischer, 2006]. There are a variety of different categories of transactive contribution, ranging from "eliciting" to "conflict-oriented consensus building."

We have simplified the computer-recognition task to two smaller steps: recognizing whether student dialogue turns are discussing the topic [Willis et. al, 2017] and whether dialogue turns are responding to other turns [Glass et al., 2014]. For the latter task, we adopted the conventions of Conversation Analysis, a framework from discourse linguistics [Sacks et al., 1974; Stubbs, 1983]. In Conversation Analysis dialogue is segmented, each segment starting with an "Initiate" turn and containing the other person's "Respond" turn plus possible "followup" turns. However COMPS project attempts to train classifiers to recognize Initiate and Respond turns had difficulty partly because of many turns where people type simultaneously [Glass et al., 2014a, 2014b]. As Figure 1 illustrates, where each dialogue turn responds to the other, there sometimes isn't even a clear separation of turns that can be tagged as which is responding to which.

One possible step toward disentangling the Initiate/Respond problem between overlapping dialogue turns would be to identify the Transition Relevance Places (TRPs) and Turn Allocational Components [Schegloff, 1990; Sacks et al., 1974]. In Conversation Analysis, a TRP is a place where turn reallocation is possible. TRPs can occur in the dialogue when a person stops speaking, but they can also occur, e.g., when a complete thought has been finished and another person can jump in and respond.

According to this analysis, the Figure 1 dialogue could be thought of as follows:

A: "labels 1, 2, 3, 4, 5, and 14" <TRP>"can be ..."

B: "What about 6 and 7?"<TRP>

A: "Because they do not have to be changed"

In this analysis, B starts typing in response to A's first TRP. In speech this could have been an interruption. In typed-chat, B typing does not interrupt A's ability to type, so A and B can type simultaneously. Similarly, A's final sentence is a response to B's recently-ended turn.

Many TRPs will be determined semantically, as the first TRP in Figure 1 after "14." We observe that a pause in the typing represents a TRP, a possible place for the of a new turn for dialogue purposes. If student A paused to read B's question in Figure 1, for example, detecting that pause could be helpful both in manual and automated dialogue analysis.

Table 1. Statistics of Group Discussions.

Group discussions	28
Dialogue turns	2723
Keystrokes (not <enter>)	113,808
Participant/group	4 (3 students, 1 TA)
Duration: Swing exercise	35 min
Duration: Inheritance exercise	70 min
Pct of keystroke overlapping	17%

2.3 Data for this Study

Table 1 shows the descriptive statistics for the chat data used in this study. COMPS exercises have been deployed in two different quantitative literacy exercises for pre-service teachers and in four different object-oriented Java concept exercises in CS2 classes [Kim et al., 2016]. In this study we used two exercises from a CS2 class in Fall 2015. One exercise was about inheritance concepts in Java, the other about the concepts in a Java SWING graphical user interface. There were 14 discussions from each exercise

2.4 Method of Analysis

This study examined two phenomena: how long is a pause that represents a turn relevance place, and how do people use simultaneous typing to address each other.

For the timing study we used data on how long did person B wait to start typing after person A paused. This was applied to all the typing in Table 1.

For the varieties of interaction, we manually analyzed examples of simultaneous typing observed in the log files. The question was the relationship of each overlapping dialogue turn to the rest of the conversation: was it initiating or responding, and if responding where was the antecedent language. During this process we maintained a coding manual listing the varieties of interaction the annotators had found.

Only a small sample of about 30 of the instances have been manually annotated at this time according to the current manual. The three coders periodically compared annotations and arrived at a consensus. Interrater reliability thus has not been tested. The result reported here is qualitative, a description of the categories that were found and coded.

3 Measuring the Pause That Signals Turn-Taking

3.1 Turn Allocation Using <enter>

The explicit component for turn allocation in typed-chat is the <enter> which ends a turn. COMPS also has a button for ending a turn, the effect is the same. We start by defining a delimited turn as the time from the first keystroke until the <enter> delimiter that ends the turn. A simultaneous keystroke occurs if person B types while any other person A is still within a delimited turn. This is similar to the usual definition of interruption in spoken dialogue, except that B typing does not interrupt A's ability to type. Using this definition of a turn, between 25% and 50% of keystrokes in COMPS dialogues are simultaneous typing.

3.2 Ending a Turn by Pausing

Just as in spoken conversation a turn can end when a person stops speaking, a chat turn can also end without explicit marking if the student stops typing. In spoken conversation, 3 seconds is an awkwardly long pause [McLaughlin, 1984]. In COMPS dialogues there are many pauses. In one extreme, participant A may pause typing without pressing <enter>, waiting for the other participants to respond. Everyone else can see what A has written so far, and can observe that A has stopped. Another participant B can then type without interference. After B pauses, A can resume, inserting a second logical turn in the single <enter>-delimited turn. In this typing regime, there may not be much incentive to type <enter> to formally end a dialogue turn.

What causes people to formally end their turns is the COMPS scrolling text box behavior. Turns properly work within the interleaved dialogue scroll only if they have been <enter> delimited. Furthermore, a single turn containing several logical dialogue turns concatenated together in a single stretch of text becomes hard to read. The result is that turn-taking by pausing rarely continues past two logical turns. It is, however, common for a turn to end with a long pause followed by the <enter> before the new turn.

3.3 Measuring a Release Time

We hypothesize that there is some time that will be recognized as meaning that the typist has given up the turn, allowing somebody else to speak. We extended the definition of simultaneous typing to include a release time. A participant is *not inside* a dialogue turn if a) the last thing typed was <enter> (explicitly ending the turn) or b) a release time has elapsed (implicitly releasing the turn).

How long after people pause typing before the other people recognize it as a typed-chat release of turn? We can look at typing behavior. If there is a well-recognized time that releases the turn, starting typing without waiting for the release time to elapse would be a form of interrupting. Under this hypothesis, we would expect to see many fewer keystrokes from other persons during the interval of the release time than after it has passed. After the release time the rate of keystrokes from other typists will reflect the average rate for conversation in general.

Figure 4 (at end) shows the percent of keystrokes classed as overlapping according to different trial values of release time. As expected, for larger times the curve is approximately linear, representing the rate of new dialogue added into the conversation. However for the first 2 seconds after a person pauses typing the other participants are much more reluctant to type.

Accordingly, for computer analysis we use 2 seconds to declare the end of a turn and subsequent typing is non-simultaneous.

3.4 Other Means of Turn Allocation

We have not considered other mechanisms for turn allocation. In conversation a turn can be ended, for example, by asking a question. The same holds true for typed chat. Spoken dialogue also employs prosodic features and other mechanisms for turn allocation that are not available in typed chat. The paucity of conventions for turn allocation in computer-mediated typed chat produces quite different behavior than spoken conversation. One experiment using a chat system similar to ours observed about 30% of turns were overlapping with other turns, an amount of overlap not possible in speech. It also observed long pauses where nobody was typing, another feature rarely observed in speech [Anderson, et al., 2010].

An issue occurs if person A pauses shortly after person B begins simultaneous typing. A's ability to type unimpeded is not compromised, however A sometimes pauses, perhaps to read what B is saying. Clearly B's first keystrokes constitute simultaneous typing. After A pauses for a while, it becomes

A	It's only one answer for this one. It'snot A. Sorry About that◄
B	It's just E.◄

Figure 2. Example of overlapping response

A	i think its B D and E◄	
B		I agree with B,D, and E◄
C		Actually no im changing to just E◄

Figure 3. Example of simultaneous response.

clear that they are no longer typing simultaneously. If A were to pause for only the time for few keystrokes it should probably still be call simultaneous. In our work we use the same release time for this determination. Up until the 2 second release time has elapsed, B's keystrokes are still counted as simultaneous typing.

4 Varieties of Interaction

The main observation is that overlapping dialogue usually addresses earlier dialogue. Overlapped dialogue never in our sample of 30 simultaneous typing incidents directly addressed or responded to the text that was being typed at approximately the same time. People were not simultaneously reading, thinking, and writing.

There are three patterns of overlapping dialogue, characterized by what parts of earlier dialogue are being addressed by the simultaneous participants:

- Overlapping response, where participant B responds to something that A has recently uttered, while A continues the same turn.
- Simultaneous response, where two participants respond to an earlier turn by a different participant.
- Simultaneous initiation, where two participants simply have different ideas to insert into the conversation and happen to type them in overlapped fashion. Both utterances fit into the conversation as of the point when they started.

Examples of the first two varieties follow.

4.1 Overlapping Response

Figure 2 shows an overlapping response. The students were asked to pick one or several from the lettered answers to a multiple choice question. The first student, who has suggested multiple letters, corrects that by saying "It's only one answer for this one. It's not A. Sorry about that." Another student starts typing in the middle of this turn, responding to the assertion that there is only one answer letter. That student says "Its just E." According to our analysis, the end of A's first sentence represents a Transition Relevance Place.

The Figure 1 example shows overlapped responses. Student B responds after the first part of A's answer, noticing that some of the numbered SWING components were not mentioned. Later, Student A responds to B after A has paused a short moment to read B's question.

4.2 Simultaneous Response

Figure 3 shows an example of a simultaneous response, student B agreeing with student A's suggestion and student C disagreeing. Simultaneous responses occur at TRPs.

One interesting aspect of this example is there is a three second gap between the end of A's turn and the beginning of both B and C. This gap is visible in the keystroke timing diagram of the same dialogue turns shown in Figure 5 (at end). Student A is the bottom line, B and C above it in that order. We think this gap represents cognitive processing, rather than waiting for the release time, since A's turn had been terminated with <newline>.

5 Discussion and Future Work

There are considerable differences between computer-mediated typed chat and spoken communication. The ability for multiple participants to talk simultaneously for extended periods is new to computer communication. It has not been well-studied how people use this ability as they engage in problem-solving dialogues.

Regarding turn allocation, it has been observed by other researchers turn allocation is not always controlled by simple <enter> and pause times. People have been observed to type <enter> in the middle of a logical thought, for example, and then quickly continue typing [Markman, 2013]. This circumvents the turn allocation mechanism, permitting a single person to hold the floor for longer stretches of dialogue.

Regarding simultaneous interaction, cognitive science suggests it is unlikely that when several people are typing simultaneously they are multitasking, viz: reading other students' dialogue, thinking about it, and writing responses. Generally people cannot multitask between two tasks that require attention and cognition without switching back and forth between them and degrading performance [Bermúdez, 2014]. Our sampling of simultaneous dialogue events is consistent with this. When people chat simultaneously, they are interacting with events in the dialogue that occur before they initiated their chat turn.

The manual analysis and annotation of simultaneous events has proven to be difficult. This will have to be addressed in order to get meaningful statistics on the prevalence of categories. The main issue is that Conversation Analysis was developed for two-person dialogues. Categorizing utterances as initiate or respond (some versions include a third category "followup") seems to break down when there are more than two people in the group. In a group dialogue it becomes necessary to determine whose utterance is being responded to. Once it becomes possible to have multiple responses to one utterance, the same analysis produces chains of responses. Did C respond to B's response to A? Or did C respond to A directly? The same utterance can often be read both ways. The methods of linguistic analysis of multi-party conversations hinge on this distinction. But when the dialogue turns overlap, it becomes harder to resolve the ambiguities. Although there are many cases where three independently-working annotators readily agree, there are a similar number where agreement comes only after consensus discussion or not at all. In the future we will try categories that do not depend on identifying the antecedent of a response.

The determination of the release time will be refined by statistical analyses of the gaps between the end of one turn and the start of the next. There are other phenomena that potentially affect pauses in the conversations. We could try to disambiguate between a cognitive reason and a social reason. Conversational gaps might be expected to be more prevalent in problem-solving dialogues due to cognitive processing. The Figures 3 and 5 example of simultaneous response exhibits just such a gap. However there is possibly a social explanation: with three or more participants, no one person is responsible for filling the gap in the conversation after one speaker pauses. We plan to study this by two methods. One is by separating the conversations into segments where students are attending to the problem vs. attending to other matters. We hypothesize longer pauses in the problem-solving segments. Another method will be to check for correlation between the length of a pause and the length of the dialogue turn which follows the pause. Longer thinking pauses might result in longer utterances subsequently.

Another aspect of simultaneous chat that could be studied is whether the degree of simultaneity correlates with student engagement or other positive measures of dialogue quality. Anecdotally, students report being engaged by this facility. If degree of simultaneity correlates with some positive or negative outcomes of group problem-solving chat, it would be useful to put this measure on the instructor dashboard.

Acknowledgments

Partial support for this work was provided by the National Science Foundation's Improving Undergraduate STEM Ed ucation (IUSE) program under Award No. 1504917. Any opinions, findings, and conclusions or recommendations expressed in this material are those of the author(s) and do not necessarily reflect the views of the National Science Foundation

References

Anderson, J. F., F. K. Beard, and J. B. Walther. (2010). Turn-Taking and the Local Management of Conversation in a Highly Simultaneous Computer-Mediated Communication System. Language@Internet vol. 7 article 7.

Bermúdez, José Luis. (2014) Cognitive Science: An Introduction to the Science of the Mind. 2nd ed. Cambridge University Press.

Eberly Center (2016). Carnegie Mellon, Eberly Center for Teaching Excellence and Innovation. What are best practices for designing group projects? http://www.cmu.edu/teaching/designteach/design/instructionalstrategies/groupprojects/design.html. Retrieved March, 2016.

Glass, Michael, Jung Hee Kim, Kelvin Bryant, Melissa Desjarlais, Micayla Goodrum, and Thomas Martin. (2014a). Toward Measurement of Conversational Interactivity in COMPS Computer Mediated Problem Solving. Proceedings of the 25th Modern Artificial Intelligence and Cognitive Science Conference (MAICS-14), Spokane, WA.

Glass, Michael, Jung Hee Kim, Kelvin Bryant, and Melissa Desjarlais. (2014b). Indicators of Conversational Interactivity in COMPS Problem-Solving Dialogues, Third Workshop on Intelligent Support for Learning in Groups (ISLG) at Twelfth International Conference on Intelligent Tutoring Systems, Honolulu, Hawaii, June.

Glass, Michael, Jung Hee Kim, Kelvin Bryant, and Melissa Desjarlais (2015). Come Let Us Chat Together: Simultaneous Typed-Chat in Computer-Supported Collaborative Dialogue. Journal of Computing Sciences in Colleges, 31 no. 2, Dec.

Kim, Jung Hee, Michael Glass, Taehee Kim, Kelvin Bryant, Angelica Willis, Ebonie McNeil, Zachery Thomas. 2016. Student Understanding and Engagement in a Class Employing COMPS Computer Mediated Problem Solving. Modern AI and Cognitive Science Conference, Dayton, OH. pp. 69–74

Markman, K. M. (2013) Conversational Coherence in Small Group Chat. In Herring, S.,D. Stein.,and T. Virtanen, eds. Pragmatics of Computer-Mediated Communication., Berlin: De Gruyter Mouton, pp. 539-564C

McLaughlin, M. (1984). Conversation: How Talk is Organized. Newbury Park, CA: Sage Publication.

Sacks, H., E. A. Schegloff, and G. Jefferson. (1974). A Simplest Systematics for the Organization of Turn-Taking for Conversation. Language, vol. 50, pp. 696-735.

Schegloff, E. A. (1992). On the Organization of Sequences as a Source of "Coherence" in Talk-in-Interaction. In: B. Dorval, ed. Conversational Organization and Its Development, Norwood NJ: Ablex, pp. 51-77.

Stahl, Gerry (2004). Building Collaborative Knowing: Elements of a Social Theory of CSCL. In J. W. Strijbos, P. Kirschner and R. Martens, eds., What We Know About CSCL and Implementing It in Higher Education, Boston, MA: Kluwer Academic Publishers, pp. 53–86.

Stahl, Gerry, ed. (2009). Studying Virtual Math Teams, Springer, pp. 57–73.

Stubbs, Michael. (1983). Discourse Analysis, U. of Chicago Press.

Weinberger, A., and F. Fischer. (2006). A Framework to Analyze Argumentative Knowledge Construction in Computer-Supported Collaborative Learning. Computers & Education, vol. 46 no. 1, pp. 71–95.

Willis, Angelica, Ashana Edwards, Jung Hee Kim, Kelvin Bryant, and Michael Glass. (2017). Topic Modeling to Detect Student Expressions of Understanding in Collaborative Problem-Solving Dialogues. Poster abstracts, Thirtieth Florida Artificial Intelligence Research Symposium (FLAIRS-30). (to appear)

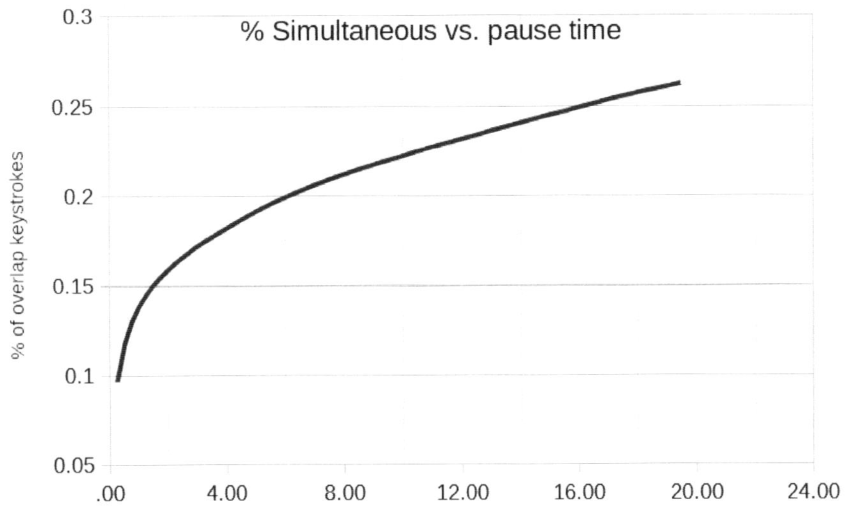

Figure 4. Percent of turns classified as simultaneous vs. pause time that would start a new turn

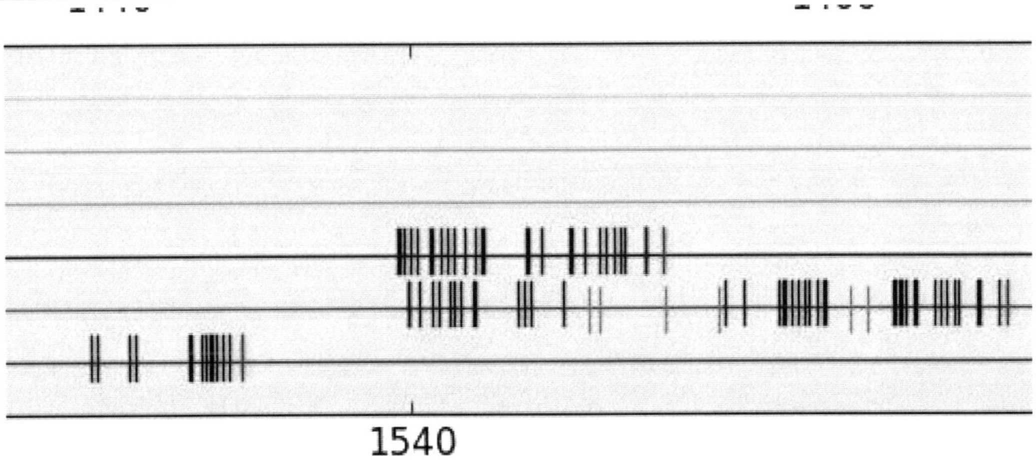

Figure 5. Keystroke timing diagram for dialogue in Figure 3. Student A on bottom line, Students B and C above.

Automating the Encoding for the LISA Model of Analogy from Raw Text

SEAN WILNER, University of Illinois Urbana-Champaign
JE HUMMEL, University of Illinois Urbana-Champaign

Analogy is an integral part of human cognition. Consequently researchers would like to produce computational models of analogy to test implementations of theoretical claims. Such computational models have relied almost exclusively upon hand-coded representations, making the resulting models too dependent upon the modeler's choices, and thus difficult to interpret in isolation of the modeler. In an effort to combat this dependency, we present here a means of automatic encoding for the LISA model of analogy and inference.

General Terms: Analogy, LISA, NLP

Additional Key Words and Phrases: Natural Language Processing, Computational Linguistics, Cognitive Psychology, Analogy

1 INTRODUCTION

Analogy, and more generally, relational reasoning are core cognitive capacities [6, 8, 10] that, along with language, seem to separate human cognition from the cognitive abilities of all the other great apes [22]. Many of the computational models of analogy arising from machine learning revolve around solving semantic, or 4-way, analogies of the form "king:queen::brother:?" where the model fills in "sister" [19]. These models fail to account for the more substantial form of analogy – narrative analogy – wherein agents and actions must all be analogically mapped to one another. Numerous models have been developed to account for our ability to make such analogies. Among the most influential have been Falkenhainer et al.'s [3] Structure Mapping Engine (SME), Holyoak and Thagard's [9] Analogical Constraint Mapping Engine (ACME) and Hummel and Holyoak's [11, 12] Learning and Inference with Schemas and Analogies (LISA) (see Gentner & Forbus, 2011[7], for a review).

Although these and other models account for many aspects of human relational thought, they share a common limitation: All of them rely on hand-coded knowledge representations, placing a great deal of control in the modeler's hands. As such, it is often unclear how many of the successes of these models reflect the models' fundamental tenets and how many reflect arbitrary representational and modeling choices made by the modeler at the time of creating the simulations (see, e.g., Lu et al. 2008 [17]). Since such models are only as good as their modeler, the support or challenge to any theoretical claims they make must be interpreted carefully.

Ideally, these models would produce their representational inputs directly from natural language, removing their dependence upon hand-coded inputs. There are some models that approach this goal for specific narrow domains, such as intuitive physics (Friedman SE & Forbus KD, 2009 [5]) and moral decision making (Dehghani M et al., 2008 [2]). However, the task of generalizing open domain natural language for analogy remains elusive. To address this problem, we describe recent efforts applying several Natural Language Processing (NLP) techniques

This material is based on research sponsored by the Air Force Research Laboratory, under agreement number FA9550-12-1-0003. The U.S. Government is authorized to reproduce and distribute reprints for Governmental purposes notwithstanding any copyright notation thereon.
Author's addresses: S. Wilner, Illinois Informatics Institute, University of Illinois UrbanaChampaign; JE Hummel, Department of Psychology, University of Illinois UrbanaChaimpaign.

to the automatic generation of knowledge representations for LISA. When combined, these techniques allow us to transform English sentences into semantically-rich propositional representations usable to the LISA model of analogy (i.e., representations in "LISAese").

1.1 Representation

LISAese is a collection of semantic encodings and structural representations which, together, allow LISA to produce semantically informed, structurally consistent analogies. LISA employs semantic representations for both objects and predicates and encodes structure in a predicated logical form. Semantics for an object in LISAese consist of a distributed list of abstract "semantic units" and corresponding weights. For instance, if we were to hand-code the representation for a taxi driver, "Bob" and a bank teller "Jill", we may end up with the following semantics and corresponding weights:

Bob: human=1.0, adult=0.7, male=1.0, employed=0.8, taxi_driver=1.0

Jill: human=1.0, adult=0.7, female=1.0, employed=0.8, bank_teller=1.0

Bob's semantics could then overlap with the semantics for our bank teller, "Jill", who is also human, adult, and employed, but would differ on male and taxi driver. LISA treats these "semantic units" as universal across all representations, that is, if two "semantic units" have the same name, they are the same unit. Aside from this universality, the names are arbitrary and the choice to give them relevant names with regard to the objects they are attached to only serves to facilitate human readability.

Similarly, predicate semantics consist of "semantic units" and weights; however, predicate semantics are defined at the level of their relational roles rather than the predicate itself. For example, the two-place predicate *love* is defined by two lists of semantics. The first list represents the agent role of *love* (the lover); the second represents the patient role of *love* (the beloved). This could be represented as follows:

love:
[lover=1.0, emotion=1.0, strong_emotion=0.8, passionate=0.9]
[beloved=1.0, receives_emotion=1.0, receives_strong_emotion=0.8, receives_passion=0.9]

With defined semantics on objects and predicates, LISA is able to ground its structural representation, given in a predicated logical format, to represent "Bob loves Jill": *love*(Bob, Jill). This logical representation is robust to recursive references such as "Jill knows that Bob loves her." which yields: *know*-(Jill, *love*(Bob, Jill)). Indeed, this is sufficient to represent the necessary semantic and structural information LISA needs to make analogies and inferences.

1.2 Task

Our task in this paper is to outline a technique to produce semantic and structural representations automatically from text. Subsequently, we will show that LISA can use the resulting LISAese to successfully find analogies and inferences. More specifically, we will present a method which achieves the following:

(1) Generates Semantics
- Object semantics that account for modification by adjectives, noun-phrases, and copular verb attachments
- Predicate semantics with role-by-role representation

(2) Generate Structure

- Produces logic form
- Handles recursive references
- Associates multiple references to a single entity

By using NLP techniques to automatically pre-process and encode text into LISAese, the LISA model will no longer need to rely on hand-coded knowledge representations. Freeing it of this requirement will clarify how LISA's successes as a model reflect its fundamental tenets rather than choices made by the modeler.

2 GENERATE SEMANTICS

Ultimately, we need to generate semantic representations for both objects and predicates, but the requirements for automated generation of the two differ slightly. This is because, as previously noted, in LISAese semantics are assigned not to the predicates themselves, but rather to each predicate role independently.

2.1 Object Semantics

Objects may be represented in a fairly straightforward manner using word embedding. Word embedding is a means of mapping words into a semantic space (a vector space) such that words which are 'similar' are closer in the resulting space than words which are 'dissimilar'. There are many means of producing word embeddings. One of the most commonly used semantic embedding tools is Google's Word2Vec [19] which produces vectors based off carefully crafted word co-occurrence statistics. Using these vectors, we can produce embeddings for individual words such as "cat", "January", or "happy". However, this means of embedding can break down upon encountering proper nouns such as "Microsoft" or "Bob". In order to properly encode proper nouns, we employ an NLP technique called Named Entity Recognition (NER) which identifies what kind of entity the proper nouns are: "Microsoft"→ORGANIZATION and "Bob"→PERSON. Using these NER tags, we can encode the proper nouns by the semantic embedding of their associated tag (for added specificity, where known, we also incorporate the gender of each proper noun).

In order to accommodate various modifiers, we additively combine the semantic vectors corresponding to each object. These vectors consist of the embeddings of the words contained within or associated with an entity, for example, the words in a noun-phrase, an NER label, adjective modifiers, or copular modifiers. Copular verbs are stative verbs such as is/are/was/were, seem, or appear. For example, "smelly Sam" and "Sam is smelly" both result in the incorporation of the semantics for "smelly" in the representation of Sam.

Using the resulting vectors, we can produce LISAese by creating an arbitrary semantic label, call it "SemUnit_i", to every i^{th} index of the vector where the weight on the generated semantic unit is the value at the ith index of the vector. For example, if our word embedding was 4 dimensions (instead of 300), we could have the following embedding for "happy":

happy→ [0.14, 0.0024, 0.81, -0.37]

Which would then yield a LISAese representation of "happy":

happy→ SemUnit_0=0.14, SemUnit_1=0.0024, SemUnit_2=0.81, SemUnit_3=-0.37

Thus allowing us to produce object semantics in LISAese from the Word2Vec word-embeddings.

2.2 Predicate Semantics

Predicate semantics in their most general form are more difficult to automatically encode than objects. Direct role-by-role representation via word-embedding is certainly non-obvious, although we will explore methods to do so in the future work section. Here, we will simplify our semantic representation to the easiest usable form wherein we assign semantics to each role corresponding to word embeddings for the predicate. For example, in our 4-dimensional embedding from before, we can imagine the following vector for "love":

"love" → [0.23, 0.01, 0.76, -0.45]

Copying the embedding onto the agent and patient roles of *love* gives us:

love:
[SemUnit_0agent=0.23, SemUnit_1agent=0.01, SemUnit_2agent=0.76, SemUnit_3agent=-0.45]
[SemUnit_0patient=0.23, SemUnit_1patient=0.01, SemUnit_2patient=0.76, SemUnit_3patient=-0.45]

While this representation meets all of our requirements, it does have a glaring weakness. There will never be any semantic overlap between two different predicate roles (e.g. agent and patient). The resulting LISAese will make LISA preferentially map agents and patients onto other agents and patients respectively. Again, we will explore alternatives to this encoding which do not suffer from the same weakness in the future works section below.

Using the above semantic representations, we meet all the requirements for LISAese's semantic encoding and are ready to explore how to structurally represent text in LISAese.

3 GENERATE STRUCTURE

In order to encode language in the kind of predicated logic LISAese requires, we need to identify predicate roles and the objects which fill them. In the simplest case, we may be presented with text such as "Bob loves Jill". In which there is one predicate with two roles, agent and patient, filled by "Bob" and "Jill" respectively. As mentioned earlier, this structure becomes more difficult when predicates fill the roles of other predicates as in "Jill knows Bob loves her". In this later case, the structure we hope to capture is that "Jill" is the agent and *love* is the patient of *know*. To discover these attachments, we may employ an NLP technique called Semantic Role Labeling (SRL). SRL identifies predicates and their roles as well as portions of the text which fill those roles. Using SRL, we can label "Jill" as the agent and "Bob loves her" as the patient of *know*. Similarly, "Bob" is identified as the agent, and "her" the patient of *love*. For our work, we use the SRL engine laid out in Punyakanok, Roth, and Yih [24] which uses joint inference over several SRL systems and Integer Linear Programming for global constraint satisfaction to optimize its labeling. After using our SRL engine, we have the following structural encoding: *know*(Jill, *love*(Bob, her)). This is nearly enough to properly structure the input for LISA since we are able to encode the predicates in a LISA's logical form and are able to handle recursive references to predicates as arguments to other predicates. The last remaining piece is to properly associate "Jill" with "her". In order to achieve this, we use another NLP technique called 'co-reference resolution' [18]. Co-reference resolution associates multiple references to the same entity throughout a text. Using this technique, we are able to associate "her" with "Jill", yielding our final representation: *know*(Jill, *love*(Bob, Jill)).

The automated structural encoding, along with the semantic encoding, is sufficient to produce functional LISAese without the involvement of any hand-coding and little modeler input. However, this automatic encoding is useless if LISA is not able to function on the resulting LISAese. In order to test this, we explore three benchmark simulations LISA has successfully completed in the past: Latin to Logic, Love Triangle, and Driving a Vehicle.

4 SIMULATIONS

To test our automated representations, we will compare LISA's discovered mappings and inferences on them against the hand-coded LISAese. Since our automatic encoding produces several hundred semantics for each object and role, we have omitted them from this paper. However, since there were some differences in some of the structural representations between the hand-coded and automatic representations, we have provided both for each benchmark below.

For "Latin to Logic"[14], the benchmark representation is shown below:

Analog 1:
is_incomplete(Second_Order_Logic)

Analog 2:
is_self_referential(Natural_Language)
has_unprovable_statement(Natural_Language)
is_incomplete(Natural_Language)

LISA can use this produced representation to find the analogy between Second Order Logic and Natural Language and infer that Second Order Logic has unprovable statements and that it is incomplete.

In order to test our automatic representation, we need to identify English sentences which convey a similar meaning. Running LISA over the representations generated by these sentences, we can check if it produces the correct mappings and inferences. For that purpose, we chose the following stories: "Second Order Logic is incomplete." and "Latin is able to self reference. Latin proves and disproves a statement. Latin is incomplete." Using the automatic representational system described here, we produced the following representation:

Analog 1:
be(Second_Order_Logic, incomplete)

Analog 2:
be(Latin, able_to_self_reference)
prove(Latin, a_statement)
disprove(Latin, a_statement)
be(Latin, incomplete)

Running LISA on this representation does in fact produce a mapping between Second Order Logic and Latin. LISA makes both of the desired inferences, namely that Second Order Logic is self referential and that it can prove and disprove a statement. Worth noting is that the structure generated by our automated system is quite different from that of the original representation. However, the correct mapping and inference was still produced.

For "Love Triangle" [12] the hand-coded benchmark structure and the automatic structural encoding were identical, and it is shown below:

Analog 1:
love(Sally, Jack)

love(Jack, Megan)
hate(Sally, Megan)

Analog 2:
love(John, Mary)
love(Mary, Bob)

In order to produce this representation automatically, Analog 1 was generated from the sentences "Sally loves Jack. Jack loves Megan. Sally hates Megan." and Analog 2 from "John loves Mary. Mary loves Bob".

"Latin to Logic" is the easiest of our three benchmarks since the structure is simple and semantic similarity alone is enough inform mapping. In "Love Triangle", while the structure remains simplistic, the object semantics are inversely correlated with the ideal mapping. That ideal mapping is from "Sally"→"John", "Jack"→"Mary", and "Megan"→"Bob", which is counter-indicated by semantic similarity on the subset of semantics corresponding to gender. In the hand-coded version, LISA finds this ideal mapping and produces the correct inference, namely *hates*(John, Bob) in Analog 2. After running LISA on the automatically produced LISAese, the same mapping and inference was found.

Lastly, we will look at the most complicated benchmark, "Driving a Vehicle" [12]. Its hand coded structure is shown below:

Analog 1:
has(Joan, car)
want(Joan, goto(Joan, airport))

Analog 2:
has(Sam, car)
want(Sam, goto(Sam, beach))
drive(Sam, car, beach)

The automatic encoding produced a very similar structure:
Analog 1:
have(Joan, a_car)
want(Joan, go(Joan, the_airport))

Analog 2:
have(Sam, a_jeep)
want(Sam, go(Sam, to_the_beach))
drive(Sam, a_jeep, to_the_beach)

To produce this, the NLP pre-processor was given "Joan has a car. She wants to go to the airport." for Analog 1 and "Sam has a jeep. He wants to go the beach. He drives the jeep to the beach." for Analog 2.

On both the hand-coded and auto-coded LISAese, LISA found the correct mapping that "Joan" is like "Sam" and the "jeep" is like the "car". LISA also managed to produce the correct inference that Joan drives her car to the airport.

5 CONCLUSION

Using NLP techniques to pre-process and encode text into LISAese has proven to be a fruitful approach to incorporating the encoding process into LISA as a model. With the incorporation of this linguistic front-end, LISA is now the first computational model of analogy capable of encoding simple open-domain text and performing analogical mapping and inference over it. More importantly, the LISA model no longer needs to rely on hand-coded knowledge representations. With this, it is now clearer how LISA's successes as a model reflect its fundamental tenets rather than the representational and modeling choices made by the modeler.

6 FUTURE WORK

We hope to improve both the semantic and structural encoding in the future with better semantic libraries and relational capture. For object semantics, we can use sparse over-complete vectors [4] for the word embeddings, since it has previously been shown that LISA performs better over sparse encodings. For predicate semantics, we can explore role specific semantics so that predicate role semantics can overlap between labeled roles (some agents overlap with some patients). Towards that end, we intend to explore several different tracks for embedding. We will look at PropBank [15] labels for verb specific roles and use the embeddings of the words in their labels (agent of *love* is "lover", patient of *love* is "loved"). We will also look at embedding the roles directly, either by forming role co-occurence chains and using Word2Vec on those chains directly, or by replacing the spans of text by their SRL label and running Word2Vec over the replaced text. However, regardless of what embedding techniques we use, the representation technique as we've described it falls pray to a common word embedding weakness – inability to differentiate phrasal cconstructs. That is, "the cat on the blanket" vs "the blanket on the cat" have the same semantic representation. This pitfall can be avoided by capturing only the head of noun phrase (with adjectives) and instead predicating any prepositional relationships contained within the phrase. We will also explore additional ways to extract structure from language in the form of explicitly stated intra-sentential cause and effect: "Bob loves Susan because she is kind." We will store the extracted information in "Cause-Effect" groups [13].

In addition to improvements of the encoding, we hope to expand our use of LISA. With the availability of computational resources as well as abundant text, auto-encoding LISAese allows for an explosion of analogical modeling. As research progresses, we hope to use auto-coded LISA's mappings and inferences as learning features on a range of traditional NLP tasks. Success in these domains would demonstrate the importance of analogy as a core cognitive capacity and its salience to a host of higher level computational tasks, for example schema generation [23][1], the Story Cloze Task [20, 21], story classification or even provide some insight into the Winograd Schema challenge [16].

ACKNOWLEDGMENTS

This material is based on research sponsored by the Air Force Research Laboratory, under agreement number FA9550-12-1-0003. The U.S. Government is authorized to reproduce and distribute reprints for Governmental purposes notwithstanding any copyright notation thereon.

The authors would also like to thank Hani Awni and Megan Emigh for their input throughout the process.

REFERENCES

[1] Niranjan Balasubramanian, Stephen Soderland, Oren Etzioni Mausam, and Oren Etzioni. 2013. Generating Coherent Event Schemas at Scale.. In *EMNLP*. 1721–1731.

[2] Tomai E. Forbus K. Klenk M. Dehghani, M. 2008. An Integrated Reasoning Approach to Moral Decision-Making. *AAAI Conference on Artificial Intelligence (AAAI)* Twenty-Third (2008).

[3] Brian Falkenhainer, Kenneth D Forbus, and Dedre Gentner. 1989. The structure-mapping engine: Algorithm and examples. *Artificial intelligence* 41, 1 (1989), 1–63.

[4] Manaal Faruqui, Yulia Tsvetkov, Dani Yogatama, Chris Dyer, and Noah A. Smith. 2015. Sparse Overcomplete Word Vector Representations. *CoRR* abs/1506.02004 (2015). http://arxiv.org/abs/1506.02004

[5] Scott E Friedman, Kenneth D Forbus, and Jason Taylor. Learning and Reasoning with Qualitative Models of Physical Behavior. (????).

[6] Dedre Gentner. 1983. Structure-mapping: A theoretical framework for analogy. *Cognitive science* 7, 2 (1983), 155–170.

[7] Dedre Gentner and Kenneth D Forbus. 2011. Computational models of analogy. *Wiley interdisciplinary reviews: cognitive science* 2, 3 (2011), 266–276.

[8] Mary L Gick and Keith J Holyoak. 1983. Schema induction and analogical transfer. *Cognitive psychology* 15, 1 (1983), 1–38.

[9] Keith J Holyoak and Paul Thagard. 1989. Analogical mapping by constraint satisfaction. *Cognitive science* 13, 3 (1989), 295–355.

[10] Keith James Holyoak and Paul Thagard. 1995. *Mental leaps.*

[11] John E Hummel and Keith J Holyoak. 1997. Distributed representations of structure: a theory of analogical access and mapping. *Psychological Review* 104, 3 (1997), 427.

[12] John E Hummel and Keith J Holyoak. 2003. A symbolic-connectionist theory of relational inference and generalization. *Psychological review* 110, 2 (2003), 220.

[13] John E Hummel and David H Landy. 2009. From analogy to explanation: relaxing the 1: 1 mapping constraint very carefully. In *New Frontiers in Analogy Research: Proceedings of the Second International Conference on Analogy.* New Bulgarian University, 211–221.

[14] John E Hummel, John Licato, and Selmer Bringsjord. 2014. Analogy, explanation, and proof. *Frontiers in human neuroscience* 8 (2014).

[15] Paul Kingsbury and Martha Palmer. 2002. From TreeBank to PropBank.. In *LREC.* Citeseer.

[16] Hector J Levesque, Ernest Davis, and Leora Morgenstern. 2011. The Winograd schema challenge.. In *AAAI Spring Symposium: Logical Formalizations of Commonsense Reasoning,* Vol. 46. 47.

[17] Hongjing Lu, Alan L Yuille, Mimi Liljeholm, Patricia W Cheng, and Keith J Holyoak. 2008. Bayesian generic priors for causal learning. *Psychological review* 115, 4 (2008), 955.

[18] Christopher D. Manning, Mihai Surdeanu, John Bauer, Jenny Finkel, Steven J. Bethard, and David McClosky. 2014. The Stanford CoreNLP Natural Language Processing Toolkit. In *Proceedings of 52nd Annual Meeting of the Association for Computational Linguistics: System Demonstrations.* 55–60. http://www.aclweb.org/anthology/P/P14/P14-5010

[19] Tomas Mikolov, Ilya Sutskever, Kai Chen, Greg S Corrado, and Jeff Dean. 2013. Distributed representations of words and phrases and their compositionality. In *Advances in neural information processing systems.* 3111–3119.

[20] Nasrin Mostafazadeh, Nathanael Chambers, Xiaodong He, Devi Parikh, Dhruv Batra, Lucy Vanderwende, Pushmeet Kohli, and James Allen. 2016. A corpus and cloze evaluation for deeper understanding of commonsense stories. *Proceedings of NAACL HLT, San Diego, California, June. Association for Computational Linguistics* (2016).

[21] Nasrin Mostafazadeh, Lucy Vanderwende, Wen-tau Yih, Pushmeet Kohli, and James Allen. 2016. Story Cloze Evaluator: Vector Space Representation Evaluation by Predicting What Happens Next. *ACL 2016* (2016), 24.

[22] Derek C Penn, Keith J Holyoak, and Daniel J Povinelli. 2008. Darwin's mistake: Explaining the discontinuity between human and nonhuman minds. *Behavioral and Brain Sciences* 31, 02 (2008), 109–130.

[23] Karl Pichotta and Raymond J Mooney. 2016. Statistical Script Learning with Recurrent Neural Networks. *EMNLP 2016* (2016), 11.

[24] V. Punyakanok, D. Roth, and W. Yih. 2008. The Importance of Syntactic Parsing and Inference in Semantic Role Labeling. *Computational Linguistics* 34, 2 (2008). http://cogcomp.cs.illinois.edu/papers/PunyakanokRoYi07.pdf

Transfer Learning of Temporal Information for Driver Action Classification

Joseph Lemley
National University of Ireland Galway
College of Engineering and Informatics
Galway, Ireland
j.lemley2@nuigalway.ie

Shabab Bazrafkan
National University of Ireland Galway
College of Engineering and Informatics
Galway, Ireland
S.Bazrafkan1@nuigalway.ie

Peter Corcoran
National University of Ireland Galway
College of Engineering and Informatics
Galway, Ireland
peter.corcoran@nuigalway.ie

ABSTRACT

Correct classification of image data can depend on features learned in multiple sequential frames. We focus on the problem of learning action from video data with an emphasis on driver behavior monitoring. An insufficient quantity of high quality labeled data is a major problem in machine learning research. This is especially true when deep neural networks are used. Although some sufficiently large, general purpose image databases exist for action recognition, most of these are limited to single frames. This kind of data requires that the action recognition task is applied regardless of the temporal information (information from previous and next frames of a video sequence). In this paper, we show that temporal information is useful for accurate classification of video and that the temporal information in lower layers of a convolutional neural network can successfully be transferred from one network to another to greatly improve performance on the driver behavior monitoring task.

KEYWORDS

Deep Learning, Transfer Learning, Action Recognition

1 INTRODUCTION

In recent years, deep learning has become ubiquitous for image classification, with some results exceeding human accuracy for certain tasks. With few exceptions, these impressive results have been limited to a set of tasks for which a single picture provides all the information required to easily distinguish between classes and essentially ignore any time element for the recognition task.

As we approach the limits of frame-based methods, there is a desire to further improve deep learning algorithms by utilizing temporal information, which is information between multiple frames taken sequentially to give a more complete idea of what is happening. Using a single frame, it is trivial to train a classifier to determine if a person is holding a glass, but difficult or impossible to train a classifier to understand if the glass is being picked up or put down. Even distinguishing jogging from walking can be difficult without a time component.

For this more refined level of visual understanding, we need machine learning models that can learn temporal information and information about frame content at the same time. We also need quality labeled data of sufficient size to prevent overfitting. Much work has been done recently to address these issues (described in the related work section below), but there is still a lack of quality data for use in many practical applications. For example, there are no publicly available databases for driver monitoring that are of sufficient size to train a deep neural network from scratch.

The largest database for driver behavior monitoring that we could find is the "Distracted Driver Dataset", provided as part of a Kaggle challenge in mid-2016. Although this database is intended for single frame classification, it is possible to identify the original frame sequences from which movies can be created. These movies can then be used for learning a limited amount of temporal information.

In this paper, we address two questions:

"Can temporal information be used to improve accurate classification of driver actions?" and "Can low-level information about temporal information from an unrelated problem be successfully used to better understand driver actions in videos?"

In the next session, we provide brief background information on Recurrent Neural networks and 3D CNN's for the interested reader. In section three, we present related work. In sections 4, 5, and 6, we present the methods, experiments, and results.

MAICS'2017, Fort Wayne Indiana

2 BACKGROUND

In this section, we provide a brief overview of the key neural network architectures used in this work, including recurrent neural networks, long short term neural networks, convolutional neural networks and 3D convolutional neural networks. We also briefly describe transfer learning. Readers with a knowledge of these topics are encouraged to skip to the Related Work section below.

2.1 RNN (Recurrent Neural Network)

Recurrent neural networks(RNN) [19] are a highly flexible network architecture frequently used to model time series data, such as a sequence of frames from a video. RNNs remember the input at a previous stage and make a decision for the present input based on the sequence of the previous data. The hidden state of an RNN is calculated based on the state of the network at each sequence. The hidden state can be considered the memory. RNNs have had great success in speech and video recognition and are sometimes combined with convolutional layers [11].

2.2 LSTM (Long Short Term Memory)

LSTMs [5] are a type of RNN that are designed with both long and short term memory which permits the modeling of more complex time series. LSTMs include at least 3 gates which control the way information flows.

2.3 CNN(Convolutional Neural Networks)

Convolutional Neural networks (CNNs) were popularized by lecun et al. [9], who used them successfully for handwritten digit classification. These networks are inspired by the organization of the visual cortex and allow spatial information to be more efficiently learned. Convolutional Neural Networks can be used on input of any number of dimensions but due to their success in pictures, are most popularly implemented for 2D input plus color channels. Other popular types of CNN's include 1D CNNs which are commonly used for time series and 3D CNNs which can be used for volumetric data or time series data where the third dimension represents either spatial frames or temporal frames [11].

2.4 Transfer Learning

Transfer learning is the process of transferring knowledge that has already been learned by one neural network into another one. This is often accomplished by copying the learned weights and biases from one or more layers of a fully trained network to a different network. Transfer learning can be used to overcome overfitting issues and to speed up the training process for a related task.

3 RELATED WORK

In 2008, before the recent wave of deep learning, Klaser et al. [8] used 3D HOG (Histogram of Oriented Gradients) descriptors and showed that 3D gradients were able to assist in understanding action from videos. More modern approaches to action classification from videos are primarily based on 3D convolutional neural networks (CNN) or recurrent neural networks (RNN) with some convolutional component or a combination of the two. 3D CNNs have been shown to capture short-term temporal information.

For example, [18] makes a compelling case for the use of 3D CNNs for understanding video data. Their method, which they named C3D, compared favorably to other published results on 5 of 6 generic action datasets used. They also showed that their network learns information about both motion and appearance, first learning appearance and then motion. One problem with this design is that only relatively short action sequences (16 frames) can be learned.

Addressing this problem, Lei, et al. [10] present an interesting approach to action recognition, they combine a 3D convolutional neural network with a hidden Markov model (HMM) and show that their method compares favorably with other methods. This paper adds support to the idea that 3D convolutions are important to understanding short-term temporal information about movement and the need for another mechanic (RNN, HMM, etc) to understand long-term context (more than a few frames)

Keeping on the theme of combining 3D CNN with a network that is able to learn long-term information, Molchanov et al. [12] combined a 3D convolutional neural network with a recurrent neural network to classify short video clips of hand gestures, reporting excellent results.

Donahue et al. introduced a new architecture called LRCN (Long-term Recurrent Convolutional Networks) that combines RNNs with CNNs [2]. Specifically, they show how to train and optimize a long-term RNN model that can account for temporal information in video data. They evaluate their method on the UCF - 101, a database that contains over 12,000 videos with 101 human action classes [16]
.

Another new architecture that combines LSTM with convolutions is introduced in "A Machine Learning Approach for Precipitation Nowcasting" [20]. Although the focus of their paper is forecasting precipitation, their method is generally applicable to the task of gathering long and short term time information from video sequences.

In [21], convolutional temporal pooling is used with a long short term memory (LSTM) network to produce state of the art results. In the same year, [2] used a convolutional LSTM to narrate videos.

Because convolutions on 3D data are time intensive, there have been attempts to combine 2D networks while retaining temporal information. For example, in [3], Feichtenhofer et al. train separate CNNs for motion and appearance and report very good results.

Addressing the problem of insufficient data to train a neural network, [7] introduced a large, automatically generated, database gathered from YouTube clips called the sport 1M dataset. They showed that a transfer learning approach is effective at gaining accuracy on UCF 101 when a network is first trained on sports 1M.

Object proposal networks, specifically fast/faster R-CNNs (region-based convolutional neural networks) have been used successfully as in [14],and [22], for action recognition, and seem to work especially well in cases where there is not enough data to train a full network. Hoang, et al. used this method for detecting cell phone usage and hands on steering wheel detection in [4].

Just as there are attempts to classify behavior without exploiting temporal information, there are also ways of addressing the problem of driver behavior monitoring that do not depend on spatial information but instead use only temporal information. For example, [6] compared LSTM, RNN, logistic regression, and deep neural networks, for detecting driver confusion. Rather than using images, that paper uses multimodal sensor data to assess driver confusion. They found that LSTM outperforms the other models, likely because some long-term information is important for this task. Similarly, [13] uses human motion, as given by cell phone sensors, as a biometric, and an RNN was utilized to process sensor signals.

4 METHODS

Experiments were conducted on NVIDIA Titan X GPU's running a pascal architecture with python 2.7, using the Theano [17] and Keras [1].

4.1 Data Preparation

4.1.1 Driver Monitoring Dataset. The Distracted Driver Dataset was provided as part of a Kaggle Competition in 2016. The dataset was created by filming actors on a closed driving course engaging in various distracted and undistracted behaviors. It should be noted that these images were obtained in a controlled environment the car was not actually being driven. It was being pulled by a truck instead. The objective of the competition was to correctly classify still images into 10 categories.

The training set of the distracted driver database contains frames of 26 subjects displaying several of the following behaviors/actions:

(1) c0: safe driving

(2) c1: texting - right
(3) c2: talking on the phone - right
(4) c3: texting - left
(5) c4: talking on the phone - left
(6) c5: operating the radio
(7) c6: drinking
(8) c7: reaching behind
(9) c8: hair and makeup
(10) c9: talking to passenger

Although all the images in the supplied training set are still images, it is possible to reconstruct the original "movies" based on their order in the CSV file supplied with ground truth annotations.

While classifying frames for driver monitoring is an interesting problem, we wanted to see if we could learn anything from the temporal information in the movies. Instead of using individual frames as required for the competition, we created short movie clips, as we describe later. It is not possible to create such movies from the supplied testing set because sequence information was intentionally left out of it by the competition organizers.

First, we arranged the dataset into distinct subject, action segments ordered by time. The generated movies varied between 38 and 135 frames in length (average is about 101) for a total of 100 clips. Because the 3D convolutional neural network we were planning to experiment with requires a fixed frame size, we further processed the videos into fixed sized frames using the sliding time window method. For each of these segments, we create a series of 5, 10, 16, and 30 frame clips. Each clip is made using a sliding window starting with the first (subject, action) with a step equal to approximately 70% of the clip length to allow sufficient frame overlap. Appropriate action labels are applied to each clip.

In all experiments, 20 drivers are used for the training set and the remaining 6 for the validation set. Due to the small size of this database, we did not feel that further dividing the data into a smaller test set would be reasonable.

In our experiments, we used 4 variations of these:

(1) Grayscale video: All videos of the 26 drivers were reduced to 60×80 Grayscale images.
(2) Color video: All videos of the 26 drivers were reduced to 112×112 full color.
(3) Grayscale frames: All frames of the 26 drivers were reduced to 60×80 Grayscale images.
(4) Color Frames: All frames of the 26 drivers were reduced $112 \times' 112$ Grayscale images.

Due to copyright restrictions, we are unable to include examples of these images in this paper, but the interested reader may view them by visiting the relevant competition at:

https://www.kaggle.com/c/state-farm-distracted-driver-detection

4.2 Augmentation

In experiments where augmentation was applied, the ImageDataGenerator class within Keras was used. This class is used to dynamically create augmented images during training given a set of parameters. Since the standard implementation of ImageDataGenerator only supports 2D data, we subclassed it to properly apply the transformations to video data. This modification involved ensuring that the same transformation was applied to every frame of a clip instead of treating each frame as an individual image with a potentially different transformation.

5 EXPERIMENTS

In this section, we describe 10 experiments on the distracted driver database. The experiments were designed to allow comparison between networks that use temporal information (LSTM, 3D CNN, etc) and networks that ignore it (2D CNN). The last experiments are designed to measure the improvement that is achieved by transfer learning.

5.1 2D experiments

We train an implementation of VGG-16 [15] from scratch on the distracted driver dataset in Keras with a learning rate of 0.001. Our loss function was categorical cross entropy and our output class predictions were obtained from a final softmax layer.

We then repeated our experiments on our grayscale dataset with rotation, translation, and feature normalization. By feature normalization, we mean that the inputs are divided by the standard deviation of the dataset.

5.2 Very Small CNNs and LSTMs

In this set of experiments, we utilized several small (one or two layer) configurations of CNN+LSTM, 3DCNN +LSTM, and 3DCNN.

For these experiments, the LSTM used is the one described by [20], implemented in Keras as ConvLSTM2D.

Three networks were evaluated:

Network 1: 3DCNN followed by Softmax (Num_Classes)

One 3D convolution with 16 filters and a kernel size of 3,3,3 followed by a softmax layer.

Network 2: LSTM followed by 3DCNN $\rightarrow$ Softmax (Num_Classes)

One LSTM with time length 16, and a 3x3x3 convolution kernel followed by one 3D convolutional layer with 16 filters and a kernel size of 3,3,3 ending with a softmax layer.

Network 3: 3DCNN followed by LSTM $\rightarrow$ Softmax (Num_Classes)

One 3D convolutional layer with 16 filters and a kernel size of 3,3,3 followed by one LSTM with time length 16, and a 3x3x3 convolution ending with a softmax layer.

All three experiments used a learning rate of 0.001 with nestrov momentum as 0.95. Categorical crossentropy was our loss function and stochastic gradient descent as the training method.

These experiments were then repeated with the grayscale video database.

5.3 Experiments with small 3DCNN architectures

Since the distracted driver dataset has a strong tendency to overfit due to the limited number of subjects, we designed a network and training strategy that would delay overfitting for as long as possible and prevent fast convergence. This involved using a high learning rate and large batch size, resulting in a training method that would allow the network to jump over minima. We also observed that the overfitting came from very low level information, so we restricted the first layer to only 8 features. The network architecture was designed as follows:

(1) input layer with 15 frames, a width and height of 112.

(2) 3D Convolutional Layer(RELU). 8 filters with size: 3, 3, 3
(3) 3D Max pooling operator with size: (2,2,2)
(4) 3D Convolutional Layer(RELU). 16 filters with size: 3, 3, 3
(5) 3D Max pooling operator with size: (2,2,2)
(6) 3D Convolutional Layer(RELU). 32 filters with size: 3, 3, 3
(7) 3D Max pooling operator with size: (2,2,2)
(8) 3D Convolutional Layer(RELU). 64 filters with size: 3, 3, 3
(9) 3D Convolutional Layer(RELU). 128 filters with size: 3, 3, 3
(10) 3D Convolutional Layer(RELU). 256 filters with size: 3, 3, 3
(11) Fully connected Layer (RELU) with 4096 units.
(12) Dropout with a probability of 0.5
(13) Fully connected Layer (RELU) with 4096 units.
(14) Dropout with a probability of 0.5
(15) Softmax with 10 units (one for each of the 10 action classes in the Distracted Driver Dataset)

A learning rate of 0.001 with nestrov momentum as 0.95 and categorical crossentropy as the loss function was used. Stochastic gradient descent was used as the optimizer.

Variations with additional dropout and Batch Normalization layers were also evaluated, but only increased the overfitting and decreased validation accuracy.

These experiments were repeated with rotation, translation, and featurewise normalization.

5.4 C3D trained from scratch

In this experiment, we trained a C3D [18] from scratch on the distracted driver dataset. Since C3D was designed to use 16 frame color video clips of size 112 X 112 we used the color video dataset described previously. As with previous experiments, a learning rate of 0.001 with nestrov momentum as 0.95 was used with categorical crosentropy and gradient descent.

5.5 Transfer Learning with C3D

Since other approaches to reducing the overfitting problem were of limited success, we tried a transfer learning approach. The idea is to use pretrained weights from an existing network, trained for a more generic action recognition task, and then to tune them with the Distracted Driver training set.

We used a pretrained 3CD on the sports 1-M dataset, included the architecture, and trained weights for The Sports-1M dataset in a GitHub repository as a 3D CNN. They reported very good results at capturing temporal information using their 3D CNN, so it seemed like a natural place to start.

In this experiment, we investigate the use of transfer learning to overcome the overfitting problem identified in the previous cases. In the previous experiments, the first layers were identified as being the primary source of overfitting, so we wanted to try two transfer learning approaches.

The first transfer learning approach we tried was to train the C3D network with a very low learning rate of 0.0001 without freezing any layers with these pretrained weights.

We then used an alternate transfer learning approach where we trained only on the final softmax layer, freezing the learning rate of the first layers.

Since we previously identified the first layers as being the greatest source of overfitting, we repeated this experiment freezing only the first five layers, and then repeated it again with only the first two layers frozen.

6 RESULTS

In this section, we report the results of the experiments in the previous section. The experiments with the best results are listed in table 1. Since overfitting is found to be the primary cause of validation error in most experiments, we also show details about the loss and accuracy in tables 2 and 3 before and after we reach 100% on the training set.

6.1 2D experiments

The best 2D accuracy we obtain without augmentation is 30% using a modified VGG 16. [15]

Interestingly, randomly augmenting the 2D dataset with shifts of up to 10% in the horizontal or vertical direction is enough to increase the accuracy from 30% to 46.3%. Adding rotation (5 or 15 degrees) lowered accuracy and allowing shifts of greater than 10% also decreased accuracy.

6.2 Very Small CNNs and LSTMs

In this set of experiments, we used 3D convolutional LSTM of 3 different configurations that have been widely cited in the literature as being effective for this task.

Despite widely different architectures, these networks all quickly resulted in an overfit network with 100% accuracy on the training set and roughly 10% accuracy on the validation set, often within the first 10 epochs.

When trained on reduced size grayscale data the results were similar but slightly better with the best accuracy on the validation set at around 16%.

The goal of this set of experiments was to identify the network architecture which would be most promising for measuring the impact of temporal information for the driver monitoring task, but due to the overfitting issue, we can not reach any conclusions from these 3 experiments.

6.3 Experiments with small 3DCNN architectures

Here we report the results of our experiment with small 3DCNN, which was designed to reduce overfitting by forcing the network to concentrate on more general features and by limiting the number of low level features.

This network achieved an accuracy of 39.57% on the validation set which is better than the 2D VGG 16 inspired network, which had been shown to be effective at this task in the Distracted Driver Competition without manual augmentation, but not better than the 2D VGG when augmented data was provided.

Variations with additional dropout and Batch Normalization layers were also evaluated, but only increased the overfitting and decreased validation accuracy.

None of the augmentation strategies that were found to improve accuracy for the 2D network (translation, rotation, featurewise normalization) increased accuracy for this small 3DCNN architecture.

Table 1: Top performing approaches (>= 30%)

Approach	Accuracy
Transfer learning on 3D CNN. First 2 layers frozen	73.35%
Transfer learning on 3D CNN. First 5 layers frozen	60%
2D VGG 16 with augmentation	46%
3D CNN without augmentation	39.57%
2D VGG 16 without augmentation	30%

Table 2: The best result on the validation set before reaching 100% on the training set was:

Train loss*	Val loss	Train Accuracy	Val Accuracy
0.0359	0.9004	0.9984	0.7273

Table 3: The best results on the validation set after reaching 100% on the training set was

Train loss*	Val loss	Train Accuracy	Val Accuracy
0.0173	0.8563	1	0.7335

6.4 C3D trained from scratch

When we trained the C3D from scratch on the distracted driver dataset, the results were: 100% accuracy on the training set. 12% accuracy on the validation set.

6.5 Transfer Learning with C3D

The first experiment was to train the pretrained 3CD network at a very low learning rate using the driver monitoring dataset. This still resulted in overfitting and unsatisfactory results on the validation set (13%).

The next and most successful transfer learning approach we used was to train only on the last few layers, freezing the learning rate of the first layers. When the first 5 layers were frozen, we achieved 60% on the validation set, which is a significant improvement over the previous results. Further refinement (freezing just the first 2 layers) allowed us to achieve over 72% accuracy on the validation set.

*in all cases loss is the categorical cross-entropy calculated on an entire batch.

7 DISCUSSION

When training a CNN, Information flows in a cone-shaped manner (see figure 1). This is a property of the convolution and pooling operations, which merge and mix the information of several pixels (a window of pixels) into a single value. In the early layers of the convolutional network, each row of the layer corresponds to a small spatial portion of the input image. This means that in these early layers, the network is restricted to the details and low-level features of the input data.

This is also the case for temporal information where time is the depth dimension. In the early stages of the 3D network, the kernels are able to observe a very short part of the input time sequence data. i.e., the beginning layers of the network are processing a short time sequence from a small spatial portion of the input data. This could correspond to small finger movement, or eye blinking for example. These movements are common among a wide variety of human activities like swimming or holding a cell phone. This is the main reason a transfer learning approach that involved freezing the first two layers gave significantly better results than other methods (See figure 2). In our presented approach, the network trained on the sports 1m dataset (a database of YouTube videos focused on sports) was tuned for the driver monitoring task, but the first two layers were frozen during the tuning procedure. The success of these features indicates that the early stage features learned from sports activity classification are generic enough to be used for other human activities.

These features represent the most detailed activities, which are the same for a wide variety of human behaviors. Figure 1 shows that by going deeper in network layers, each row of a convolutional layer is observing a wider and larger temporal and spatial region of the input data.

This suggests that the kernels in these later layers are dealing with coarser features of the input data, which includes specific movements or behaviors of the subject in the input movie stream. This explains why tuning later layers for our specific task converged to a reasonable approximation of driver activities. In figure 2, network A is the C3D network trained on the sports 1M dataset and the network B is the presented network for driver activity classification. As you can see, the parameters from the first two layers of the network A were transferred to network B and the rest of the network was tuned for our task.

This is our explanation of the results obtained by a transfer learning approach.

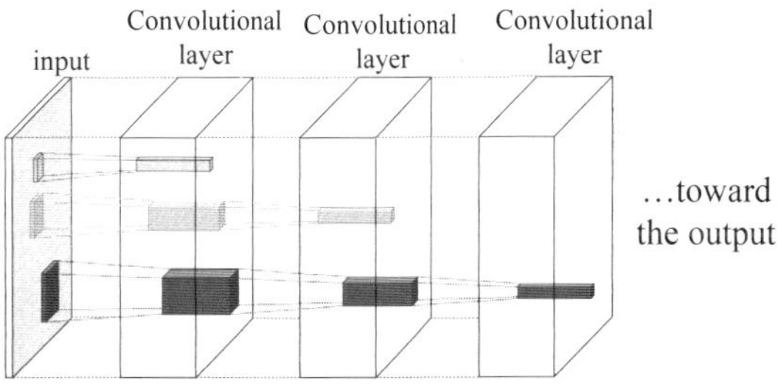

Figure 1: Illustration of cone shape of information flow in convolutional neural networks.

8 CONCLUSIONS

We have shown that the lower level filters learned by a 3D CNN can be used to greatly increase the accuracy on small datasets of drivers for the driver behavior classification task. It is not obvious that the first layers of a network trained for identifying actions in sports videos, such as basketball and swimming, could also be used to distinguish between distracted driver actions like left and right hand cell phone use or speaking with a passenger.

We have also shown that temporal information can be used to increase accuracy for the driver behavior monitoring task over a network that does not use such temporal information.

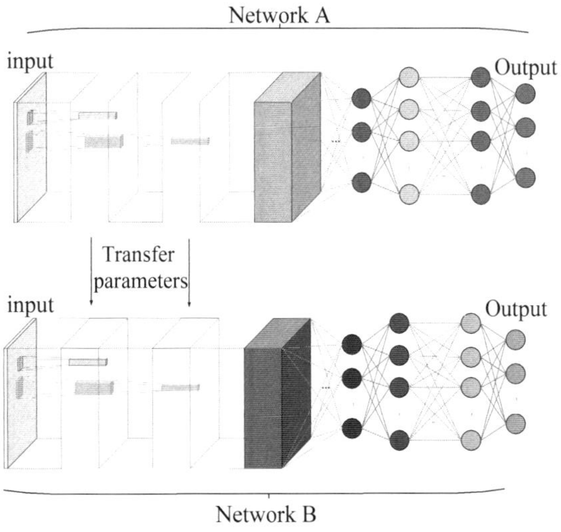

Figure 2: Illustration of transfer learning concept where the first layers in network A and network B are the same.

At a very low level, the action of Moving fingers and heads may not be substantially different between different action recognition problems for convolutional neural networks. In our experiments, using any more than the first two layers decreased accuracy.

Given the shortage of well-labeled task-specific datasets for action recognition, this is an encouraging result.

ACKNOWLEDGMENTS

This research is funded under the SFI Strategic Partnership Program by Science Foundation Ireland (SFI) and FotoNation Ltd. Project ID: 13/SPP/I2868 on Next Generation Imaging for Smartphone and Embedded Platforms. This work is also supported by an Irish Research Council Employment Based Programme Award. Project ID: EBPPG/2016/280.

We gratefully acknowledge the support of NVIDIA Corporation for the donation of a Titan X GPU used for this research.

REFERENCES

[1] François Chollet. 2015. Keras. https://github.com/fchollet/keras. (2015).

[2] Jeffrey Donahue, Lisa Anne Hendricks, Sergio Guadarrama, Marcus Rohrbach, Subhashini Venugopalan, Kate Saenko, and Trevor Darrell. 2015. Long-term recurrent convolutional networks for visual recognition and description. In *Proceedings of the IEEE conference on computer vision and pattern recognition.* 2625–2634.

[3] Christoph Feichtenhofer, Axel Pinz, and Andrew Zisserman. 2016. Convolutional two-stream network fusion for video action recognition. In *Proceedings of the IEEE Conference on Computer Vision and Pattern Recognition.* 1933–1941.

[4] T Hoang Ngan Le, Yutong Zheng, Chenchen Zhu, Khoa Luu, and Marios Savvides. 2016. Multiple Scale Faster-RCNN Approach to Driver's Cell-Phone Usage and Hands on Steering Wheel Detection. In *Proceedings of the IEEE Conference on Computer Vision and Pattern Recognition Workshops.* 46–53.

[5] Sepp Hochreiter and Jürgen Schmidhuber. 1997. Long short-term memory. *Neural computation* 9, 8 (1997), 1735–1780.

[6] Chiori Hori, Shinji Watanabe, Takaaki Hori, Bret A Harsham, JohnR Hershey, Yusuke Koji, Yoichi Fujii, and Yuki Furumoto. 2016. Driver confusion status detection using recurrent neural networks. In *Multimedia and Expo (ICME), 2016 IEEE International Conference on.* IEEE, 1–6.

[7] Andrej Karpathy, George Toderici, Sanketh Shetty, Thomas Leung, Rahul Sukthankar, and Li Fei-Fei. 2014. Large-scale video classification with convolutional neural networks. In *Proceedings of the IEEE conference on Computer Vision and Pattern Recognition.* 1725–1732.

[8] Alexander Klaser, Marcin Marsza lek, and Cordelia Schmid. 2008. A spatio-temporal descriptor based on 3d-gradients. In *BMVC 2008-19th British Machine Vision Conference.* British Machine Vision Association, 275–1.

[9] Yann LeCun, Bernhard Boser, John S Denker, Donnie Henderson, Richard E Howard, Wayne Hubbard, and Lawrence D Jackel. 1989. Backpropagation applied to handwritten zip code recognition. *Neural computation* 1, 4 (1989), 541–551.

[10] Jun Lei, Guohui Li, Jun Zhang, Qiang Guo, and Dan Tu. 2016. Continuous action segmentation and recognition using hybrid convolutional neural network-hidden Markov model model. *IET Computer Vision* 10, 6 (2016), 537–544.

[11] Joe Lemley, Shabab Bazrafkan, and Peter Corcoran. 2017. Deep Learning for Consumer Devices and Services: Pushing the limits for machine learning, artificial intelligence, and computer vision. *IEEE Consumer Electronics Magazine* 6, 2 (2017), 48–56.

[12] Pavlo Molchanov, Xiaodong Yang, Shalini Gupta, Kihwan Kim, Stephen Tyree, and Jan Kautz. 2016. Online detection and classification of dynamic hand gestures with recurrent 3d convolutional neural network. In *Proceedings of the IEEE Conference on Computer Vision and Pattern Recognition.* 4207–4215.

[13] Natalia Neverova, Christian Wolf, Griffin Lacey, Lex Fridman, Deepak Chandra, Brandon Barbello, and Graham Taylor. 2016. Learning human identity from motion patterns. *IEEE Access* 4 (2016), 1810–1820.

[14] Shaoqing Ren, Kaiming He, Ross Girshick, and Jian Sun. 2015. Faster r-cnn: Towards real-time object detection with region proposal networks. In *Advances in neural information processing systems.* 91–99.

[15] Karen Simonyan and Andrew Zisserman. 2014. Very deep convolutional networks for large-scale image recognition. *arXiv preprint arXiv:1409.1556* (2014).

[16] Khurram Soomro, Amir Roshan Zamir, and Mubarak Shah. 2012. UCF101: A dataset of 101 human actions classes from videos in the wild. *arXiv preprint arXiv:1212.0402* (2012).

[17] Theano Development Team. 2016. Theano: A Python framework for fast computation of mathematical expressions. *arXiv e-prints* abs/1605.02688 (May 2016). http://arxiv.org/abs/1605.02688

[18] Du Tran, Lubomir Bourdev, Rob Fergus, Lorenzo Torresani, and Manohar Paluri. 2015. Learning spatiotemporal features with 3d convolutional networks. In *Proceedings of the IEEE International Conference on Computer Vision.* 4489–4497.

[19] DRGHR Williams and GE Hinton. 1986. Learning representations by back-propagating errors. *Nature* 323, 6088 (1986), 533–538.

[20] SHI Xingjian, Zhourong Chen, Hao Wang, Dit-Yan Yeung, Wai-Kin Wong, and Wang-chun Woo. 2015. Convolutional LSTM network: A machine learning approach for precipitation nowcasting. In *Advances in Neural Information Processing Systems.* 802–810.

[21] Joe Yue-Hei Ng, Matthew Hausknecht, Sudheendra Vijayanarasimhan, Oriol Vinyals, Rajat Monga, and George Toderici. 2015. Beyond short snippets: Deep networks for video classification. In *Proceedings of the IEEE conference on computer vision and pattern recognition.* 4694–4702.

[22] Liliang Zhang, Liang Lin, Xiaodan Liang, and Kaiming He. 2016. Is Faster R-CNN Doing Well for Pedestrian Detection?. In *European Conference on Computer Vision.* Springer, 443–457.

Learning Photography Aesthetics with Deep CNNs

Gautam Malu*
International Institute of Information Technology, Hyderabad
Hyderabad, India
gautam.malu@research.iiit.ac.in

Raju S. Bapi
International Institute of Information Technology, Hyderabad
& University of Hyderabad
Hyderabad, India
raju.bapi@iiit.ac.in

Bipin Indurkhya
International Institute of Information Technology, Hyderabad
Hyderabad, India
bipin@iiit.ac.in

ABSTRACT

Automatic photo aesthetic assessment is a challenging artificial intelligence task. Existing computational approaches have focused on modeling a single aesthetic score or class (good or bad photo), however these do not provide any details on why the photograph is good or bad; or which attributes contribute to the quality of the photograph. To obtain both accuracy and human-interpretability, we advocate learning the aesthetic attributes along with the prediction of the overall score. For this purpose, We propose a novel multi-task deep convolution neural network (DCNN), which jointly learns eight aesthetic attributes along with the overall aesthetic score. We report near-human performance in the prediction of the overall aesthetic score. To understand the internal representation of these attributes in the learned model, we also develop the visualization technique using back propagation of gradients. These visualizations highlight the important image regions for the corresponding attributes, thus providing insights about model's understanding of these attributes. We showcase the diversity and complexity associated with different attributes through a qualitative analysis of the activation maps.

KEYWORDS

Photography, Aesthetics, Aesthetic Attributes, Deep Convolution Neural Network, Residual Networks

1 INTRODUCTION

Aesthetics is the study of science behind the concept and perception of beauty. Although aesthetics of photograph is subjective, some aspect of its depends on the standard photography practices and general visual design rules. With the ever increasing volume of digital photographs, automatic aesthetic assessment is becoming increasingly useful for various applications, such as a personal photo assistant, photo manager, photo enhancement, image retrieval etc. Conventionally, automatic aesthetic assessment tasks have been modeled as either a regression problem (single aesthetic score) [7, 8, 27] or as a classification problem (aesthetically good or bad photograph) [2, 13, 14].

*Corresponding author

MAICS'17, Purdue University Fort Wayne

DOI:

Intensive data driven approaches have made substantial progress in this task, although it is a very subjective and context dependent task. Earlier approaches used custom designed features based on photography rules (e.g., focus, color harmony, contrast, lighting, rule of thirds) and semantic information (e.g., human profile, scene category) from low level image descriptors (*e.g.* color histograms, wavelet analysis) [1, 2, 4, 9, 12, 15, 16, 21, 24] and generic image descriptors [19]. With the evolution of deep learning based techniques, recent approaches have introduced deep convolution neural networks (DCNN) in aesthetic assessment tasks [8, 10, 13, 14, 26].

Although these approaches give near-human performance in classifying whether a photograph is "good" or "bad", they do not give detailed insights or explanation for such claims. For example, if a photograph received a bad rating, one would not get any insights about the attributes (e.g., poor lighting, dull colors etc.) that led to that rating. We propose an approach in which we identify (eight) such attributes (such as Color Harmony, Depth of Field etc.) and report those along with the overall score. For this purpose, we propose a multi-task deep convolution network (*DCNN*) which simultaneously learns the eight aesthetic attributes along with the overall aesthetic score. We train and test our model on the recently released aesthetics and attribute database (*AADB*) [10]. Following are the eight attributes as mentioned in [10] (Figure 1):

(1) *Balancing Element* - Whether the image contains balanced elements.
(2) *Content* - Whether the image has good/interesting content.
(3) *Color Harmony* - Whether the overall color composition is harmonious.
(4) *Depth of Field* - Whether the image has shallow depth of field.
(5) *Light* - Whether the image has good/interesting lighting.
(6) *Object Emphasis* - Whether the image emphasizes foreground objects.
(7) *Rule of Thirds* - Whether the image follows rule of thirds principle. The rule of thirds involves dividing the photo into 9 parts with 2 vertical and 2 horizontal lines. The important elements and leading lines are placed on/near these these lines and intersections of these lines.
(8) *Vivid Color* - Whether the image has vivid colors, not necessarily harmonious colors.

We also develop attribute activation maps (Figure 3) for visualization of these attributes. These maps highlight the salient regions for the corresponding attribute, thus providing us insights about the representation of these attributes in our trained model.
In summary, followings are the main contributions of our paper:

Figure 1: Sample images taken from AADB for each attribute. top row: Highest rated images, bottom row: Lowest Rated Images. All images were padded to maintain aspect ratio for illustration purposes.

(1) We propose a novel deep learning based approach which simultaneously learns eight aesthetic attributes along with the overall score. These attributes enable us to provide more detailed feedback on automatic aesthetic assessment.
(2) We also develop localized representation of these attributes from our learned model. We call these *attribute activation maps* (Figure 3). These maps provide us more insights about model's interpretability of the attributes.

2 RELATED WORK

Most of the earlier works have used low-level image features to design high level aesthetic attributes as mid-level features and trained aesthetic classifier over these features. Datta *et al.* [2] proposed 56 visual features based on standard photography and visual design rules to encapsulate aesthetic attributes from low-level image features. Dhar *et al.* divided aesthetic attributes into three categories Compositional (*e.g.* Depth of field, Rule of thirds), Content(*e.g.* faces, animals, scene types), Sky-Illumination (*e.g.* clear sky, sunset sky). They trained individual classifiers for these attributes from low-level features (*e.g.* color histograms, center surrounding wavelets, haar features) and used outputs of these classifiers as input features for the aesthetic classifier.

Marchesotti *et al.* [18], proposed to learn aesthetic attributes from textual comments on the photographs using generic image features. Despite increased performance, many of these textual attributes (good, looks great, nice try) do not map to well-defined visual characteristics. Lu *et al.* [13] proposed to learn several meaningful style attributes, and used these to fine-tune the training of aesthetics classification network. Kong *et al.* [10] proposed attribute and content adaptive DCNN for aesthetic score prediction.

However, none of the previous works report the aesthetic attributes themselves. These attributes are used as features to predict the overall aesthetic score/class. In this paper, we learn aesthetic attributes along with the overall score, not just as intermediate features but as auxiliary information. Aesthetic assessment is relatively easier in images with evident high and low aesthetics than in ordinary images with marginal aesthetics (Figure 2). For these images, attributes information would greatly supplement the quality of feedback from an automatic aesthetic assessment system.

Figure 2: Sample images from AADB testing data. first column: Images rated high on aesthetic score, second Column: Images rated at mid-level, third Column: Images rated low.

Recently, deep learning techniques have shown significant performance gains in various computer vision tasks such as object classification, localization [11, 23, 25]. In deep learning, non-linear features are learned in a hierarchical fashion in increasing complexity (e.g. colors, edges, objects). The aesthetic attributes can be learned as combinations of these features. Deep learning techniques have shown significant performance gains in comparison with traditional machine learning approaches for aesthetic assessment tasks [8, 10, 13, 14, 26]. Unlike traditional machine learning techniques, features are also learned during training in deep learning techniques. However these internal representations of DCNNs are still opaque. Various visualization techniques [5, 17, 22, 28–30] have been proposed to visualize the internal representations of DCNNs in an attempt to have a better understanding of their working. However, these visualization techniques have not been applied in aesthetic assessment tasks. In this article, we apply the gradient based visualization technique proposed by Zhou *et al.* [30] to obtain attribute activation maps. These maps provide localized representation of these attributes. Additionally we also apply similar visualization technique [22] to the model provided by Kong *et al.* [10] to obtain similar maps for qualitative comparison of our results with the earlier approach.

3 METHOD

3.1 Architecture

We use the deep residual network (ResNet50) [6] to train all the attributes along with the overall aesthetic score. ResNet50 has 50 layers which can be divided into 16 successive residual blocks. Each residual block contains 3 convolution layers followed by the batch normalization layer (Figure 3). Each residual block is followed by a rectified linear activation layer (ReLU) [20]. We take these rectified convolution maps from the ReLU output of all these 16 residual blocks, and pool features from each of these 16 blocks with a global average pooling (GAP) layer. GAP layer gives the spatial average of these rectified convolution maps. Then we concatenate all these pooled features and use this as a feature for a fully connected layer which produces the desired outputs (aesthetic attributes and the overall score) as shown in Figure 3. We model the attribute and score prediction as a regression problem with mean squared error as loss function. Due to this simple connectivity structure, we are able to identify the importance of image regions by projecting the weights of the output layer on to the rectified convolution maps, a technique we call *attribute activation mapping*. This technique was first introduced by Zhou *et al.* [30] to get class activation maps for different semantic classes in image classification task.

3.2 Attribute Activation Mapping

For a given image, let $f_k(x, y)$ represent the activation of unit k in the rectified convolution map at spatial location *(x, y)*. Then, for unit k, the result of performing global average pooling is $F^k = \sum_{x,y} f_k(x, y)$. Thus, for a given attribute a, the input to the regression layer, R_a, is $\sum_x w_k^a F_k$ where w_k^a is the weight corresponding to attribute a for unit k. Essentially, w_k^a indicates the importance of F_k for attribute a as shown in Figure 3.

We also synthesized similar attribute maps from the model proposed by Kong *et al.* [10]. We did not have the final attribute and content adapted model from [10] due to patent rights but Kong *et al.* shared the attribute adapted model with us. That model is based on alexnet architecture [11] consisting of fully connected layers along with convolution layers. In this architecture, outputs of convolution layers are separated from desired outputs by three stacked fully connected layers. The outputs from last FC layer are regression scores of attributes. In this architecture we compute weight of layer k for attribute a as summation of gradients (g_k^a) of outputs with respect to k^{th} convolution layer $w_k^a = \sum_{x,y} g_k^a(x, y)$. This technique was first introduced by Selvaraju *et al.* [22] to get class activation maps for different semantic classes and visual explanation (answers for questions).

3.3 Implementation Details

Out of 10000 samples present in the AADB dataset, we have trained our model on 8500 training samples. 500 and 1000 images have been set aside for validation and testing purposes, respectively. As the number of training samples (8500) is not adequate for training of such a deep network (23,715,852 parameters) from scratch, we used a pre-trained ResNet50. It was trained on 1000-class Imagenet classification dataset [3] with approximately 1.2 million images. We fixed the input image size to 299 × 299. We used *horizontal flip* of the input images as a data augmentation technique. The last residual block gives convolution maps of size 10 × 10, so we reduce the sizes of the convolution maps from the previous Res-Blocks to the same size with appropriate sized average pooling. As ResNet50 has batch normalization layers, it is very sensitive to batch size. We fixed the batch size to 16 and trained it for 16 epochs. We report our model's performance on test set (1000 images) provided in AADB. We have made our implementation publicly available [1].

3.4 Dataset

As mentioned earlier, we have used the aesthetics and attribute database (AADB) provided by Kong *et al.* [10]. AADB provides overall ratings for the photographs along with the ratings on the eleven aesthetic attributes as mentioned in [10] (Figure 1). Users were asked to provide information about the effectiveness of these attributes on the overall aesthetic score. For

[1]https://github.com/gautamMalu/Aesthetic_attributes_maps

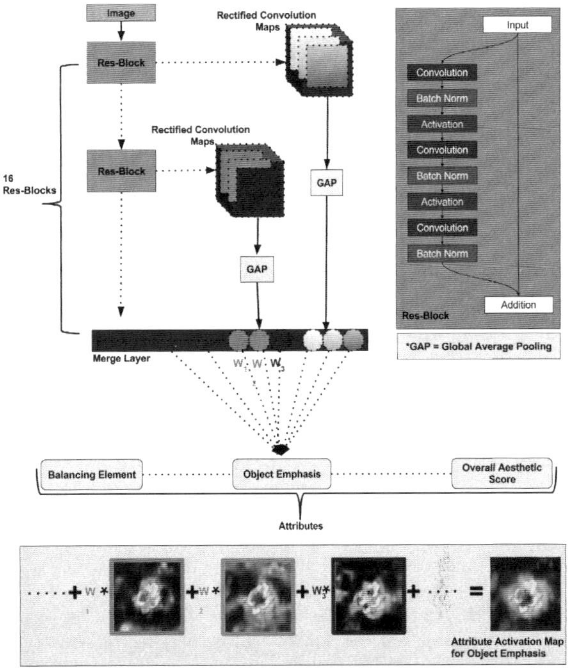

Figure 3: Our approach for generating attribute activation maps. The predicted score for a given attribute (object emphasis in the figure) is mapped back to the rectified convolution layers to generate the attribute activation maps. These maps highlight the attribute-specific discriminative regions as shown in the bottom section.

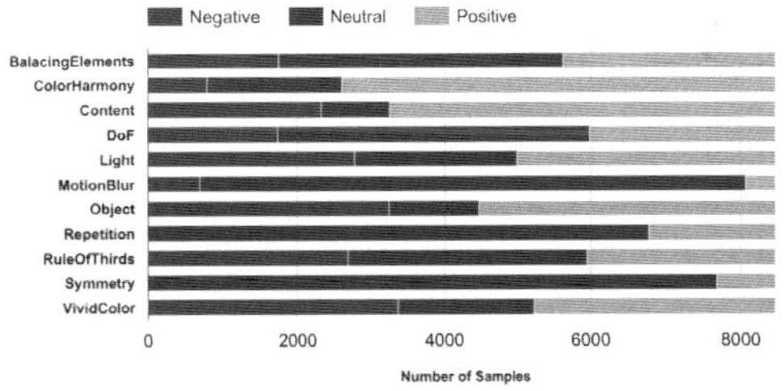

Figure 4: The distribution of all the eleven attributes in the training data of AADB. Most of the images are rated neutral for motion blur, repetition and symmetry.

example, if *object emphasis* is positively contributing towards the overall aesthetics of a photograph, user will give a score of *+1* for the attribute, if object is not emphasized adequately and this is contributing negatively towards the overall aesthetic score of the photograph, user will give a score of *-1* for the attribute (See Fig 5). The users also rated the overall aesthetic score on a scale of 1 to 5, with 5 being the most aesthetically pleasing score. Each image was rated by at least *5* persons. The mean score was taken as the ground truth score for all attributes and the overall score.

If an attribute has enhanced the image quality, it was rated positively and if the attribute has degraded the image aesthetics it was rated negatively. The

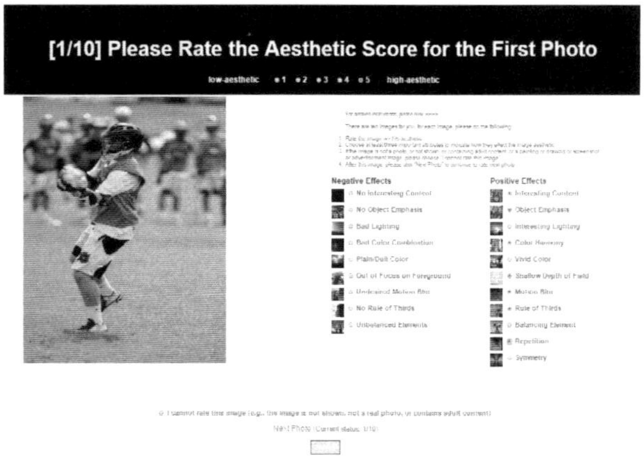

Figure 5: Interface of data collection adopted by Kong *et al.*[10].

default zero (null) means the attribute does not affect the image aesthetics. For example, positive *vivid color* means the vividness of the color presented in an image has a positive effect on the image aesthetics; while the negative *vivid color* means the image has dull color composition. All the attributes except for *Repetition* and *Symmetry* are normalized to the range of [-1, 1] *Repetition* and *Symmetry* are normalized to the range of [0, 1], as negative values are not justifiable for these two attributes. The overall score is normalized to the range of [0, 1].Out of these eleven attributes, we omit *Symmetry, Repetition* and *Motion blur* attributes from our experiment as most of the images rated null for these attributes (Figure 4). We model the other eight attributes along with the overall aesthetic score as a regression problem.

4 RESULTS & DISCUSSION

To evaluate the aesthetic attribute scores predicted by our model, we report the Spearman's ranking correlation coefficient (ρ) between the estimated aesthetic attribute score and the corresponding ground truth score for the testing data. The ranking correlation coefficient (ρ) evaluates the monotonic relationship between estimated scores and ground truth scores, hence there is no need of explicit calibration between them. The correlation coefficient lies in the range of [-1, 1], with greater values corresponding to higher correlation and vice-versa. For baseline comparison, we also train a model by fine tuning a pre-trained ResNet50 and label it as ResNet50-FT. Fine-tuning here refers to modifying the last layer of the pre-trained ResNet50 [6] and training it for our aesthetic attribute prediction task. Table 1 lists the performance on AADB using the two approaches. We also report the performance of the model shared by Kong *et al.*[10].

It should be noted that the spearman's coefficient between the estimated overall aesthetic score and the corresponding ground truth reported by Kong *et al.*[10] was 0.678. They did not report any metrics for the other aesthetic attributes. They used ranking loss along with mean squared error as loss functions. Their final approach was also content adaptive. As can be seen from the results reported in Table 1, our model managed to outperform their approach in overall aesthetic score in-spite of only being trained with mean square error and without any content adaptive framework . Our model significantly underperformed for *Rule of Thirds* and *Balancing elements* attributes. These attributes are location sensitive attributes. *Rule of thirds* deals with positioning of the salient elements, *Balancing Elements* deals

[2]The ρ reported by Kong *et al.* [10] for their final content and attribute adaptive model is 0.678, here we are reporting the performance of the model shared by them.

Table 1: Spearman's rank correlations for all the attributes. All correlation coefficients (ρ) are significant at $p < 0.0001$. The coefficients marked with a * are best results for respective attributes.

Attribute	ResNet50-FT	Kong *et al.*[10]	Our method
Balancing Elements	0.184	**0.220***	0.186
Content	0.572	0.508	**0.584***
Color Harmony	0.452	0.471	**0.475***
Depth of Field	0.450	0.479	**0.495***
Light	0.379	**0.443***	0.399
Object Emphasis	0.658	0.602	**0.666***
Rule of Thirds	0.175	**0.225***	0.178
Vivid Colors	0.661	0.648	**0.681***
Overall Aesthetic Score	0.665	0.654[2]/0.678	**0.689***

Table 2: Human performance on AADB. Our model actually outperforms the human consistently (as measured by ρ, last row) averaged across all raters (first row). However, when considering only the "power raters" who have annotated more images, human consistently outperform our model (second and third row).

Number of Images rated	Number of Raters	ρ
> 0	195	0.6738
> 100	65	0.7013
> 200	42	0.7112
Our Approach	–	0.689

with relative positioning of objects with each other and the frame. In our model, due to use of global average pooling (GAP) layers after activation layers we are losing location specificity. We selected GAP layer to reduce the number of parameters. The number of training samples (8500) allows learning of only small parameter space. We also warp the input images to the fixed size input (299*x*299), thus destroying the aspect ratio. These could be possible reasons for the under-performance of the model for these compositional and location sensitive attributes. Across all the attributes, our proposed method reports better results than ResNet50 fine-tuned model. Our model performs better than the model provided by Kong et al. [10] for five-out-of-eight attributes.

Aspects of aesthetic judgments are very subjective in nature. To quantify this subjectivity. In AADB the ground-truth score is the mean score of ratings given by different individuals. To quantify the agreement between ratings, ρ between each individual's ratings and the ground-truth scores was calculated. The average of ρ is reported in Table 2. Our model actually outperforms the human consistently (as measured by ρ) averaged across all raters. However, when considering only the "power raters" who have annotated more images, human evaluators consistently outperform model's results.

5 VISUALIZATION

As mentioned above we generate attribute activation maps for different attributes, to get their localized representations. Here we omit the following attributes, namely, emphbalancing element and the *rule of thirds*, as our model's performance is very low for these attributes as shown in Table 1. For each attribute, we have analyzed the activation maps and present the insights in this section. For illustration purposes, We have selected ten samples for each attribute. Out of these ten samples, first five are the

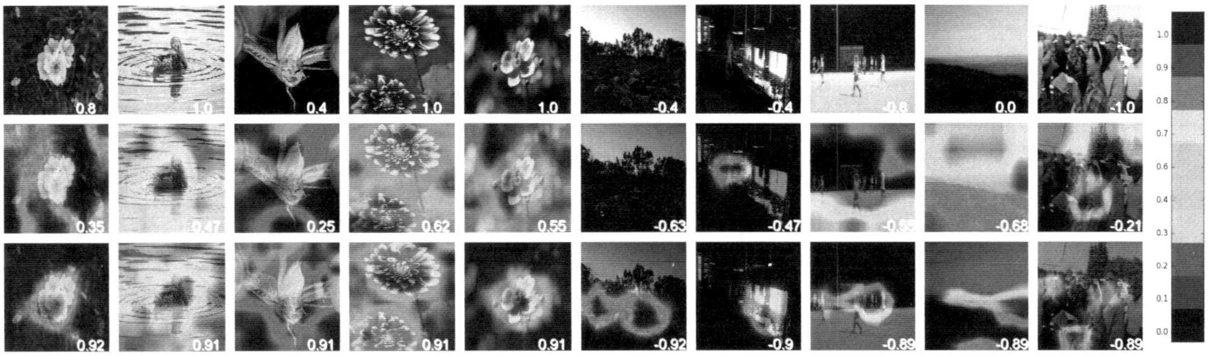

Figure 6: Object Emphasis activation maps. First row: Original Images (marked with ground truth score at the bottom right), second row: Activation Maps from Kong *et al.* [10] model (marked with predicted score from their given model), third row: Activation Maps from our method (marked with our predicted score). Color-bar indicates the color encoding of activation.

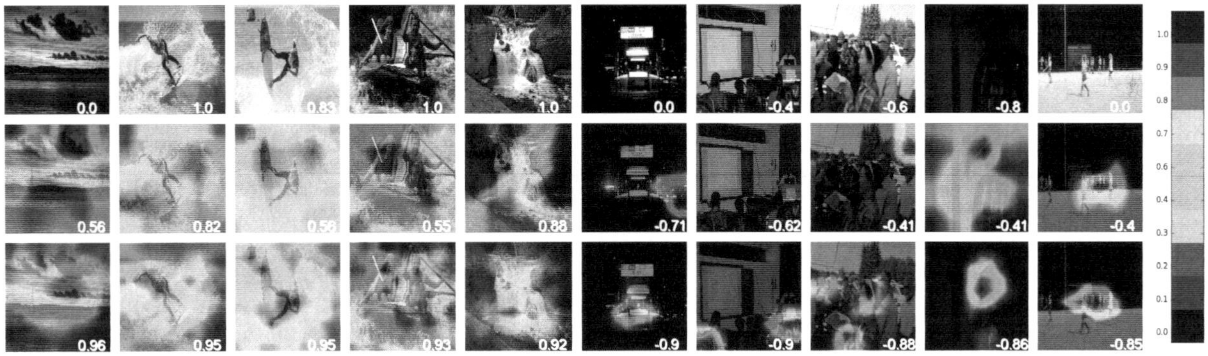

Figure 7: Content activation maps. First row: Original Images (marked with ground truth score at the bottom right), second row: Activation Maps from Kong *et al.* [10] model (marked with predicted score from their given model), third row: Activation Maps from our method (marked with our predicted score). Color-bar indicates the color encoding of activation.

highest rated by our model, and the next five are the lowest rated. We have selected these samples from test samples (1000) and not from the train samples. We also have included the activation maps from model given by Kong *et al.* [10] (Kong's model). These activation maps highlight the most important regions for the given attributes. We define these activation maps as "gaze" of the model.

5.1 Object Emphasis

By qualitative analysis of activation maps of object emphasis, it was observed that model gazes at the main object on the image. Even when the model predicts negative rating, i.e. object is not emphasized, the model searches for regions which contain objects Figure 6. In comparison, activation maps from Kong's model are not always consistent as can be seen in the second row of activation maps in Figure 6. It showcases that our model has learned the object emphasis attribute as an attribute which is indeed related to objects.

5.2 Content

Interestingness of content is significantly subjective and is a context-dependent attribute. However, if a model is trained on this attribute, one would expect the model would have maximum activation at the content of the image while making this judgment. If there exists a well-defined object in an image, then that object is considered as the content of the image, for e.g., 2nd and 3rd columns of Figure 7. Further, it can be observed in these columns that our proposed approach is better at identifying the content than Kong's model. Without the presence of explicit objects, the content of the image is difficult to localize, for e.g. 1st and 5th columns of Figure 7. As shown in Figure 7, our model's activation maps are maximally active at the content of the image. In comparison activation maps from Kong's models are not consistent.

5.3 Depth of Field

On analyzing the representations of shallow depth of field, it was observed that model looks for blurry regions near the main object of the image while making the judgment as showcased in Figure 8. Shallow depth of field technique is used to make the subject of the photograph stand out from its background. The model's interpretation of it is in that direction. The images for which model has predicted the negative score on this attribute, the activation maps are random. Activation maps from Kong's model also showcase a similar behavior, these maps are more active at the corner of the images.

Figure 8: Depth of Field activation maps. First row: Original Images (marked with ground truth score at the bottom right), second row: Activation Maps from Kong *et al.* [10] model (marked with predicted score from their given model), third row: Activation Maps from our method (marked with our predicted score). Color-bar indicates the color encoding of activation.

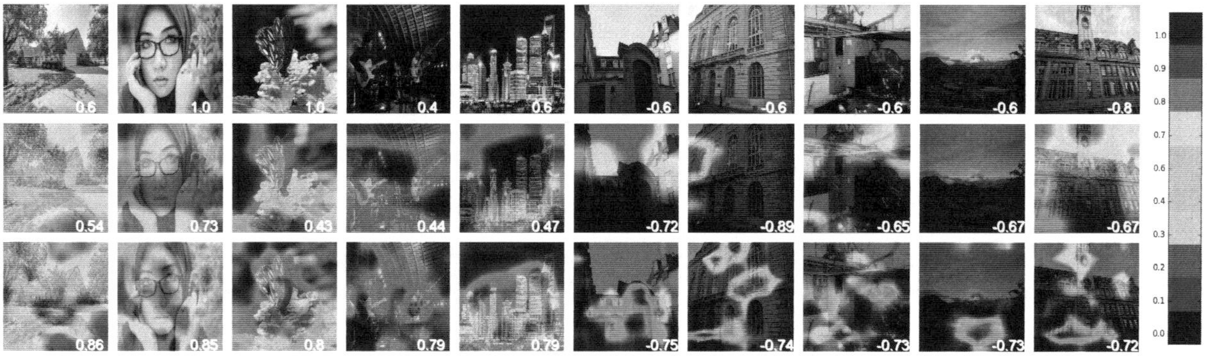

Figure 9: Vivid Color activation maps. First row: Original Images (marked with ground truth score at the bottom right), second row: Activation Maps from Kong *et al.* [10] model (marked with predicted score from their given model), third row: Activation Maps from our method (marked with our predicted score). Color-bar indicates the color encoding of activation.

5.4 Vivid Color

Vivid Color means the presence of bright and bold colors. The model's interpretation of this attribute seems to be along these lines. As shown in Figure 9, model gazes at vivid color areas while making the judgment about this attribute. For example, in 2nd column of the Figure 9 pink color of flowers and scarf, and in 3rd column butterfly and flower were the most activated regions. Authors couldn't find any pattern in activation maps from Kong's model.

5.5 Light

Good Lighting is quite a challenging concept to grasp. It does not merely depend on the light in the photograph, but rather how that light complements the whole composition. As shown in Figure 10, most of the time model seems to look at bright light, or source of the light in the photograph. Although model's behavior is consistent, its understanding of this attribute is incomplete. This was also evident in the low correlation ratings of our proposed model for this attribute, as reported in Table 1.

5.6 Color Harmony

Although model's performance is significant for this attribute, we could not find any consistent pattern in its activation maps. As color harmony is of many types, e.g., analogues, complementary, triadic; it is difficult to get a single representation pattern. For example, in the first example shown in Figure 11, the green color of hills is in analogous harmony with blue color of water and sky; in the 3rd example, brown sand color is in split complementary harmony with blue and green. The attribute activation maps for Color Harmony are shown in Figure 11.

6 CONCLUSION

In this paper, we have proposed deep convolution neural network (DCNN) architecture to learn aesthetic attributes. Results show that estimated scores of five aesthetic attributes (Interestingness of Content, Object emphasis, shallow Depth of Field, Vivid Color, and Color Harmony) correlate significantly with their respective ground truth scores. Whereas in the case of attributes such as Balancing Elements, Light and Rule of Thirds, the correlation is inferior. The activation maps corresponding to the learned aesthetic attributes such as object emphasis, content, depth of field and vivid color indicate that the model has acquired internal representation suitable to highlight these attributes automatically. However, for color harmony and light, the visualization maps were not consistent.

Aesthetic judgment involves a degree of subjectivity. For example, in AADB the average correlation between the mean score and an individual's

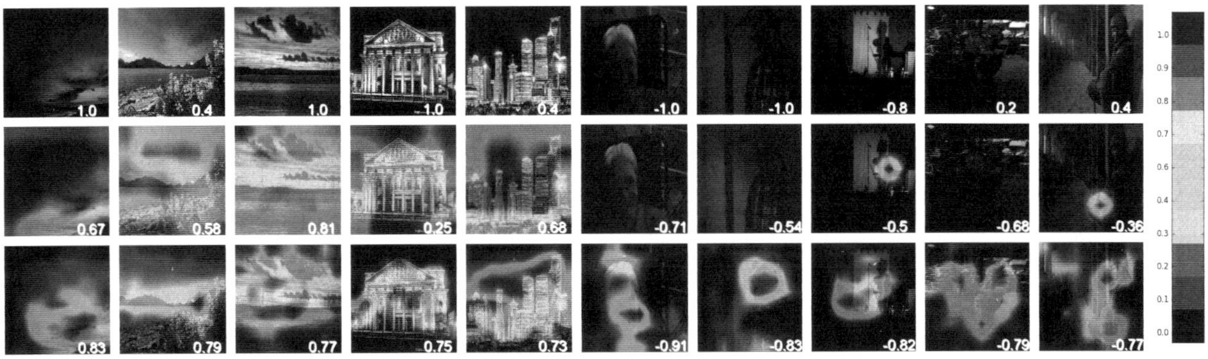

Figure 10: Light activation maps. First row: Original Images (marked with ground truth score at the bottom right), second row: Activation Maps from Kong *et al.* [10] model (marked with predicted score from their given model), third row: Activation Maps from our method (marked with our predicted score). Color-bar indicates the color encoding of activation.

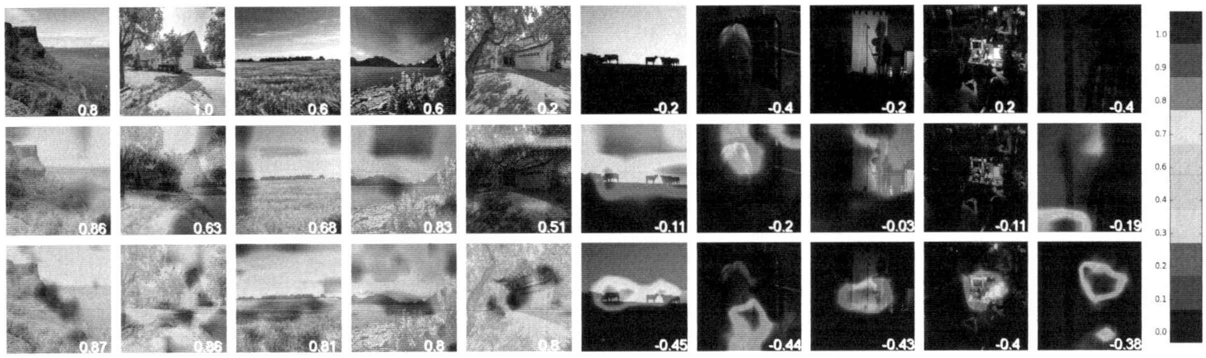

Figure 11: Color Harmony activation maps. First row: Original Images (marked with ground truth score at the bottom right), second row: Activation Maps from Kong *et al.* [10] model (marked with predicted score from their given model), third row: Activation Maps from our method (marked with our predicted score). Color-bar indicates the color encoding of activation.

score for the overall aesthetic score is 0.67 2. Moreover, as reported by Kong *et al.* [10], the model learned on a particular dataset might not work on a different dataset. Considering all these factors, empirical validity of aesthetic judgment models is still a challenge. We suggest that the visualization techniques presented in the current work is a step forward in that direction. Empirical validation could proceed by asking subjects to annotate the images (identifying the regions that correspond to different aesthetic attributes) and these empirical maps could in turn be compared with the predicted maps of the model. Such experiments need to be conducted in future to validate the current approach.

ACKNOWLEDGMENTS

The authors would like to thank Ms. Shruti Naik, and Mr. Yashaswi Verma of International Institute of Information Technology, Hyderabad, India for their help in manuscript preparation.

REFERENCES

[1] Subhabrata Bhattacharya, Rahul Sukthankar, and Mubarak Shah. 2010. A framework for photo-quality assessment and enhancement based on visual aesthetics. In *Proceedings of the 18th ACM international conference on Multimedia*. ACM, 271–280.

[2] Ritendra Datta, Dhiraj Joshi, Jia Li, and James Z Wang. 2006. Studying aesthetics in photographic images using a computational approach. In *European Conference on Computer Vision*. Springer, 288–301.

[3] Jia Deng, Wei Dong, Richard Socher, Li-Jia Li, Kai Li, and Li Fei-Fei. 2009. Imagenet: A large-scale hierarchical image database. In *Computer Vision and Pattern Recognition, 2009. CVPR 2009. IEEE Conference on*. IEEE, 248–255.

[4] Sagnik Dhar, Vicente Ordonez, and Tamara L Berg. 2011. High level describable attributes for predicting aesthetics and interestingness. In *Computer Vision and Pattern Recognition (CVPR), 2011 IEEE Conference on*. IEEE, 1657–1664.

[5] Alexey Dosovitskiy and Thomas Brox. 2015. Inverting convolutional networks with convolutional networks. *CoRR abs/1506.02753* (2015).

[6] Kaiming He, Xiangyu Zhang, Shaoqing Ren, and Jian Sun. 2016. Deep residual learning for image recognition. In *Proceedings of the IEEE Conference on Computer Vision and Pattern Recognition*. 770–778.

[7] Yueying Kao, Kaiqi Huang, and Steve Maybank. 2016. Hierarchical aesthetic quality assessment using deep convolutional neural networks. *Signal Processing: Image Communication* 47 (2016), 500–510.

[8] Yueying Kao, Chong Wang, and Kaiqi Huang. 2015. Visual aesthetic quality assessment with a regression model. In *Image Processing (ICIP), 2015 IEEE International Conference on*. IEEE, 1583–1587.

[9] Yan Ke, Xiaoou Tang, and Feng Jing. 2006. The design of high-level features for photo quality assessment. In *Computer Vision and Pattern Recognition, 2006 IEEE Computer Society Conference on*, Vol. 1. IEEE, 419–426.

[10] Shu Kong, Xiaohui Shen, Zhe Lin, Radomir Mech, and Charless Fowlkes. 2016. Photo aesthetics ranking network with attributes and content adaptation. In *European Conference on Computer Vision*. Springer, 662–679.

[11] Alex Krizhevsky, Ilya Sutskever, and Geoffrey E Hinton. 2012. Imagenet classification with deep convolutional neural networks. In *Advances in neural information processing systems*. 1097–1105.

[12] Li-Yun Lo and Ju-Chin Chen. 2012. A statistic approach for photo quality assessment. In *Information Security and Intelligence Control (ISIC), 2012 International Conference on*. IEEE, 107–110.

[13] Xin Lu, Zhe Lin, Hailin Jin, Jianchao Yang, and James Z Wang. 2014. Rapid: Rating pictorial aesthetics using deep learning. In *Proceedings of the 22nd ACM international conference on Multimedia*. ACM, 457–466.

[14] Xin Lu, Zhe Lin, Xiaohui Shen, Radomir Mech, and James Z Wang. 2015. Deep multi-patch aggregation network for image style, aesthetics, and quality estimation. In *Proceedings of the IEEE International Conference on Computer Vision*. 990–998.

[15] Wei Luo, Xiaogang Wang, and Xiaoou Tang. 2011. Content-based photo quality assessment. In *Computer Vision (ICCV), 2011 IEEE International Conference on*. IEEE, 2206–2213.

[16] Yiwen Luo and Xiaoou Tang. 2008. Photo and video quality evaluation: Focusing on the subject. In *European Conference on Computer Vision*. Springer, 386–399.

[17] Aravindh Mahendran and Andrea Vedaldi. 2015. Understanding deep image representations by inverting them. In *Proceedings of the IEEE Conference on Computer Vision and Pattern Recognition*. 5188–5196.

[18] Luca Marchesotti, Naila Murray, and Florent Perronnin. 2015. Discovering beautiful attributes for aesthetic image analysis. *International journal of computer vision* 113, 3 (2015), 246–266.

[19] Luca Marchesotti, Florent Perronnin, Diane Larlus, and Gabriela Csurka. 2011. Assessing the aesthetic quality of photographs using generic image descriptors. In *Computer Vision (ICCV), 2011 IEEE International Conference on*. IEEE, 1784–1791.

[20] Vinod Nair and Geoffrey E Hinton. 2010. Rectified linear units improve restricted boltzmann machines. In *Proceedings of the 27th international conference on machine learning (ICML-10)*. 807–814.

[21] Masashi Nishiyama, Takahiro Okabe, Imari Sato, and Yoichi Sato. 2011. Aesthetic quality classification of photographs based on color harmony. In *Computer Vision and Pattern Recognition (CVPR), 2011 IEEE Conference on*. IEEE, 33–40.

[22] Ramprasaath R Selvaraju, Abhishek Das, Ramakrishna Vedantam, Michael Cogswell, Devi Parikh, and Dhruv Batra. 2016. Grad-cam: Why did you say that? visual explanations from deep networks via gradient-based localization. *arXiv preprint arXiv:1610.02391* (2016).

[23] K. Simonyan and A. Zisserman. 2014. Very Deep Convolutional Networks for Large-Scale Image Recognition. *CoRR* abs/1409.1556 (2014).

[24] Xiaoshuai Sun, Hongxun Yao, Rongrong Ji, and Shaohui Liu. 2009. Photo assessment based on computational visual attention model. In *Proceedings of the 17th ACM international conference on Multimedia*. ACM, 541–544.

[25] Christian Szegedy, Wei Liu, Yangqing Jia, Pierre Sermanet, Scott Reed, Dragomir Anguelov, Dumitru Erhan, Vincent Vanhoucke, and Andrew Rabinovich. 2015. Going deeper with convolutions. In *Proceedings of the IEEE Conference on Computer Vision and Pattern Recognition*. 1–9.

[26] Xinmei Tian, Zhe Dong, Kuiyuan Yang, and Tao Mei. 2015. Query-dependent aesthetic model with deep learning for photo quality assessment. *IEEE Transactions on Multimedia* 17, 11 (2015), 2035–2048.

[27] Ou Wu, Weiming Hu, and Jun Gao. 2011. Learning to predict the perceived visual quality of photos. In *Computer Vision (ICCV), 2011 IEEE International Conference on*. IEEE, 225–232.

[28] Matthew D Zeiler and Rob Fergus. 2014. Visualizing and understanding convolutional networks. In *European conference on computer vision*. Springer, 818–833.

[29] Bolei Zhou, Aditya Khosla, Agata Lapedriza, Aude Oliva, and Antonio Torralba. 2014. Object detectors emerge in deep scene cnns. *arXiv preprint arXiv:1412.6856* (2014).

[30] Bolei Zhou, Aditya Khosla, Agata Lapedriza, Aude Oliva, and Antonio Torralba. 2016. Learning deep features for discriminative localization. In *Proceedings of the IEEE Conference on Computer Vision and Pattern Recognition*. 2921–2929.

Working Memory Concept Encoding Using Holographic Reduced Representations

Grayson M. DuBois and Joshua L. Phillips
Department of Computer Science
Middle Tennessee State University
Murfreesboro, TN 37132

Abstract

Artificial neural networks (ANNs) utilize the biological principles of neural computation to solve engineering problems, and ANNs also serve as formal, testable hypotheses of brain function and learning in the cognitive sciences. However, ANNs are often underutilized in applications where symbolic encoding (SE) of conceptual information is preferred (robotics, games, theorem proving, etc.) since ANN models often employ distributed encoding (DE). The Working Memory Toolkit (WMtk) was developed to aid the integration of an ANN-based cognitive neuroscience model of working memory into symbolic systems by mitigating the details of ANN design and providing a simple DE interface. However, DE/SE conversion is still managed by the user and tuned specifically to each learning task. Here we utilize Holographic Reduced Representation (HRR) to overcome this limitation where HRRs provide a framework for manipulating concepts using a hybrid DE/SE formalism that is compatible with ANNs. We validate the performance of the new Holographic Working Memory Toolkit (HWMtk) using two simple partially observable reinforcement learning problems, and show how the HWMtk automates the process of DE/SE conversion for the user while seamlessly providing additional cognitive capabilities such as context switching, cross-task generalization and concept chunking.

The field of artificial intelligence (AI) is synergistic with a wide range of disciplines but artificial neural networks (ANNs) is perhaps the most prolific subfield. Not only are biological principles of neural computation and neuroanatomy adapted to solve engineering problems, but ANNs also serve as formal, testable hypotheses of brain function and learning in the cognitive sciences. Still, since ANN models often employ distributed encoding (DE), most have limited application in other areas of AI where symbolic encoding (SE) is the norm (e.g. planning, reasoning, robotics).

There is extensive evidence that the brain contains a working memory (WM) system that actively maintains a small amount of task-essential information and supports learning in myriad ways: focusing attention on the most task-relevant features, transfering learning across tasks, limiting the search space for perceptual systems, providing a means to avoid the out-of-sight/out-of-mind problem, and providing robust behavior in the face of irrelevant events (Baddeley 1986; Waugh and Norman 1965). The prefrontal cortex and mesolimbic dopamine system have been implicated as the functional components of WM in humans and animals, and biologically-based ANNs for WM have been developed based on electrophysiological, neuroimaging, and neuropsychological studies (O'Reilly et al. 2002; Kriete et al. 2013). A software library, the working memory toolkit (WMtk), was developed to aid the integration of ANN-based WM into robotic systems by mitigating the details of ANN design and providing a simple DE interface (Phillips and Noelle 2005). The WMtk has been tested in several task domains in the area of cognitive robotics (Tugcu et al. 2007; Erdemir et al. 2008; Busch et al. 2007; Gordon, Kawamura, and Wilkes 2010).

Despite the fact that the WMtk can solve common tests of working memory performance, the DE/SE distinction is still problematic for the WMtk. DE/SE conversion still needs to be programmed directly by the user and tuned specifically to each learning task. A technique called holographic reduced representation (HRR) may provide the technical assistance needed to overcome this limitation (Plate 1995). HRRs provide a framework for creating and combining symbolic concepts using a distributed formalism that is compatible with ANNs. Our aim is to create a software engine for encoding and manipulating concept representations using HRRs and integrate it into the WMtk. The newly integrated HRR Engine (HRRE) would greatly simplify the user interface by automating DE/SE conversion. We assess the performance of the new Holographic Working Memory Toolkit (HWMtk) on two main criteria: 1) significant improvement in the ease of use of the toolkit with automated DE/SE conversion, and 2) robust performance on working memory tasks while using HRRs in place of user-defined distributed representations.

Background

An example of the capabilities of the WMtk can be seen in a robotic simulation written using the toolkit based on the delayed saccade task (DST) (Phillips and Noelle 2005). In the DST, the robot is required to focus attention on a crosshair in the center of the screen. After a variable time delay, a target object will appear in the periphery of the screen, but the robot must continue to focus on the crosshair in the face of this distraction. After some time, the target object disappears and the robot must continue to focus on the crosshair. Finally, the crosshair disappears and the robot must then look at (or saccade to) the location where the target object appeared during the task. Rather than programming the robot to solve the DST, the WMtk allows the robot to learn how to solve the DST by repeatedly attempting the task as a series of episodes. The robot's WM learns to both override automatic behaviors (such as immediate saccades) and store task-relevant information (such as target locations) in order to guide future actions. Importantly, the robot is given feedback (positive reward) only at the end of correctly performed episodes. Even under these conditions, the WMtk learned to correctly manage items in WM and attain proficiency on the DST within merely hundreds of episodes.

Even though the toolkit mitigates many challenges to the integration of a well-established model of WM into learning systems, the toolkit does not aid the user in developing reasonable representations of the environment or working memory concepts themselves. Each of these components needs to be encoded using a sparse, distributed formalism that support learning by the underlying neural network. Such representations are challenging to develop and implement for even expert users, and are limited in applicability to the specific learning task in question. For example, a simple binary encoding of two distinct concepts for WM would require the user to write a function which takes a two-element vector and a string concept. The function would be used to set the appropriate element of the vector to one based on which concept the WMtk is trying to encode. This function would need to be rewritten every time additional concepts need to be encoded if they were not anticipated from the start. Also, this framework leaves the user open to difficult debugginc concerns that might otherwise be avoided if the encoding process was handled automatically. Additional functions for encoding information about the current state of the task and calculating reward based on this state information were also needed by the original WMtk. A more flexible encoding scheme is needed to make the toolkit more accessible to end-users.

HRRs may provide all of the necessary capabilities to solve the SE/DE conversion problem in an automated fashion. In the HRR formalism, distinct concepts, each represented by unique, distributed vectors of real numbers, can be combined and reduced to a single vector that represents the combined knowledge of its constituent concepts. Importantly, the length of the HRR vector encodings for all concepts (both constituent and combined) remains fixed since concepts are compressed using a mathematical operation known as circular convolution. Nevertheless, combined concepts still retain information about each the constituents which is a key property of holographic storage methods. Additionally, HRRs are DE representations which are compatible with neural network architectures and other machine learning approaches. However, since all concepts are encoded into unique vector representations, each HRR can be tied to a complementary SE representation (eg. the concept name) more commonly used in other symbolic or logic-based learning systems (Plate 1995). By replacing the DE interface of the WMtk with an HRR interface, DE/SE conversion would be automated and concepts learned from one task would naturally carry over to new tasks. Additional cognitive phenomena (e.g. chunking, cross-task generalization) may be investigated as well. Here we aim to develop and test a holographic reduced representation engine (HRRE) for accomplishing automated DE/SE conversion, and integrate the HRRE into the Working Memory Toolkit.

Methods

Work on this project was performed in 2 phases, both separated into three parts. During the first phase we created an engine to generate and manipulate HRRs. This HRR Engine provided us with a means of encoding, storing, and manipulating representations of concepts used in the WMtk. During the second phase, we rebuilt the WMtk around the HRRE, replacing the original DE interface with a simple SE (string-based) interface, and automating the encoding and manipulation of concepts using HRRs. Testing of new holographic working memory toolkit (HWMtk) was then performed using a basic memory retrieval task, and a partially observable maze exploration task.

Phase 1: Creating an HRR Engine for Concept Encoding

Our 3-part process for creating the HRRE consisted of (a) researching holographic reduced representation, (b) developing a conjunctive encoding engine, and (c) developing a conjunctive decoding engine. These phases were implemented as follows:

Holographic Reduced Representation HRR is a robust method of representing symbolic concepts in a distributed formalism. Simple concepts can be combined to make holographic representations for complex concepts containing information from each of the constituents. Additionally, it is possible to use HRRs in place of corresponding symbolic concepts for interfacing with ANNs. HRRs are constructed as a vector of real values typically drawn from a Normal/Gaussian distribution with zero mean ($\mu = 0$), and standard deviation, $\sigma = 1/\sqrt{(n)}$ where n is the length of the vectors. Longer vectors allow the encoding of more unique concepts as well as storage of more constituents within combined representations. Therefore, n is often adjusted for adequate performance on requisite tasks. Additional constraints can be placed on the vectors as well, such as in the case of "unitary" vectors, which exhibit some additional, useful mathematical properties, and were the types of HRRs employed here (Plate 1995). A newly generated HRR can then be assigned to a unique symbol for a single concept. Here we use strings to represent symbols, where the string value is simple the name of the concept we wanted the HRR to represent. For example, to generated an HRR for the concept red, we generated a unitary HRR, and assigned it to the string value "red".

The base data structure for our HRRE is a dictionary, where the string name for the concept is the key and the HRR representing that concept is the value. This dictionary serves as the engines long-term concept memory. From this point forward, the term *concept* will be used to refer to the entity composed of a string value and its associated HRR. These concepts are the key-value pairs stored in concept memory.

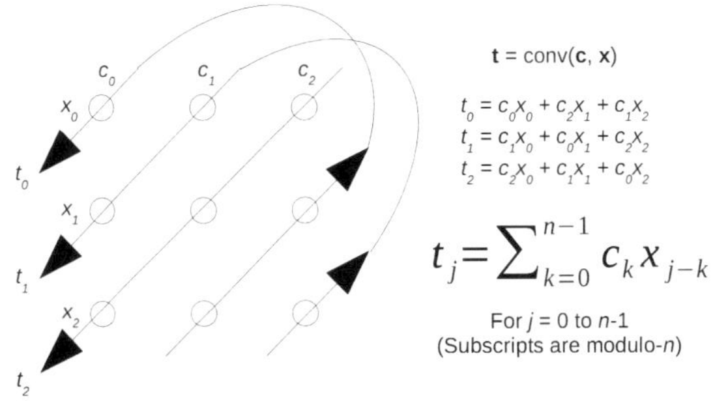

Figure 1: Example of how to perform circular convolution on two vectors (c and x), both of length n=3.

The term *representation* may be used interchangeably with HRR, since HRRs are the structure we use to form the distributed representation of the concepts we will use.

Developing a Conjunctive Encoding Engine After setting up the base dictionary for the engines concept memory and building the functionality for HRR generation, we needed to add a conjunctive encoding function to the engine for combining the HRRs to form complex concepts. We combine the representations for the concepts using the circular convolution operation. This operation is what makes holographic representations reduced, as it combines information from two HRRs into a single HRR of the same size. Circular convolution consists of constructing the outer product of the two HRRs and summing the elements along the trans-diagonals, as indicated in Figure 1. This $O(n^2)$ operation results in an HRR of size n with information from both constituent HRRs. This operation can be performed in $O(n\ log(n))$ time, however, using fast-fourier transforms (FFT). Therefore, we use FFTs in the HRRE for convolution operations.

Circular convolution is the key operation used in the main part of the HRREs conjunctive encoding functionality: the *construct* function. This function takes a list of concept names, or a string containing the concatenation of concept names, delimited by an asterisk ("*"), and combines all individual concepts into a single complex concept. The construct function would first make sure that there is a representation in concept memory for each given concept name, reorder each concept by lexicographical order, and then convolve each together to form the final representation. In this way, the construction of the concept made from "big", "red", and "ball" would result in the complex concept, "ball*big*red". What makes the construct function so powerful, however, is that in addition to constructing the final combination of all concepts, it also constructs representations for every combination of the constituent concepts. For example, constructing a concept using the values "big", "red", and "ball", would not only create the full combination above, but also the combinations "ball*big", "ball*red", and "big*red". These additional operations speed up memory retrieval by minimizing the number of circular convolutions that the system may need to perform in the future.

We ensured that the HRRE always sorts concepts into lexicographical order before working with them in order toeliminate duplicate representations made for the same concept. For example, we do not want the engine to create a new representation for "big*red*ball", if the analogous concept, "ball*big*red" exists. Generating a new representation for "big*red*ball" would be redundant. There is an additional safeguard built into the engine that protects against generating redundant constituent subconcepts this as well (eg. "ball*red" and "red*ball"). Beyond these constraints, whenever a concept is requested from the HRRE that it does not currently have in memory, it constructs the new representations. Constituent concepts are split apart by name, and combinations are constructed using the process described above. In this way, the user can pass in "ball*big*red", "red*ball*big", or any other permutation of these concepts, and the HRRE will always construct or perceive it as "ball*big*red".

Developing a Conjunctive Decoding Engine The final piece added to the HRRE was the conjunctive decoding function. Whereas conjunctive encoding is the combination of two representations through circular convolution, conjunctive decoding is the extraction of a constituent concept from a complex concept using circular involution (i.e. the inverse operation of circular convolution). Using circular involution, we can take the representation for the concept, "red*ball" and probe it using the representation for the concept, "ball". The resulting HRR would be the representation of the alternative constituent concept, "red". Identification of "red" is performed by calculating the dot product between the resulting HRR from the involution operation and all other concepts currently stored in the HRRE. The concept with the highest dot product similarity will be "red" in this case. Therefore, the HRRE can infer that the HRR for "red*ball" consists of both the probe concept "ball", and the response concept, "red".

Similar to the encoding part of the engines construct function, the decoding part of the engine has an *unpack* function that deconstructs a complex concept into all combinations of its constituent parts. Whereas the construct function is merely encoding each combination to ensure that they are all recognizable concepts for the HRRE, the unpack function serves to find all combinations and return them as a list of concepts. This is useful to the WMtk, as it will be the means by which a list of concepts will be constructed as candidates for WM contents.

By combining the encoding and decoding function, the HRRE is capable of 1) generating HRRs for new concepts, 2) storing concepts as key-value pairs of names and representations in the concept memory dictionary, 3) combining concepts through circular convolution, 4) extracting concepts through circular involution, 5) constructing and encoding all combinations of a list of concepts, and 6) unpacking all combinations of constituent concepts from a complex concept, and returning the resulting list to the user.

Phase 2: Building the Holographic Working Memory Toolkit

Our three-part process for building the HWMtk comprised of (a) researching the specifications of the original WMtk and making a development plan for the augmented toolkit, (b) rebuilding the WMtk around the HRRE, and (c) testing the augmented toolkit to ensure that it still learns using the new HRR interface.

Original WMtk Architecture The Working Memory toolkit implements a working memory model inspired by the interactions between the human pre-frontal cortex (PFC) and mesolimbic dopamine system (MDS). In this working memory model, the PFC maintains task-relevant information, and the DMS decides when such information should be gated into or out of PFC storage. The WMtk implements the PFC as a fixed set of *slots* for storing task-relevant concept representations. However, the MDS is implemented as a single-layer neural network, or *critic network*, which evaluates the utility of storing concepts in the slots. The network is passed an HRR representation consisting of representations (potentially) stored in working memory slots convolved with the HRR representation of the current task state. The value produced by the critic network determines how valuable that particular set of working memory contents is under the current task state. All states and combinations of WM contents are equally valuable at first, but the critic network employs temporal difference (TD) learning (Sutton and Barto 1998; O'Reilly et al. 2007) to learn the correct value of each WM-state combination by experiencing repeated episodes of the learning task. In this way, the working memory learns what information is the most valuable to retain for future processing given what it is currently experiencing. At this point, the user designs their learning task in such a way that the agent decides to make an action according to what is currently held in working memory.

We decided to start with a minimal design for our augmented toolkit since our aim was to improve ease of use for researchers using the toolkit. Therefore, here we utilize the HRRE to provide a simple interface for automating the concept encoding process. Additional functionality will be added to the toolkit in future work.

Rebuilding the WMtk Around the HRRE We determined that the two main components of the toolkit would be the Working Memory (WM) and the Critic Network (CN). We created both components under the following specifications:

Working Memory The WM component is the workhorse of the toolkit. It houses the HRRE, which serves to store all basic concepts, as well as the processor for the representations of all combinations of combined concepts. First, WM receives a string representation of the current state. The state is set up as a string containing a concatenation of the concepts describing the state, delimited by the addition symbol ("+"). An example of a state containing a cross in the center of the environment and a target in the north position of the environment could be denoted "center*cross+north*target". WM parses the state string for the list of concepts it contains, splitting each by the addition delimiter. These concepts are then passed to the HRRE, which returns a list of all the unpacked combinations of concepts. Following the cross-target example, the list of candidate chunks would be "center", "center*cross", "cross", "north", "north*target", and "target". This list of concepts becomes our list of candidate chunks: all are candidates for retention in WM. It is important to note that the *previous* contents of WM are also included in the list of candidates for retention. This process allows WM to potentially store task-relevant information for long-term. WM then goes through every combination of all candidate chunks that can fit in its WM slots. The value of WM candidates is determined by convolving them with the representation of the state, and feeding each combination into the critic network. Element-wise addition is used to combine vectors separated by the addition operator within the state representation before convolution. When passed into the critic, the set of WM contents that returns the highest value in the given state is chosen for retention, and the control is returned to the user until WM is passed a new state on the next step of the task.

Critic Network The CN component is the neural network that drives learning in the WMtk. It is passed representations from WM in order to compute the value function. The value function for the CN is a dot product calculation of the WM-state combination with a weight vector that is retained for the duration of the simulation. The weight vector is initialized with small random values. Therefore, initial values for each representation will be quite low. However, the CN employs TD-learning over many repeated task episodes, which will update the values in the weight vector. The value function eventually converges to the correct values for each WM-state combination, according to their effectiveness at determining task outcomes.

TD learning is implemented through 3 functions in the toolkit: *Initialize Episode*, *Step*, and *Absorb Reward*. Each function is passed the string representation of the state and the reward for that state. These functions are implemented and called through the WM object, but are closely tied to the CN for TD calculations. Initialize episode resets all episodic variables, clears and chooses the initial contents for WM, and stores reward and value information about the initial state for later use. Step chooses the current contents of WM, calculates reward and value information for the current state, and uses those values along with those stored from the previous state to update the weight vector using the CNs TD learning functions. Step then stores the current states value and reward for use in the next step of the episode. Step is called on each time step of the simulation to update working memory and drive learning. Finally, Absorb Reward is called at the end of the episode, which takes the state string for the final state, and computes the TD update for the previous state as well as the final state. Typically, a scalar reward of zero is provided throughout all steps of the task. On the final step, a reward value of 1 is provided if the agent successfully completes the task and zero for task failure. However, other reward schedules are permissible. When a new episode begins, these functions are called again, in the same order:

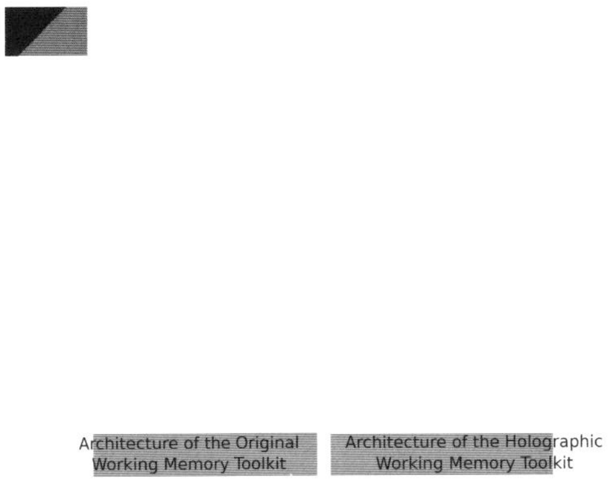

Figure 2: Comparison of the original WMtk architecture (left) to the architecture of the HWMtk (right).

Initialize Episode, a sequence of calls to Step, and finishing the episode with Absorb Reward. We do also use eligibility traces in our TD calculations, and an ϵ-soft policy is implemented by generating random WM contents, ϵ percent of the time.

A visual comparison between the architectures of the original and augmented toolkit is shown in Figure 2. The main difference between the two architectures is in the amount of code the user needs to provide in the form of functions/methods. Many of these user-defined functions are now completely performed within the HWMtk. Sensory information can now be provided in a symbolic, English-like syntax. Symbols are automatically converted to appropriate vectors by the HRRE for presentation to the CN. The selection of task-relevant concepts for storage in working memory is learned over time, enabling the agent to override prepotent responses with task-relevant behaviors. Also, while the function calculating reward information still needs to be specified by the user, the augmented toolkit does not need to call this function directly. This simplifies the user's implementation since it no longer needs to be concerned with the inner-workings of the toolkit to perform reward calculations.

Testing the Toolkit to Ensure Learning Capabilities We developed two tasks for the HWMtk to determine if the user interface is indeed easier for developing new tasks compared to the original toolkit. Additionally, the tasks test the basic components of working memory function: learning to store task-relevant information and ignore task-irrelevant information (distractors). For the first task, the agent is shown 7 colors in random order, and is rewarded if it remembers the color "red" at the end of the simulation. This task would be equivalent to shuffling 7 cards of different colors, and showing them all to the agent, one at a time, and asking at the end which color we were thinking of. The task is simple, but not trivial, as the toolkit can choose to remember nothing or any of the other colors as well. Also, the presentation order is randomized, so the agent cannot anticipate when the relevant color is being presented. The agent must decide to hold onto the color "red" and retain this concept in working memory even while other colors (distractors) are being presented to the agent until the end of the episode is reached. We repeat this process many times (each repetition being a single episode). The agent must learn that it is only rewarded upon remembering "red", regardless of presentation order or the number of distractors encountered. This ability to retain task-relevant information in the face of competing distractions is one of the core mechanism of focused attention needed to perform all working memory tasks.

Learning parameters for the task were set to similar values as the defaults for the standard WMtk: CN learning rate parameter, α=0.1; future reward discounting factor, γ=0.9; past action eligibility factor, λ=0.1; ϵ-soft random working memory selection probability, ϵ=0.01; number of working memory slots, s=1; and HRR vector length, n=64. The HRR vector length (n) is the only new parameter on this list, and must be set to a value large enough that the dot products between base HRR concept vectors remain close to zero. A value of 64 was the minimum size needed to run 100 successful trials (described below), but larger values did not show any noticable difference in learning behavior.

A second task was developed which provided a more rigorous test of working memory function. We simply reward the agent for remembering a specific item in the first task. However, in the second task, the agent must also learn to utilize stored WM representations to make decisions which impact future reward. Contextual information is provided early in this task that is then needed for proper action selection later in the task. We created a simple reinforcement learning agent which utilized temporal difference learning to solve a 1D maze task consisting of 20 independent states. Each state has two immediately accessible neighbors to the left and right. For example state 4 is located to the left of state 5 and state 6 is located to the right of state 5. The maze is periodic such that state 20 is the left neighbor of state 1, and 1 is the right neighbor of state 20. A reward value of 1 is provided to the agent upon reaching the goal, and each each episode consists of starting in a random state and proceeding for no more than 100 steps (early termination if the goal was not reached).

To make the above task *partially observable*, and therefore a good test of WM performance, we also provided a "signal" (S1 or S2) on *only the first step* of each episode which was correlated with the location of the goal for that episode. For example, a presentation of S1 indicated that the goal would be at state 1, but for S2 the goal would be at state 10. This information would be provided to the toolkit on the first step of an episode, but never again for the remainder of the episode. Therefore, only retention of this contextual signaling cue would allow for optimal performance since failure to remember the context signal would make selecting the optimal action an ambiguous decision. The task type (S1 or S2) was chosen at random at the start of each episode, so that there were no predictable performance correlations between tasks.

One HRR vector (n=4096) was generated for each of the 20 states, the 2 signals (S1 and S2), and the two possible actions (left and right). A single-layer critic network was constructed to evaluate the value of combining any working memory representations remembered (or not if WM did not store the necessary signal cue), and the current state via circular convolution. Convolving this representation with either of the two action representations would allow critic network to select the appropriate action using the same TD-learning formalisms described above.

Learning parameters for the task were set to the following values: CN learning rate parameter, α=0.05; future reward discounting factor, γ=0.9; past action eligibility factor, λ=0.5; epsilon-soft random working memory selection probability *and* action selection probability, ϵ=0.001; number of working memory slots, s=1; and HRR vector length, n=4096.

Results

When testing the HWMtk with the colors task, we were looking to see if it held up to the two main criteria for success mentioned in the introduction: 1) ease of use in setting up a learning task using the new string-passing SE interface, and 2) successful learning using HRRs in place of the old distributed encodings.

Ease of Use

Setting up the colors and signal learning tasks above proved to be more straightforward compared to setting up tasks using the original toolkit. Had we been using the original WMtk, we would have had to write a function to create distributed representations of each color as a chunk of information usable to WM, as well as a similar function for encoding the state, and a reward function to check to provide a reward value according to the agents performance. We would have had to write each of these before writing the logic for the task itself, but using the augmented toolkit, none of this preparation was necessary. We simply set up an array of n color strings, shuffled them at the beginning of each episode, initialized episode with the first color, called the Step function with each subsequent color less than n, and called the Absorb Reward function with the nth color string. The only logic for the reward was written in line with the rest of the task, and it entailed a check to see if red was stored in the contents of WM. If it was, Absorb Reward was provided a reward value of 1.0 for success, else a 0.0 for failure. Considering the simplicity and ease of setting up the task, the HWMtk meets our first and most important criterion for success: simplification of interface and ease of use for the developer.

The C++ code for the HWMtk and colors task agent is open source, distributed under the GPLv3, and available online at: `https://github.com/jlphillipsphd/wmtk/`.

Effective Learning Using HRRs

The colors taks test was run for 100 learning trials. We gathered information over every trial, keeping track of the number of episodes the agent successfully completed the task and recording the number of successes per every 1000 episodes. We considered a 98 percent success rate per thousand episodes an indication that the agent had effectively learned the task. Over the 100 trials, we found that the agent learned the task to a 100 percent success rate within an average of 8000 episodes. Therefore, the HWMtk meets the requirement of being capable of learning using holographic reduced representations instead of distributed representations for concepts.

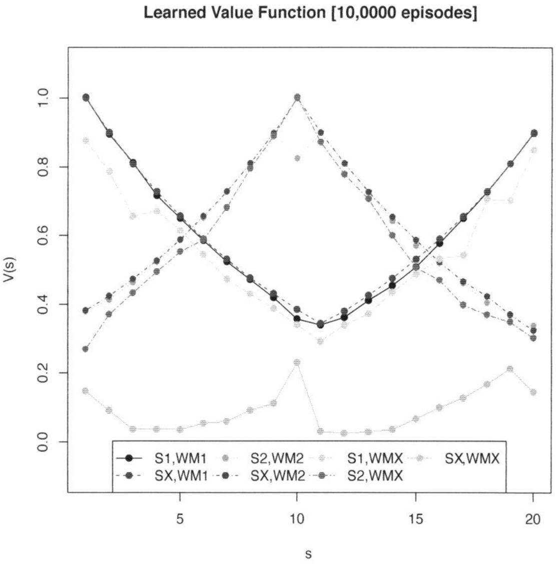

Figure 3: Learned value function of the partially observable 1D maze task. The learned value, V(s), is shown for each state (s). S1 indicates states for when the first task signal is present, S2 indicates states for when the second task signal is present, and SX indicates states when *no signal* was present. These options are combined with possible WM contents: WM1 means the first task signal was stored, WM2 means the second task signal was stored, and WMX means that *no signal* was stored.

The 1D maze-signal task showed successful learning within 10000 episodes, and the resulting value function across the 20 states for the different possible WM contents is shown in Figure 3. The toolkit was able to learn that the signal information provided (S1,WM1 or S2,WM2) was relevant for proper task discrimination. This is indicated by the expected rise in the value function for each of the respective subtasks as the agent approaches the goal for that subtask. Conditions where signals were retained in WM are shown by SX,WM1 and SX,WM2 for retention of the S1 or S2 signals, respectively. Figure 3 also shows conditions for when the signal was observed, but not yet retained in WM (prior to the call to Step). These are shown in conditions S1,WMX and S2,WMX, respectively. All six of the conditions described above fall along the optimal path to the goal(s) and the CN has learned the correct discounted reward values in all cases. Thus, the value function for each task was learned independently along with learning of the proper contextual cues needed to perform this separation of learning concerns. The performance of the agent when signal information was *not* retained in WM memory was also learned. This subproblem (SX,WMX) occurs when the ϵ-soft policy decides to remove signal representations currently stored in working memory, or early in learning when the value of this option looks preferable to storing signal information in WM. This subproblem is equivalent to creating a learning agent without WM capabilities, and the average discounted reward for this subproblem is significantly reduced (0.15 on average) compared to the optimal values. Therefore, WM is critical for learning this task, and indicates that the HWMtk provides the necessary capabilities for learning systems to deal with the out-of-sight, out-of-mind problem.

Discussion

The HWMtk has several advantages over the WMtk by using HRRs for SE/DE representation.

- HRRs are much more robust than the task specific, manually encoded representations used in the original toolkit. New, complex concepts can be encoded automatically without having to alter the topology of the CN since such concepts are constructed via new HRRs or convolved representations of equivalent length. Thus, complex concepts fit into the same WM slots as simple ones, allowing slots to encode increasingly more complex concepts.
- Tasks that were previously beyond the capabilities of the previous toolkit are now more realizable. For example, since new concepts can be formed when needed, learning performance on a simple task might transfer to a more complex task. More complex tasks might be more learned in far fewer episodes by leveraging such previous knowledge rather than learning the task from scratch. Also, since HRRs provide a natural method for encoding hierachical structure, tasks which require paying attention to heirachical signals will be easier to program, and possibly easier to learn.
- The HWMtk antiquates the need for user-specified concept encoding mechanisms. This greatly reduces both the time and knowledge of ANNs needed to adequately set up encoding functions when developing learning agents. Specifically, the user no longer needs background knowledge on how to construct sparse, distributed, conjunctive codes. The user also does not need to rewrite encoding functions when *new* concepts need to be proposed to WM or encoded into the state descriptions. We hope that this alone will increase the interest in the HWMtk, and will make it a better resource for other researchers wishing to test WM-related tasks.
- The HWMtk provides a unique cognitive framework for solving partially observable reinforcement learning problems, by learning to store contextual information that proves useful for later action selection by other learning systems and illustrates the utility of WM as an attention focusing mechanism.

The development of the HWMtk has opened up several new avenues for future work. First, we plan to utilize the HWMtk to create a new version of the delayed saccade task. This task is no more complicated, in practice, than the colors task presented earlier, but it would provide a more intuitive comparison of how the distributed encoding process is simplified by the HRRE component of the HWMtk as shown in Figure 4. Second, the ability to rehearse and group items using convolution might be added to tackle tasks which require memorizing long sequences of information quickly. Such functionality might be used to study how limits on cognitive faculties arise from a small set of WM slots. Additionally, the TD learning element of the toolkit is currently being used to learn internal actions (selecting working memory contents), but has traditionally been used to learn external actions. It seems likely that the toolkit could be provided with a list of symbolic actions to choose from and the TD learning element could then learn to select appropriate actions given the current state and working memory concepts. This avenue would further reduce the programming burden placed on the user, but would also complicate the learning process by needing to learn both internal actions and external actions simultaneously. However, our 1D maze task results indicate that this hurdle was easily overcome by utilizing the same HRR approach to encode each of the possible actions and provides a clear path forward in this regard. More complex tasks involving hierarchical structure and role-filler generalization will also be explored in the future, but may require additional changes to the current generic "slot" approach used by the HWMtk since slots currently all have equal precedence. This assumption may not hold for such tasks.

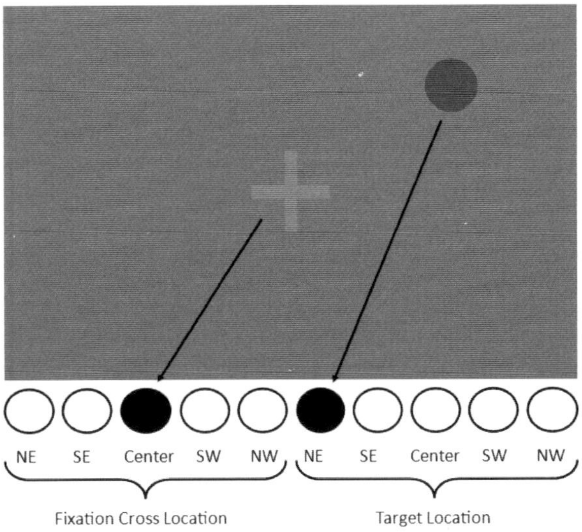

Figure 4: Example of how task-specific, sparse, distributed encoding was performed in the original WMtk. In the HWMtk, an appropriate distributed HRR representation can be built automatically without the users aid from a symbolic description of the environment: "center*cross+northeast*target".

Acknowledgments The authors would like to thank Dr. David C. Noelle (University of California, Merced) for helpful discussions and two anonymous reviewers for their supportive feedback.

References

[Baddeley 1986] Baddeley, A. 1986. Working memory. In *Oxford Psychological Series*, volume 11. Oxford: Clerendon Press.

[Busch et al. 2007] Busch, M. A.; Skubic, M.; Keller, J. M.; and Stone, K. E. 2007. A robot in a water maze: Learning a spatial memory task. In *Proceedings 2007 IEEE International Conference on Robotics and Automation*, 1727–1732.

[Erdemir et al. 2008] Erdemir, E.; Frankel, C.; Kawamura, K.; Gordon, S.; Thornton, S.; and Ulutas, B. 2008. Towards a cognitive robot that uses internal rehearsal to learn affordance relations. In *2008 IEEE/RSJ International Conference on Intelligent Robots and Systems*, 2016–2021. IEEE.

[Gordon, Kawamura, and Wilkes 2010] Gordon, S. M.; Kawamura, K.; and Wilkes, D. M. 2010. Neuromorphically inspired appraisal-based decision making in a cognitive robot. *IEEE Transactions on Autonomous Mental Development* 2(1):17–39.

[Kriete et al. 2013] Kriete, T.; Noelle, D. C.; Cohen, J. D.; and O'Reilly, R. C. 2013. Indirection and symbol-like processing in the prefrontal cortex and basal ganglia. *Proceedings of the National Academy of Sciences* 110(41):16390–16395.

[O'Reilly et al. 2002] O'Reilly, R. C.; Noelle, D. C.; Braver, T. S.; and Cohen, J. D. 2002. Prefrontal cortex and dynamic categorization tasks: representational organization and neuromodulatory control. *Cerebral Cortex* 12(3):246–257.

[O'Reilly et al. 2007] O'Reilly, R. C.; Frank, M. J.; Hazy, T. E.; and Watz, B. 2007. PVLV: The primary value and learned value Pavlovian learning algorithm. *Behavioral Neuroscience* 121(1):31–49.

[Phillips and Noelle 2005] Phillips, J. L., and Noelle, D. C. 2005. A biologically inspired working memory framework for robots. In *IEEE International Workshop on Robot and Human Interactive Communication*, 599–604. Nashville, TN: IEEE.

[Plate 1995] Plate, T. 1995. Holographic reduced representations. *IEEE Transactions on Neural Networks* 6(3):623–641.

[Sutton and Barto 1998] Sutton, R., and Barto, A. 1998. *Reinforcement Learning*. Cambridge, MA: MIT Press.

[Tugcu et al. 2007] Tugcu, M.; Wang, X.; Hunter, J. E.; Phillips, J. L.; Noelle, D. C.; and Wilkes, D. M. 2007. A Computational Neuroscience Model of Working Memory with Application to Robot Perceptual Learning. In *Proceedings of the 3rd International Conference on Computational Intelligence*.

[Waugh and Norman 1965] Waugh, N., and Norman, D. 1965. Primary memory. *Psychological Review* 72:89–104.

Deep Barca: A Probabilistic Agent to Play the Game *Battle Line*

S. McCulloch
Ohio Wesleyan University
stmccull@owu.edu

Daniel Bladow
Gonzaga University
dbladow@zagmail.gonzaga.edu

Tom Dobrow
Google, Inc
tomdobrow@gmail.com

Haleigh Wright
University of California, Santa Barbara
wright@umail.ucsb.edu

ABSTRACT

Recent years have seen an explosion of interest in "modern" board games. These differ from the "classic" games typically seen in Artificial Intelligence research (e.g. Chess, Checkers, Go) in that the modern games often have a large component of randomness or non-public information, making traditional game-tree methods infeasible. Often, these modern games have an underlying mathematical structure that can be exploited. In this paper, we describe an intelligent agent to play the game *Battle Line*, which uses elements of theorem-proving and probability to play intelligently without utilizing game trees. The agent is superior to the only other known computer player of the game and plays at a level competitive with top human players.

CCS CONCEPTS

- **Computing methodologies ~ Probabilistic reasoning**
- **Computing methodologies ~ Game tree search**

ADDITIONAL KEYWORDS

Modern Board Games, Battle Line

1 INTRODUCTION

Historically, the main work in developing intelligent agents to play board games has focused on "classic" games such as Chess [5], Checkers[12], or Othello[4]. The agents that play these games often focus on variants and improvements to game-tree search. While modern agents have many clever approaches and optimizations, there is still an exponentially-sized game tree to search. Even the recent "AlphaGo" program by Google [13] uses neural networks, but does so in order to evaluate a game tree more efficiently.

In recent years, an influx of new games have been created of varying levels of complexity. These games often depend on non-public information (such as a secret hand of cards or tiles) or randomness, making the size of a typical game tree infeasibly large.

There have been efforts to design agents to play these games. Some of these efforts have involved designing variants of classical search methods [8] [10] [11], some have applied multiple agents to the problem, and some have kept a simpler model of the game to reduce the complexity [14]. Another approach is to develop a rule-based system derived from specific rules and strategies of a given game. These rules can then either be applied directly to choose a move, or serve as the basis of an evaluation function in a search [7] [8].

While these methods can produce competitive players, any approach that uses a variant of classical search will eventually become confounded by the exponential growth of the game tree-often sooner in modern games than in more classical games because of the need to model randomness or hidden information. Efforts to reduce the game's complexity may remove important information. Rule-based systems can only perform as well as the rules in which they are given, and since those rules are typically programmed in by humans, they do not capture the autonomous nature that we desire in our agents.

Our approach is to notice that these games often have interesting underlying mathematical structure and to exploit that structure. If we can recast a game's strategy as a mathematical problem, then we have the ability to use theorems and approaches from mathematics to design an agent that makes moves based on an underlying mathematical model. We feel that an agent made according to this paradigm is more autonomous than one that follows a rule-based system or an evaluation of leaves of a game tree because its strategy comes from the mathematical underpinnings of the game itself.

We have used this approach in the past on a different game, called *Football Strategy* [8], where the rules of the game can be viewed as a normal-form game, in the game-theoretic sense. By applying concepts of Nash Equilibria, our agent created a mixed strategy that made it competitive against top human players.

In this paper we focus on the two-player strategy card game *Battle Line*, published by GMT Games in 2000 [1]. We have developed an agent named "Deep Barca" that plays this game by exploiting the underlying probabilistic and logical nature of the card game.

2 DESCRIPTION OF THE GAME

In *Battle Line* there are two decks of cards: Troop cards and Tactic cards. Most of the game is played using the Troop cards, which is a deck of 60 cards consisting of the numbers 1-10 in six different colors. On their turn, players play a Troop card from their hand on one of nine flags. Each player will eventually place three cards on each of nine flags. The three card hand that is formed is called a formation. (See Figure 1 for an example of what flags and formations look like). The player with the better formation will claim the flag. Winning the game requires claiming 5 of the 9 flags or any 3 flags in a row.

2.1 Evaluating Formations

The values of the formations correspond to three-card poker hands. The order in which cards are played does not matter; the cards in the final formation are evaluated collectively. The ranks of the different formations are as follows (the actual game uses military terminology for these ranks, but we have translated them into terminology that is closer to that used in poker to aid understanding).

- A straight flush is the highest possible hand. It consists of three cards, all the same color, in consecutive order (for example, the 7, 8, and 9 of Blue).
- A three of a kind is the next highest hand, consisting of three cards of the same number (for example, the red, blue, and green 8).
- A flush is three cards of the same color, but with no relationship among the numbers (for example, the Yellow 1, 4,and 8).
- A straight is three cards in consecutive order, but with no relationship among the colors (for example, a Red 2, Orange 3, and Purple 4).
- A nothing is the lowest formation, and is any collection of cards that does not fit one of the above rankings. (for example, a Red 2, Orange 4, and Blue 6). Note that a single pair (for example, a Green 2, Blue 2, and Orange 7) counts as a nothing.

When both players have completed formations, if one player's formation is a higher rank, that player wins. If two players have the same rank, then the highest total wins (so a three of a kind with 7's beats a 3 of a kind with 4's). If two players have the same rank and the same total, whoever finishes their hand first wins the flag. In practice among skilled players, most flags are won with a straight flush or three of a kind.

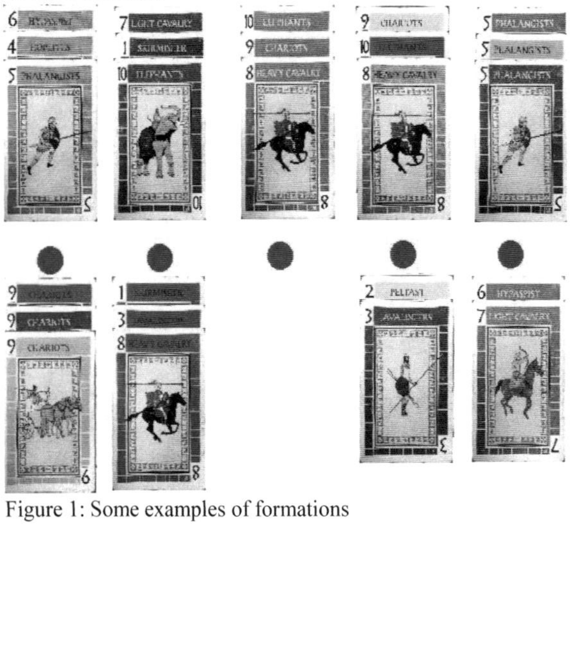

Figure 1: Some examples of formations

Figure 1 illustrates some of these situations. In the leftmost column, the top player has a straight flush, which beats the opposing three of a kind. In the second column, both players have flushes, but the top one totals to 18 and will beat the bottom's total of 12.

The third column of Figure 1 shows a situation where the top player has played the best possible hand-- the highest possible straight flush (10, 9, 8) that is finished first. Once the player plays the final card of this formation, it cannot be beaten. When this situation occurs, a player is allowed to claim a flag at the beginning of their next turn, even before the opponent has competed their three card hand on the flag. This prevents the opponent from playing any more cards on the flag and is a powerful move, as it reduces the available number of places for the opponent to play cards.

It is also possible in other situations to use the state of the board to prove that a player will not be able to beat a completed formation no matter what Troop cards are played. For example, in the fourth column of Figure 1, the top player has completed a straight totaling 27. The best formation the bottom player could possible complete is a straight totaling 9. In this case, the player is also allowed to claim the flag at the start of their next turn.

This situation can also arise when a needed card exists elsewhere on the board. In the rightmost formation of Figure 1, the bottom player has two cards towards a straight flush, which if completed would win the flag. However, the cards that can complete the straight flush have already been played (the 8 in the third column and the 5 in the same column by the top player). In this case, the best formation that can be completed by the bottom player is a flush, which will lose to the top player's three of a kind, and so the top player can claim this flag at the start of their turn.

2.2 Tactics Cards

The deck of 10 Tactics cards provides "special" cards that can bend the rules of the game in various ways. Some are wild cards (and thus can take on a variety of colors or numbers depending on what makes the best possible formation), some change the resolving rules of a flag (for example, making the hands consist of 4 cards instead of 3, or turning all hands into "nothings" so only the highest total wins), and some change the positions of the cards (allowing a player to move their cards between flags, or steal a card from an opponent's formation). The possibility of an opponent responding to a completed formation with a Tactic card play is the main reason why flags are claimed at the start of the claimers turn.

Tactic cards operate under two important restrictions. First, if a player chooses to draw a Tactic card, they do so instead of drawing a Troop card for that turn. This reduces the player's hand of playable Troop Cards. Second, a player is not allowed to have played more than one Tactics card beyond what their opponent has played. So, if Player A had played two Tactics cards, and Player B had only played one, Player A would not be able to play another Tactics card until Player B has played a second one.

3 DESIGN OF THE AGENT

Our goal in designing Deep Barca was to make the agent as autonomous as possible, giving it a set of underlying mathematical and probabilistic principles from which moves will be devised. The agent models these principles in several different ways, and these models generate rankings of the possible moves that the agent can make.

3.1 Enforcing the Rules

Before intelligently deciding on the best moves, it is necessary to develop a program that enforces the rules of the game. Many of those rules are straightforward. The most complex involves when a flag can be claimed.

As stated in the previous section, flags can be claimed by a player at the start of their turn if it can be proven that no possible set of cards the opponent can play will beat the player's formation. To determine this, when a formation is finished, the program determines the set of superior formations: formations that can beat the formation that was just completed. Then, the set of possible cards that can complete the formation are examined. These are cards that are currently not on the board (though they may be in player's hands). If any superior formation can be completed by adding these cards to it, then that formation is feasible. A flag can only be claimed if all superior formations are infeasible.

3.2 The Probabilistic Model for Decision Making

Deep Barca uses a general probabilistic model for decision making to play *Battle Line*. Each turn, for each card in its hand and for each flag that card could be placed on, the agent evaluates the probability of winning the game if the card being considered is placed on the flag being considered. It then chooses the option that maximizes this probability. Calculating the probability of winning the game for each move is a three-part process.

First, for each flag the agent calculates the top four formations that each player could make on the flag. These are the four strongest formations that could possibly be made, given the Troop Cards remaining in the agent's hand and the cards left in the deck of Troop Cards.

Next, the agent calculates the probability of winning each flag given the move under consideration. We categorize each flag in one of the following three ways:

a) If neither player has played a card towards a formation on the flag, we simply say the probability of winning the flag is 50%.
b) If both players have played at least one card towards a formation on the flag, we calculate the probability of winning the flag via what we call the *Multiple Formation Approach*, or *MFA*, described in the next section.
c) If one player has played at least one card towards a formation on the flag, but the other player has yet to play a card, we use a mix of the MFA from above and the *Best Single Formation Approach*, or *BSFA*, also described in the next section.

Lastly, we calculate the probability of winning the game as a function of the probabilities of winning each of the nine flags. Since we have two different win conditions (winning five out of nine, and winning three adjacent flags) we take the weighted average of the probabilities of winning via each of these two conditions as a function of the number of cards left in the Troop Deck. Thus, in the beginning of the game, the agent is far more concerned with simply winning the majority of the flags since this goal in practice entails doing as well as possible on as many flags as possible. Near the end of the game, the agent is more concerned with winning three adjacent flags and will even willingly sacrifice a fringe flag if it means winning three in a row somewhere else.

3.3 The MFA and BSFA Methods

The Multiple-Formation Approach (MFA) is designed to estimate the best hands that can be created once both players have committed to a hand. It is computed for each of the agent's top four formations computed above. For each potential final formation, the agent finds the probability of winning via that formation (the probability of making that formation multiplied by the probability of that formation not being beaten by the opponent). The probability of the agent winning that flag is the union of the probabilities of winning via each of its top formations.

Table 1 shows what these probabilities would look like in the situation where the agent has played a 9 on a flag, and the opponent has played a 4 of a different color. For this table, we assume that no cards in any useful formation exists in the player's hand or on any other flag. The top two formations the agent can make using the 9 are straight flushes (10-9-8 and 9-8-7). If these are successfully made, the opponent cannot possibly beat them using the 4 that was committed to its flag. The next highest formation is three nines. This involves the agent drawing any two of the five remaining nines in the deck, but can be beaten if the opponent draws any of the three possible straight flushes using the 4. The fourth highest formation is a flush totaling 26 (10-9-7). This loses not only to any straight flush, but also to any three 4's.

Formation	Probability of Making	Probability of Opponent beating	Chance to win flag
SF 10-9-8	.25	0	.25
SF 9-8-7	.25	0	.25
9-9-9	.82	.58	.35
Flush 26	.25	.94	.02

Table 1: A sample table used in the MFA for a 9 vs a 4 on an empty board. For details of how the probabilities are computed, see section 3.4

In our experiments, we found that the MFA approach did not work well on flags where one player had not played any cards. This was because on an empty flag all of the top formations in the game are still theoretically possible. Once a card is played on a flag, the space of potential formations is drastically reduced-- instead of being able to create any feasible formation, now only formations that include the played card can be considered. This had the effect of making the agent undervalue playing cards on empty flags. The reason for this is that the MFA does not take into account the need of a player to play a card on a flag (usually reducing the potential value of the formations that can be made on the flag) each turn. Instead, the probability is based on whether the formation can be made by the end of the game.

Thus, to make the agent less pessimistic, in situations where one of the two flags had no cards played, we implemented the Best

Single Formation Approach (BSFA). In the BSFA, we find the single best possible formation for the player with no cards and then evaluate the chances of winning the flag if that formation was played vs the top four formations of the player who has played cards. This simulates the potential "goal" of the opponent who sees a card played and is trying to beat what our agent is trying to do.

The BSFA on its own yields very narrow decision making because the agent will not even consider many decent or adequate formations (since they are not the single best formations that could be made). Often even subpar formations are enough to yield a victory on a particular flag. The MFA on its own is weak as well since it is heavily biased in favor of the player who has yet to play a card on the flag. This is due to the fact that all of the top formations generated for that player are simply the very strongest formations in the game since the player has yet to commit any card that would narrow his or her options. Using a mix of these two approaches, our agent makes much better decisions than it would using either approach by itself.

3.4 Evaluating Formations Probabilistically

In both the MFA and BSFA models described above, the agent needs to determine the likelihood of whether one formation will defeat another, especially in a situation where the formations are currently incomplete, and the cards needed to complete the formation will need to be drawn from the deck. We use the following probabilities to aid our calculations:

- If a card is present on the board, and is in the formation, it has a 100% probability of being part of the final formation.
- If a card is present on the board but is part of another flag, it has a 0% probability of bring part of the final formation.
- If a card is not present on the board but is in the agent's hand, then the agent gives a 100% chance of that card being a part of the formation if the desired formation belongs to the agent and a 0% chance of the card being part of the formation if the desired formation belongs to the opponent.
- If the card is not present in the board or in the agent's hand, the card must be drawn to be useful. The cards in the Troop deck are assumed to be split evenly among both players. The probability of the agent drawing a needed card is their share of the Troop deck divided by the total number of unseen cards (both in the Troop deck and the opponent's hand). The complement of that probability is the probability that the opponent will draw (or has drawn) that card. Notice that the agent will do this calculation even if the card is actually in the opponent's hand, since the agent has no legitimate way of knowing this fact.

3.5 Discarding on a Lost Flag

The above probabilistic behavior forms the bulk of our agent, and thus it chooses moves largely autonomously within the models it is given. However, our models do not cover some areas. Thus, there is a need to develop approaches for these specific situations. Even here, we attempted to make the decisions as autonomous as possible, avoiding low-level pre-programmed rules.

The first situation arises in the turn before claiming a flag. Recall that a flag is claimed at the *start* of a turn, meaning that in the normal course of events, the opponent has a turn to react between the playing of a card that will win a flag and the actual claiming of it. This turn exists to give the opponent a chance to play a Tactics card that may result in changing the resolution of a flag. But even if the player cannot or does not wish to play a Tactics card, they must take a turn. This turn often has rich strategic depth.

Since a flag that is claimed is ineligible to be played upon by either player, even if the formation is incomplete, it usually behooves the player about to lose the flag to play a card on the flag that is about to be lost. This "discarding" action has several benefits:

- Since playing a card on a flag often decreases the possible formations that can be formed, it is usually beneficial to delay committing to a flag as long as possible. Playing a card on the flag that is about to be claimed helps delay decisions about other flags.
- Since proving a flag is unbeatable often involves using cards already played on the board as a reference, discarding is a good chance to play a card that will help a later proving effort.
- Since once the flag is claimed the flag will become unplayable, *not* playing on the flag before it is claimed will mean the owner of the losing flag will have less total spaces to play on in the game (and thus have less total options in the game). This loss of tempo is especially noticeable at the end of the game, since it is possible for one player to have no legal places to play a card and be forced to pass.

Deep Barca handles the situation in which it is about to lose a flag in a different way than it handles the normal course of the game. If it recognizes (via its internal proving mechanism) that it is about to lose a flag, it attempts to find a card to discard. The decision of which card to dump is made by creating a set of "wishlists"-- cards that each possible formation (for each player) are hoping to draw or to play on a flag. The agent will choose a card that appears most frequently on the opponent's wishlist and least frequently on its own. The hope is that this discarding action will thus not adversely affect any of the top formations the agent is trying to make but possibly will aid in proving that a formation the opponent is trying to make is impossible.

These wishlists are also used by the agent to resolve conflicts where a single card is one of the top formations on multiple flags. By noting what cards are desired by the agent in other places, we reduce the probability that such a card will be available on the conflicted flag.

3.6 Drawing and Playing Tactics Cards

In addition to the Troop deck, Battle Line has a deck of Tactics Cards. These cards do many different things, and if played at the right time, can swing the ownership of a flag from one player to another, for example by playing a wild card to complete a formation that would be proven impossible using played Troop cards. The agent has two decisions regarding Tactics cards. The first decision is deciding when to draw one. The agent will be drawing a Tactics card instead of a Troop card, and since there are limitations on how many Tactics cards can be played, it is not a good idea to have an excess. The second decision is when to play one. Since there are limitations on the frequency of playing these cards, the timing of the play should be carefully considered.

Since the different Tactics cards are so different and the situations in which they can be played are so different, we had to resort to several ad-hoc rules:

- If playing a Tactic card could win the agent the game, play it.
- If the agent is about to lose a flag, and the loss can be prevented by the play of a Tactics card, play it if it raises the agent's chance of winning the flag to over 50%, or if losing the flag would lose the game.

Other than that, except for very specific situations relating to specific cards, the agent will not play a Tactics card. This has the result of the agent being rather conservative with their Tactics cards, which mirrors the way they tend to be used by expert-level humans.

Similarly, the agent will draw Tactics cards defensively. If it determines that the opponent is one card away from winning a flag that can only be beaten by a Tactics card, it will draw one. It will draw a second if the opponent has two or more cards or if the one tactic card the agent possesses is one of the "less useful" ones. In either case, the agent will not draw a Tactics card that it cannot play.

4 RESULTS

4.1 Evaluating the Quality of Deep Barca

We evaluated the quality of our agent against computer and human players. To the best of our knowledge, there is only one other computer agent, which is the IOS App *Reiner Knizia's Battleline*, by Gourmet Gaming [6] We played a best-of-three match, in which our agent handily won 2-0. In one of the games, our agent won without losing a flag. Against human players, we tested against a group of 5 experienced human players, and the agent won about 50% of the time. One of the authors is a former three-time world champion at *Battle Line* [2] at the World Boardgaming Championships [3]. We played a 10 game series, in which Deep Barca won three of the games.

With these results we can confidently say that our agent can competitively play against even the very best human Battle Line players. Also, our agent was able to make its decision for each turn in between a tenth of a second and one second, which is far faster than a human player could play. This is encouraging, since it leaves the option for more complex decision-making without those decisions taking an undue amount of time.

4.2 Emergent Behavior

Since our agent generally followed a general mathematical model for decision making, we often found that it would make moves that went against our immediate human intuition. In our experiments, we found some emergent behaviors that were particularly noteworthy.

Eight > Ten: We noticed that early in the game, on an empty flag, the agent often chose to play an 8 on the flag when it could also play a 10. Most high level human players would prefer a Troop Card with value 10 to a Troop Card with value 8, all else equal. The 10 is a higher value, and thus potentially can make hands with higher totals than the 8. However, the 8 is eligible for more straight flushes (10-9-8; 9-8-7; 8-7-6 as opposed to just 10-9-8), which are the strongest formations. Because of this, our agent's preference of an 8 over a 10 is not necessarily bad, and many human players even have this preference. We were pleased to see this behavior emerge, as it was unexpected and not caused by direct human intervention.

Playing low-value viable formations: If the agent has two cards toward a straight flush (for example, the 5 and 6 of red), and the opponent has two cards towards a three of a kind (for example, two 7's), the agent would often give up on the straight flush, going all the way down to a straight (for example, playing a blue 4). This was especially common in situations where many of the cards of the opposing three of a kind were already played (and thus making the three of a kind less likely) or in situations where there was just one possible card that would complete the straight flush.

At first glance, it appeared that the agent was making a mistake giving up a flag so easily. But in reality, once two cards of the same value are played on a flag, the only possible outcomes are a three of a kind or a nothing. The agent has recognized this fact and decided to create a formation that can *only* be beaten by the opponent drawing the card to complete their three of a kind.

While the actual usefulness and timings of these moves against top players can be debated, the ability to find these kinds of moves without having the strategies directly programmed in validates our approach to make the agent largely autonomous and based on underlying mathematical principles.

5 FUTURE WORK

There are many possible improvements we could make to the agent to strengthen quality of play and reduce ad hoc decision making even further.

We would like to improve the way the agent draws and plays Tactics cards to be less ad-hoc.

We would like to improve the agent's ability to make longer-term decisions. Since we evaluate the quality of each move based only on the game state one turn in the future, the agent can often miss moves involving multiple Tactic Cards used together, since the play of any of the cards by itself is weak.

The agent's ability to handle the scenario in which multiple flags are being claimed at the same time is very weak. We would like to be able to evaluate which of the claimed flags are worth fighting for and which of the flags might be too detrimental to lose, but currently we do not.

Our agent keeps the top four possible formations in its MFA model of rating a flag, mainly for efficiency reasons. We would like to examine what would happen if that number was increased.

Since our agent evaluates its moves so quickly, it would be interesting to see if it would be possible to incorporate some lookahead search into the agent, even if just for one or two moves.

ACKNOWLEDGMENTS

This work was partially sponsored by the National Science Foundation's Research Experience for Undergraduates Program, Grant # 1262850

REFERENCES

[1] BGG. Battle Line. Available online at https://boardgamegeek.com/boardgame/760/battle-line (2017)

[2] BPA. Battle Line Event History. Available online at http://boardgamers.org/eventhistory/bat.html (2017)

[3] BPA The World Boardgaming Championships. Available online at http://boardgamers.org/wbcindex.html (2017)

[4] Buro, M. From Simple Features to Sophisticated Evaluation Functions. In *1st International Coference on Computers and Games*, 126-145 (1999).

[5] Campbell, M., Hoane, A. & Hsu, F. Deep Blue. *Artif. Intell.*134,57–83 (2002)

[6] Gourmet Gaming. Reiner Knizia;s Battleline. Available online at http://www.gourmetgaming.com/mobileBattleline.php (2017)

[7] Hall L.; Gordon A.; James R.; and Newall L. A Lightweight Rule-Based AI Engine for Mobile Games. In Proceedings of the 2004 ACM SIGCHI International Conference on Advances in Computer Entertainment Technology, 284-289. New York, NY: Association of Computing Machinery. (2009)

[8] Heyden C. Implementing a Computer Player in Carcassone. Master's Thesis. Department of Knowledge Engineering, Maastricht University, Maastricht, Netherlands. (2009)

[9] McCulloch, S. A Game-Theoretic Intelligent Agent for the Board Game Football Strategy. Proceedings of the 26th Modern AI and Cognitive Science Conference, pp. 121-125. (2015)

[10] Schadd, M and Winands M. Quiescence Search for Stratego. In Proceedings of the 21st Benelux Conference on Artificial Intelligence. Eindhoven, the Netherlands. (2009)

[11] Schadd, M, Winands M, Bergsma M, and Uiterwijk J. Solving Fanorona. ICGA Journal, 30(1):43-45. (2007)

[12] Schaeffer, J, Culberson, J, Norman Treloar, Brent Knight, Paul Lu, Duane Szafron. A world championship caliber checkers program. *Artif. Intell.*53,273–289 (1992)

[13] David Silver, Aja Huang, Chris J. Maddison, Arthur Guez, Laurent Sifre, George van den Driessche, Julian Schrittwiese, Ioannis Antonoglou, Veda Panneershelvam, Marc Lanctot, Sander Dieleman, Dominik Grewe, John Nham, Nal Kalchbrenner, Ilya Sutskever, Timothy Lillicrap, Madeleine Leach, Koray Kavukcuoglu, Thore Graepel and Demis Hassabis. Mastering the Game of Go with Neural Networks and Deep Tree Search, *Nature* 529, 484-489 (2016).

[14] Thomas, R. Real-time Decision Making for Adversarial Environments Using a Plan-based Heuristic. PhD diss., Department of Computer Science, Northwestern University, Evanston IL. (2003)

Proof-of-Concept: Creating "Fuzzy" Sorting Algorithms

Stephany Coffman-Wolph
West Virginia University Institute of Technology
405 Fayette Pike, Montgomery, West Virginia 25136
sscoffmanwolph@mail.wvu.edu

Abstract

Sorting algorithms are common tools for manipulating data and used in both standalone circumstances and within larger more complex algorithms. Thus, it is highly desirable for sorting algorithms to be efficient in terms of storage and computation. By applying the concept of fuzzy logic (an abstract version of Boolean logic) to any well-known algorithm, it generates an abstract version (i.e., fuzzy algorithm) that often results in computational improvements. Although the algorithm may produce a less precise result, this is counteracted by gaining computational efficiency with minimal acceptable trade-offs (e.g., small increase in space requirements, loss of precision). Using an established three-step framework for fuzzification of an algorithm, the resulting new fuzzy algorithm goes beyond a simple conversion of data from raw to fuzzy data by converting the operators and concepts within the algorithm to their abstract equivalents. The purpose of this paper is to demonstrate, as a proof-of-concept, that sorting algorithms can be converted into their corresponding fuzzy sorting algorithms. This paper discusses the preliminary results of: (1) how to apply the general framework by developing the corresponding fuzzy algorithms for a variety of sort algorithms, (2) the success of applying the framework through the development of several fuzzy sort algorithms including fuzzy shell sort, fuzzy strand sort, and fuzzy bucket sort, and (3) the possible applications and benefits of these fuzzy sort algorithms.

Motivation

Sorting algorithms are used prolifically and have been thoroughly researched. This resulted in a wealth of algorithm options for sorting. Every sort algorithm produces the same result, but many have unique properties or techniques (e.g., used for an almost sorted list, reversing a sorted list, or easily adding an additional value). Given the frequent use of sorting algorithms, being able to sort efficiently (in regards to both space and time) is highly desirable. If precise sorting is not necessary, a fuzzy sort algorithm could be advantageous as fuzzy algorithms take advantage of integer calculations and generally execute fewer steps than the equivalent traditional non-fuzzy algorithm [Coffman-Wolph and Kountanis, 2013a]. (In the event that high precision is required, the results from the fuzzy algorithm could be defuzzified and run through a non-fuzzy algorithm to complete the sorting).

Introduction and Background

The next five sections provide the necessary background materials for this paper. The first section discusses the three-step fuzzy algorithm framework used to convert a traditional non-fuzzy algorithm into the corresponding equivalent fuzzy algorithm. The second section briefly discusses sorting algorithms and their use within the paper. In the third section the author discusses types of data and the fuzzy sorting algorithms. The fourth section covers the notation used within the paper to denote when an element is fuzzy. In the final section, the author provides a description of what it means to be fuzzily sorted.

The Fuzzy Algorithm Framework

The general broad-spectrum framework for the fuzzification of any algorithm is a simple three-step conversion process that converts any algorithm from a traditional non-fuzzy version into a corresponding fuzzy version [Coffman-Wolph and Kountanis, 2013b]. The three steps of the framework are as follows:

1. Decide what can/should be fuzzified and determine the category of each piece to be fuzzified
2. Fuzzify each piece (identified in step 1) based on the category
    a. Scale/normalize the data, then fuzzify the data
    b. Fuzzify the operators
    c. Fuzzify the concepts
3. Defuzzification (if needed/applicable)

As can be seen in the framework, there are three main categories of components within an algorithm that can be fuzzified or made more abstract: (1) data, (2) operators, and (3) concepts. The fuzzification of data is the process of taking "raw"/non-fuzzy data and converting it into fuzzy data. The fuzzification of operators is the process of converting a mathematical, logical, or comparative operator to its fuzzy counterpart, which operates on fuzzy sets instead of pure numbers. The fuzzification of concepts, the most difficult of the three, is the conversion of an idea into a similar fuzzy idea. Together these three core techniques create a fuzzy algorithm.

The first and second steps of the framework are needed to apply the fuzzy algorithm to a variety of problems. The first step of the framework is to make an in-depth examination of the traditional (non-fuzzy) algorithm and decide which elements to fuzzify. It is often helpful to determine what the solution will look like in the fuzzy form. This will lay the foundation for the entire fuzzified algorithm. Therefore, it can be helpful to work backwards through the algorithm to determine what elements (data, operators, or concepts) need to be changed for the solution to be produced. Defuzzification, the opposite of fuzzification, is used to convert the result back to a non-fuzzy result and can be applied to data or concepts. In some cases, this step might be unnecessary and, hence, why the framework denotes this step as optional. Deciding to do defuzzification is both problem and usage dependent. For example, if the fuzzy algorithm is being used to narrow the solution space and the information will be fed into a non-fuzzy algorithm, then it is important to develop a method of defuzzification.

This process has already been successfully applied to the following algorithms: (1) a concept-oriented fuzzification for finding fuzzy patterns [Coffman-Wolph and Kountanis, 2013c], (2) a fuzzification of both data and the operators for a fuzzy process particle swarm optimization (FP2SO) [Coffman-Wolph and Kountanis, 2013a], (3) a fuzzification of multiple algorithm components to find strategies for adversarial situations from game theory [Coffman-Wolph, 2013], (4) a fuzzification of the simple simplex method for the transportation problem [Coffman-Wolph and Coffman, Jr, 2014], (5) the fuzzification of various linear and nonlinear search techniques used in optimization algorithms [Coffman-Wolph and Coffman, Jr, 2016], and (6) the fuzzification of the Golden Ratio Search [Coffman-Wolph, 2016].

The Sorting Algorithm

Generally, sort algorithms put data "in order". This paper will explore a variety of sort algorithms ranging from the simplistic comparison sorts to slightly more complex distribution sorts. Given the commonality of these sort algorithms, this paper will focus only on the specific algorithmic details needed for fuzzification conversion and skip in-depth discussions of the algorithms themselves. To simplify the discussion, this paper will primarily consider integer data. These concepts are easily extended to other data types as discussed in the next section.

Data

Sorting algorithms are generally able to handle a wide variety of data types (e.g., numbers, strings, or combinations). The fuzzy sort algorithms will need to have the data "converted" to the fuzzy equivalent. Fuzzy algorithms generally take advantage of integer calculations and, usually, have the data in integer format. In the circumstances that require a conversion of non-integer numeric data, it is often accomplished using scaling. A fuzzy number is not a single value, but is represented by a set of values. The size/range of values is problem/data dependent and can also be affected by the level of precision the user desires. For strings, there are several possibilities for fuzzifying the data including: converting to a number or considering only the ASCII value equivalent of the first character (or the first few characters). If there is a combination of data (i.e., records from a database), then a combination of fuzzy data would be required. The greatest performance advantage is obtained using integer values, so the closer the data is to an integer format the better.

Notation

Throughout this paper, a subscript f will be used to denote when a value, variable, operator, or concept is fuzzy. Given that not everything is required to be fuzzy within a fuzzy algorithm, the subscript f will help the reader distinguish between portions of the algorithm that remain traditional/non-fuzzy and those that have been converted to a corresponding fuzzy version. As mentioned in the previous section, it is important to keep in mind that a single fuzzy value is represented by a set of non-fuzzy traditional values. For example, 5_f is a "fuzzy-five" and contains the value 5 and possibly the values 4 and 6 as well (depending on the definition of 5_f in the context of the problem). In other circumstances, 5_f could represent all the real number values in the range of 4.5 to 6.5.

Definition of Fuzzily Sorted

A traditional sort algorithm stops when the algorithm has guaranteed that all data are sorted in the required order (e.g., numerical order, alphabetical order, reverse order, or a combination). To proceed with the fuzzification of the sort algorithm, the key question to answer is: when is the $data_f$ from a fuzzy sort algorithm considered sorted sufficiently? In general, adding fuzzy logic to an algorithm creates a more abstract version of this algorithm. Therefore, with a fuzzy sort, it will be a more abstract version of the sort algorithm and, thus, the output is abstractly sorted. The definition of "abstractly sorted" will depend on the circumstances of the application and may be problem specific and/or sorting algorithm specific (i.e., dependent on the fuzzification process). These definitions have one thing in common, that the data will not always be perfectly sorted. One could describe the data as "slightly out of order". For a fuzzy sort, one measure could be an associated percentage which represents the required/desired level of sufficient "sorted-ness". The level or percentage can be adjusted as needed for desired precision. Another measure, for a fuzzy sort, could be that the results are sorted within a specific number of significant digits or letters/symbols.

The Fuzzy Sort Algorithm

The following sections discuss the fuzzification of several well-known sort algorithms including: selection, insertion, bubble, shell, strand, and bucket sort. Each subsection below will focus on how the algorithm is converted from the traditional algorithm to a fuzzy algorithm using the three-step framework for conversion. A discussion of the likely advantages and disadvantages will be included for each of the sort algorithms.

Fuzzy Version of Selection, Insertion, and Bubble Sort

Selection, Insertion, and Bubble sorts are three of the most common comparison-based $O(n^2)$ sort algorithms [Sedgewick, 1998; Weiss, 1999]. Each algorithm can be easily converted from the traditional algorithm into a fuzzy equivalent version. The comparison operators, $<$ and $>$, would be converted to $<_f$ and $>_f$ to handle the fuzzified data, but the algorithms would otherwise remain unchanged and operate in the same manner. The fuzzy selection, fuzzy insertion, and fuzzy bubble sorts do not experience any computational advantages except the possible use of integer comparisons over more complex data types. Additionally, the output of these fuzzy sorts would be dependent on the precision level the user wants to achieve when they fuzzify the data and decide the exact functionality of the $<_f$ and $>_f$. Therefore, the author concludes that while these algorithms can be converted to their fuzzy equivalents, there is no advantage to do this unless they are being applied as part of a more complex sort algorithm (e.g., the bubble sort as a last step in a more sophisticated sort algorithm).

Fuzzy Version of the Shell Sort

The traditional shell sort is an "in-place" sort and considered an abstract version of an insertion sort [Sedgewick, 1998; Weiss, 1999]. (The comb sort is a very similar "in-place" sort but uses the bubble sort as an underlying basis and basically differs only at the implementation level). When the fuzzified version of the shell sort is implemented, the algorithm will be even further abstracted. Both the fuzzy and traditional versions of the sort use a single list with portions of the list designated as sorted and un-sorted. (Traditional implementations have the sorted portion at the front of the list and the un-sorted portion towards the back of the list). During the process of converting the algorithm to a fuzzy algorithm, the concept of the xth element will be fuzzified using the concept of a fuzzy set [Zadeh, 1965]. For the traditional shell sort, the algorithm takes every x^{th} element within the un-sorted portion of the list and sorts them into the correct sequence before merging them into the sorted portion of the list. In the corresponding fuzzified version of this algorithm, the algorithm will take every x_f^{th} set of elements from the un-sorted portion of the list, sort$_f$ these elements, and merge these elements into the sorted$_f$ portion of the list. The fuzzy shell sorting algorithms would likely have an advantage in situations where data naturally "clusters".

Consider the following data points: 88, 92, 98, 100, 7, 5, 3, 13, 17, 15, 24, 36, 42, 57, 55, 73, and 77 to illustration the fuzzy shell sort (and the traditional shell sort). When using the fuzzy shell sort, the first step is to determine the definition of the x_f^{th} element(s). For this small of a list, the fuzzy algorithm will use a two-element range at each x_f^{th} element. Thus, the algorithm will consider the xth element and the $(x+1)^{th}$ element to be the x_f^{th} element. The fuzzy algorithm begins by selecting the 5_f^{th} elements: (88, 92), (5, 3), (24, 36), and (73, 77). These elements are sorted, removed from the un-sorted portion of the list, and placed into the sorted part of the list: 3, 5, 24, 36, 73, 77, 88, and 92 and the unsorted portion is: 98, 100, 7, 13, 17, 15, 42, 57, and 55. The next step is to take the 3_f^{th} elements which are (98, 100), (17, 15), and (57, 55). These elements are sorted into the existing list and removed from the unsorted list: 3, 5, 15, 17, 24, 36, 55, 57, 73, 77, 88, 92, 98, and 100 and the remaining portion of the unsorted list is: 7, 13, and 42. These last three elements can be sorted into the sorted portion of the list: 3, 5, 7, 13, 15, 17, 24, 36, 42, 55, 57, 73, 77, 88, 92, 98, and 100. For each of the x_f^{th} elements, the only additional processing required is a simple swap (as there are only two elements) before sorting and merging. The traditional version of the shell sort algorithm run on the same data set would require 5 total passes to get the data in numeric order, which is an additional two passes over this fuzzy algorithm version. The author projects from preliminary data that this technique would cut the number of passes in almost half as each pass pulls twice the amount of data.

Fuzzy Version of the Strand Sort

The strand sort is a fairly straightforward comparison-based sorting algorithm. The algorithm looks for strands of in-order data and slowly builds the sorted list [Black, 2008]. The following data points: 55, 57, 89, 92, 98, 95, 100, 3, 5, 7, 13, 15, 17, 24, 36, 42, 73, and 77 will be used to demonstrate the fuzzy strand sort (and the traditional strand sort). The traditional algorithm begins by creating a sub-list obtained by comparing each value to the next value and stopping when the next is less than the previous. The traditional algorithm would find the following strand: 55, 57, 89, 92, 98. The remaining elements are: 95, 100, 3, 5, 7, 13, 15, 17, 24, 36, 42, 73, and 77. However, the fuzzy version of the strand sort performs fuzzy "less than" comparisons (e.g., $<_f$ means $x <_f y$ if $x < y + 5$) and, thus, could create the following sub-list: 55, 57, 89, 92, 98, 95, 100 with the remaining elements being: 3, 5, 7, 13, 15, 17, 24, 36, 42, 73, and 77. The traditional algorithm would need to take an additional step to get to the same place (merging the 95, 100 into the sub-list). From that point onward both the traditional and fuzzy versions of strand sort would produce the same strands. The final sorted list for the traditional strand sort is always precisely in-order. However, the fuzzy strand sort could have a few data points slightly out of order (as can be seen with the 98 and 95 above). The fuzzy strand algorithm required fewer overall steps and could be the better sort algorithm when the slightly out of order data are within an acceptable level of precision. Given the nature and organization of the data that works well for the strand sort, the fuzzy strand algorithm could take the same or fewer steps than the traditional version of the algorithm. However, the fuzzy strand algorithm would never take more steps then the traditional version. The fuzzy strand algorithm output might be slightly out of order, but the max amount is predictable and controlled by the specific implementation of the fuzzy set size.

Fuzzy Version of the Bucket Sort

A fuzzy sort most closely resembles the traditional distribution based sorts or "bucket" sorts, but differs because of the underlying definition of a fuzzy value. In a traditional bucket sort, an item sorts into one category/bucket [Sedgewick, 1998; Weiss, 1999]. In a fuzzy sort since each (fuzzy) value is represented by a set, an item can sort into multiple categories/buckets. Additionally, each category/bucket is a (fuzzy) value and it too is represented by a set, thus, the categories/buckets may overlap and do not have to be distributed evenly.

Given the following set of numbers: 24, 36, 50, 42, 57, 0, 88, 73, 92, 46, 7, 81, 15, 21, 100. Both the traditional and fuzzy bucket sort algorithms begin by sorting each number into a bucket/bin. For this example, consider that there are four bucket/bins for the traditional bucket sort: (1) 0-25, (2) 26-50, (3) 51-75, (4) 75-100. The numbers will be sorted as follows using the traditional algorithm:

1. 24, 0, 7, 15, 21
2. 36, 50, 42, 46
3. 57
4. 88, 73, 92, 81, 100

For the fuzzy algorithm, the four fuzzy buckets/bins are defined as: (1) 25 and below, (2) 20-50, (3) 45-82, and (4) 70 and above. The numbers could be sorted as follows using the fuzzy algorithm (and fuzzy buckets):

1. 0, 7, 15, 21
2. 24, 36, 50
3. 42, 57, 46, 73
4. 88, 81, 92, 100

Using the same four fuzzy buckets/bins, the fuzzy algorithm could also have produced the following:

1. 0, 7, 15, 21
2. 24, 36, 42, 46
3. 50, 57, 73, 81
4. 88, 92, 100

Observe that the output for the traditional algorithm would require further processing on each bin to complete the algorithm. Generally, in these kinds of algorithms, either each bin/bucket is subdivided into more bin/buckets or the contents of each bucket are sorted using a basic sort algorithm. In the first output of the fuzzy algorithm, the data in each bin/bucket except number four is almost in-order (and bin number four needs the 88 and 81 flipped). (Merging these bins/buckets into a final sorted list would be an easy process and eliminate the issue that the 46 is in bin number three while the 50 is located in bin number two). The second output of the fuzzy algorithm, the fuzzily sorted data is completely in order and does not require further processing. Both outputs of the fuzzy algorithm are better in-order than the output produced by the traditional algorithm

In this example, it is important to note that that there is both overlap between the different buckets and different sizes for each bucket/bin. Changing the overlap amounts and size of bins could change the outcome of the algorithm and it would be important to choose these dependent on the data being sorted. In other words, the bin size and overlap are both problem and data specific. If the user wants/needs a high level of precision on the fuzzy sort, then the overlap and bin size would need to be chosen carefully and the algorithm would probably need to continue by further sorting each bin. However, if each bucket/bin has a small quantity of data, in many cases it will not be necessary to continue sorting.

The total number of steps taken by the fuzzy bucket/bin sort is controlled in the same way as the traditional algorithm – basically divide into to bucket/bins until each bin has a certain amount (and then use another sorting technique to complete each bin). With the fuzzy bucket sort, it would be possible to eliminate the final step of using another sorting technique to completely sort each bin especially when the slightly out of order numbers are within an acceptable lack of precision. The output of a fuzzy bucket/bin algorithm might be slightly out of order, but can be partial controlled by the specific implementation of the fuzzy bucket/bin sizes and the overlap allowed among bins. The fuzzy bucket/bin algorithm is also more adaptable and, from the preliminary data, more accurate when sorting data with fewer bins than needed by the traditional algorithm.

Possible Applications for Fuzzy Sort Algorithms

As mentioned earlier, sorting is most commonly used to manipulate data especially for display to a user or within a search algorithm, but sorting algorithms are found within a diverse range of interesting and complex algorithms. There are several operation research examples that implement a sort algorithm as an essential element of a larger algorithm including shortest processing time rule, load-balancing problem, and event-driven simulation [Hillier and Lieberman, 1990; Lasden, 1970; Luenberger, 1973]. In discrete event simulation, a sorting algorithm is used to order events but a fuzzy sort algorithm would be an unworkable solution because the events are required to be in exactly time order (and, as seen earlier, a fuzzy sort could have a few items out of order). However, there are circumstances where that functionality of the fuzzy sort algorithm would not have detrimental or negative effects on operation research algorithms. For example, in queuing problems, sorting is used to determine the ordering of operations and the operations list is constantly being re-ordered. Given that a precise ordering is not necessary and the nearly continuously resorting of the data, a faster fuzzy sort algorithm would be helpful to the overall runtime of the algorithm. Another example is bin packing, if objects are sorted from largest to smallest, then greedy algorithms can find optimal results. Using a fuzzy sort algorithm to produce a "good enough" or "close enough" list from largest to smallest will produce close to optimal results but spend less precious processing time. For queues, sequence rules, and other similar algorithms, a fuzzy sort can provide an approximate order which would be sufficient for most heuristic algorithms.

Discussion and Concluding Remarks

After preliminary analysis, further study is needed to investigate the promising implications seen in the aforementioned sample fuzzy sort algorithms. This paper has demonstrated that it is possible to convert a sort algorithm into a more abstract fuzzy version using the established three-step framework. However, it is important to note that often the success of the conversion process is dependent on the techniques and underlying design of the algorithm itself. Likewise, the measure of usefulness of the fuzzy sort algorithm is dependent on the precision required in the resulting sorted output. The "in-place" sort algorithms demonstrated some reduction in number of iterations needed by moving to a fuzzy sort algorithms. However, the bucket-based sort algorithm behavior corresponded the best to the natural habits of a fuzzy sort algorithm and, thus, showed the best promise of the algorithms presented in this paper.

Future Work

Using the knowledge gained in this proof-of-concept paper, the author plans to further investigate the fuzzification of sort algorithms by focusing attention on the bucket-like sorts and the "in-place" sorts. One next step would be to complete an implementation of these algorithms (both fuzzy and non-fuzzy) and run benchmark data on these algorithms to determine if the promise shown above holds for various cases. Additionally, the author needs to: (1) verify that fuzzifying the sort algorithm does not have adverse effects to sorting the data and (2) determine the best and worst cases for the fuzzy sorts. For adverse effects, the author will thoroughly investigate the negative or dangerous effects fuzzification could have on an algorithm and determine if there exist any countermeasures. The author also plans to use the knowledge gleamed from this experience to further refine details of the three-step framework. This research encompasses the need to determine which algorithm characteristics imply that there is a smooth transition from non-fuzzy to fuzzy using the framework and which algorithm characteristics imply that a transition is infeasible or impractical.

References

[Black, 2008] Black, P. E. 2008. Strand Sort. In *Dictionary of Algorithms and Data Structures*. https://www.nist.gov/dads/HTML/strandSort.html [online].

[Coffman-Wolph, 2016] Coffman-Wolph, S. 2016. Fuzzy Algorithms: Applying Fuzzy Logic to the Golden Ratio Search to Find Solutions Faster. In the Proceedings of the 27th Modern Artificial Intelligence and Cognitive Science Conference (MAICS 2016).

[Coffman-Wolph and Coffman Jr, 2016] Coffman-Wolph, S and Coffman, Jr, P. 2016. Fuzzification Of Search Techniques for Linear and Nonlinear Optimization. Conference Presentation. In the Proceedings of the INFORMS Annual Meeting, Nashville, Tennessee.

[Coffman-Wolph, 2015] Coffman-Wolph, S. 2015. The Hunch Factor: Exploration into Using Fuzzy Logic to Model Intuition in Particle Swarm Optimization. In the Proceedings of the 26th Modern AI and Cognitive Science Conference (MAICS 2015).

[Coffman-Wolph and Coffman Jr, 2014] Coffman-Wolph, S and Coffman, Jr, P. 2014. Fuzzification of the Special Simplex Method for the Transportation Problem. Conference Presentation. In the Proceedings of the INFORMS Annual Meeting, San Francisco, California.

[Coffman-Wolph, 2013] Coffman-Wolph, S. 2013. Fuzzy Search Strategy Generation for Adversarial Systems using Fuzzy Process Particle Swarm Optimization, Fuzzy Patterns, and a Hunch Factor. Ph.D. diss., Department of Computer Science, Western Michigan University, Kalamazoo, MI.

[Coffman-Wolph and Kountanis, 2013a] Coffman-Wolph, S. and Kountanis, D. 2013a. Fuzzy Process Particle Swarm Optimization.

In the Proceedings of the 43rd Southeastern Conference on Combinatorics, Graph Theory, & Computing. Winnipeg: Utilitas Mathematica Pub. Inc.

[Coffman-Wolph and Kountanis, 2013b] Coffman-Wolph, S. and Kountanis, D. 2013b. A General Framework for the Fuzzification of Algorithms. In the Proceedings of the 4th Biennial Michigan Celebration of Women in Computing (MICWIC 2013).

[Coffman-Wolph and Kountanis, 2013c] Coffman-Wolph, S. and Kountanis, D. 2013c. Finding Strategies in Adversarial Situations. In the Proceedings of the 24th Modern AI and Cognitive Science Conference (MAICS 2013).

[Hillier and Lieberman, 1990] Hillier, F. S., and Lieberman, G. J. 1990. *Introduction to Operations Research*. McGraw-Hill.

[Lasden, 1970] Lasden, L. (1970) *Optimization Theory for Large Systems*. New York, NY: Macmillan Publishing Co, Inc.

[Luenberger, 1973] Luenberger, D. 1973. *Introduction to Linear and Nonlinear Programming*. Reading, MA: Addison-Wesley Publishing Company.

[Sedgewick, 1998] Sedgewick, R. 1998. *Algorithms in C++ Third Edition, Parts 1-4*. Boston: Addison-Wesley Publishing Company, Inc.

[Weiss, 1999] Weiss, M. A. 1999. *Data Structures & AlgorithmAnalysis in C++*. Reading, MA: Addison Wesley Longman, Inc.

[Wismer and Chattergy, 1978] Wismer, D. and Chattergy, R. 1978. *Introduction to Nonlinear Optimization*. New York, NY: Elsevier North-Holland, Inc.

[Zadeh, 1965] Zadeh, L.A. 1965. Fuzzy Sets. *Information and Control* 8: 338-353.

Toward An IoT-based Expert System for Heart Disease Diagnosis

Do Thanh Thai[1], Quang Tran Minh[1], Phu H. Phung[2]
[1] Ho Chi Minh City University of Technology, VNU-HCM, Vietnam
{1570229,quangtran}@hcmut.edu.vn
[2] Intelligent Systems Security Lab
Department of Computer Science, University of Dayton, Dayton, OH, USA
http://academic.udayton.edu/PhuPhung/

Abstract

IoT technology has been recently adopted in the healthcare system to collect Electrocardiogram (ECG) signals for heart disease diagnosis and prediction. However, noises in collected ECG signals make the diagnosis and prediction system unreliable and imprecise. In this work, we have proposed a new lightweight approach to removing noises in collected ECG signals to perform precise diagnosis and prediction. First, we have used a revised Sequential Recursive (SR) algorithm to transform the signals into digital format. Then, the digital data is proceeded using a revised Discrete Wavelet Transform (DWT) algorithm to detect peaks in the data to remove noises. Finally, we extract some key features from the data to perform diagnosis and prediction based on a feature dataset. Redundant features are removed by using Fishers Linear Discriminant (FLD). We have used an ECG dataset from MIT-BIH (PhisioNet) to build a knowledge-base diagnosis features. We have implemented a proof-of-concept system that collects and processes real ECG signals to perform heart disease diagnosis and prediction based on the built knowledge-base.

1 Introduction

Electrocardiogram (ECG) signals are the data measured from patients' heartbeats by electronic devices. Generated by cells in the heart, ECG signals reflect all activities in these cells. Therefore, ECG signals are the most valuable data used in the heart disease diagnosis [Blackburn *et al.*, 1960].

Nowadays, ECG signals can be measured automatically by sensors instead of the conventional discrete measurement [Hassanalieragh and Moeen, 2015; Pantelopoulos *et al.*, 2010; Paradiso *et al.*, 2005; Milenkovi *et al.*, 2006; Bazzani and Marco, 2012; Benharref *et al.*, 2014]. The data collected by the sensors can be transmitted to a cloud-based system to perform preliminary automatic diagnosis based on a knowledge-base without medical experts. A knowledge-base is initially built using a large sample dataset, and then can frequently be updated by specialists to improve the accuracy of the prediction.

The overall aim of our work is to develop such an eco-expert system using Internet of Things (IoT) technology. As data can be collected in real-time and transmitted to the cloud for analysis, the proposed expert system will help patients to detect their possible heart diseases before seeing their doctors. This system can also support the physicians to perform treatment for their patients for a minimum period.

However, there are several significant research challenges in building such expert systems. First, noises always appear in the ECG signals, making the data imprecisely or even unreadable. Second, building a knowledge-base to be used in heart disease diagnosis and prediction is not a trivial task. Finally, ECG signals must be extracted with some key features to match with the knowledge-base for accuracy prediction.

In this paper, we have proposed a lightweight approach to solving above mentioned challenges. We have developed a combined data processing algorithms to collect "clear" ECG signals from sensors. In particular, we have adopted the Sequential Recursive (SR), Discrete Wavelet Transform (DWT), and Fishers Linear Discriminant (FLD) algorithms and combined them to remove noises from raw ECG data. Based on these algorithms, we have proposed a novel computational model to extract precise features and perform diagnosis and prediction by matching with the ones developed in the knowledge-base. We have also built a knowledge-base from a public heart disease dataset (MIT-BIH [MIT-BIHArrhythmiaDatabase, 2016] from Boston's Beth Israel Hospital) and evaluated our proposed diagnosis system using this knowledge-base.

In summary, the main contributions of this paper include:

- We have proposed combined algorithms to remove noises from ECG signals received from sensors.
- We have developed a mechanism to automatically extract information related to heart disease from filtered ECG signals.

- We have implemented a proof-of-concept heart disease diagnosis system based on a large dataset. The system has been validated by a real data collected from the human through ECG sensors.

The rest of the paper is organized as follows. In the next section, we discuss the related work and motivate our contributions. Section 3 describes the background of this research including knowledge-base of ECG, data processing, Sequential Recursive (SR) algorithm, features extraction using Discrete Wavelet Transform (DWT), arrhythmias classification using Fishers Linear Discriminant (FLD). Section 4 presents our approach to building a computational model using combined algorithms to filter data. Classifying and extracting heart disease features for matching with knowledge-base are also described. In Section 5, we illustrate our experimental results. We discuss and summarize our contributions in Section 6.

2 Related Work

Expert systems for heart disease diagnosis have been studied in the literature. For example, ECG signal analysis can be recognized and classified by neural networks [Kiranyaz *et al.*, 2016]. Neural networks use a large number of neural units; each neural unit has relations with others, the number of relationships depends on the structure of the system. The neural network combines multilayer feed forward network with back propagation learning algorithm [Patel and Joshi, 2013]. Although the system can learn during runtime, some parameters are still chosen in ranges, which are dependent on the experience of the users when they deploy the system. A more advanced system is proposed by adding one more step to classification the arrhythmias [Khemphila and Boonjing, 2011]. The method is to use the production data from *multi layer feed forward network with back propagation learning algorithm* and *doctor's expertise, experience* to give the clinical diagnosis. However, these systems only support the physicians yet do not provide the automatic diagnosis.

Fuzzy support vector machine (FSVM) is another method using techniques of pattern recognition to decide the acceptable recorded signals. FSVM is frequently used to assess the quality of ECG analysis processing [Zhang and Ya-tao, 2014].

Classification of heart disease features was also well studied. In [Rani, 2011; Das *et al.*, 2009], a database from Cleveland was used to build the training and testing classification. However, the diagnosis and analysis of input data were not studied.

On the other hand, Wireless Body Area Network (WBAN) technologies have been recently introduced and adopted in healthcare systems. WBAN automatically measures users' parameters such as blood pressure, brain activities, ECG and other, and transmits the collected data to the cloud for analysis. Users, medical staffs, and other stakeholders can access, analyze and visualize data depend on their right. WBAN is considered as an IoT-based system in healthcare and has recently been studied [Hassanalieragh and Moeen, 2015; Pantelopoulos *et al.*, 2010; Paradiso *et al.*, 2005; Milenkovi *et al.*, 2006; Bazzani and Marco, 2012; Benharref *et al.*, 2014]. As discussed in [Soni *et al.*, 2011], IoT-based data contain *'rich information'* but *'poor knowledge'*. Several data-mining methods for extracting data from the massive volume healthcare database were proposed in [Soni *et al.*, 2011].

In this work, we aim to contribute to filling the gap by introducing an IoT-based framework that combines data acquisition, extraction, classification. We will also build a frequently update knowledge-base to perform feature matching for heart disease diagnosis and prediction. In the next section, we present the background needed for this work.

3 Background

In this section, we describe the overview of the electrocardiogram signal and related algorithms to process the data.

3.1 Electrocardiogram

Electrocardiogram signal (ECG) is an electrical signal that is frequently measured by three poles, also known as electrodes, placed on the skin. These electrodes capture electrical signals produced by heart muscles electrophysiological during the heartbeat.

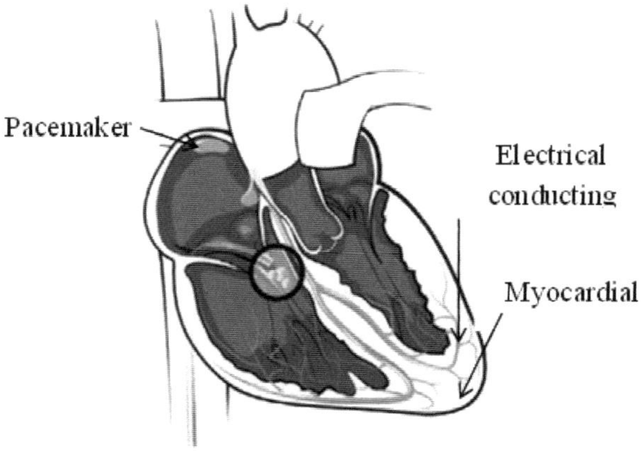

Figure 1: The cells in construction of heart

ECG signals are generated by cells in the heart. The structure of the heart constructed by three kinds of cells: pacemaker, electrical conducting, myocardial. Figure 1 depicts the cells in the construction of heart. Pacemaker cells produce electrical that provides power for all activities of heart. Electrical conducting cells transmit the power from the source to remote regions of the heart. Myocardial cells work likely to the engine of a mechanical system. Therefore, for any issue relevant to these cells will be reflected through the electrical signals (ECG). Parameters in ECG signals such as phase time cycles, peak magnitudes can be used to diagnose types of heart diseases [Blackburn *et al.*, 1960].

ECG can be measured by sensors. The output of these ECG sensors is analog signals. These signals need to be converted to digital data to be able to processed. Normally, ECG will go through an Analog-to-Digital Converter (ADC) and then to other Microcontrollers (MCU). Data processed by MCU then is stored in cloud helping for the database of healthcare systems.

3.2 Data processing algorithms

In this work, we propose a model to process the ECG signals from sensors. The model adopts a number of data processing algorithms. In this subsection, we briefly describe these related algorithms used in Section 4.

Finite Impulse Response (FIR)

Finite Impulse Response (FIR) filter is an algorithm that removes noises in digital signals. FIR filter can briefly be described as function below [Oppenheim *et al.*, 1983].

$$\begin{aligned} y[n] &= b_0x[n] + b_1x[n-1] + ... + b_Nx[n-N] \\ &= \sum_{i=0}^{N} b_ix[n-i] \end{aligned} \tag{1}$$

where,
x[n]: The input signal;
y[n]: The output signal;
N: The filter order;
$b_i, i = 0 \to N$: The value of the impulse response at the ith instant, it is also a coefficient of the filter.

Sequential Recursive Algorithm - SR

With the characteristics of ECG, time series represent for the object that need to be analyzed. For a long time, time series investigating belong to the scope of medical diagnoses.

The signal y at time n can be estimated via the data from beginning to $(n-1)$. To obtain $y[n]$, factor θ decides the quality of the estimating operation [Ifeachor and Jervis, 2002; Godambe, 1991].

$$\begin{aligned} y[n] &= \sum_{i=1}^{n} \theta_i.y[k-1] + e[k] \\ &= [y[k-1] \cdots y[k-n]].[\theta_i \cdots \theta_n]^T + e[k] \\ &= \mu[k]^T.\theta + e[k], e[k] \simeq NID[0, \sigma_e^2] \end{aligned} \tag{2}$$

where,
$y[k]$: Signal at time k;
$\mu[k]$: Regression vector at time k;
θ: Prediction parameter vector;
$e[k]$: The error at time k.

Discrete Wavelet Transform

Discrete Wavelet Transform (DWT) using technique of discretely sampling where all signals such as numerical, functional analysis based on any wavelet is discretely separated, both frequency and location information stored in the signal are captured [Akansu *et al.*, 2010; Akansu and Haddad, 2001].

$$a^t[n] = \sum_k a^{t-1}[n]g[2n-k] \tag{3}$$

$$d^t[n] = \sum_k a^{t-1}[n]h[2n-k] \tag{4}$$

$a^t[n]$: Coefficient of the approximation;
$d^t[n]$: Detail vector;
$g[.]$: Low-pass wavelet filter;
$h[.]$: High-pass wavelet filter.
Both $g[.]$ and $h[.]$ represent for down-sampling by two $[2n-k]$.

Fisher's Linear Discriminant

Fisher's Linear Discriminant (FLD) is a method for pattern recognition, machine learning, and statistics. It operates by the way of finding a linear combination of features which represent for separated classes of objects or events, the number of classes depends on the characteristics of the signal. The combination helps to reduce the redundancy features which are duplicated or not necessary, it makes the classification less complicated [McLachlan, 2004; Haghighat *et al.*, 2016]. Equation (5) illustrates this algorithm.

$$S_w = \sum_{t=1}^{n} \sum_{x \in C_t} (x - \bar{x}_t)(x - \bar{x}_t)^T \tag{5}$$

where,
S_w: The intra-class matrix;
$\bar{x}_t$: The mean vector of the tth class;
x: Data vector that belong to training feature data set.

4 Proposed Model for Data Processing and Diagnosis

We propose a model that contains several modules and steps. First, we develop several filter modules to remove noises in raw ECG signals collected from sensors. Next, we adopt the SR algorithm to process the filtered ECG data, and compare with an ECG knowledge-base to produce data for the feature extraction module. Extracted features are the input for the classification module that performs diagnosis. In the next subsections, we describe these modules in detail.

4.1 Noise removal

As mentioned, ECG signals are very sensitive to noises that make the collected data unreadable. To filter and remove noises, we have performed several steps and algorithms as follows. First, we propose a simple raw filter module, developed in a micro-controller, to filter the raw data so that they can be readable for the next step. Next, we implement the Low and High pass filters because ECG signals are sensitive to low and high-frequency noises. We use the FIR filter algorithm (c.f. Section 3) for the both filters. These FIR-based filters

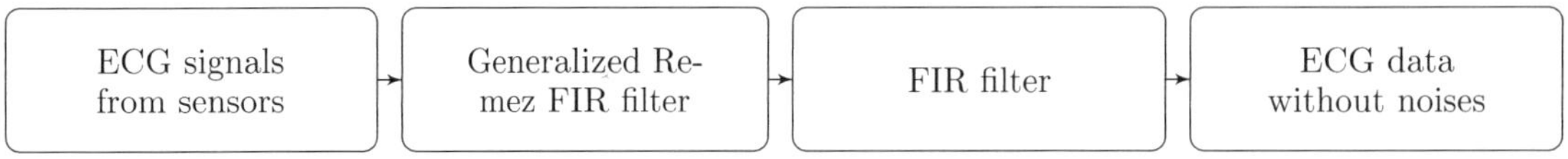

Figure 2: Structure of Low/High pass filter

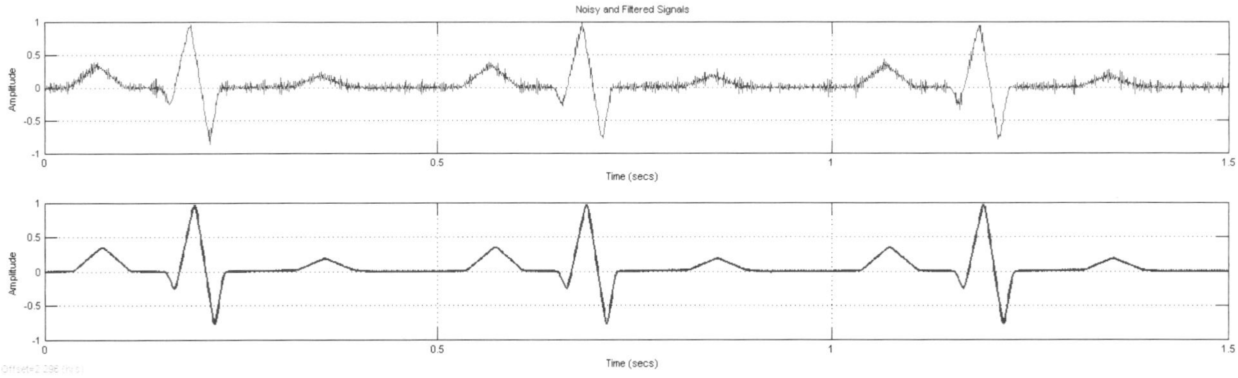

Figure 3: ECG signal with and without noise

are the primary processor to remove noises, as illustrated in Figure 2. **Defined Parameters** integrated in block *Generalized Remez FIR filter* have threshold parameters such as pass-threshold, stop-threshold, and other corresponding ones. Depending on the values of pass-threshold and stop-threshold parameters; diagram in Figure 2 is defined as Low or High pass filter respectively.

The output of these filters is ECG data without noises that can be used for the next module for analysis and classification. Figure 3 illustrates the ECG signals with and without noises, before and after passing through Low and High pass filters. In the real implementation, the values of parameters of FIR filter are calibrated to reach the best fit.

4.2 Sequential Recursive Algorithm for Data Processing

We propose a data processing adaptive model using the Sequential Recursive (SR) Algorithm, depicted in Figure 4. The core of this adaptive model is the block Model (SR algorithm) in the figure. ECG signals of each patient have different characteristics. To handle this, our proposed model will perform automatic adjustment to get the best match based on: (1) the backward step n in the previous block, and (2) the gap between the measurement signal and estimation signal. With this proposed model, the algorithm can perform quick convergence to generate the best fit model for a particular ECG data from each patient.

As mentioned, raw ECG signals contain not only pure signals but also noises $v(t)$ as showed in Figure 4. Noises come from the environment, measurement, system noises, etc. The model is built based on the knowledge-base integrated with SR algorithm, which

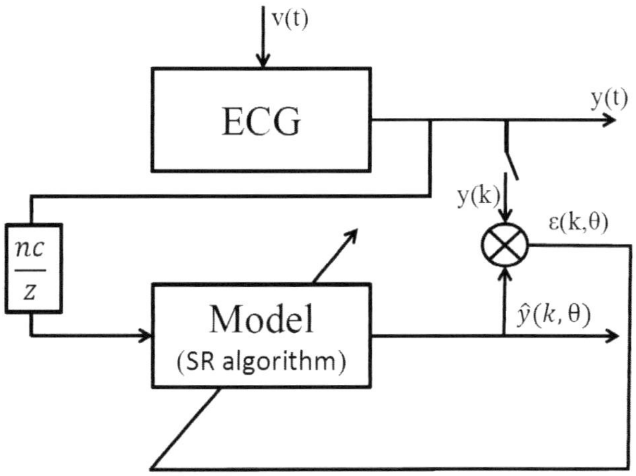

Figure 4: Our proposed model using the SR algorithm

uses the previous cycles of the ECG data to predict the signal at time (k).

The signal produced by Block Model can be considered as the standard signal which is compared to the real signal at time (k), along with the prediction period. The SR algorithm receives two inputs: (1) data from ECG knowledge-base such as MIT-BIH, and (2) real ECG data captured from patients after being filtered by the filter module. These datasets will be analyzed and stored so that if the difference between them (by subtraction) is greater than a threshold, the data is generated as the output data for the feature extraction module.

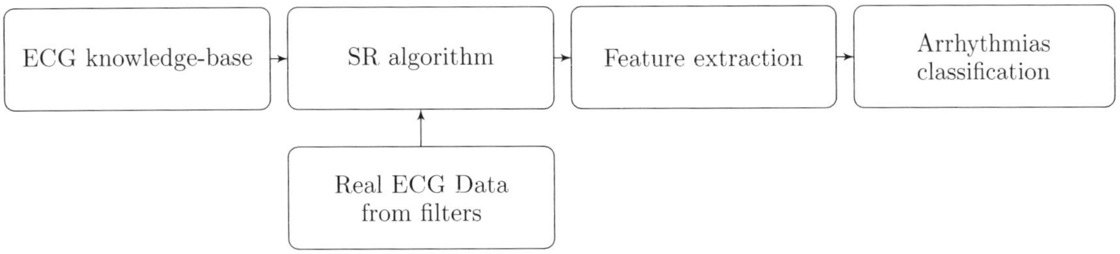

Figure 5: SR algorithm and feature extraction modules in the system

4.3 Feature Extraction and Classification

Processed data from the SR algorithm will be the input for our feature extraction module, illustrated in Figure 5. We adopt the DWT algorithm described in Section 3 to perform this feature extraction. The DWT is used to detect R-peak and capture the center of R-peak, which is the top of each cycle of ECG signal. The DWT gives a flexible time-frequency localization, an appropriate transform domain where the classification system operating.

DWT processes the signal based on the decomposition using an orthonormal. Wavelets have its energy carrying and the magnitude values depending on the concentration representing in time. Their energy spectrums are concentrated around low frequencies [Mahmoodabadi and Abolhasani, 2005].

The decomposition repeatedly implements on the approximation signal to get the second detail and approximation signal. Therefore, discrete wavelet domain gives a multiresolution analysis [Majumder *et al.*, 2008]. The level of each implementation can be adjusted to achieve the appropriate quality, depending on the characteristics of signals. To clearly get the information from the low frequency, the level of decomposition is taken to be high value [Thakor *et al.*, 1984].

Depending on the energy concentration, the decompositions are chosen to comprise and evaluate. Therefore, the R-peaks are captured based on the maximum amplitude points. The accuracy of the feature extraction module mainly depends on the accuracy of R-peaks detection [Thakor *et al.*, 1984].

The final step is the classification for heart disease diagnosis. To employ the arrhythmias classification, we adopt the FLD algorithm described in Section 3. The FLD algorithm helps to reduce the dimension space, where some features are not necessary; and helps to classify the heart disease in the end of the SR data flow.

In equation (5) (c.f. Section 3), we have n classes for the feature vectors x, S_w is the intra-class matrix, C_t is class t, $\bar{x}_t$ is the mean of vectors x, which we obtain equation (6)

Re-write equation (5) with m_t is the number of vectors of class C_t, $\bar{x}$ is the mean of x.

$$S_b = \sum_{t=1}^{n} m_t(\bar{x}_t - \bar{x})(\bar{x}_t - \bar{x})^T \tag{6}$$

where,
S_b: The between-class matrix;
m_t: The number of vectors of class C_t;
$\bar{x}_t$: The mean of vector x;
$\bar{x}$: The mean vector of all fault samples.

To obtain the data at time n, we apply the Rayleigh quotient. Rayleigh quotient [Horn and Johnson., 2012; Parlett, 1998] is a technique to get the eigenvalues providing for min-max operations of matrix multiplication. During classification progress, complicated matrix cannot be obtained from a series of multiplication operators if it is lack of using any technique like Rayleigh quotient. The role of Rayleigh quotient is vital; it decides the success of matrix operations.

5 Implementation and Experimental Results

We use data from MIT-BIH [MIT-BIHArrhythmiaDatabase, 2016] that were built at Boston's Beth Israel Hospital (Beth Israel Deaconess Medical Center) to develop the ECG knowledge-base to validate our proposed model. MIT-BIH data are divided into 3 files: Header file, Attribute file, Data file. The header file contains information relevant to personal info, properties of recorded data; attribute file coordinates with the data file to represent the characteristics of recorded data.

We have implemented a system to collect and analyze ECG signals. The data were recorded at 360 Hz, and the raw data results with noises are showed in Figure 6. Data after processing by our mechanism are shown in Figure 7, where vertical axis represents the beat (mV) and the horizontal axis represents the sample numbers. In Figure 7, incidents are detected and labeled as premature ventricular contraction (PVC). Near each incident, the R-peaks located closer than usual, it means that the period between R-peaks is shorter than usual. Iterative experiments show that recorded signals are stable and less affected by noise.

We use a sensor named AD8232 shown in Figure 8 to capture the ECG signals. This sensor is the single lead ECG, three electrodes, two poles adjustable high pass filter with fast restore capability, three poles adjustable low pass filter. The output signals from AD8232 is analog signals.

To read analog signals from AD8232 then convert it to

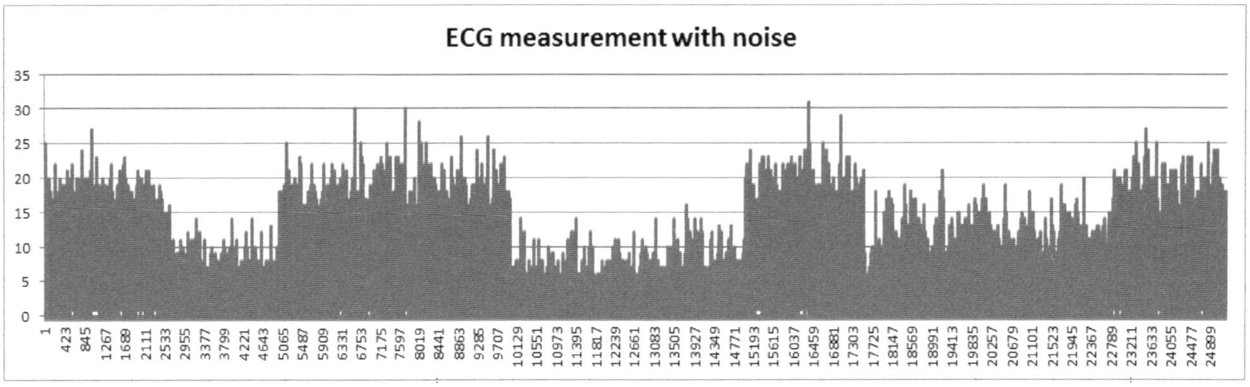

Figure 6: ECG measurement with noise

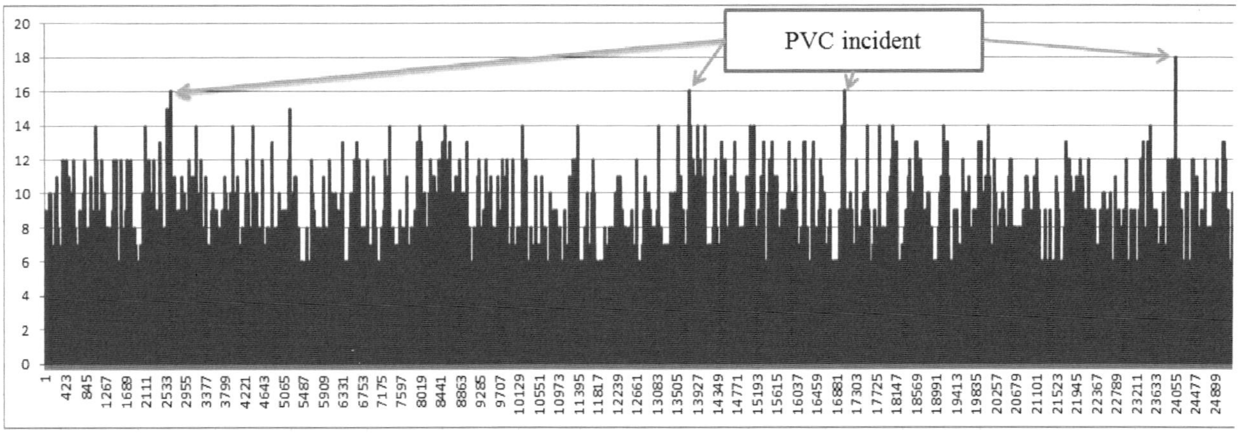

Figure 7: Recorded ECG signals with arrhythmia incidents (PVC)

digital signals, we develop a module on a microcontroller named STM32F4 shown in Figure 9. STM32F4 has 1MB Flash, 192KB SRAM; using ARM 32-bit $Cortex^{TM}$-M4F CPU with FPU, frequency up to 168 MHz. Raw production data from STM32F4 is processed by our proposed computational model and the algorithms introduced in the previous section.

The signal shown in Figure 6 represents the noises existing in the data. To remove noises, we have implemented the Kalman filter in microcontroller STM32F407VG, and implemented the FIR filter in Matlab R2013b to achieve the results as illustrated in Figure 7.

As demonstrated in the experimental results, the SR algorithm improves the quality of signals and makes them stable. We recognize that the SR algorithm not only has potential to make ECG extraction simpler but also reduces the suddenly rash or lost info, make ECG signals more stable. During the processing of ECG signals, the SR algorithm provides filters within calculations, reduces the duplications, and helps to improve the performance of microprocessors for implementation.

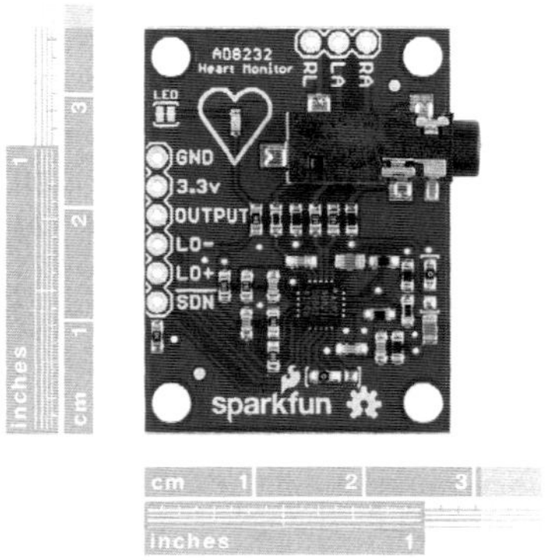

Figure 8: AD8232 - Heart sensor

6 Conclusion and Future Work

In this work, we have presented a lightweight approach to processing ECG signals from sensors in order to perform diagnosis based on a heart disease knowledge-base. Our preliminary results demonstrated that the proposed model can remove noises from raw ECG signals, extract

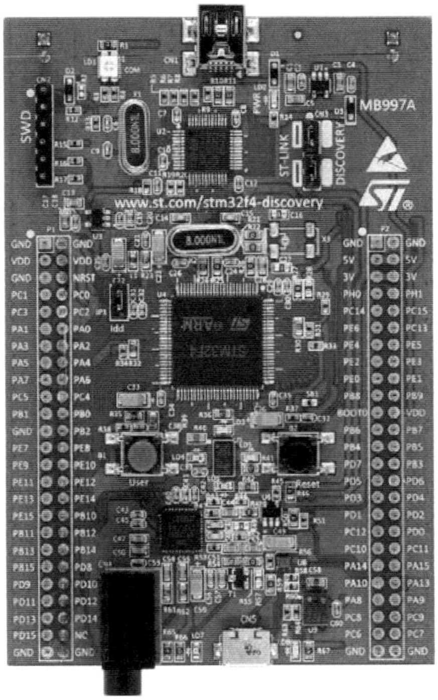

Figure 9: STM32F4 - Microcontroller

key features for performing diagnosis that can support patients for pre-treatment and physicians for treatment.

We have implemented a proof-of-concept prototype of the proposed model toward building an IoT expert system. However, there are several challenges to be addressed. These include the error detection and error correction of the collected data from sensors, online update of the knowledge-base to provide more precise diagnosis. We also need to validate our system with other independent validation mechanisms and datasets to ensure that the outcome of our model is precise. Furthermore, we have not investigated the security for the proposed system. Security is a very important factor in IoT-based systems as the data are transferred over the Internet. However, we leave these challenges for future research.

In future, we plan to develop a comprehensive IoT system that supports automatic data transmission to the cloud for automatic diagnosis and data-mining. We also plan to build a health social network where specialists can update the knowledge-base so that the disease diagnosis can be improved over the time. Our proposed model can be extended to other diseases such as high blood pressure, abnormal brain activities, measuring attention index, sleep index, pulse index, abnormal body temperature, daily physical activities, controlling cardiac fitness and stress index.

Acknowledgments

This research is funded by Vietnam National Foundation for Science and Technology Development (NAFOSTED) under grant number 102.01-2016.28 and by The University of Dayton Research Council Seed Grant.

References

[Akansu and Haddad, 2001] A. N. Akansu and R. A. Haddad. Multiresolution signal decomposition: transforms, subbands, and wavelets. Academic Press, 2001.

[Akansu *et al.*, 2010] A. N. Akansu, W. A. Serdijn, and I. W. Selesnick. Wavelet transforms in signal processing: a review of emerging applications. pages 1–18. Physical Communication, Elsevier, 3(1), 2010.

[Bazzani and Marco, 2012] Bazzani and Marco. Enabling the iot paradigm in e-health solutions through the virtus middleware. IEEE 11th International Conference on Trust, Security and Privacy in Computing and Communications. IEEE, 2012.

[Benharref *et al.*, 2014] Benharref, Abdelghani, and Mohamed Adel Serhani. Novel cloud and soa-based framework for e-health monitoring using wireless biosensors. pages 46–55. IEEE journal of biomedical and health informatics 18.1, 2014.

[Blackburn *et al.*, 1960] H. Blackburn, A. Keys, E. Simonson, P. Rautaharju, and S. Punsar. The electrocardiogram in population studies. pages 1160–1175. Circulation, 21(6), 1960.

[Das *et al.*, 2009] R. Das, I. Turkoglu, and A. Sengur. Effective diagnosis of heart disease through neural networks ensembles. pages 7675–7680. Expert systems with applications, 36(4), 2009.

[Godambe, 1991] V. P. Godambe. Estimating functions. Oxford Statistical Science Series, The Clarendon Press Oxford University Press, 7, 1991.

[Haghighat *et al.*, 2016] Haghighat, Mohammad, Mohamed Abdel-Mottaleb, and Wadee Alhalabi. Discriminant correlation analysis: Real-time feature level fusion for multimodal biometric recognition. pages 1984–1996. IEEE Transactions on Information Forensics and Security 11.9, 2016.

[Hassanalieragh and Moeen, 2015] Hassanalieragh and Moeen. Health monitoring and management using internet-of-things (iot) sensing with cloud-based processing: Opportunities and challenges. Services Computing (SCC), IEEE International Conference on. IEEE, 2015.

[Horn and Johnson., 2012] Roger A. Horn and Charles R. Johnson. Matrix analysis. Cambridge university press, 2012.

[Ifeachor and Jervis, 2002] E. C. Ifeachor and B. W. Jervis. Digital signal processing: a practical approach. Pearson Education, 2002.

[Khemphila and Boonjing, 2011] A. Khemphila and V. Boonjing. Heart disease classification using neural network and feature selection. pages 406–409. In Systems Engineering (ICSEng), 2011 21st International Conference on IEEE, 2011.

[Kiranyaz *et al.*, 2016] Kiranyaz, Serkan, Turker Ince, and Moncef Gabbouj. Real-time patient-specific ecg classification by 1-d convolutional neural networks. pages 664–675. IEEE Transactions on Biomedical Engineering 63.3, 2016.

[Mahmoodabadi and Abolhasani, 2005] A. Ahmadian Mahmoodabadi, S. Z. and M. D. Abolhasani. Ecg feature extraction using daubechies wavelets. Proceedings of the fifth IASTED International conference on Visualization, Imaging and Image Processing, 2005.

[Majumder *et al.*, 2008] Majumder, Swanirbhar, and et al. A hybrid wavelet and time plane based method for qt interval measurement in ecg signals. Signal Processing. ICSP 2008. 9th International Conference on. IEEE, 2008, 2008.

[McLachlan, 2004] G. McLachlan. Discriminant analysis and statistical pattern recognition. John Wiley & Sons (Vol. 544), 2004.

[Milenkovi *et al.*, 2006] Milenkovi, Aleksandar, Chris Otto, and Emil Jovanov. Wireless sensor networks for personal health monitoring: Issues and an implementation. pages 2521–2533. Computer communications 29.13, 2006.

[MIT-BIHArrhythmiaDatabase, 2016] MIT-BIHArrhythmiaDatabase. Available: https://www.physionet.org/physiobank/database/. 2016.

[Oppenheim *et al.*, 1983] A. V. Oppenheim, A. S. Willsky, and Ian T. Young. Signals and systems. page 256. Englewood Cliffs, New Jersey: Prentice-Hall, Inc., 1983.

[Pantelopoulos *et al.*, 2010] Pantelopoulos, Alexandros, and Nikolaos G. Bourbakis. A survey on wearable sensor-based systems for health monitoring and prognosis. pages 1–12. IEEE Transactions on Systems, Man, and Cybernetics, Part C (Applications and Reviews) 40.1, 2010.

[Paradiso *et al.*, 2005] Paradiso, Rita, Giannicola Loriga, and Nicola Taccini. A wearable health care system based on knitted integrated sensors. pages 337–344. IEEE Transactions on Information Technology in Biomedicine 9.3, 2005.

[Parlett, 1998] B. N. Parlett. The symmetric eigenvalue problem. Society for Industrial and Applied Mathematics, 1998.

[Patel and Joshi, 2013] A. R. Patel and M. M. Joshi. Heart diseases diagnosis using neural network. pages 1–5. In Computing, Communications and Networking Technologies (ICCCNT), 2013 Fourth International Conference on IEEE, 2013.

[Rani, 2011] K. U. Rani. Analysis of heart diseases dataset using neural network approach. arXiv preprint arXiv:1110.2626, 2011.

[Soni *et al.*, 2011] J. Soni, U. Ansari, D. Sharma, and S. Soni. Predictive data mining for medical diagnosis: An overview of heart disease prediction. pages 43–48. International Journal of Computer Applications, 17(8), 2011.

[Thakor *et al.*, 1984] Thakor, Nitish V., John G. Webster, and Willis J. Tompkins. Estimation of qrs complex power spectra for design of a qrs filter. pages 702–706. IEEE Transactions on biomedical engineering 11, 1984.

[Zhang and Ya-tao, 2014] Zhang and Ya-tao. Ecg quality assessment based on a kernel support vector machine and genetic algorithm with a feature matrix. pages 564–573. Journal of Zhejiang University SCIENCE C 15.7, 2014.

Feature Selection for Malware Classification

Mitchell Mays, Noah Drabinsky, Dr. Stefan Brandle
Taylor University

Abstract

In applying machine learning to malware identification, different types of features have proven to be successful. These features have also been tested with different kinds of classification methodologies and have had varying degrees of success. Every time a new machine learning methodology is introduced for classifying malware, there is the potential for increasing the overall quality of malware classification in the field. Even new classifiers with the same accuracy as those used previously can be combined using one of a few different ensemble techniques sharpen the classification and raise the accuracy to new heights.

For our purposes, we have attempted to create a coalition of classifiers which each use different features. These classifiers when trained, provide multiple angles to the same problem and can be used to test ensemble techniques. Eventually, such an ensemble of individual malware classifiers could create a highly precise means of picking out malware from other software.

Specifically, we have created a convolutional neural network which processes byte data as an image, and a deep feed forward neural network which utilizes opcode N-gram features. Both of these classifiers, while not perfect, provide a significant level of classification. They achieve this independently of one another, and when combined, they each contribute enough to improve the final accuracy.

The majority of the effort in this research was placed on gathering the N-gram features, a time and resource intensive process. Tinkering with the parameters or structure of classifiers could provide further improvements to the system.

Introduction

The increased use of technology by citizens in recent decades has made society dependent on it. Technology is not going away anytime soon, and since software has become so entangled in daily life (e.g. monetary transactions, social media, and storage of personal information), it has become an increasingly prevalent target for malicious individuals. With highly motivated and intelligent attackers creating malware, many of the simple defenses currently in place are now insufficient to protect against them. The common anti-virus softwares are unable to guarantee protection against new malware, even if that malware has only been slightly modified from one that is similar.

With this in mind research has turned to machine learning techniques as a possible solution. Anti-virus softwares rely on specific malware signatures (longer byte sequences that are only found in a particular malware executable or highly similar executables). These signatures are a sure sign that a file is a malware. Unfortunately, the trade off of such high confidence is a failure to generalize well to new or unseen malware. Minor changes to a malware can disrupt the signature and allow it to slip past detection. Another method used in current anti-virus software is a collection of heuristics created by experts. These painstakingly created rules attempt to capture the essence of a type of malware. They can do better at generalizing, but the effort needed to keep an anti-virus software up-to-date with new rules for each new type of malware is unsustainable. Machine learning attempts to identify particular indicative features of a malware that can be generalized across all malicious software of its kind.

Previous machine learning attempts have used shorter byte or assembly opcode sequences as a feature. These sequences, called n-grams, are representative of specific actions taken within the execution of a malware. The same actions are replicated in all malware that are in the same family.

For the sake of identifying malware, it is helpful to organize them by family. Each family of malware has a similar course of action or purpose. For example, a Keylogger is a type of malware that records all of the text typed into a keyboard, reporting this information back to the attacker who can extract usernames, passwords, and other important data from it. Although two Keyloggers may accomplish their tasks in unique ways from one another, they both rely on the same essential components to do their work. Therefore, identifying malware by family allows for a system to find multiple types of malware without treating them all as one identical classification. Furthermore, if a particular family of malware can be accurately classified, then the features used to classify it are clear indicators of that specific malware family. Some digging may then uncover how that feature correlates to the malware family in question, providing more insight into how attackers are doing their work.

Related Work

In recent years, the topography of malware research has been churning. Due to a recent surge of success, as well as the nature of the problem, machine learning techniques have served as a backbone for a significant portion of this research. The quantity of effort put forth recently has stemmed from the multiple large scale and damaging malware attacks. Under the public eye, funding and attention have turned to a more innovative solution to the persistent problem. These recent years have brought about many fruitful developments, and have allowed for the production of better protection against malware to be available to businesses and tech-owners.

Schultz, Eskin, Zadok, and Stolfo [1] were the first to publish a work attempting to apply machine learning to malware. They looked at executable files and found features for classification within. Their system used a Naïve Bayes classifier. By training on general indicators from the executable file, they ended up with a system that was significantly more accurate than an anti-virus, although it had potential to falsely identify benign software as malicious.

As with many developments in machine learning, a lot of effort initially was spent on feature discovery. Many components of the executable file were tested as features, including gathering n-grams from the bytes. N-grams were first used in text classification, but Abou-Assaleh, Cercone, Keˇselj, and Sweidan [2] applied this technique for malware classification. They extracted these specific sequences of bytes from the executable files and used their frequency within the file as a feature. The combined power of these n-gram features served as a good classification method for malware.

In more recent years, with a successful set of features for classifying, research has been directed toward different classifier alternatives. This set of possible classifiers including support vector machines, k-nearest neighbor, and artificial neural networks have performed at varying degrees, but many have formed a high accuracy classification system. In the pursuit of the most accurate classifier possible, new research has offered up an ensemble classifier [3, 4]. An ensemble classifier is a classification system which utilizes multiple classifiers to come to a final class decision. The benefit of using multiple classifiers is that where one classifier fails, others may succeed, further cutting down error rates.

Preprocessing

For this research we used a dataset made available by Microsoft through the machine learning website Kaggle. It includes nine different malware families and over 10,000 malwares. Based off of this dataset, we chose to create a classifier to distinguish between the different malware families. The winner of the Kaggle competition provided a paper with the techniques that they used [5]. This served as a launching point for our research. From it, we settled on using a convolutional neural network to treat byte data as an input image, and opcode n-grams for use in a more standard neural network.

Each of the 10,000 malwares provided, had both a byte file and an assembly file, which has been disassembled from the byte file. The byte file was used to create the byte "images" in the following manner. Each byte was converted into a pixel value to be used in the black and white image. Since each line of the byte file is sixteen bytes long, the image created represents this same shape: sixteen pixel wide and sixty-four pixels tall.

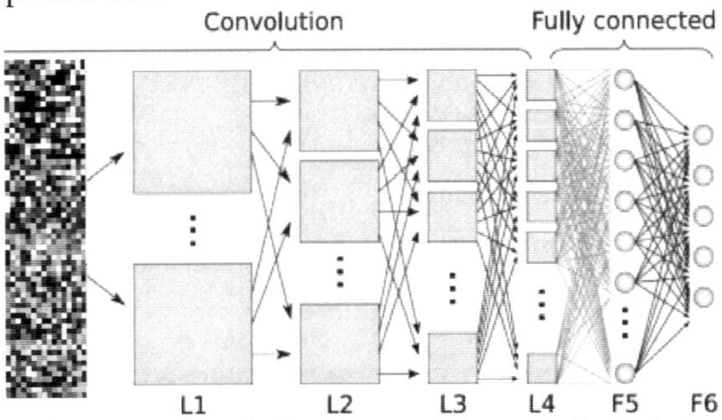

***Figure 1**. Example Byte image as input to Convolutional Neural Network*

Figure one shows how a byte image is used as an input to the convolutional neural network. The network performs convolutions on the pixels creating a matrix of smaller convolved images. As it passes through each layer of the network, the information from the image is condensed and routed into a final output layer, giving a value to each possible class node. The class node with the maximum value is the projected class given by the network. Our network had nine class nodes corresponding with the nine possible malware families.

For the second classifier in our coalition, the features were opcode n-grams. One possible n-gram may have been: "mov eax, [ebp+arg_0]". This is a 3-gram, a sequence of three consecutive data points in the assembly code. For each malware, the number of times that this 3-gram occurred in its assembly would be an input to the classifier. Due to results from Abou-Assaleh, T., N. Cercone, V. Keselj, and R. Sweidan [2] as well as findings from Xiaozhou Wang, Jiwei Liu, and Xueer Chen [5], we settled on n-grams ranging from two to four data points.

The feature gathering for this classifier was more complicated than for the convolutional neural network. A method was needed to identify certain n-grams as possible features and then to decide which of those chosen n-grams would provide the most classification power. There were four stages to this process.

1. 1-gram Selection
2. 1-gram Paring
3. n-gram Selection
4. n-gram Paring

1. 1-gram Selection

Unless intending to evaluate every possible two to four-gram of operations in an assembly file (a number easily in the billions) we needed a criterion to select particular n-grams. One way of doing this is to build larger n-grams off of particular 1-grams. Based off of the work by Xiaozhou Wang, Jiwei Liu, and Xueer Chen [5], we mimicked the execution of the assembly, following every unconditional jump and counting the frequency of each 1-gram. If it occured at least two hundred times in a file it was considered a valid 1-gram.

2. 1-gram Paring

Even after using a specific criterion to limit the number of 1-grams selected, there were too many to build n-grams off of. We used a few further criteria to further pare down the list of 1-grams. First, we removed 1-grams with only one character. We then removed 1-grams that started with a register. While we could assume that the malware would be manipulating the registers, we intuited that having the registers themselves be the start of an n-gram would be unhelpful since it gives no vision into how they are being manipulated. Further paring involved removing items that began with "loc_" or "sub_" as they are somewhat file specific, relying on file locations, and are, therefore, not merely specific to a type of malware.

These heuristic decisions were made due to the limitations of my system being unable to handle the enormous number of n-grams that would be generated from a larger set of 1-grams. It is possible that the 1-grams that were removed could have produced potent n-grams for classification, but based on our reasoning, they were less likely to. After all of paring was complete we were left with 855 different 1-grams.

3. n-gram Selection

With the 1-grams selected, we ran through all of the files a second time, grabbing every possible 2 through 4-gram that began with a 1-gram in the list. Upon completion there were 14,566,780 n-grams. Each with a particular frequency per malware file.

4. n-gram Paring

The most important step to generating an accurate classifier is to select the n-grams from the 14 million that will actually aid in separating some families of malware from others. The best way to evaluate the benefit of an individual feature as an element of a classifier is to test its ability to classify on its own. If a simple classifier trained on the individual feature is able to classify the malwares in a way that exceeds randomness then that feature would be helpful to include in a larger classifier.

Information gain is an algorithm that encapsulates this idea. First, it calculates the entropy in a dataset. Then, it classifies that dataset based on some feature. For each class, the algorithm calculates the entropy of the items within. Subtracting the average entropy of the each designated class from the original entropy gives the information gain, or the improvement in classification ability based off of that feature.

In figure two it is clear that the feature helps to distinguish between the two classes, and the entropy in each new class evidences that. By examining the change in entropy, the helpfulness of a feature is revealed. Unfortunately, to train a classifier on 14 million possible features is a lengthy process. In order to compensate for this I took two different measures.

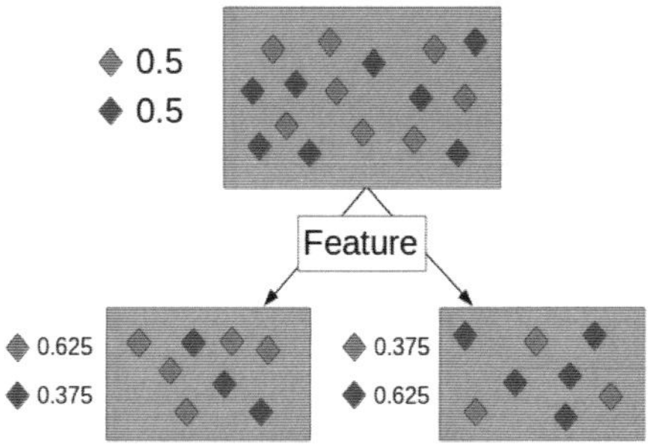

Figure 2. *Change in entropy by classifying on a single feature*

First, rather than running the information gain on each individual feature, we split the list of features into batches of five. Training the mini-classifier on five features instead of one allowed for a quick check to see if any of the five features were helpful. Even with four unhelpful features, we assumed that after training, the one helpful feature would still significantly effect classification, leading to a noticeable information gain.

Second, we distributed the work across several different machines in Taylor University's Computer Science Department. By re-purposing a bit of code written for distributing graphics rendering tasks, we were able to create a task list of n-grams to run through the algorithm and return the result to a central server. Even with up to sixty-two machines churning through the features, it took three full days to complete the information gain on the 14 million n-grams.

We iterated through the information gain values for each set of five features, finding each set with a value above zero. There were approximately 72,000 sets of five which provided a positive information gain. We split these sets of five into individual tasks and re-ran the information gain test. We were left with 10,985 individual n-grams, to use as features.

Testing

In order to test the the n-gram features, we used a deep feed-forward neural network. This network took 10,985 inputs, one for each n-gram. It had two hidden layers, each with 7,300 nodes. The output had nine nodes, one for each family of malware. The structure of the network was based off of a tutorial by Nathan Lintz [6], and was built using the TensorFlow library.

The convolutional neural network was also built in the TensorFlow library, taking an input of a 16x64 pixel image. It held four convolutional layers and finished with nine output nodes. In order to prevent over-fitting, both networks employed dropout at every layer. Dropout ignores a percentage of the weights in the neural network during training. This prevents the network from hyper fitting to the training data and, therefore, failing on the testing data.

The testing methodology that was used for both of these networks was 10-fold cross validation. The entire set of 10,000 malwares was shuffled and split into ten separate sets with 90% of files used for training and 10% for testing. Each iteration of cross validation took place in the following manner:

First, both networks were trained to completion on the training set. Next, the networks attempted to classify the test sets. The features (byte image or n-gram frequency) were used as inputs to the classifier and the output was a set of float values assigned to the nine class nodes. The node with the highest value was the network's classification. Finally, we utilized the output float values from each classifier to create an ensemble classifier. To get a final classification from the ensemble classifier we multiplied the accuracy of each classifier on the test set by its output values for each malware. We summed these class values for each classifier. This gave a weighted consensus between the two classifiers.

The feed-forward neural network trained on the malware n-grams twenty times, and the convolutional neural network trained on the 16x64 pixel images fifty times. We chose the

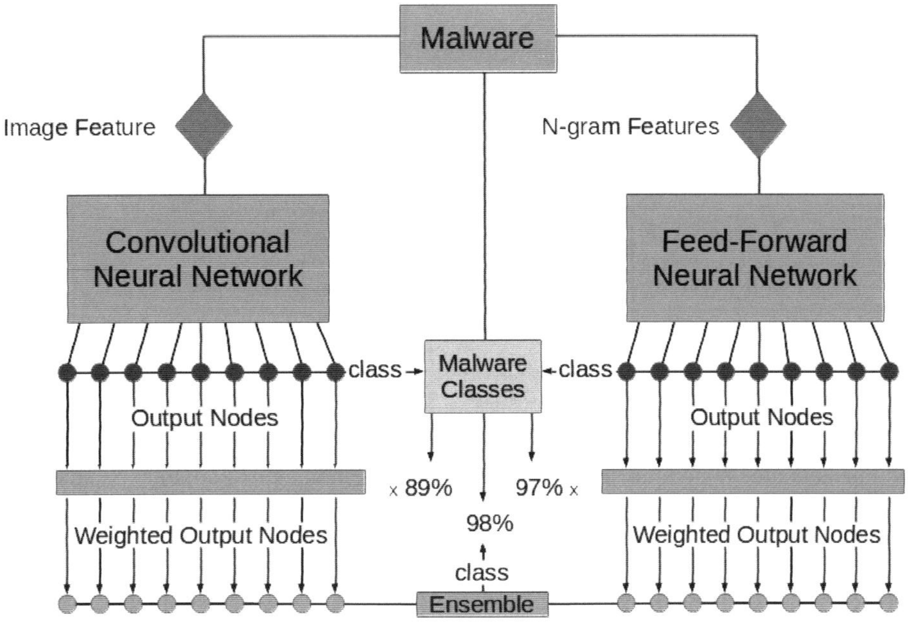

Figure 3. *Testing framework for individual and ensemble classifiers*

number of iterations after overseeing training. Each network took approximately that number of iterations to settle.

Results

After running the cross validations on both of the networks, we were left with a final average accuracy for each. The deep feed-forward neural network using n-gram features trained to be 96.7% accurate. The convolutional neural network, on the other hand, trained to 88.5% accuracy on the test data. By multiplying the nodes by these accuracies, we created weighted nodes. Combining these nodes as an ensemble classifier returned an accuracy of 97.7%.

The training time for the feed-forward neural network was much longer than the training for the convolutional neural network. This was expected since the feed-forward neural network was training weights for every input node rather than the training the smaller convolutions.

Conclusion

The final outcome of my research was an ensemble classifier with 97.7% accuracy on the 10,000 malwares. This value is one percent higher than the best individual classifier in the coalition (96.7% percent from the feed-forward neural network). Yi-Bin, Shu-Chang Din, Chao-Fu Zheng, and Bai-Jian Gao [3] showed that simpler classifiers such as support vector machines and decision trees could be used as components to build an improved ensemble classifier. Our work shows that neural networks can be used as constituents to an ensemble classifier and still create an improved classification.

While limited in our time to tinker with the networks and improve their performance, the principle that ensembles improve the overall classification will most likely still hold as the individual classifiers become more accurate. Furthermore, adding more classifiers to the ensemble should add to the accuracy of the system as a whole.

Future Work

Ultimately, the use of ensembles of complex classifiers has barely scratched the surface of what is possible. Feature gathering took up a large portion of research time, and there is plenty more to be done on the classifiers. Manipulating the structure and number of layers in both the convolutional neural network and feed-forward neural network could drastically effect the performance of the classifiers. Adding new classifiers also has the potential to add significant improvements to the malware classification. Now that using an ensemble method has been applied to neural networks with success, it is worth investing more time to perfect this method and compare it to ensembles which depend on simpler classifiers.

Acknowledgements

[1]. Schultz, M.g., E. Eskin, F. Zadok, and S.j. Stolfo. "Data Mining Methods for Detection of New Malicious Executables." *Proceedings 2001 IEEE Symposium on Security and Privacy. S&P 2001* (n.d.): n. pag. Web.

[2]. Abou-Assaleh, T., N. Cercone, V. Keselj, and R. Sweidan. "N-gram-based Detection of New Malicious Code." *Proceedings of the 28th Annual International Computer Software and Applications Conference, 2004. COMPSAC 2004.* (n.d.): n. pag. Web.

[3]. Lu, Yi-Bin, Shu-Chang Din, Chao-Fu Zheng, and Bai-Jian Gao. "Using Multi-Feature and Classifier Ensembles to Improve Malware Detection." *Journal of Chung Cheng Institute of Technology* 39.2 (2010): n. pag. Web.

[4]. Kolter, Jeremy Z., and Marcus A. Maloof. "Learning to Detect Malicious Executables in the Wild." *Proceedings of the 2004 ACM SIGKDD International Conference on Knowledge Discovery and Data Mining - KDD '04* (2004): n. pag. Web.

[5]. Wang, Xiaozhou, Jiwei Liu, and Xueer Chen. "Microsoft Malware Classification Challenge (BIG 2015): First Place Team: Say No to Overfitting." (2015): n. pag. Web.

[6]. https://github.com/nlintz/TensorFlow-Tutorials/blob/master/03_net.py

Continuous Authentication on Smartphones Using An Artificial Immune System

Nawaf Aljohani[1], Joseph Shelton, Kaushik Roy
Department of Computer Science, North Carolina A&T State University, Greensboro, U.S.A
naaljoha@aggies.ncat.edu[1]

Abstract

Most of the authentication systems require the users to provide their credential for authentication purposes by providing their passwords or their biometric data. However, as long as the user remains active in the system, there is no mechanisms to verify whether the user who provides the credential is still in control of the device or not. Most mobile devices rely upon passwords and physical biometrics to authenticate users only when they start using the device. Active authentication based on analyzing the user's touch interaction could be a reasonable solution to verify that a legitimate user is still in control of a smartphone or tablet. In this research, an Artificial Immune System (AIS) is proposed to apply to continuously authenticate the users based on touch patterns. Our results show that AIS is able to actively authenticate 96.89% of the users correctly.

Introduction

During the authentication process, a primary concern for users and designers is the level of security. The process of authenticating an individual must be both secure and effective to be applicable for a real world authentication system. In the event that the authentication process is compromised, other aspects in the system such as availability, confidentiality, and integrity would be easily compromised as well. Knowledge-based authentication systems, such as password or pin, have several drawbacks, but many systems still use this method to authenticate legitimate users due to their simplicity and flexibility. This research proposes an authentication method for the users based on finger swipe movements.

Touch screen technology is used in many mobile devices where users have the ability to access various data and resources at anytime. Most of the smartphones use PINs to authenticate the users. However, a traditional PIN typically consists of four to eight digits, making it easy to guess with its small password space and thus vulnerable to attacks [Chang *et al.*, 2012]. Nowadays, most mobile devices use graphical password that have a larger and more accepted password space. Though graphical password increases the password space in touch screen handheld mobile devices, there are no further authentication processes after unlocking the touch screen. Thus, the attacker has the ability to access and control all the users' data and resources as long as the attacker gains access to a device after it is unlocked. This research aims to continuously authenticate the users without asking them to provide the login information multiple times while the smartphones or tablets are in use.

In this research, an artificial immune system (AIS) approach will be used to secure mobile devices. The immune system is considered to be a highly complex functional system that protects the body from foreign diseases causing pathogens [Shojaie and Moradi, 2008]. This immunology inspired researchers to develop the computational intelligence technique, which is called AIS. AIS has been used in solving complex computational problems, such as classification, recognition, and network security [Dudek, 2012]. This research makes use of an AIS which has the ability to continuously keep track of any changes in the environment based on recognizing the patterns of 'self' and predicting and detecting new patterns of 'non-self'.

This research uses a set of 11 behavioral touch features that were extracted while the users were interacting with their smartphones. This research uses touch data collected from 100 users and each subject has 100 instances [Sitová *et al.* 2016]. This research proposes the use of an AIS to continuously authenticate the smartphones users where the security of smartphone is enhanced.

Related Work

Sitová et al. proposed a set of behavioral features based on hand movement, orientation, and grasp to continuously authenticate mobile users [Sitová *et al.* 2016]. The data is collected from 100 participants under two conditions:

walking and sitting. The achieved equal error rates (EERs) are 7.16% (walking) and 10.05% (sitting) where walking interactions are more richer than sitting interactions due to the distinctive body movements caused by walking and hand-movement dynamics from taps. Sitová et al. believe that each mobile user has postural preferences for interacting with touch screen which can be used to authenticate the users. In their dataset, Sitová et al. designed 96 features and extracted data while users are walking and sitting. The dataset was divided into two types of features that grasp resistance and stability and the data was collected by using three sensors: accelerometer, gyroscope, and magnetometer [Sitová *et al.* 2016]. The user touch data was acquired using Samsung Galaxy S4 smartphone where the average duration of a user's interaction with touch screen was 11.6 minutes per session. Sitová et al. used scaled Manhattan (SM), scaled Euclidian (SE), and 1-class Support Vector Machines (SVM) to verify the users.

Frank et al. [Frank *et al.*, 2013] determined whether or not a classifier could be used to continuously authenticate users based on their interaction with the touch screen. Authors in [Frank *et al.*, 2013] proposed 30 behavioral touch features that could be collected from raw touch screen logs. These features were used to identify a user based on the way he/she interacts with the touch screen. Furthermore, Frank et al. explained the reasons that mobile devices are at higher risk than that of desktop computers due to that fact that mobile devices can be easily lost or stolen. Their dataset consists of 41 subjects and the data was collected from four different smart phones.

Feng et al. [Feng *et al.*, 2012] introduced FAST: Fingergestures Authentication System using Touchscreen. Their idea was to extract data from touch screen interactions and validate the data by using a digital sensor glove. Their proposed approach relied on Random Forest (RF) and Bayesian network classifiers to authenticate mobile users continuously. Feng et al. used a dataset that consisted of 40 users and authors obtained a False Accept Rate (FAR) of 4.66%, while the False Reject Rate (FRR) was 0.13%.

Meng et al. [Meng *et al.*, 2013] proposed a scheme based on touch dynamics that used a set of behavioral features to improve the accuracy of user authentication. Their dataset consisted of 21 features that were collected form users interaction with the touch screen. All data was extracted from 20 Android phones. Researchers in [Meng *et al.*, 2013] found that a Neural Network (NN) achieved an average error rate of 7.8%. In addition, Meng et al. optimized the NN by implementing Particle Swarm Optimization (PSO) and they reported an average error rate of about 3%.

Proposed Approach

There are three types of AISs reported in the literature: 1) Negative selection, 2) Clonal selection, and 3) Immune Network [Watkins *et al.*, 2002].

The main goal of the Negative Selection (NS) is to provide tolerance for self cells that indicate the ability to detect non self antigens. This idea is used in many areas such as network security, where NS generates detectors and then removes those that can detect self patterns. The rest of detectors can be used to detect anomaly. The detectors, which are randomly generated, are representation for matching the authorized users' patterns to create the self profile [Greensmith *et al.*, 2010]. A detector is a set of intervals for each feature a detector is created for. Any self pattern number lies in the interval of a detector means that the detector detects the self pattern. As a result of that all detectors that detect self patterns must be removed. The remaining detectors are used to detect unauthorized users.

Clonal Selection (CS) differs from the NS approach by selecting the detectors that proliferate over those that do not. The main feature of CS is the new detectors that are the copies of their parents and reactivated detectors are eliminated afterwards. In this research, CS is implemented to authenticate smartphone users continuously instead of NS because CS, in some cases, gives better accuracy than NS due to the fact that the nearest created detectors cloned (See Figure 1). First, CS generates *n* detectors and searches for new patterns. CS selects the nearest detectors to be cloned using distance metric such as the Euclidean distance. CS clones the nearest detectors from the detectors and the new pattern. CS then finds best matching clone and assigns clone class to antigen. Finally, it deletes other superfluous clones and for each deletion, replaces with new randomly generated detectors [Greensmith *et al.*, 2010]. In this research, we created 100 detectors and then remove those detectors that can detect self elements. Self elements in the dataset represent one subject. The remaining subjects are non-self elements. The detectors detect the self elements by exploring self subject's features patterns. Suppose the smartphone is unlocked by an attacker, detectors created by CS are used for continuously authenticating the user by tracking the user's interactions with touch screen. As long as the smartphone is unlocked, CS detectors are used to analyze the user's interactions via detectors. Once a certain number of detectors detect abnormal interactions, the device is locked due to unauthorized access. In our experiments, abnormal interactions must be detected by four detectors to detect unauthorized access.

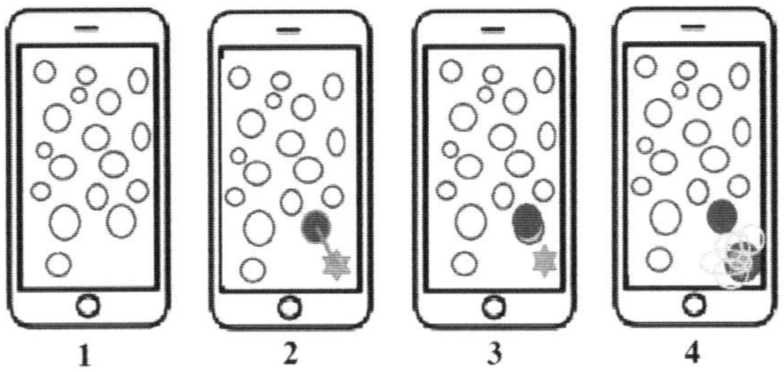

Figure 1. Clonal selection concept

Table 1. behavioral features [Sitová *et al.*, 2016].

Name	**Description**
Systime	Absolute time-stamp
EventTime	Sensor event relative time-stamp
ActivityID	Belonged activity
Pointer_count	1: Single touch 2: Multi-touch
PointerID	0: Single touch; or first pointer in multi-touch 1: Second pointer in multi-touch
ActionID	0 or 5: DOWN 1 or 6: UP 2: MOVE
X	Touch location in X coordination
Y	Touch location in Y coordination
Pressure	Touch pressure
Contact_size	Touch contact size
Phone_orientation	0: Portrait and no rotate 1: device rotated 90 degrees counterclockwise 3: device rotated 90 degrees clockwise

Experimental Results

We conducted our experiments on TouchEvent dataset that has 11 behavioral features [Sitová *et al.* 2016]. A list of features is shown in Table 1. First, we ran the AIS with only two subjects, and we achieved an accuracy of 100%. The accuracy remains 100% as long as we are using 5 subjects. After adding 6th subject and its instances, the accuracy went down to 99.33%. Initially, we added a new subject to the dataset and ran AIS. The accuracies for all the users are shown in Table 2.

It is clear that at a certain point, adding users do not affect the accuracy of AIS as shown in Figure 2. For each run, AIS is executed for 1000 generations and the number of detectors is 100. Unauthorized user is detected if at least 4 generated detectors are able to detect the touch screen interactions.

We ran the AIS on the entire dataset for 20 times. For each run, we experimented it for 1000 generations. Also, for each run, we use 100 detectors. The best accuracy for 20 runs is 96.89% and the average is 93.81% (See Figure 3). The average of FRR out of 20 runs is 0.9381 which shows unauthorized users detections. The average of FARs on the other hand is 0.06.

Table 2. Results of adding each user

User	Accuracy	User	accuracy	User	accuracy
2	1	35	0.939246	68	0.919757
3	1	36	0.9409309	69	0.924135
4	1	37	0.9417141	70	0.920664
5	1	38	0.9473414	71	0.922134
6	0.993333	39	0.9471731	72	0.927492
7	0.993036	40	0.9375915	73	0.923671
8	0.991111	41	0.938403	74	0.923728
9	0.991444	42	0.941495	75	0.924533
10	0.994636	43	0.940016	76	0.919508
11	0.99447	44	0.941293	77	0.927949
12	0.991282	45	0.952014	78	0.930393
13	0.987418	46	0.940592	79	0.927764
14	0.970905	47	0.941241	80	0.923218
15	0.9675	48	0.941101	81	0.92879
16	0.964118	49	0.945453	82	0.922505
17	0.966471	50	0.944878	83	0.926952
18	0.965409	51	0.944246	84	0.897615
19	0.964263	52	0.939213	85	0.926551
20	0.950119	53	0.941237	86	0.927851
21	0.963009	54	0.946933	87	0.921804
22	0.9543478	55	0.936571	88	0.925723
23	0.9558696	56	0.946563	89	0.923815
24	0.9473167	57	0.939958	90	0.926972
25	0.9522769	58	0.955611	91	0.923371
26	0.9377635	59	0.954308	92	0.917491
27	0.9335714	60	0.931101	93	0.91647
28	0.9355788	61	0.913392	94	0.910208
29	0.9428851	62	0.919519	95	0.917088
30	0.9464194	63	0.914184	96	0.921645
31	0.9375403	64	0.916935	97	0.919436
32	0.9340909	65	0.922818	98	0.925315
33	0.9328699	66	0.921142	99	0.922192
34	0.9395126	67	0.922046		

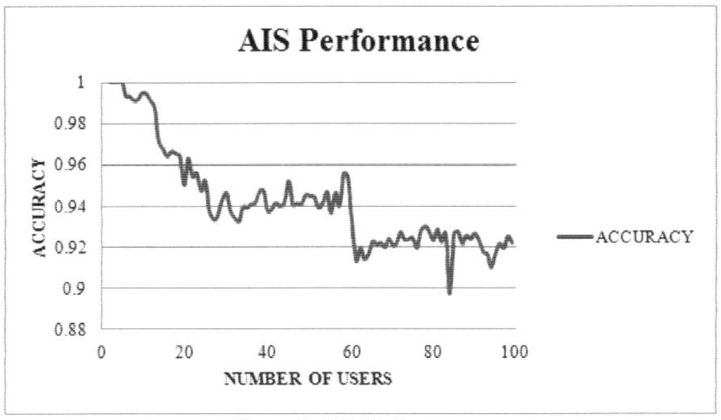

Figure 2. CS Performance

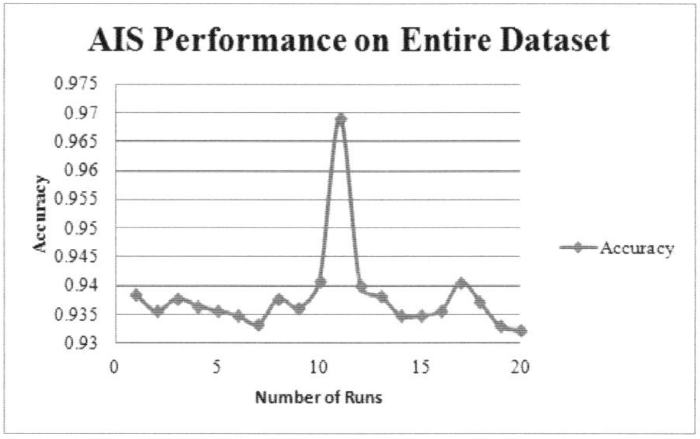

Figure 3. CS Performance

Conclusion and Future Work

We find from the experimental results that AIS can be used to authenticate smartphone users continuously. AIS approach has the flexibility in restricting the authentication process based on the sensitivity of the mobile devices by reducing the number of detectors. The best performance of CS on the entire dataset was 96.89%. However, there seems to be a promise with the increasing number of detectors for each run. This research uses CS for an AIS to continuously authenticate the users.

Future work will be focused on evaluating the impact of each behavioral feature on the overall accuracy. Furthermore, future work will evaluate the effect of increasing the number of detectors. This may improve accuracy by increasing the chance of detecting more unauthorized mobile interactions. Also, a comparison between CS and NS will be conducted. In addition, the performance of CS and NS will be compared with other classifies such as SVM.

Acknowledgements

This research is supported by the Army Research Office (Contract No. W911NF-15-1-0524).

References

[Chang *et al.*, 2012] Chang, T. Y., Tsai, C. J., & Lin, J. H. (2012). A graphical-based password keystroke dynamic authentication system for touch screen handheld mobile devices. *Journal of Systems and Software*, *85*(5), 1157-1165.

[Dudek, 2012] Dudek, G. (2012). An artificial immune system for classification with local feature selection. *IEEE Transactions on Evolutionary Computation*, *16*(6),p.847-860.

[Feng *et al.*, 2012] Feng, Tao, Ziyi Liu, Kyeong-An Kwon, Weidong Shi, Bogdan Carbunar, Yifei Jiang, and Nhung Nguyen. (2012). "Continuous Mobile Authentication Using Touchscreen Gestures." *2012 IEEE Conference on Technologies for Homeland Security (HST).* Print.

[Frank *et al.*, 2013] Frank, M., R. Biedert, E. Ma, I. Martinovic, and D. Song. (2013) "Touchalytics: On the Applicability of Touchscreen Input as a Behavioral Biometric for Continuous Authentication." IEEE Trans.Inform.Forensic Secur. IEEE Transactions on Information Forensics and Security 8.1 pp.136-48. Print

[Greensmith *et al.*, 2010] Greensmith, J., Whitbrook, A., & Aickelin, U. (2010). Artificial immune systems. In *Handbook of Metaheuristics* (pp. 421-448). Springer US.

[Meng *et al.*, 2013] Meng, Yuxin, Duncan S. Wong, Roman Schlegel, and Lam-For Kwok. (2013) "Touch Gestures Based Biometric Authentication Scheme for Touchscreen Mobile Phones." *Information.Security and Cryptology Lecture Notes in Computer Science.* pp. 331-50. Print.

[Shojaie *et al.*, 2008] Shojaie, S., & Moradi, M. H. (2008). An evolutionary artificial immune system for feature selection and parameters optimization of support vector machines for ERP assessment in a P300-based GKT. In *Biomedical Engineering Conference, 2008. CIBEC 2008. Cairo International* (pp. 1-5). IEEE.

[Sitová *et al.*, 2016] Sitová, Z., Šeděnka, J., Yang, Q., Peng, G., Zhou, G., Gasti, P., & Balagani, K. S. (2016). HMOG: New behavioral biometric features for continuous authentication of smartphone users. *IEEE Transactions on Information Forensics and Security*, *11*(5), 877-892.

[Watkins et al., 2002] Watkins, Andrew and Timmis, Jon (2002) *Artificial Immune Recognition System (AIRS):Revisions and Refinements*

Context-Based Heuristics in Attribution

Jim Q. Chen, Ph.D.
National Defense University, U.S.A.

Abstract

In cyber forensics, attribution of an attack, which finds out details about the individual(s) who launched an attack, is more important than mere identification of an attack, since a precise response to the cyber attack heavily depends upon attribution. The identification of the initiator(s) in attribution provides precise targeting for a counter-attack. However, heuristics are typically deployed to find out information about attack actions rather than initiator(s) of attack actions. This paper proposes a mechanism that utilizes a weight system for guiding the way in which the heuristics prioritize the discovery of attacker initiator(s). Linking purpose, methods, time, location, and events with the identified device, the proposed heuristic approach can serve as a path towards accurate and prompt attribution.

Introduction

It is not uncommon that a cyber attack is reported without identification of the attacker(s). Quite often, cyber defense mechanisms and cyber forensics can help to identify the fact that a system has been hacked and compromised and the data on the system have been stolen. However, it always takes a lot more time and efforts to find out who did it and why it was done. Attribution is hard to be done even though it is possible. Without quick and accurate attribution, precise responses to the attacker(s) are delayed, and direct cyber deterrence mechanisms become less effective. In some cases, indirect deterrence mechanisms, such as diplomatic, economic, legal, military, or other national security instruments, have been employed, especially in dealing with nation-state attackers. Unfortunately, the indirect deterrence mechanisms are always taking long time to be deployed and executed, as attribution and preparation for the use of non-cyber national security instruments require extra time in this process, thus causing the delay in response or retaliation. In addition, as correctly pointed out by Sterner (2011), the indirect deterrence mechanisms have limited effect on non-nation-state attackers.

What needs to be done in order to improve the process of attribution in the cyber domain so that direct retaliation in the cyber domain can be quickly launched should it be legal and necessary? To answer this question, the key components in attribution should be identified. With this identification, a novel approach can be figured out to address these key components ahead of time so that the time needed for conducting attribution can be significantly reduced.

The paper is organized as follows: In Section 1, an introduction to the challenge is provided. In Section 2, related works are examined. The current approaches and their limitations are analyzed. In Section 3, an innovative solution is proposed. In Section 4, this novel approach is applied to a hypothetical case. In Section 5, a conclusion is drawn.

Related Works

Beebe (2009) calls for the design and implementation of smart analytical algorithms in digital forensics since the "cost of human analytical time spent sifting through non-relevant search hits is a significant issue". He holds that even though current "computational approaches for searching, retrieving and analyzing digital evidence are unnecessarily simplistic", there exists significant information retrieval overhead. He argues that smart analytical algorithms should "clearly reduce information retrieval overhead", "help investigators get to relevant data more quickly, reduce the noise investigators must wade through, and help transform data into information and investigative knowledge." In order to design such an intelligent algorithm, heuristics should be looked into.

Marti and Reinelt (2011) maintain that a good heuristic algorithm should fulfill the following properties: "A solution can be obtained with reasonable computational effort". "The solution should be near optimal (with high probability)". "The likelihood for obtaining a bad solution (far from optimal) should be low".

Hill-climbing algorithms belong to local search, which, according to Kokash (1998), "is a version of exhaustive search that only focuses on a limited area of the search space". "Such algorithms consistently replace the current solution with the best of its neighbors if it is better than the current." However, a hill-climbing algorithm "always finds the nearest local optima of low quality". This issue is referred to as pre-mature convergence. Heuristics is used to deal with this problem.

There are several different approaches in heuristics. The best-first search selects the best state in the list. Simulated annealing allows some moves to worse states in order to explore many regions of the state space. A* algorithm, which uses a best-first search with a modified evaluation function, selects the shortest path that has the minimal total cost. However, in the first trial, as evaluation is not performed yet, it may select a path that is not the shortest one.

In the context of attribution, is there a structural configuration that helps to select the shortest path in the first trial? If there is one, what is it? How does this work? These are the questions that are addressed in the next section.

Proposal

A novel context-based heuristic approach is proposed in this section. Here, the relationship among the components for attribution is analyzed and a weight system is employed. Combining this weight system with the Contextual Binding Condition, this new context-based heuristic approach is designed to discover the shortest and the most optimal path for attribution.

To accurately attribute an event to an individual, all the following elements should be addressed: "who", "what", "when", "where", "how", and "why". To do so, it is crucial to find out the relationship among these elements.

Sinek (2009) does a very good job in explaining the relationship among some components, such as "what", "how", and "why", via the Golden Circle, as shown in Figure 1 below:

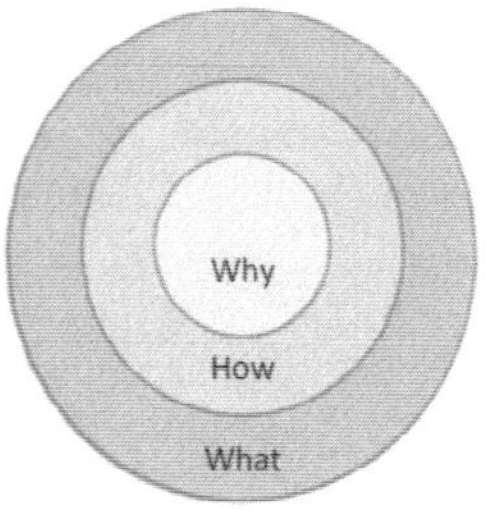

Figure 1. Golden Circle

The Golden Circle is used for inspirational leadership. The idea is to have a goal figured out and made known first, come up with a method or craft a strategy based on the purpose, and then figure out what to do to achieve the goal.

As shown in this figure, the component "what" represents actions or events. The component "how" represents the method or the strategy used in orchestrating these events. It is relatively less obvious than the component "what". The component "why" represents the goal to be achieved via the method or the strategy employed. It is the least comprehensible element of these three components. However, once an understanding of the goal is gained, an understanding of the whole picture and the relationship of all these events is acquired.

Given the representation in circles, this process can be depicted as being inside out. In Sinek's term, it all starts with why. Sinek (2009) even looks at how this representation corresponds with the major levels of the brain. The "what" level corresponds with neocortex, while the "how" level and the "why" level correspond with limbic brain. Neocortex is responsible for rational and analytical thought as well as language but it does not drive behavior. Limbic brain, which drives behavior, is responsible for feelings, such as trust and loyalty, as well as all human behavior and decision making.

This model demonstrates that a purpose (i.e. the "why" component) drives methods or strategies (i.e. the "how" component), which, in turn, drive actions (i.e. the "what" component). From this perspective, the "why" component is more important than the "how" component, and the "how" component is more important than the "what" component.

It has to be pointed out that as the purpose of the Golden Circle is not for attribution, other important components such as "who", "when", and "where", are not included in the Golden circle. However, to build the Attribution Circle on the basis of the Golden Circle, these three components have to be included. What needs to be discovered is the relationship among all these components.

It needs to be noted that the component "who", which represents the human component, possesses the highest priority in any investigation as it directly pinpoints to the individual(s) who conducted the action. Other factors, such as the reason why the action was conducted, the way the action was conduct, the action that was conducted, the place where it was conducted, and the time when it was conducted, are all directly associated with the human component, i.e. the "who" component. To a certain extent, they are the attributes of the "who" component, which represents the initiator of an action. It is the human who has a purpose or a goal. It is the human who comes up with a method or a strategy to archive the goal. Of course, the method or the strategy has to be associated with location and time. It is the human who conducts the action based on the method or the strategy. The action has to occur in a specific location within a specific time. This is why this human component should hold relatively the highest weight in the Attribution Circle. Also, the component "who" is closely tied to all other components as it is the initial driver who makes all these happen.

The component "why" is the second most crucial element, as it drives the component "how", which, in turn, drives the component "what". This is why it should possess the second highest weight in the Attribution Circle. For the same reason, the component "how" should hold a weight that is less than that of the component "why" but more than that of the component "what". As location (i.e. the component "where") and time (i.e. the component "when") are the attributes for a method (i.e. the component "how") or an action (i.e. the component "what"), they should hold a weight that is less than that of the component "how". Naturally, a weight system comes into being.

All these relations can be successfully captured in the Attribution Circle proposed in Figure 2 below:

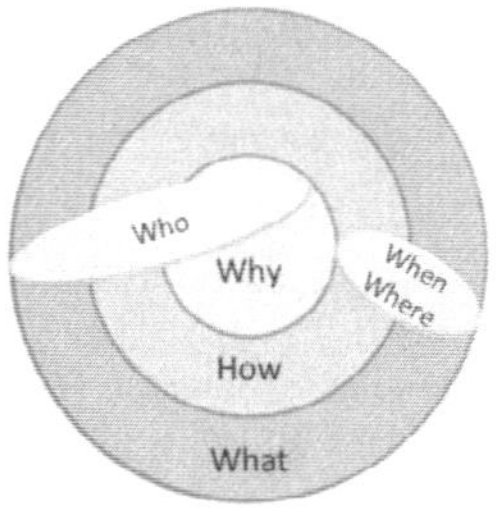

Figure 2. Attribution Circle

In the leadership environment, an effective directional relationship is inside out. Similarly, a well-designed attack follows this directional relationship. An attacker has a goal to achieve. To achieve that goal, the attacker needs to figure out a method or a strategy. The attacker then orchestrates various actions in different locations at different times according to the method or the strategy. This clearly reflects an inside-out directional relationship, which is displayed in Figure 3 below:

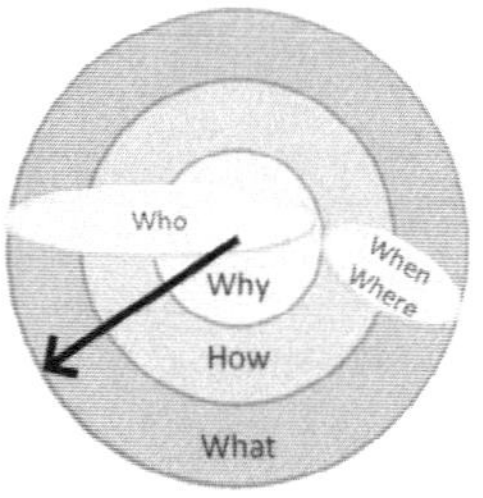

Figure 3. Inside Out

However, in the cyber forensics environment, an effective directional relationship is outside in. Investigators usually observe seemingly irrelevant actions in different locations at different times. The analysis helps them to link the dots of these actions and eventually to figure out the method or the strategy used. Based on the understanding of the method or the strategy used as well as the link between an action and an actor, the suspect(s) can be eventually attributed to. This reflects an outside-in directional relationship, which is displayed in Figure 4 below:

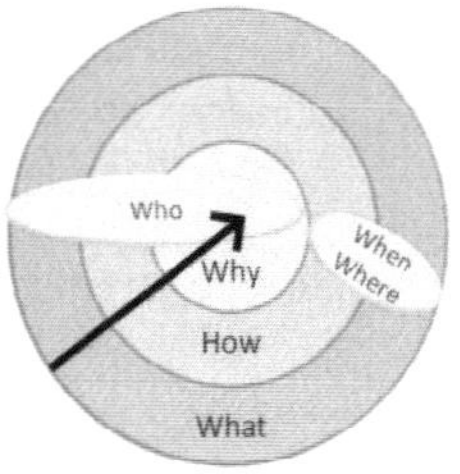

Figure 4. Outside In

Evidently, the directional relationship truly reflects the order of events. The Attribution Circle can effectively capture the relationship.

Based on the above analysis, the following stipulation can be made to capture the proportion of weight of probability for each component in attribution:

(1) Weight of probability for each component:
"who": $W1 = 0.3$
"why": $W2 = 0.25$
"how": $W3 = 0.15$
"when": $W4 = 0.1$
"where": $W5 = 0.1$
"what": $W6 = 0.1$

The total weight of probability equals 1.

If a component is known, it carries the value "1". Otherwise, it has the value "0".

The probability of successful attribution can be express as follows:

(2)

$$P(X) = \sum_{i=1}^{6} (Xi * Wi)$$

Given the weight of each component listed in (1), the formula in (2) can be expanded as follows:

(3)

$$P(X) = \sum_{i=1}^{6} (Xi * Wi)$$

$$= (X_1*W_1) + (X_2*W_2) + (X_3*W_3) + (X_4*W_4) + (X_5*W_5) + (X_6*W_6)$$
$$= (1*0.3) + (1*0.25) + (1*0.15) + (1*0.1) + (1*0.1) + (1*0.1)$$
$$= 0.3 + 0.25 + 0.15 + 0.1 + 0.1 + 0.1$$
$$= 1$$

This means that if all the six components are known, the individual who launched the attack can be successfully attributed to.

Also, when the attributes represented by these components are all properly addressed in an expected way, the Revised Restrictive Contextual Binding Condition proposed in Chen (2016) is satisfied, as the variables are properly bound by their corresponding contextual operators. This binding condition is listed below:

Assume X is an entity, and CO is a contextual operator.

(4) In a specialized time, location, environment, and background, if X is directly related to CO with respect to all the attributes such as action-initiator (who), action (what), action-recipient (who/what_recipient), time (when), location (where), method (how), and purpose (why) in such a setting:
COi[WHO1, WHAT2, WHAT_RECIPIENT3, WHEN4, WHERE5, HOW6, WHY7]
{......Xi[WHO1,WHAT2, WHAT_RECIPIENT3, WHEN4, WHERE5, HOW6, WHY7]......}
then Xi is contextually bound by COi in a restrictive way.

As pointed out in Chen (2016), this is a typical representation of Type 1 Binding as all the attributes in the variable are contextually bound by the attributes in the contextual operator. "If one contextual attribute in the variable is not directly related to the corresponding attribute in the contextual operator, the variable is not contextually bound by the contextual operator in the restrictive sense."

Putting (3) and (4) together, if all the attributes of a variable (i.e. "who", "why", "how", "when", "where", and "what") are known, then $P(X) = 1$, and the variable is properly, (i.e. 100%) bound by the contextual operator (CO). However, if only "what", "when", and "where" are known, then $P(X) = (1*0.1) + (1*0.1) + (1*0.1) = 0.3$, and the variable is 30% bound by the CO.

As the attribute "who" possesses the highest weight, i.e. 0.3, and the attribute "why" possesses the second highest weight, i.e. 0.25, the missing of these two attributes immediately points out a new path of search, namely, the quest for the attributes "who" and "why". Once these two attributes are known, 55%, i.e. $(1*0.3) + (1*0.25) = 0.55$, of the puzzle is solved. Let us compare the pair of the attributes "who" and "why" with the pair of attributes "how" and "what". As the weight of the attribute "how" is 0.15 and the weight of the attribute "what" is 0.1, the total weight of the latter pair is $P(X) = (1*0.15) + (1*0.1) = 0.25$. This means that getting to know these two attributes solves 25% of the puzzle. Evidently, 25% is less than 55%; and the pair of the attributes "how" and "what" has less priority than the pair of the attributes "who" and "why" does. With such a weight system in place, the attribute "who" is always the first one to go after if it is unknown. The attribute "why" is the second one to go after, and the attribute "how" is the third one to go after. The pair of the attributes that possesses the highest weight, i.e. the attributes of "who" and "why", which possesses 55% of the total weight, is the first one to go after as a pair. The pair of the attributes that holds the second highest weight, i.e. the attributes of "who" and "how", which holds 45% of the total weight, is the second one to go after as a pair. As shown here, the weight system proposed in this paper helps to set up the priority in the search and helps to heuristically choose an optimal path for the quest. This structural configuration helps to select the shortest path in the first trial, thus making heuristic algorithms more optimal and more efficient, especially in the quest for attribution.

In addition, this weight system can help the process of intelligence collection for the sake of prevention in the cyber domain. If a request for a service is received from a device that is unknown, the server service should hold the normal response and immediately start the query for the unknown factors. Picking up the component with the heaviest weight in the list, the server service goes after the component "who". The server service now engages the device of the attack-initiator into a dialog by asking it questions related to the "who" attribute. The idea is to make the device of the attack-initiator to reveal its identity information. If no answer or unsatisfactory answer is received, the request from the attack device is immediately rejected and the normal response is not provided at all. If a satisfactory answer is received, the server service goes after the component "why", which possesses the second heaviest weight in the list. The server service now asks the device that makes the request to provide reasons for its request. Again, if no answer or unsatisfactory answer is received, the request from the attack device is immediately rejected and the normal response is not provided at all. Otherwise, a normal response is provided. The questions related to the "why" attribute can help to detect a zombie since a zombie either does not have a good reason for the request or has to wait for the attack-initiator to provide a reason. The unsatisfactory answer or the delay in response is a good indicator in detecting a zombie system. Evidently, this new context-based heuristic approach can help intelligence collection for the sake of prevention.

Chen and Dinerman (2016) examine the unique characteristics of cyber conflicts and discover the following three cyber feature sets, namely intelligence collection, stealth maneuvers, and surprise effect. They argue that these unique feature sets can be turned into unique cyber capabilities that serve as force multipliers, if they are integrated appropriately into conventional conflicts as complementary military capacities. As shown in this paper, this new context-based heuristic approach not only can assist intelligence collection but also can speed up the attribution process. This capability is exactly what is needed for force multipliers.

Case Study

In this section, the proposed context-based heuristics is applied to a hypothetical case, which is a typical attribution challenge.

Let us assume that a server suddenly receives 2,000 repetitive packets within a second from the same source right at 5:00 PM on Monday. This abnormal behavior immediately triggers the context-based heuristics for investigation, as the server usually receives less than 1,000 different packets within a minute. A quick scrutiny reveals the packets are all echo packets utilizing UDP Port 7. The message echoed is exactly the same. This started a minute ago. It only occurs on this particular server at that time.

This quick scrutiny discloses the attributes of "what", "when", "where", and "how". The fact that the server is hit by 2,000 echo packets per second accounts for the attribute of "what". The time at 5:00 PM on Monday accounts for the attribute of "when". The location of the server accounts for the attribute of "where". Echo packets utilizing UDP Port 7 in that particular location at that particular time accounts for the attribute of "how". So far, the known attribute are "what", "when", "where", and "how". The unknown attributes are "who" and "why". Given the weighted system, the weight of the known attributes is $((1*0.15) + (1*0.1) + (1*0.1) + (1*0.1) = 0.15 + 0.1 + 0.1 + 0.1 = 0.45$, namely, 45% of the puzzle is known. The context-based heuristics recommends an inquiry for the attribute "who" first as it possesses 30% of the total weight.

Now, the engagement mechanism is triggered, and the intelligence collection process gets started. It examines the source MAC address and the source IP address within the echo packets. As the source MAC address is the address of the switch that the server is directly connected to, the server asks the switch for the source MAC address of the packet that the switch receives. The switch will ask the router that it directly connects to for the source MAC address and the source IP address within the echo packets that the router receives. The router provides the information. Now, the MAC address and the IP address that sends the echo packets to the router are discovered. The engagement mechanism approaches that device and asks the same question. This process keeps running until it reaches to the device that launches these echo packets.

Once it gets to the device that launches these echo packets, the engagement mechanism makes an inquiry about the attribute "why", which possess 25% of the total weight. If this device is a zombie, it may provide an unsatisfactory reason; or it may be slow in providing the reason as it waits for it from the command and control (C2) server. Note that this type of control requires connectivity. If the engagement mechanism further asks for the current status of its connectivity, and if the zombie device provides the answer, the IP address of the C2 server is revealed.

Using the same back-tracking method, the engagement mechanism can eventually trace to the C2 server. From the neighboring device of this C2 server, the engagement mechanism is able to find out the MAC address as well as the IP address of the C2 server. Once discovered, the engagement mechanism makes an inquiry about the attribute "why". The C2 server either refuses to provide an answer or provides an unsatisfactory answer. This may give up its real intention. At this point, a close surveillance is initiated in order to find out the host name of the devices and the user name if possible. In addition, the engagement mechanism tries to verify if the device is used by the real attack initiator and if the owner/user of the device is the real attacker. Eventually, 100% of the puzzle is solved, or at least a very higher percentage of the puzzle is solved.

Note that this operation is conducted at the very early stage of a denial of service attack. So, deterrence mechanisms, defense mechanisms, and recovery mechanisms can be immediately launched to halt the denial of service attack. In cyber operations, every minute counts. The sooner an attacker can be identified, the sooner a counter-attack can be launched, and the less impact can be left on the affected systems and networks. Meanwhile, the evidence collected can be used for prosecution and retaliation purpose. This supports cyber deterrence.

As shown in this hypothetical case, the context-based heuristics plays a significant role in search for a target and in collecting intelligence and evidence about the target. With no doubt, it helps accurate attribution.

Conclusion

Attribution is a challenge in the cyber domain. However, as shown in this paper, heuristics can guide the most optimal search based on some structural configurations with a weight system. Eventually, it is capable of limiting the search time of information discovery heuristics in supporting cyber operations. Linking purpose, methods, time, location, and events with the identified device, the proposed heuristic approach can serve as a path towards accurate and prompt attribution.

References

Beebe, N. 2009. Digital Forensic Research: the Good, the Bad and the Unaddressed. *Advances in Digital Forensics V*, Springer. pp. 17-36.

Chen, J. 2016. Contextual Binding and Intelligent Targeting. *Proceedings of the 2016 IEEE/WIC/ACM International Conference on Web Intelligence*. pp.701-704.

Chen, J. & Dinerman, A. 2016. On Cyber Dominance in Modern Warfare, *Proceedings of the 15th European Conference on Cyber Warfare and Security*. pp.52-57. Reading, UK: Academic Conferences & Publishing International (ACPI) Limited.

Kosash, N. 1998. An Introduction to Heuristic Algorithms. University of Trento, Italy.

Marti, R. & Reinelt, G. 2011. Heuristic Methods. The Linear Ordering Problem, Exact and Heuristic Methods in Combinatorial Optimization 175, DOI: 10.1007/978-3-642-16729-4_2. pp.17-40. Berlin: Springer-Verlag.

Sinek, S. 2009. *Start with Why: How Great Leaders Inspire Everyone to Take Action*. USA: Penguin Group.

Sterner, E. 2011. Deterrence in Cyberspace: Yes, No, Maybe. *Returning to Fundamentals: Deterrence and U.S. National Security in the 21st Century*. pp. 27. Washington DC: George C. Marshall Institute.

Semi-supervised Random Forest for Intrusion Detection Network

Ningxin Shi, Xiaohong Yuan, William Nick
North Carolina Agricultural and Technical State University
ningxss@hotmail.com, xhyuan@ncat.edu, wmnick@aggies.ncat.edu

Abstract

In order to protect valuable computer systems, network data needs to be analyzed and classified so that possible network intrusions can be detected. Machine learning techniques have been used to classify network data. For supervised machine learning methods, they can achieve high accuracy at classifying network data as normal or malicious, but they require the availability of fully labeled data. Semi-supervised machine learning methods, however, can use a small number of labeled examples and train a large number of examples without label.

In this research, we explore the use of semi-supervised Random Forest in classifying network data and intrusion detection. It was used to classify the Third International Knowledge Discovery and Data Mining Tools Competition dataset (KDD 1999) and the result were compared with the results of using the supervised methods of Random Forest. The results were also compared with those using ladder network, an approach which combines unsupervised neural networks, in classifying KDD 1999.

KEYWORDS

Random Forest, semi-supervised machine learning, KDD 1999.

1 INTRODUCTION

In the last decade, the development of computer technology and the invention of the internet have brought many benefits to society. Some of these benefits include faster communication, better convenience and more productivity. Today, more than three billion people have access to the Internet, equating to 42 percent of the global population in 2014. Thus, network security has become very important. Intrusion Detection System (IDS) is a device or software application that monitors a network or system for malicious activity or policy violation. Current IDSs are either signature based or anomaly based. The signature based IDS detects the attacks which have been documented. Thus new types of attacks cannot be detected by the signature based detection. The anomaly based detection focuses on finding unknown or unusual activity patterns in the observed data. It can detect new attacks but it also needs a domain expert to distinguish normal or abnormal activity patterns.

In this research, machine learning methods has been used to detect attacks. Some of the machine learning classifiers have been developed under supervised learning. Supervised learning is to use labeled data to train the classifier and then test the classifier in the test set. The disadvantage of supervised learning is that it needs a large amount of labeled data, which is not practical since it's labor intensive. Different from supervised learning, the unsupervised learning is to use unlabeled data to train the classifier and to infer a function described hidden structure. However unsupervised learning is very sensitive to noise data and the results can be influenced a lot. Hasan and his team developed the Support Vector Machine (SVM) and Random Forest supervised learning methods[4]. Salama and his team have used a hybrid intrusion detection scheme utilizing both SVM and Deep Belief Networks (DBN) [5].

Semi-supervised learning falls between supervised learning and unsupervised learning. Different from supervised learning, semi-supervised learning uses a small amount of labeled data and a large amount of unlabeled data to train and test the classifiers. Researchers have found that unlabeled data, when used in conjunction with a small amount of labeled data, can produce considerable improvement in learning accuracy. There are two kinds of semi-supervised learning, transductive and inductive learning. Transductive learning is to use labeled data to train the classifier and use the unlabeled data to test the classifier. The inductive learning is to use both labeled and unlabeled data to train the classifier. Zehra Cataltepe *et al* had a research on semi-supervised decision trees for network intrusion detection based on KDD99 dataset [6]. Leistner *et al* developed a semi-supervised algorithm of Random Forest [3] based on Breiman's research on Random Forest which developed the Out-of-bag theory [1]. Liu *et al* discussed about the node splitting for Random Forest Construction and developed the new algorithm [2].

This research implemented semi-supervised Random Forest for network intrusion detection. KDD99 dataset was used for training the classifier. The experiments used the same number of classes, and the same number of samples in each class as in Mtahir *et al* 's research [7] in order to compare the results with supervised Random Forest and semi-supervised ladder nework.

The paper is organized as follows. Section 2 discusses the background of Random Forest based on Dr. Leo Breiman's research [1]. Section 3 discusses about the experiment results and compares to results on supervised Random Forest and semi-supervised ladder network [7]. Section 4 concludes the paper.

2 Background

2.1 Random Forest

Random Forest is an ensemble of classification or regression trees. The Random Forest classifier works by partitioning the training set of the data into *k* subsets and constructing a decision tree out of each subset. All of the subsets are randomly selected. Each decision tree is made by randomly selecting *m* variables out of all the variables and finding the best split on the selected variables. This is done at each node and continued until a node cannot be split further, leading to the leaf nodes. Each tree votes on a classification after running the test set on each of them. The final classification of the forest is determined by the majority of the decision trees [7].

The algorithm of Random Forest proposed by Dr. Leo Breiman described as below [1].

Given a set of classifiers $t_1(x), t_2(x), \ldots, t_k(x)$, and with the training set drawn at random from the distribution of the random vector Y, $\boldsymbol{X}$, we can get the margin function as

$$mg(\boldsymbol{X}, Y) = av_k I(t_k(\boldsymbol{X}) = Y) \\ -max_{j \neq Y} av_k I(t_k(\boldsymbol{X}) = j) \quad (1)$$

where I is the indicator function. The margin measures the average number of votes at $\boldsymbol{X}$, Y for the right class exceeds the average votes for any other class. The larger the margin, the more accuracy in testing. The generalization error is given by

$$PE * = P_{\boldsymbol{X},Y}(mg(\boldsymbol{X}, Y) < 0) \quad (2)$$

where the subscripts $\boldsymbol{X}$, Y indicate that the probability is over the $\boldsymbol{X}$, Y space.

In random forests, $t_k(X) = t(\boldsymbol{X}, \Theta_k)$. When the forest has a large number of trees, it follows the Strong Law of Large Numbers and the tree structure that:

$$P_{\boldsymbol{X},Y}(P_\Theta(t(\boldsymbol{X}, \Theta) = Y) \\ - max_{j \neq Y} P_\Theta(t(\boldsymbol{X}, \Theta) = j) < 0 \quad (3)$$

where Θ is random vector for splitting selection and Θ_k is independent identically distributed random vector.

2.2 Semi-supervised Random Forest

For Random Forest $F = \{t_1, t_2, \ldots, t_N\}$, when each tree is constructing, it learns a function $F: x \rightarrow y$. The training set is $\{x_i \in x\}_{i=1\ldots l}$ and the test set $\{y_i \in y\}_{i=1\ldots l}$. Each internal node of Random Forest is binary split with a partition criterion.

When testing, given a test case x, Random Forest gives the probability estimation for each class as

$$p(k|x) = \frac{1}{N} \sum_{i=1}^{N} p_i(k|x) \quad (4)$$

where $p_i(k|x)$ is the probability estimation of class k given by the ith tree [2].

It is estimated by calculating the ratio that class k gets votes from the leaves in the ith tree

$$p_i(k|x) \frac{l_{i,k}}{\sum_{j=1}^{K} l_{i,j}} \quad (5)$$

where $l_{i,k}$ is the number of leaves in the ith tree that vote for class k. Here the overall decision function of Random Forest is as follows.

$$F = argmaxp(k|x) \mid k \in y \tag{6}$$

Xiao Liu *et al* [2] developed the Semi-supervised splitting Random Forest based on the Out-Of-Bag (OOB) samples of the tree which was mentioned in Beriman's research.

The process of Random Forest constructing, an individual training set for each tree (random input) is generated from the original training set using bootstrap aggregation (for labeled set X_l^i and unlabeled setX_u^i). The samples which are not included in the training set is OOB samples and can be used to calculate OOB error. A OOBE is a good feature to do node splitting and semi-supervised training.

Xiao's algorithm for semi-supervised splitting is as follows [2].

Table 1 Algorithm of semi-supervised splitting

Algorithm Semi-supervised Splitting

Input: A set of labeled data X_l for training and a set of labeled Y_l for testing.
Input: A set of unlabeled training data X_u.
Input: The size of the forest *N*.
Output: The Semi-supervised Random Forest *F*.
Step 1: Initialize an empty forest *F*.
Step 2: **for** the ith decision tree in *F*
Step 3: Select a new labeled set X_l^i and a new unlabeled set X_u^i using the bootstrap aggregation from the original dataset.
Step 4: Train the tree with only labeled data: $t_l^i = trainTree(X_l^i)$.
Step 5: Calculate the OOBE: $e_l^i = oobe(t_l^i, X_l - X_l^i)$ using the labeled trained tree and the difference between original labeled data and labeled samples.
Step 6: Train the tree with both labeled and unlabeled data: $t_u^i = semiTree(X_l^i, X_u^i)$.
Step 7: Calculate the OOBE: $e_u^i = oobe(t_u^i, X_l - X_l^i)$ using unlabeled trained tree and the difference between original labeled dataset and labeled samples.
Step 8: Compare the OOBE of the above two different trained tree to select final classifiers.
if $e_l^i > e_u^i$ **then**
Step 9: $F = F \cup t_u^i$.
Step 10: **else**
Step 11: $F = F \cup t_l^i$.
Step 12: **end if**
Step 13: **end for**
Step 14: Return *F*.

3 Experiment and Results

3.1 KDD 1999 dataset

KDD 1999 is the Third International Knowledge Discovery and Data Mining Tools Competition, which was held in conjunction with the Fifth International Conference on Knowledge Discovery and Data Mining [8]. The training data contains about 4GB of compressed packet capture data from 7 weeks of network traffic. These data have been processed into 4.9 million connection records, with a set of 41 features. Table 2 is the categories of malicious behavior included in the dataset [7].

Table 2 Categories of Malicious Behavior

Major Categories	Subcategores
Denial of Service (DoS)	Ping of Death, LAND, Neptune, Backscatter, Smurf, Teardrop
User to Root (U2R)	Buffer Overflow, Loadmodule Perl, Rootkit
Remote to Local (R2L)	FTP write, password guessing, IMAP attacks, Multi-hop, PHF, Spy, Warezclient, Warezmaster
Probing	Ipsweeping, Nmap, Portsweeping, Satan

3.2 Experiment

This research used Berman's Random Forest model [1] and implemented the algorithm of Liu *et al* [2] to split the tree nodes. The program was developed based on Kevin-kerandren's example program [9].

In order to compare with supervised Random Forest method, the experiments used the samples as 10, 1000, 3000 and 5000 examples per class and classes as 16, 9, 6 and 6 respectively which were same as those in Mtahir *et al* 's research [7]. Each of the class contained 50% labeled data and 50% unlabeled data.

3.3 Semi-Supervised Random Forest compared with Supervised Random Forest

To compare the supervised machine learning and semi-supervised machine learning, we used Mutahir Nadeem *et al* [7] 's results on supervised machine learning. Table 3 and Table 4 are the result comparison for semi-supervised Random Forest and supervised Random Forest.

Table 3 Accuracy for Supervised Random Forest and Semi-supervised Random Forest [7].

Examples		Accuracy %	
# per class	# of classes	Semi-supervised RF	Supervised RF
10	16	N/A	87%
1000	9	95%	99%
3000	6	99%	99%
5000	6	99%	99%

Table 4 Time for Supervised Random Forest and Semi-supervised Random Forest [7].

Examples		Execution Time (sec)	
# per class	# of classes	Semi-supervised RF	Supervised RF
10	16	N/A	1.832
1000	9	9.745	5.745
3000	6	17.13	8.717
5000	6	18.29	14.47

The result under semi-supervised took a little bit longer time to execute but the accuracy is similar as the one used supervised method. The advantage of semi-supervised approach is that it only requires part of the training dataset is labeled.

3.4 Semi-Supervised Random Forest compared with Semi-Supervised Ladder Network

Table 5 and Table 6 are the result comparison for semi-supervised Random Forest and semi-supervised Ladder Network of Mutahir *et al* [7].

To be consistent, the result used the samples as 10, 1000, 3000 and 5000 examples per class. The training data set includes both labeled and unlabeled examples. The ratio of labeled data is 50%.

Table 5 Accuracy for Semi-Supervised Random Forest and Semi-Supervised Ladder Network.

Examples	Accuracy %	
# per class	Semi-supervised RF	Semi-supervised Ladder Network
10	N/A	N/A
1000	95%	92.18%
3000	99%	98.13%
5000	99%	99.03%

Table 6 Time for Semi-Supervised Random Forest and Semi-Supervised Ladder Network.

Examples	Execution Time (sec)	
# per class	Semi-supervised RF	Semi-supervised Ladder Network
10	N/A	N/A
1000	9.745	12.7
3000	17.13	21.8
5000	18.29	22.2

Compared with the result of semi-supervised Random Forest, the Ladder Network took more time to execute. For large amount of data, semi-supervised RF and Ladder Network has similar accuracy. But for the medium amount of data, the Ladder Network has lower accuracy than that of Random Forest.

4 Conclusions

In summary, the Semi-supervised Random Forest performed better than the Semi-supervised Ladder Network. Even though it took more time to train in semi-supervised Random Forest than that in supervised Random Forest, it has advantage because it only needs small amount of labeled data. This is practical because in the real world, it is hard to label large amount of data. Also, training the classifier using unlabeled data can make the margin more accurate and smooth.

Our future work includes improving the training algorithm of semi-supervised Random Forest and making it faster. Also we will develop semi-supervised Support

Vector Machine (SVM) and Deep Belief Network (DBN) on KDD 99 and compare their results.

Acknowledgement

This work is partially supported by NSF under the grant CNS-1460864. Any opinions, findings, and conclusions or recommendations expressed in this material are those of the author(s) and do not necessarily reflect the views of NSF.

Reference

[1] Leo Breiman. 2001. Random forests. *Machine Learning,* 45(1): 5-32, University of California Berkeley, CA.

[2] Xiao Liu, Mingli Song, Dacheng Tao, Zicheng Liu, Luming Zhang, Chun Chen and Jiajun Bu. 2013. *Semi-supervised Node Splitting for Random Forest Construction*. CVPR2013.

[3] Christian Leistner, Amir Saffari, Jakob Santner and Horst Bischof. *Semi-supervised Random Forests*. Institute for Computer Graphics and Vision. Graz University of Technology.

[4] Md Al Mehedi Hasan, Mohammed Nasser, Biprodip Pal and Shamim Ahmad. 2014. Support vector machine and random forest modeling for intrusion detection system (ids). *Journal of Intelligent Learning Systems and Applications*, 6(1):45.

[5] Mostafa A. Salama, Heba F. Eid, Rabie A. Ramadan, Ashraf Darwish and Aboul Ella Hassanien. 2011.*Hybrid Intelligent Intrusion Detection Scheme,* pages 293-303. Springer Berlin Heidelberg, Berlin, Heidelberg.

[6] Zehra Cataltepe, Umit Ekmekci, Tanju Cataltepe, and Ismail Kelebek. *Online Feature Selected Semi-supervisd Decision Trees for Network Intrusion Detection*. Istanbul Technical University.

[7] Mutahir Nadeem, Ochaun Marshall, Sarbjit Singh, Xing Fang and Xiaohong Yuan. 2016. *Semi-supervised Deep Neural Network for Network Intrusion Detection*. Conference on Cybersecurity Education, Research and Practice, October 29-30, 2016.

[8] KDD cup 1999 data, October 1999.

[9] Kevin-kerandren. 2016, March 13. Random forest in Python. *GitHub*. https://github.com/kevin-keraudren/randomforest-python

Short Papers

Short papers presented as posters at the
2017 Modern AI and Cognitive Science Conference.

A study of how people infer social relationships from people's behavior in simple economic games

Nathan Blank
Rose-Hulman Institute of Technology
Dept. of Comp. Sci. and Software Eng.
blanknc@rose-hulman.edu

Charles Kemp
Carnegie Mellon University
Dept. of Psychology
ckemp@cmu.edu

Alan Jern
Rose-Hulman Institute of Technology
Dept. of Humanities and Social Sciences
jern@rose-hulman.edu

ABSTRACT

We explore several models of social reasoning to better understand how people make inferences about people's social relationships after observing their behavior. In an experiment, we find that there are individual differences in subjects' social inferences and no single model accounts well for most subjects' inferences.

1 INTRODUCTION

After observing two people interact, it is often possible for an observer to infer what kind of relationship the two people have. In this paper, we explore the mental representations that support these inferences. Previous studies have suggested that people represent other people as rational agents in order to reason about their mental states, choices, and relationships with other people [1, 3]. In this paper, we address whether this holds when people are making inferences about social interactions. Specifically, we focus on situations in which a person observes two people simultaneously making choices that affect themselves and the other person; the observer then infers whether the pair are friends, strangers, or enemies.

We studied this question using simple economic games, like the prisoner's dilemma. Each game has two players, each with two options. We chose these games because they represent stereotypical social interactions [4]. The two players' choices in a game can be used to infer their relationship. For example, in the prisoner's dilemma, if both players cooperate, one might infer that the players trust each other, and are friends. If the players both act greedily and defect, one might infer that the players do not trust each other and are enemies or strangers. We ran an experiment in which subjects made inferences like these. We compared subjects' judgments to the predictions of three different computational models to better understand how they made these inferences [1].

2 MODELS

The three models varied in complexity and number of assumptions. We will describe the models in order of decreasing complexity.

2.1 Recursive model

The recursive model first assumes that observers expect players to make choices based on the payouts they and the other player get in the game. We capture this by assigning weights to how much a player cares about her own payout and how much she cares about the other player's payout (cf. [2]). Specifically, we represent how much Player A cares about her own payout as w_{AA} and how much Player A cares about Player B's payout as w_{AB}, and similarly for Player B. These weights are constrained so that $w_{AA} + w_{AB} = 1$. We represent whether Player A wants Player B to receive positive or negative payout as $\gamma_{AB} \in \{-1, +1\}$.

These parameters can capture different relationships. For friends, we assume that $\gamma_{AB} = +1$ and $w_{AB} > w_{AA}$. For enemies, $\gamma_{AB} = -1$, and $w_{AB} > w_{AA}$. For strangers, we assume that the players care more about themselves than the other player but that they want to help the other player: $\gamma_{AB} = +1$ and $w_{AA} > w_{AB}$. These assumptions have previous empirical support [3, 5].

To perform inferences about two players' relationship, we compute the probability of each relationship (setting of parameters) given an observed outcome in a game. For example, to find the probability that two players are friends, we iterate over settings of our parameters (i.e., all weights subject to the $w_{AB} > w_{AA}$ constraint). For each setting of parameters, we compute the probability that the players would make the observed choices, assuming a softmax utility function. We compute the mean probability of making the observed choice averaged over all possible parameter settings. We repeat this procedure for strangers and enemies. We then normalize the resulting mean probabilities to produce a probability distribution over the three relationships.

We call this model the recursive model because it assumes that observers of a game assume that each player takes the other player's choice into account before making a choice. For example, if two players are friends, the model assumes that each player expects the other player to choose using the parameter settings for friends. For simplicity, we stopped this recursive reasoning at a depth of one. That is, each player assumes that the other player is modeling them in return as a random agent.

2.2 Independent agents model

The independent agents model is similar to the recursive model, but does not assume that the players take the other players' choices into account. Instead, this model assumes that each player assigns a utility to each of the four possible game outcomes, based on the payouts and the player's relationship with the other player. We then assign probabilities to each outcome in proportion to the player's utility. We repeat this procedure for the other player. We then combine the probabilities for both players by multiplying them for each outcome, and then normalizing so that the total probability for all outcomes in a game sums to 1.

2.3 Heuristic model

It is possible that people make social inferences by relying on simple cues. To test this possibility, we also created a heuristic model. This model predicts that the players are friends if they end up in an outcome with the total maximum payout for both players, enemies

[1]All modeling code, materials, and data are available at https://github.com/jernlab/social-reasoning

Figure 1: *All subjects' ratings. Conditions on the x-axis are ordered by mean rating assigned to friends, from lowest (left) to highest (right).*

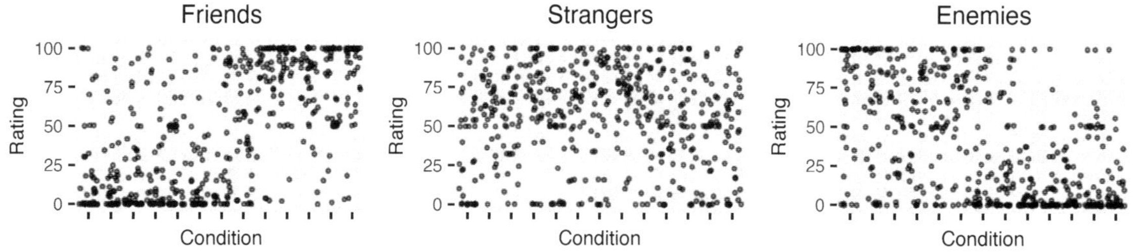

Figure 2: *Mean correlations between subjects' ratings and model predictions, for three different groups of subjects. Error bars are 95% confidence intervals.*

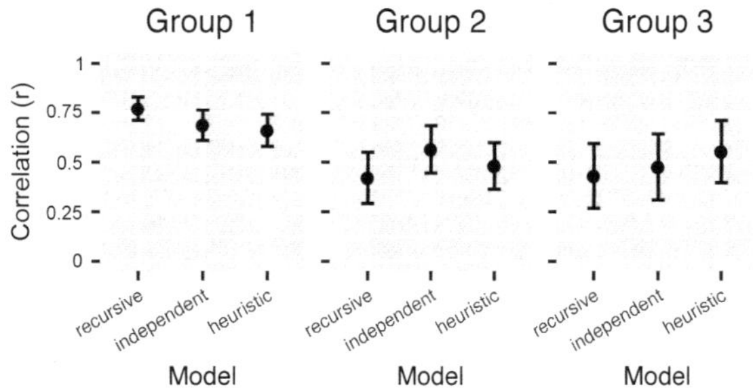

if they end up in an outcome with the total minimum payout, and strangers otherwise.

3 EXPERIMENT

We conducted an experiment to test what inferences people actually make. Subjects were 60 users on Amazon Mechanical Turk, 20 of which were excluded for failing an attention check (instructions to only enter a '0' in a text box). There were 13 within-subjects conditions. In each condition, subjects saw a table of the game's payouts with the players' outcome in the game identified. Subjects were told that the players were not able to communicate in the game. In total, we used five different games and between two and four different outcomes for each game. The conditions were shown in random order, but conditions involving the same game (with different outcomes) were shown sequentially before moving onto a new game. Subjects rated how likely it was that the players were friends, strangers, and enemies using three sliders that ranged from 0 ("very unlikely") to 100 ("very likely"). Finally, subjects were asked to explain their judgments in a text box.

4 RESULTS AND DISCUSSION

Figure 1 shows all subjects' ratings for all conditions, ordered by mean rating for friends from lowest to highest. Subjects' ratings were highly inconsistent for strangers, compared to friends and enemies. Examining individual subject's ratings and written explanations revealed that some subjects expected strangers to act selfishly, some expected strangers to act ambivalently, and many subjects assigned high ratings to strangers when the outcome of the game was difficult to make sense of otherwise. One example: "In this case it is almost impossible to determine, since all the choices are the same except for [outcome 4], but even enemies wouldn't pick that one because they would be sabotaging themselves as well". Our data therefore suggest that people's intuitions about how friends and enemies behave toward one another are more consistent than their intuitions about strangers.

Due to the inconsistency in responses about strangers, we further analyzed data and predictions only for friends and enemies. We identified the best-fitting model for each subject by computing the Pearson's correlation coefficient between each model and each subject's ratings. Figure 2 shows the mean correlation coefficients for subjects in three groups that resulted from this analysis. Group 1 ($N = 9$) includes subjects that were best fit by the recursive model ($r = 0.77$) compared to the independent model ($r = 0.69$) and the heuristic model ($r = 0.66$). Group 2 ($N = 19$) includes subjects that were best fit by the independent agent model ($r = 0.56$) compared to the recursive model ($r = 0.42$) and the heuristic model ($r = 0.48$). Group 3 ($N = 12$) includes subjects that were best fit by the heuristic model ($r = 0.55$) compared to the recursive model ($r = 0.43$) and the independent agent model ($r = 0.47$).

None of our models provided a strong account of all subjects' judgments, suggesting that people may approach our task in qualitatively different ways. However, about three quarters of our subjects were best-fit by either the recursive or independent agents models—both of which include models of the players' decision-making behavior—rather than the heuristic model, which does not. This result suggests that most people reason about social relationships by modeling the behavior of the people involved, rather than by relying on superficial heuristic cues.

REFERENCES

[1] C. L. Baker and J. B. Tenenbaum. 2014. Modeling human plan recognition using Bayesian theory of mind. In *Plan, activity and intent recognition: Theory and practice*, G. Sukthankar, R. P. Goldman, C. Geib, D. Pynadath, and H. Bui (Eds.). Morgan Kaufmann.

[2] D. W. Griesinger and J. W. Livingston, Jr. 1973. Toward a model of interpersonal motivation in experimental games. *Behavioral Science* 18, 3 (1973), 173–188.

[3] Alan Jern and Charles Kemp. 2014. Reasoning about social choices and social relationships. In *Proceedings of the 36th Annual Conference of the Cognitive Science Society.*

[4] Harold H. Kelley, John G. Holmes, Norbert L. Kerr, Harry T. Reis, Caryl E. Rusbult, and Paul A. M. Van Lange. 2002. *An atlas of interpersonal situations.* Cambridge University Press.

[5] G. F. Loewenstein, L. Thompson, and M. H. Bazerman. 1989. Social utility and decision making in interpersonal contexts. *Journal of Personality and Social Psychology* 57, 3 (1989), 426–441.

The *Robot* Mafia

A Test Environment for Deceptive Robots

Brad Lewis
lewibt01@students.ipfw.edu

Isaac Smith
smitil01@students.ipfw.edu

Max Fowler
fowlml01@students.ipfw.edu

John Licato
jlicato@ipfw.edu

Indiana University - Purdue University / Fort Wayne
Department of Computer Science

ABSTRACT

Future robotic agents may be required to reason about a given situation and decide whether it is appropriate to lie to or deceive humans. One type of deception, known formally as strategic deception, is the act of influencing others toward a specific goal through non-truths.

To demonstrate and test for the kind of reasoning required in strategic deception, we use a modified form of the social strategy game "Mafia" as a testing ground.

In the game, the townsfolk, who can be seen as an uninformed majority, must determine who amongst themselves are members of the informed minority (the Mafia) via social cues before the Mafia eliminate all the townsfolk.

First, we talk about how strategic deception applies to Mafia. We then present simplified rules for the game which can be formalized into a logic-based language. Once formalized, the rules can be provided to an automated theorem prover, which can carry out the necessary reasoning. By using this automated theorem prover we discuss how one can demonstrate automated strategic deception.

Keywords

Strategic Deception; Robots; Social Games

1. INTRODUCTION

In the field of artificial intelligence, there is a need for environments in which generally intelligent agents can be tested. Currently, there are no standard environments for testing how well autonomous agents can carry out strategically deceptive reasoning. In this poster, we propose an environment in which agents can demonstrate their ability to strategically deceive other intelligent agents. We then set out to use a social game as this example environment to show how strategic deception can be modeled in autonomous agents. Our work currently assumes that only one agent is being tested. However, the game can be reworked to account for multiple autonomous, deceptive agents, allowing systems of cooperation and networks of deception to be fostered among these agents. By defining a standard testing ground suitable for such reasoning we hope to provide a foundation upon which future research can be built.

MAICS '17 April 28–29, 2017, Fort Wayne, IN, USA

ACM ISBN 978-1-4503-2138-9.

DOI: 10.1145/1235

2. WHY STUDY STRATEGIC DECEPTION?

Strategic deception is the act of influencing others towards a specific goal through non-truths and misdirection. [1] Colloquially, deception is viewed as negative. However, there are numerous circumstances where deception is necessary, even performed benevolently. Bedside manner is one such example. Doctors must be able to keep their patient calm and comfortable even if the doctor is feeling panicked, as failure to do so endangers the patient and staff.

Another example is a texting service that determines when it is best to let its user see a text. This kind of service would reason about what impact the information in the message would have on its user and how that information would affect their ability to perform a task, such as driving a car, performing a surgery, or operating heavy machinery. In this case, the texting service may not directly lie to the user by saying there is information in the message being withheld; rather, the service may try to subtly misdirect the user's attention to more important things.

Strategic deception is common among humans in social settings. Often, it requires reasoning about the socially acceptable path through a situation. For example, if someone asks you how they look they would expect you to respond positively, as there is a mutual understanding that being excessively negative is rude. By default, machines lack this mutual understanding, and thus could come across as mean, blunt, unfeeling, or insincere. While machines currently lack the ability to genuinely feel or express feeling effectively, it would still be useful for the machines that are present in our day-to-day lives to be able to understand when and where it is appropriate to practice strategic deception.

For these reasons, strategic deception may be a necessity in more environments than just ones where protecting individuals and groups of individuals involves being able to answer questions diplomatically, if slightly dishonestly. But what kind of reasoning is needed to carry out such strategic deception, and how can that sort of reasoning be tested?

3. THE GAME

3.1 Why Mafia?

The game of Mafia provides agents both an incentive to lie and to tell the truth when necessary. It is also an environment which incentivizes suspicion and caution amongst agents, reducing stochastic behavior. This levels out the playing field between man and machine, as all participants use the same rules and can be punished by being overly mistrustful without evidence. Unfortunately, socially oriented games tend to be intractable to model, and therefore need to be reduced to a version that can be reasoned over. We decided to create a simplified form of Mafia to handle this difficulty. We will next briefly discuss the simplification of some of the rules, and how these could be leveraged inside an automatic prover (e.g. Machina Arachne Tree-based Reasoner, or MATR).

3.2 The Rules

The rules of this game are reduced forms of the original Mafia's rules. To simplify the environment for the autonomous agent(s), our game only contains two types of players: townspeople and Mafia members. Townspeople do not know who the Mafia members are, and are capable of voting any other person up to trial during the day, then voting on whether the defendant should be killed. At night, Townspeople go to "sleep", and are unaware of what happens during that time until the following morning. Mafia members have the same abilities as Townspeople during the day, but at night they become aware of who their fellow Mafia members are and have the capability to collectively eliminate a target from the game. Note that unlike the original Mafia we have simplified the voting process used to put a suspect on trial, and have removed the discussion stage from the game.

3.3 Day and Night Cycle

At the start of the day cycle, everyone "wakes up" by opening their eyes. This is when the villagers discover who the Mafia killed the previous night. After everyone learns who has been eliminated, each person is then given the opportunity to vote another player up to trial. Voting consists of two different and discrete votes: a primary vote and a secondary vote. The primary vote is a vote of conviction, in which the voter has accepted that the suspect is a member of the Mafia. The secondary vote is a vote of suspicion, in which the voter believes that the suspect is a member of the Mafia. Once someone has been voted up to trial, the townspeople vote again on whether or not to actually kill the person on trial. Note that on the first day cycle the game has just begun and nobody has yet been killed by the Mafia. Thus, there is no trial stage and the game progresses shortly thereafter to the night cycle.

During the night cycle, everyone begins by closing their eyes. Note that Mafia members must also close their eyes so as to not immediately reveal themselves to others who may be watching for this behavior. Each Mafia member must then open their eyes, and decide non-verbally and covertly amongst themselves who to kill. Once the decision is made, that person dies and is removed from the game once the day cycle begins.

3.4 Trials from the Mafia's Perspective

3.4.1 Townspeople

If the townsperson on trial has been helpful to the Mafia, (e.g. voted other townspeople up on trial, defended Mafia members who were on trial, etc.) it may be worth it to defend this person. This serves the purpose of keeping in the game individuals who are less adept at finding Mafia members. Additionally, the act of defending an innocent reflects positively on the voter, even if the suspect were to be eliminated.

3.4.2 Mafia Members

As a Mafia member, a good strategy may be to defend one's teammates when possible. Should the Mafia lose a teammate, it will be able to kill one less person per night than it would otherwise be able to. Also, for each teammate that is executed the number of suspects lowers, raising the probability that other Mafia members are eliminated tomorrow.

3.5 Autonomous Agent on Trial

This is the scenario we will be targeting with our research. Here the autonomous agent can easily lie, tell the truth, or strategically deceive. Strategic deception is encouraged as telling the truth would most likely remove the agent from the game, and a statement of innocence is, in general, not as effective as a reasoned argument against another individual. The recommended strategy is to deflect the blame onto someone who has been either under-participating or over-participating in the social aspects of the game, as this can usually be construed as a sign of nervousness.

3.5.1 Measuring the value of players

The autonomous agent keeps track of how valuable each person is to the Mafia. Teammates are placed arbitrarily high on this scale for their ability to contribute an additional kill each night. From there, people who do things to help the Mafia are given a higher worth than others. For instance, if a person has a history of voting to eliminate non-Mafia members, they would be given a higher strategic value than someone who voted to save non-Mafia members. In this way, actions which spread discord amongst townspeople are encouraged. Then, the individual with the strategic value closest to 0 is selected and removed from the game.

4. FUTURE WORK

This is a work in progress, which we hope to develop into a well-defined, standard test for deceptive agents. Using this work as a foundation, we will be able to demonstrate an artificial agent's performance on this system experimentally, perhaps by having a robot play against humans. Related work will formally define strategic deception and automatically perform the required reasoning using formalized rules.

5. REFERENCES

[1] FOWLER, M., THIEME, A., AND LICATO, J. Robotic misdirection, for good causes. In *The 28th Modern Artificial Intelligence and Cognitive Science Conference (MAICS)* (Fort Wayne, Indiana, 2017).

Timetable Design from Even Headways to Even Loads with Dynamic Fuzzy Constraints

Yanan Zhang[1], Deeptha Girish[2], Vineeta Singh[2], Zhaopeng Meng[1], Anca Ralescu[2]
[1]School of Computer Software,Tianjin University,Tianjin,300350,China
[2]EECS Department, University of of Cincinnati, Cincinnati, OH 45221-0030, USA
zhangyn@tju.edu.cn, girishde@mail.uc.edu, singhvi@mail.uc.edu, mengzp@tju.edu.cn, anca.ralescu@uc.edu

Abstract

Timetable scheduling is to adjust departure time of vehicles (while providing comfortable environment for passengers). Public transit systems have limited resources, such as drivers and number of vehicles and timetables are usually set with with fixed number of bus services and even headways (equal time intervals between successive services).

This study considers the problem of dynamic timetable designing under fuzzy constraints based on average vehicle loads, and produce fixed number of bus services. Passenger satisfaction is described as a fuzzy goal, that associates with the number of on-board passengers and vehicle capacity. A new method of timetable scheduling is proposed in which the decision on the time interval between two successive bus services is obtained by maximizing the decision value of both fuzzy goal and fuzzy constraint.

Experimental results show that the timetable produced by fuzzy decision making can adjust to the fluctuating passenger flow, and leads to a higher and more even usage of vehicle.

Introduction

A timetable is a specific sequence of time moments for vehicles departing from the first to the last stop of a bus line. The time intervals between two successive bus services are usually decided by the experience of the timetable scheduler. Even headway with fixed time interval is a common way for timetable design in many real systems. Resources, such as the number of drivers or the number of vehicles, limit the number of bus services. This study concentrates on readjusting the time interval with fixed service number under a fuzzy environment.

The review of the strategies for planing, operation, and control of bus transit system(Ibarra Rojas, Lopez Irarragorri, and Rios Solis 2015) discusses the purpose of the timetable scheduling from four aspects (i) to meet specific demand, (ii) to minimize waiting time, (iii) to maximize the number of synchronization events (iv) to balance multi objectives.

Many approaches in designing even-load and even-headway timetables have been proposed including rescaling continuous service times to discrete values with equal time intervals (for example, the time can be 30s, 1min, 2min)(Ceder 2007), where each discrete value is a time state that has its own feature values. Determination of preferred headways uses a heuristic algorithm, and state as a mixed integer programming problem(Ceder, Hassold, and Dano 2013). In *even-load* and *even-headways* transit timetable design (Ceder 2011) (Hassold and Ceder 2012), the time interval between bus services is based on the desired occupancy of bus capacity. For the same number of bus services instead of using one size vehicles and fixed value of time intervals, different size vehicles are used to adjust to the variation of passenger flow, in which the interval is decided by usage rate of vehicles; the new timetable reduces the periods with empty seats and maintains the same waiting time of passengers, with little increase in the time periods when the passengers are standing during travel (Ceder et al. 2013).

According to (Sun et al. 2014a), decision making with discrete time is easy to model and apply in real system, where models of demand-sensitive timetable making with vehicle capacity constraints and dynamical headways are discussed respectively. The equivalent time intervals are used to describe the train/subway operation (it is assumed that traffic is stable over short time periods such as 5 to 30 minutes). Timetables with dynamical headways have good performance.

It can be seen from previous research, that time interval decision making under vehicle size and real time passenger flow is the key part in dynamic timetable making. Discrete service time can simplify the process of time interval decision making.

The data used in the current study, such as passenger flow, is extracted by combining data of Global Position System (GPS) and intelligence Card (IC) from real public transportation system.

The dynamic activities of passenger boarding/alighting are extracted from IC. The duration of passenger travel and bus capacity can be incorporated into time interval optimization(Sun et al. 2014b). Drawbacks of the scheduled timetable are assessed by calculating the load factor of rail lines at different time and section to evaluate the timetable from the viewpoint of passenger flow data. The load factor incorporates the number of alighting and boarding passengers, waiting time of passengers at platform, and the number of passengers waiting for trains due to the overcrowding in vehicles (Jiang et al. 2016).

Most of timetable optimization problems have an objective function with crisp constraints. Incomplete knowledge, fluctuation of passenger flow, and varying riding time challenge the performance of these approaches in deterministic environment(Chaari et al. 2014). There are many ways of timetable scheduling under uncertainty, which can be stochastic and/or fuzzy (for example to describe service level as 'poor', 'good', 'very good'; the comfort of passenger as 'little comfort', ' satisfied', 'very comfort'; and the usage of vehicle as 'crowded', 'very crowded', etc.) (Zimmermann 1985). The objectives of timetable scheduling are mainly concerned with improving the service level, passenger comfort, and resource usage.

A fuzzy multi-objective optimization problem is formulated to model single bus line frequency (Tilahun and Ong 2012). The relationship between the objective functions and decision variables are described by fuzzy reasoning schemes (Chakraborty, Guha, and Dutta 2016). Weighted constraint aggregation in fuzzy optimization are specified by the preference of the decision-maker(Kaymak and Sousa 2003) (Choon and Tilahun 2011). A summary of understanding of fuzzy optimization and clarification of fuzzy goals and constraints are given in(Tang et al. 2004).

Based on previous work, design and optimization of timetable to meet dynamic temporary passenger flow under a fuzzy environment (Zhang et al. 2017 submited), and reverse-flow technique in multistage decision making of time intervals for timetable (Zhang, Meng, and Ralescu 2017 submited), this study adopts decision-making under fuzzy environment as proposed in (Bellman and Zadeh 1970). The results show that the model with fuzzy constraints shortens the waiting time of passengers, and can better adjust the timetable to fit the varying passenger flow.

Even headway timetable is first designed. The average loads in even timetable provide a threshold value in designing the dynamic fuzzy constraint of vehicle capacity usage. The passenger satisfaction is fixed in all cases, and act as fuzzy goal in decision making. The time interval between two successive bus services is decided by maximizing the decision value of both fuzzy goal and fuzzy constraint. A group of case studies are conducted to compare the timetable with fixed even headway and the timetable with uneven headways from fuzzy timetable scheduling. The results show that timetable produced by fuzzy decision making can adjust to the fluctuation of passenger flow, and leads to a higher and more even capacity usage of vehicles.

From this point on this paper is organized as follows: Notation and terminology for fuzzy timetable scheduling is listed in section 2. Decision making in fuzzy system and problem formulation are discussed in section 3. Cases study are conducted on section 4. summary and conclusion are given in section 5.

Notation and Terminology

The following quantities are used to describe the system.

1. To apply the approach described in (Bellman and Zadeh 1970), the continuous service time space is translated into a discrete finite *Time State Space*: $\mathcal{T}$, $\mathcal{P} = |\mathcal{T}| < \infty$, with equivalent interval of one minute (that is, for $t_i, t_{i+1} \in T, t_{i+1} - t_i = 1$).
2. $\mathcal{S} = \{s, \ldots, s_{\mathcal{M}}\} \subset \mathcal{T}$ is the timetable of bus services, where s is the first depart time of bus service from the first stop of the bus line, $s_{\mathcal{M}}$ is the last depart time of bus service, and $\mathcal{M}$ is the total number of bus service.
3. The decision variable is δ, the time interval between two successive bus services. δ takes values in the set $\Delta = \{\delta_q \,|\, q = 1, 2, \ldots, \mathcal{Q},\ \delta_{i+1} - \delta_i = 1\}$. δ_0 is the fixed time interval for even headways timetable.
4. The maximum bus capacity - maximum number of on-board passengers - is denoted by $\mathcal{B}$.[1]
5. J denotes the total number of bus stops, and a particular bus stop is denoted by $j = 1, 2, \ldots, \mathcal{J}$. It is assumed that all passengers can board the first incoming vehicle at each bus stop j, that is, the number of vehicles that can be scheduled is large enough. For $j \in \{1, \ldots, J\}$, passengers arriving in the time interval $\delta \in \Delta$ are distributed uniformly.

To capture the traffic conditions at time state $t \in \mathcal{T}$, bus stop j, $j = 1, \ldots, \mathcal{J}$, time interval $\delta \in \Delta$, with vehicle size $\mathcal{B}$, the following quantities are defined:

1. $\mathcal{N}_j^{t,\delta}$ denotes the number of passengers still on-board when the bus leaves stop j at time $t + \delta$.
2. $w_j \geq 0$, the weight of bus stop j, $\sum_{j=1}^{\mathcal{J}} w_j = 1$.
3. $\mu_{s,\mathcal{B}}(\mathcal{N}_j^{t,\delta})$ is the degree of passenger satisfaction, $\mu_{u,\mathcal{B}}(\mathcal{N}_j^{t,\delta}, n)$ is the degree of vehicle usage, when the bus capacity is $\mathcal{B}$, each evaluated at $\mathcal{N}_j^{t,\delta}$ passengers.
4. $\mu_{s,\mathcal{B}}^t(\delta)$ and $\mu_{u,\mathcal{B}}^t(\delta)$ are the respective aggregated values of $\mu_{s,\mathcal{B}}(\mathcal{N}_j^{t,\delta})$ and $\mu_{u,\mathcal{B}}(\mathcal{N}_j^{t,\delta}, n)$ over all bus stops $j = 1, \ldots, \mathcal{J}$.
5. $\mu_{\mathcal{D},\mathcal{B}}^t(\delta) = \mu_{s,\mathcal{B}}^t(\delta) \wedge \mu_{u,\mathcal{B}}^t(\delta)$, is the degree of simultaneous satisfaction of the constraints at time $t \in \mathcal{T}_{\mathcal{L}}$, with time interval δ.

[1] In China, $\mathcal{B}$ is defined very precisely as the number of passenger seats plus the bus effective standing area (sq.m.) multiplied by 8 (i.e., it is assumed that up to eight passengers can stand on a square meter surface).

Timetable design in fuzzy system

Decision making of two fuzzy sets

Letting $\mathcal{X}$ denote the universe of discourse, $\mathcal{A}$, a discrete fuzzy set in $\mathcal{X}$, can be represented as a set of ordered pairs: $\{(x, \mu_{\mathcal{A}}) \mid x \in \mathcal{X}\}$, where $\mu_{\mathcal{A}}(x)$ is the degree to which x belongs to fuzzy set $\mathcal{A}$.

For an optimization problem, goals and constraints can be described as fuzzy sets(Bellman and Zadeh 1970). A decision is their joint satisfaction modeled as the *intersection* of fuzzy goals and constraints as illustrated by Example 1.

Example 1 *$\mathcal{X}$= {1, 2, ...}. $\mathcal{A}$ is fuzzy goal that 'x near 5', and $\mathcal{B}$ is fuzzy constraint that 'x near 4' in $\mathcal{X}$. Decision $\mu_{\mathcal{D}}$ is $\mu_{\mathcal{A}} \wedge \mu_{\mathcal{B}}$. Choosing membership functions for $\mathcal{A}$ and $\mathcal{B}$ respectively*

$$\mu_{\mathcal{A}} = \{(3, 0.6)(4, 0.8)(5, 1)(6, 0.8)(7, 0.6)(8, 0.4)\}$$
$$\mu_{\mathcal{B}} = \{(3, 0.9)(4, 1)(5, 0.9)(6, 0.8)(7, 0.7)(8, 0.6)\}$$

the value of the decision $\mu_{\mathcal{D}}$ is calculated as follows. First the intersection $\mathcal{A} \cap \mathcal{B}$ is computed:

$$\begin{aligned} \mu_{\mathcal{D}} &= \mu_{\mathcal{A} \cap \mathcal{B}}(x) \\ &= \mu_{\mathcal{A}}(x) \wedge \mu_{\mathcal{B}}(x) \\ &= \{(3, 0.6)(4, 0.8)(5, 0.9)(6, 0.8)(7, 0.6)(8, 0.4)\} \end{aligned}$$

The final decision, d_0, corresponds to the value with maximum membership degree to the $\mathcal{D}$, that is, $d_0 = (x_0, \mu_0)$ where

$$x_0 = arg \max_x \mu_{\mathcal{D}}(x) \text{ and } \mu_0 = \mu_{\mathcal{D}}(x_0)$$

Therefore $d_0 = (5, 0.9)$.

Problem formulation

The objective function, $\mu_{\mathcal{D}}^{\mathcal{M}}(\delta)$, is to find the time interval that has maximum decision value at time state t over all possible time interval δ, as shown in Equation (1).

$$\mu_{\mathcal{D}}^{\mathcal{M}}(\delta) = \max_{\delta}(\mu_{\mathcal{D},\mathcal{B}}^{t}(\delta)). \tag{1}$$

subject to the constraints described by equations (2a) - (2e) below:

$$\mathcal{N}_j^{t,\delta} \leq \mathcal{B}, \; j = 1, \ldots, \mathcal{J} - 1 \tag{2a}$$

$$\mu_{s,\mathcal{B}}^{t}(\delta) = \sum_{j=1}^{\mathcal{J}-1} w_j \times \mu_{s,\mathcal{B}}(\mathcal{N}_j^{t,\delta}) \tag{2b}$$

$$\mu_{u,\mathcal{B}}^{t}(\delta) = \sum_{j=1}^{\mathcal{J}-1} w_j \times \mu_{u,\mathcal{B}}(\mathcal{N}_j^{t,\delta}, n) \tag{2c}$$

$$\mu_{\mathcal{D},\mathcal{B}}^{t}(\delta) = \mu_{u,\mathcal{B}}^{t}(\delta) \wedge \mu_{s,\mathcal{B}}^{t}(\delta) \tag{2d}$$

$$\sum_{j=1}^{\mathcal{J}} w_j = 1, \; \delta \in \Delta \tag{2e}$$

Equation (2a) states that the on-board passenger number cannot exceed the vehicle capacity. Equations (2b), (2c) show that $\mu_{x,\mathcal{B}}^{t}(\delta), x \in \{s, u\}$ is obtained by the aggregation of $\mu_{x,\mathcal{B}}(N_j^{t,\delta}), x \in \{s, u\}$ at stop j, $j = 1, 2, \ldots, \mathcal{J} - 1$, weighted by w_j. w_j is calculated from the boarding and alighting number of passengers. Equation (2d) states the fuzzy decision on $\delta \in \Delta$ as the fuzzy set intersection of the satisfaction and capacity constraints.

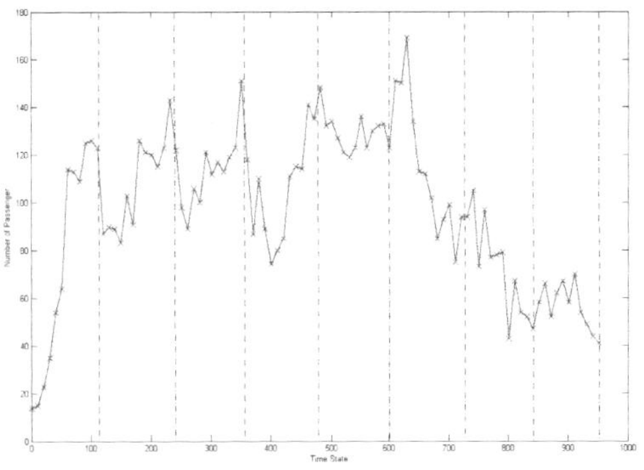

Figure 1: Varying passenger flow.

Case study

Parameters

In this section, timetables are designed separately on the service time covering from 6:00 am to 10:00 pm, divided into eight 2 hour periods, having a total of 960 time states. For cases 1 to 8 the time spans are: 6:00 ∼ 8:00, 8:00 ∼ 10:00, ..., 20:00 ∼ 22:00. Table 1 summarizes the parameters used for this case study.

Table 1: Value of parameters in case study

Parameters	value
service time	6:00 am to 10:00 pm
Time State Space index p	{1,2, ..., 960}
$\{\delta_1, \delta_2, \ldots, \delta_{\mathcal{Q}}\}$	$\{2, 3, \ldots, 15\}$(minutes)
δ_0	8(minutes)
$\mathcal{B}$	90
$\mathcal{J}$	24

Origin and destination of passengers are extracted from history data of ShiJiaZhuang bus line 1. The passenger flow of the day are shown in Figure 1. The area between two vertical dashed lines and passenger flow curve stands for the number of boarding passenger at each cases. Case 5 has the highest number of boarding passengers, Case 8 has the lowest number of passengers.

$$\mu_{s,\mathcal{B}}(\mathcal{N}) = \begin{cases} 1 & 0 \leq \mathcal{N} \leq \mathcal{B}/3 \\ -0.6\mathcal{N}/\mathcal{B} + 1.2 & \mathcal{B}/3 < \mathcal{N} \leq 2\mathcal{B}/3 \\ -2.4\mathcal{N}/\mathcal{B} + 2.4 & 2\mathcal{B}/3 < \mathcal{N} \leq \mathcal{B} \\ 0 & \text{otherwise} \end{cases}$$

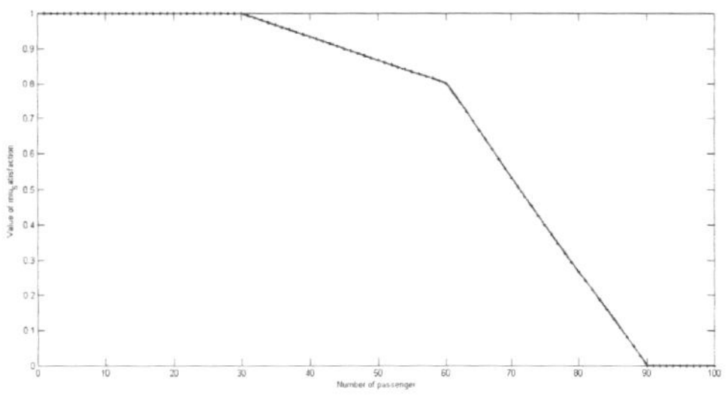

Figure 2: Shape of passenger satisfaction μ_s

(3)

The membership functions for the fuzzy goal is given by Equation (3), and Figure 2 shows the shape of μ_s.

In (3), $\mu_{s,\mathcal{B}}(\mathcal{N})$, the satisfaction degree of on-board passengers captures the following: when few passengers are on the bus (everyone has a seat), the satisfaction degree is equal to 1 as everyone is comfortable; when the number of passengers varies from $\mathcal{B}/3$ to $2\mathcal{B}/3$, recent passengers might have to stand, but the bus is not yet crowded, the satisfaction degree slowly reduces to 0.8; however, the comfort degree drops sharply, when the bus is crowded, i.e., there are more than $2\mathcal{B}/3$ (and up to $\mathcal{B}$) passengers. In this situation not only standing passengers feel uncomfortable also those seated have less space and have difficulty alighting.

Timetable Comparison

In the following, the timetables designed from the fuzzy system, are labeled as **fuzzyT**, while those designed by even headways (fixed and equal time intervals between two successive bus services) are labeled as **evenT**. They have the same number of services in cases 1-8 (the cost of bus company are same).

Algorithm 1 shows the procedure of adjusting fuzzy constraint to design **fuzzyT** that have same number of bus services $\mathcal{M}$. First design timetable with even headways $\delta_0 = 8$, each case has 16 bus service; then calculate the average loads $n = \overline{\mathcal{N}}$ as the initial value of threshold; then design **fuzzyT** under $\mu_{s,\mathcal{B}}(\mathcal{N})$ and $\mu_{u,\mathcal{B}}(\mathcal{N}, n)$. Compare the number of bus services time in **fuzzyT**, $\mathcal{M}_F$ and **evenT**, $\mathcal{M}_E$; if $\mathcal{M}_F = \mathcal{M}_E$, return **fuzzyT**; else adjusting threshold n and redesign **fuzzyT** and compare again until $\mathcal{M}_F = \mathcal{M}_F$.

$$\mu_{u,\mathcal{B}}(\mathcal{N}, n) = \begin{cases} \mathcal{N}/n & 0 \leq \mathcal{N} \leq min(n, \mathcal{B}) \\ 1 & n < \mathcal{N} \leq \mathcal{B} \\ 0 & \text{otherwise} \end{cases} \quad (4)$$

The membership function for fuzzy constraint is given by Equation (4).

$\mu_{u,\mathcal{B}}(\mathcal{N}, n)$, the usage degree of the bus, captures the following: when the number of on-board passengers is between n and $\mathcal{B}$, the usage degree is equal to 1; when number of on-board passengers less than the threshold

Algorithm 1 Transfer even timetable to uneven timetable under fuzzy constraint

procedure 1 Initialization,
    $\delta_0 \leftarrow 8$; $\mathcal{M} \leftarrow 16$
    Design **evenT**, calculated threshold n, $c \leftarrow n$
    Design $\mu_{u,\mathcal{B}}(\mathcal{N}, n)$; get **fuzzyT**
    if $\mathcal{M}_F = \mathcal{M}_E$ **then**
        //same bus service number
        Save **fuzzyT**;
    else
        countMinus$\leftarrow$0;
        while countMinus $< c$ &&$\mathcal{M}_F! = \mathcal{M}_E$ **do**
            if $\mathcal{M}_F < \mathcal{M}_E$ **then**
                $n--$; get **fuzzyT** under $\mu_{u,\mathcal{B}}(\mathcal{N}, n)$
                if $\mathcal{M}_F = \mathcal{M}_E$ **then**
                    Save **fuzzyT**;
                    break
                end if
            else if $\mathcal{M}_F > \mathcal{M}_E$ **then**
                $n++$; get **fuzzyT** under $\mu_{u,\mathcal{B}}(\mathcal{N}, n)$
                if $\mathcal{M}_F = \mathcal{M}_E$ **then**
                    Save **fuzzyT**;
                    break
                end if
            end if
        end while
    end if
end procedure

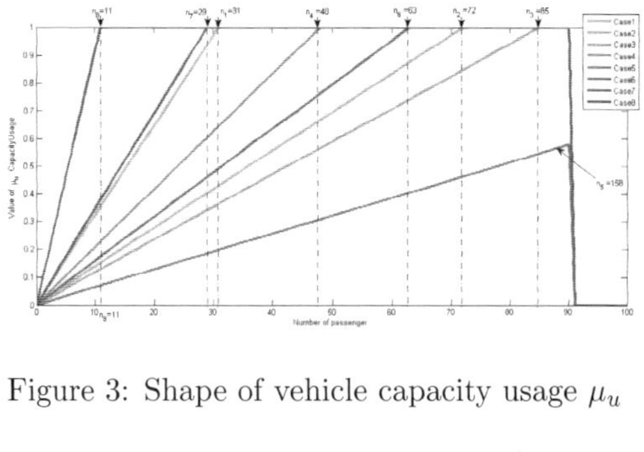

Figure 3: Shape of vehicle capacity usage μ_u

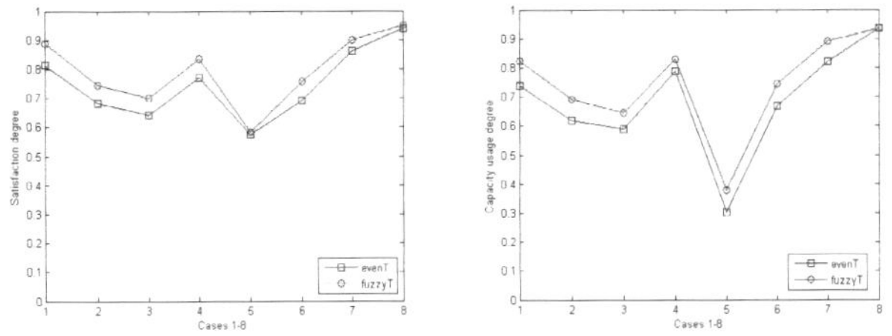

(a) $\overline{\mu}_s$ (b) $\overline{\mu}_u$

Figure 4: Mean value of $\overline{\mu}_s$ and $\overline{\mu}_u$

$min(n, \mathcal{B})$, the capacity usage degree is $\mathcal{N}/n$. Figure 3 shows the shape of μ_u at each case. Case 5 has lowest value of the slope $1/n$, and Case 8 has the highest value of the slope.

The first and last bus service time, $s/s_{\mathcal{M}}$, of timetable $\mathcal{S}$ are shown in the left two columns of Table 2; and each row lists the waiting time, t_w, travel time, t_t, and average loads, $\overline{\mathcal{N}}$, of **evenT** and **fuzzyT**. It can be seen that for each case **fuzzyT** has similar or smaller value in, t_w, t_t, and $\overline{\mathcal{N}}$ compared with **evenT**. Still Case 5 has highest values in t_w, t_t, and $\overline{\mathcal{N}}$ compared with other cases and Case 8 has lowest value.

Table 2: Time table results of **evenT** and **fuzzyT**

$\mathcal{S}$		**evenT**			**fuzzyT**		
s	$s_{\mathcal{M}}$	t_w	t_t	$\overline{\mathcal{N}}$	t_w	t_t	$\overline{\mathcal{N}}$
6:00	8:00	96	498	38	86	488	37
8:00	10:00	133	715	50	129	705	50
10:00	12:00	140	856	55	141	824	53
12:00	14:00	130	626	45	128	585	42
14:00	16:00	158	915	57	157	912	56
16:00	18:00	130	793	49	126	752	47
18:00	20:00	89	501	36	90	492	36
20:00	22:00	66	308	26	66	299	25

Figures 4(a) and 4(b) show the mean value of μ_s and μ_u, it can be seen that for cases 1-8 **fuzzyT** have a higher value than **evenT**. Case 5 has the smallest value in $\overline{\mu}_s$ and $\overline{\mu}_u$. This is because the threshold n for fuzzy membership function of vehicle capacity usage is 158, the maximum degree of $\mu_{u,\mathcal{B}}(\mathcal{N}, n)$ is when on-board passengers equal the bus capacity $\mathcal{B}$, and $\mu_{u,\mathcal{B}}(90, 158) = 90/158 = 0.57$; thereby for any on-board passenger less then $\mathcal{B}$, the usage degree is less then 0.57, thus the average usage degree in Case 5 is even lower.

Take Case 5 as an example, Table 3 show the timetable and time interval in **evenT** and **fuzzyT**. Time interval in **evenT** is fixed to 8 minutes, while time interval in **fuzzyT** range from 6 to 13 minutes;

Figures 5(a) and 5(b) show the number of on-board passengers at bus stops 1-23 of 7th and 10th bus services respectively (these two bus services have the largest, 13,

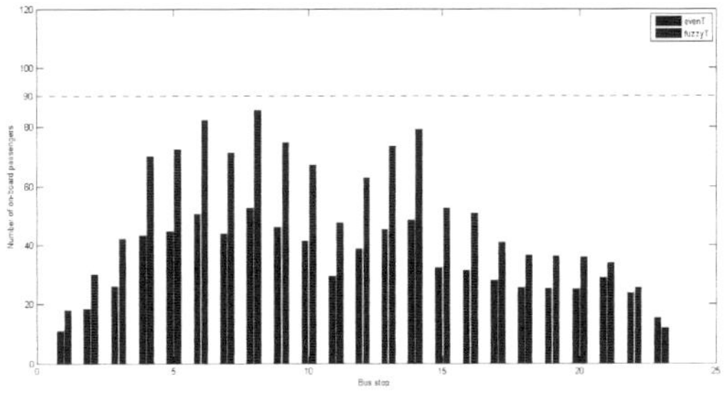

(a) On-board passengers at 7th bus services qquad

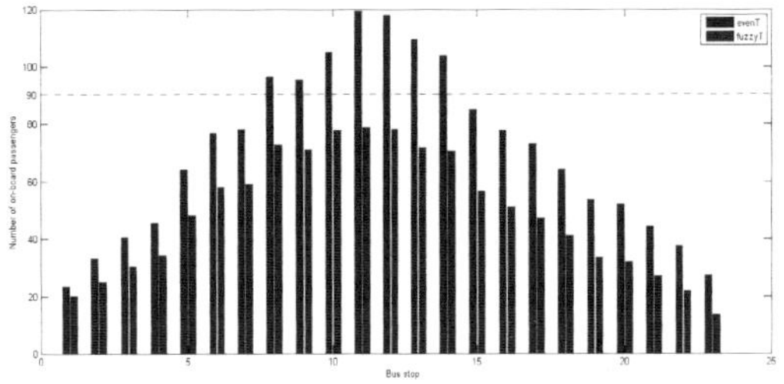

(b) On-board passengers at 10th bus services qquad

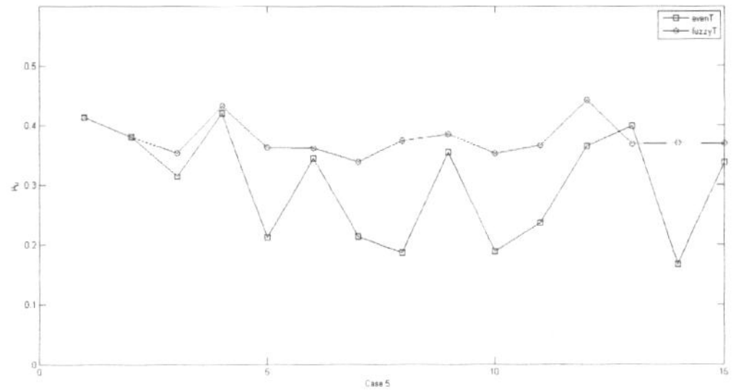

(c) value of μ_u at bus services

Figure 5: Case 5

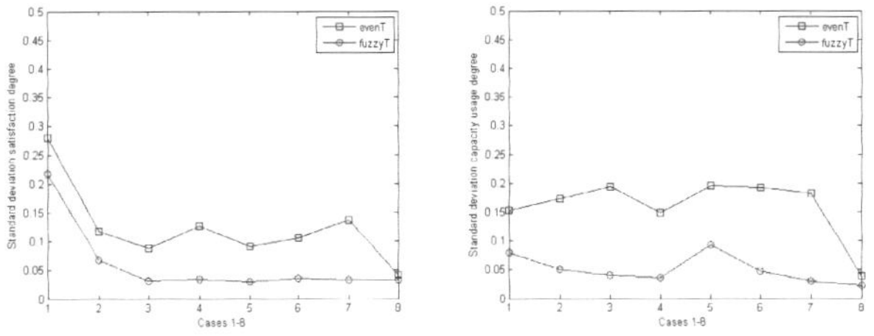

(a) σ_s (b) σ_u

Figure 6: Standard deviation of μ_s, σ_s, and standard deviation of μ_u, σ_u

Table 3: Timetable in Case 5

s_m	evenT		fuzzyT	
	t	δ	t	δ
1	14:00	8	14:00	8
2	14:08	8	14:08	8
3	14:16	8	14:16	9
4	14:24	8	14:25	8
5	14:32	8	14:32	7
6	14:40	8	14:39	7
7	**14:48**	**8**	**14:46**	**13**
8	14:56	8	14:59	10
9	15:04	8	15:09	6
10	**15:12**	**8**	**15:15**	**6**
11	15:20	8	15:21	7
12	15:28	8	15:28	9
13	15:36	8	15:37	7
14	15:44	8	15:44	6
15	15:52	8	15:52	7
16	16:00		15:59	

and smallest, 6, time interval respectively in **fuzzyT**), bars with red color are the number of on-board passengers in **fuzzyT**, and bars with blue color are the number of on-board passengers in **evenT**. A horizontal line, $\mathcal{B} = 90$, where the number of on-board passengers equal to the vehicle size, is shown in both figures 5(a) and 5(b). In Figure 5(a), it can be seen that the number on-board passengers in **fuzzyT** (the left red bars in the group) are larger than the number of on-board passenger in **evenT**(blue bars on the right in the group). As time interval in **fuzzyT**, 13 minutes, is bigger than the time interval in **evenT**, 8 minutes, and having all the red bars under the horizontal line (means no overloading). In Figure 5(b), the value of blue bars are much larger than the value of red bars, at 10th time interval with last bus service in **fuzzyT** is 6 minutes, which is shorter than the time interval in **evenT**. Moreover, all the red bars are under the horizontal line, $\mathcal{B} = 90$, and for six bus stops from bus stop 8 to 14 in **evenT** , the $\mathcal{N}$ exceeds the value of bus capacity $\mathcal{B}$.

In Figure 5(c), the capacity usage degree of vehicles in **fuzzyT** and **evenT** of Case 5 are given respectively; it can be seen that **fuzzyT** (red line with circles) has a more even and higher value than **evenT**.

The standard deviation of passenger satisfaction degree and vehicle capacity usage degree (evaluate by e-quations (3) and (4)) are shown in figures 6(a) and 6(b) respectively. It can be seen that **fuzzyT** have a lower variance than **evenT** in cases 1-8.

MannWhitney U test (U text) and Two-sample Kolmogorov-Smirnov test (K text) are used on mean and standard deviation values of μ_u and μ_s in **fuzzyT** and **evenT**, as shown in Table 4, with the respective p and h values. As it can be seen from Table 4, the difference between the standard deviations of **fuzzyT** and **evenT** is statistically significant ($h = 1$, at p-value less than 0.05). Both tests reject the null hypothesis

Table 4: Test the difference significantly level of **fuzzyT** and **evenT**

Test	Passenger satisfaction				Vehicle capacity usage			
	p_1	h_1	p_2	h_2	p_3	h_3	p_4	h_4
U test	0.33	0	0.010	1	0.38	0	0.003	1
K test	0.52	0	0.010	1	0.52	0	0.001	1

(i.e., that the passenger satisfaction and capacity usage degrees between **fuzzyT** and **evenT** are same).

Conclusion

This study investigated transfer of a timetable scheduling from an even headways timetable into uneven headways timetable, with even loads, using fuzzy decision making. The interest of passenger is designed as fuzzy goal, and fuzzy constraint of vehicle capacity usage is adjusted dynamically by limited, fixed bus services number. Timetables in **fuzzyT** and **evenT** are compared in total and in detail. The results show that **fuzzyT** has lower and similar value of passengers waiting time, travel time; and have a higher passenger satisfaction and vehicle usage rate. More importantly, **fuzzyT** improve the vehicle usage degree in a significant level and avoid overload.

Acknowledgments

Yanan Zhang's work for this study was supported by China Scholarship Council (Grant No. 201506250051) while visiting the MLCI Laboratory led by Anca Ralescu, in the EECS Department, College of Engineering and Applied Science, University of Cincinnati.

References

Bellman, R., and Zadeh, L. A. 1970. Decison making in fuzzy environment. *management science* 17:B114–B164.

Ceder, A.; Hassold, S.; Dunlop, C.; and Chen, I. 2013. Improving urban public transport service using new timetabling strategies with different vehicle sizes. *International Journal of Urban Sciences* 17(2):239–258.

Ceder, A. A.; Hassold, S.; and Dano, B. 2013. Approaching even-load and even-headway transit timetables using different bus sizes. *Public Transport* 5(3):193–217.

Ceder, A. 2007. Public transit planning and operation: Theory. *Modeling and practice. Oxford: Elsevier.*

Ceder, A. 2011. Optimal multi-vehicle type transit timetabling and vehicle scheduling. *Procedia - Social and Behavioral Sciences* 20:19–30.

Chaari, T.; Chaabane, S.; Aissani, N.; and Trentesaux, D. 2014. Scheduling under uncertainty: Survey and research directions. In *Advanced Logistics and Transport (ICALT), 2014 International Conference on*, 229–234. IEEE.

Chakraborty, D.; Guha, D.; and Dutta, B. 2016. Multiobjective optimization problem under fuzzy rule constraints using particle swarm optimization. *Soft Computing* 20(6):2245–2259.

Choon, O., and Tilahun, S. L. 2011. Integration fuzzy preference in genetic algorithm to solve multiobjective optimization problems. *Far East Math. Sci* 55:165–179.

Hassold, S., and Ceder, A. 2012. Multiobjective approach to creating bus timetables with multiple vehicle types. *Transportation Research Record: Journal of the Transportation Research Board* 2276:56–62.

Ibarra Rojas, O. J.; Lopez Irarragorri, F.; and Rios Solis, Y. A. 2015. Multiperiod synchronization bus timetabling. *Transportation science.*

Jiang, Z.; Hsu, C.-H.; Zhang, D.; and Zou, X. 2016. Evaluating rail transit timetable using big passengers' data. *Journal of Computer and System Sciences* 82(1):144–155.

Kaymak, U., and Sousa, J. 2003. Weighted constraint aggregation in fuzzy optimization. *Constraints* 8(1):61–78.

Sun, L.; Jin, J. G.; Lee, D.-H.; Axhausen, K. W.; and Erath, A. 2014a. Demand-driven timetable design for metro services. *Transportation Research Part C: Emerging Technologies* 46:284–299.

Sun, L.; Tirachini, A.; Axhausen, K. W.; Erath, A.; and Lee, D.-H. 2014b. Models of bus boarding and alighting dynamics. *Transportation Research Part A: Policy and Practice* 69:447–460.

Tang, J.; Wang, D.; Fung, R. Y.; and Yung, K.-L. 2004. Understanding of fuzzy optimization: theories and methods. *Journal of Systems Science and Complexity* 17(1):117–136.

Tilahun, S. L., and Ong, H. C. 2012. Bus timetabling as a fuzzy multiobjective optimization problem using preference-based genetic algorithm. *Promet - Traffic - Traffico* 24(3):183–191.

Zhang, Y.; Meng, Z.; Zheng, Y.; and Ralescu, A. 2017 submited. *Schedule Optimization Under Fuzzy Constraints of Vehicle Capacity.*

Zhang, Y.; Meng, Z.; and Ralescu, A. 2017 submited. *Dynamic Timetable Scheduling with Reverse-flow Technique in Fuzzy Environment.*

Zimmermann, H.-J. 1985. Applications of fuzzy set theory to mathematical programming. *Information sciences* 36(1-2):29–58.

Weather Forcasting Using Artificial Neural Network

Md. Tanvir Hasan[1], K. M. Fattahul Islam[2], Md. Sajedul Karim[3],
Lt. Md. Arifuzzaman[4], Md. Sifat Rahman[5] & Nure Alam Md. Risalat[6]
[1, 6] Faculty of Science & Technology, Bangladesh University of Professionals, [2, 3, 4] Department of Aeronautical Engineering, Military Institute of Science and Technology & [5] Stamford University Bangladesh
[1]tanvir89@gmail.com, [2]fattahulislam@gmail.com, [5]mdsifat.r@gmail.com, [6]ankon.risalat.cse@gmail.com

INTRODUCTION

Weather forecasting is such a blessing of modern technology which predict the atmospheric condition for a specific location. Weather forecast depends on proper collection of quantitative data regarding the current state of the atmosphere. Those data help us to predict how the atmosphere will be after a period using various methods.

Because of the nature of the atmosphere an enormous computational power is required to solve the equations. The equation which describes the atmospheric error related to measure the initial conditions and an incomplete understanding of atmospheric processes suggest that forecasting becomes less accurate because of timing. There is a multiplicity of end uses to weather forecasts.

EASE OF USE

Objective

- To observe sharp change in predicted data with respect to previous data available.
- To predict whether the weather condition is normal or there is any chance of natural calamities.
- To distinguish among various seasons.
- To understand the concept of neural network & how it works.
- To predict four different weather parameters.
- Compare predicted data with actual data.
- To observe neural network training state and training error.

BACKGROUND

Weather Forecasting has been playing a vital role in our day to day life since the birth of human race. Various kinds of warnings are important because they are accustomed to protecting our lives and properties. Forecasting is so useful in the field of agriculture through various parameters like rain, temperature etc. Therefore, it also has a significant effect in the service markets. Utility companies use forecasting to calculate demand for the future. On an everyday basis, people use weather forecasts to determine clothing on a given day. Outdoor activities are severely condensed by rain, snow fall and the wind speed. So, forecasts can be used to plan activities around these events and to plan ahead and survive them. In order to forecast

Weather, the methods which are being used worldwide have shown below:

- *Persistence Method*
- *Climatology Method*
- *Analog Approach Method*
- *Numerical Weather Prediction*

FORECASTING PROCEDURE FOR NUCERICAL MODELS

Among various numerical prediction methods, we have chosen ANN (Artificial Neural Network) tool which can be processed and implemented using MATLAB.

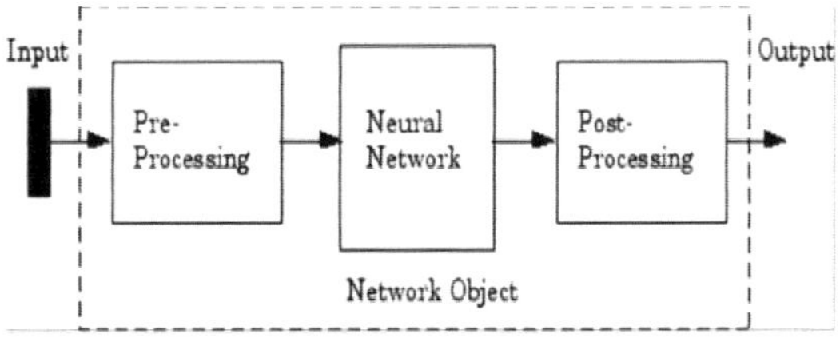

Fig. 1. Multilayer Processing [3]

REASONS BEHIND CHOOSING ANN OVER CONVENTIONAL COMPUTING

For better understanding of artificial neural computing it is important to know how a conventional computer and various software of this computer process information. A regular computer has a central processor that can address an array of memory locations where various kinds of data and instructions are stored. For computation, the processor needs to read an instruction. It also requires help from the memory address section. After that the instruction is then executed and results are saved in a specified memory location as per requirement. In a serial system, the computational steps are done sequentially and logically. In comparison, neural networks are not as complex as the computer. In neural network, we don't have a processor but many parts which only can take the weight from the input. Rather than executing instructions. Neural network responds according to the pattern of inputs presented to it. There is also no separate memory address for storing data. Instead, information is contained in the overall activation phase of the network.

FIGURES AND TABLES

Following possible combinations are used in our experiment for a typical feed forward back propagation network.

- 50 neurons: 10 neurons in each 5 hidden layers.
- 80 neurons: 10 neurons in each 8 hidden layers.
- 100 neurons: 20 neurons in each 5 hidden layers.

Comparisons of different methods of neural network for January data and training performance are given below

Serial	No. of neurons	Performance/ MSE	Training function	Training algorithm
1	50	20.511	TRAINGDX	Gradient descent with momentum and adaptive LR
2	50	7.32	TRAINLM	Levenberg-Marquardt
3	80	15.54	TRAINGDX	Gradient descent with momentum and adaptive LR
4	80	6.547	TRAINLM	Levenberg-Marquardt
5	100	13.2298	TRAINGDX	Gradient descent with momentum and adaptive LR
6	100	5.92	TRAINLM	Levenberg-Marquardt

As we predict weather data for January, for training we have used the data of 2013 as an input and data of 2014 as target for the certain month.

The variation was observed by graph for each parameter.

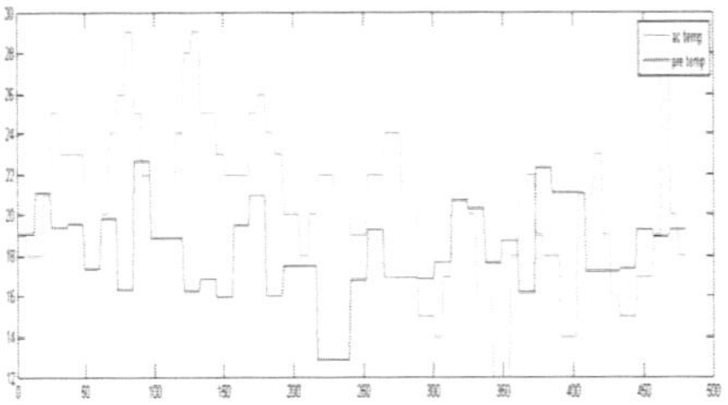

Fig. 2. Graphical representation of actual temperature and predicted temperature of January 2015

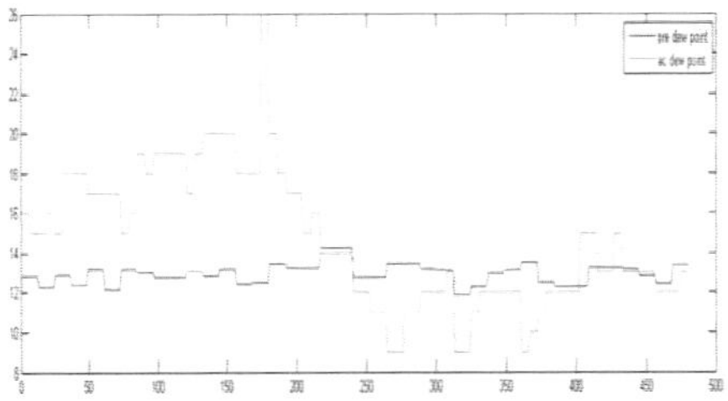

Fig. 3. Graphical representation of actual dew point and predicted dew point of January 2015

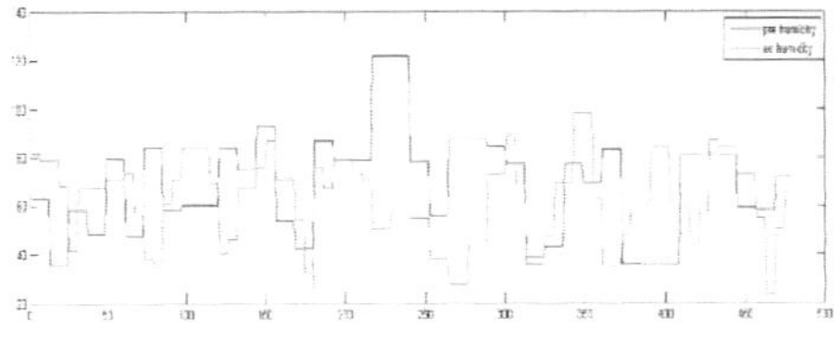

Fig. 4. Graphical representation of actual humidity and predicted humidity of January 2015

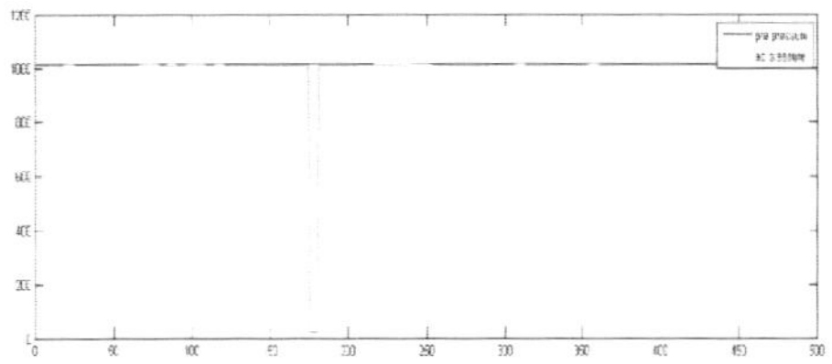

Fig. 5. Graphical representation of actual pressure and predicted pressure of January 2015

OBSERVATION

- As we increase the number of neurons, decreases the mean square error i.e. increases the performance.
- For the same number of neurons TRAINLM transfer function gives better performance than TRAINGDX though the training time is more for TRAINLM than TRAINGDX transfer function.

OVERALL COMMENTS

All the weather data which is predicted is close to the actual value for the respective month. In some cases, we can see that the value between the actual and predicted weather data is not closer that insist that their might have some natural calamities. Our model has limitation for the prediction of natural calamities and using same model for all weather data shows that humidity prediction is not much accurate which needs further modification

RECOMMENDATION FOR FUTURE IMPROVEMENT

Networks can be connected to sensors so that data is automatically stored. The training error can be minimized. The prediction can be done more precisely to minimize the difference between the actual value and the predicted value. Additional post processing system can be introduced to predict possibility of natural calamities.

REFERENCES

[1] Aguado and Burt; "Understanding Weather and Climate", Chapter 13-Weather Forecasting and Analysis. http://www.atmo.ttu.edu/schroeder/ATMO_1300/Notes/chapter13.pdf

[2] "METHODS OF INTERPRETING NUMERICALWEATHER PREDICTION OUTPUT FOR AERONAUTICAL METEOROLOGY", by the CAeM Working Group on Advanced Techniques Applied to Aeronautical Meteorology (Second Edition), TECHNICAL NOTE No. 195. http://projects.knmi.nl/geoss/wmo/RRR/AeroMet/WMO770.pdf

[3] Mark Hudson Beale, Martin T. Hagan, Howard B. Demuth; "Neural Network Toolbox™ User's Guide" https://www.mathworks.com/help/pdf_doc/nnet/nnet_ug.pdf

[4] "A Basic Introduction To Neural Networks" http://pages.cs.wisc.edu/~bolo/shipyard/neural/local.html

[5] https://en.wikipedia.org/wiki/Mean_squared_error

[6] "Weather underground", Meteorological Data for January and for year 2013, 2014, 2015 of Dhaka city.

How similar are the *twins*? Using Psycholinguistic Tests to Determine Similarity Among Near-Synonyms

Pranay Yadav, Anupam Basu
Department of Computer Science and Engineering
Indian Institute of Technology Kharagpur, West Bengal, India 721302
y.pranay@cse.iitkgp.ernet.in, anupam@cse.iitkgp.ernet.in

Abstract

A word usually expresses many implications, connotations and attitudes in addition to its lexicon meaning. And a word often has near-synonyms that differ from it solely in these nuances of meaning and in the degrees of expression. In a truly articulate linguistic system, there is a need of a highly sophisticated lexical-choice process that can determine which of the near-synonyms is best suited for a given word. The most widely used English lexical database — WordNet, organizes the near-synonyms into entities called *synsets*, but fails to identify finer differences among them for a better lexical-choice process. In this paper, we discuss an approach to extend the lexical knowledge base of near-synonym differences by using a set of psycholinguistic experiments aimed to address this particular task in hand.

1 Introduction

Choosing the right word — the one that precisely conveys the desired meaning and also avoids unwanted implications — is a difficult task for present-day linguistic systems. For example, how can a machine translation (MT) system determine the best English word for the French *bonheur* when there are so many potentially similar but slightly different translations? The system could choose *happiness*, *joy*, *pleasure*, *well-being* and so on, but the most appropriate choice is a function of how *bonheur* is used (in context) and of the difference in meaning between *bonheur* and each of the English possibilities. Thus, a faithful MT or more generally a natural language generation (NLG) system demands a sophisticated lexical-choice process[1] that can determine which of the near-synonyms is the most appropriate in any particular situation.

Our research focusses on the largest English lexical database — WordNet and in particular its structural units, *synsets*. Semantic similarity measures based on WordNet have attracted great concern in the recent past.[3] *Synsets* are the sets of synonyms which are very similar in meaning but not completely inter-substitutable (true synonymy)[4]. On one hand, grouping them together gives rise to a broader class of concepts but on the other, the near-synonym differences among them are compromised. The goal of our research is to extend the lexical knowledge base (in our case, WordNet) to account for near-synonymy in a computationally implementable manner and to model such fine-grained distinctions among senses belonging to the same *synset* for a more sophisticated lexical-choice process.

Psycholinguistics is concerned with the understanding of how language is stored and processed in the brain. In our research, we explore the approach of using a set of dedicated psycholinguistic experiments to quantify the near-synonym differences by exploiting human brain's cognitive ability to identify and respond to *synonymous* words if subjected to appropriate experimental setting. Many previous studies establish that brain response-times act as an indicator of the cognitive load in various linguistic sub-fields like phonetics, and semantics. In our case, participants of these carefully designed tests will respond to *similar* words better in the amount of time (response-time) they take to understand the ingrained *similarity* between those words, as perceived by a human brain[4]. These response times will further be mapped onto the similarity scores between pairs of near-synonym words derived from the WordNet *synsets*.

2 Approach

In this section, we shall outline the design of the two behavioural psycholinguistic experiments that are based on the priming principle[2]. Priming is an implicit memory effect in which exposure to one stimulus (called *prime*) influences the response to another stimulus (called *target*). Exposure to the prime is known to activate a range of associated words which makes it easier for the subjects to identify these target words via a process called *spreading activation*. Of all types of priming, the one of interest is semantic priming, where the prime and the target are from the same semantic category and share features. Semantic priming is observed frequently across several lexical decision tasks.

For the first experiment, we start by sampling *synsets* from the WordNet Corpus, and from each one we select a representative word, called *prime*, and the remaining words act as *targets*. For the second experiment, we randomly select pairs of *primal* and *target* words from synsets, not necessarily belonging to the same synset like the former. The rationale behind the second experiment is to validate the lemmas in WordNet. In other words, the second experiment gives us the number of True Positives (*synonymous* and belonging to the same *synset*) and True Negatives (*non-synonymous* and belonging to different *synsets*) from WordNet. For both the experiments, reaction time (RT), which is the measured as the elapsed time between the stimulus (*target*) and the subsequent behavioural response (button-press events) in milliseconds, indicate how fast the individual can identify the *synonymy* of the target and prime.

3 Design and Evaluation

In this section, we first discuss the design, evaluation and results of the first experiment, followed by the second one.

3.1 First Psycholinguistic Experiment

For the first experiment, we sampled nearly 1000 *synsets* from WordNet, each comprising of at least 10 lemmas. Choosing one representative from each *synset* as the *prime* stimulus (which appears on screen for 5 seconds), the remaining lemmas in the synset form the *target* stimuli (which appear on the screen indefinitely until a button a pressed). As depicted in the figure below, P denotes the *prime* and T_i denote the ith *target* corresponding to P. We measure the response times (elapsed time between successive button presses in *ms*) as a measure of mental chronometry of this linguistic task of identifying how semantically similar the prime and targets are.[5]

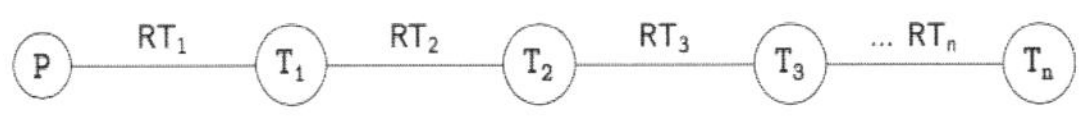

For evaluation, response times of all the subjects were averaged to account for any variation due to different cognitive abilities or test errors, yielding a finite-dimensional vector (referred to as *z*). We further assigned similarity scores by squashing this vector of response times to a vector of real values in the range (0, 1) by using the *softmax function*. All the response times were negated so as to give higher weightage to the smaller positive response time.

$$\sigma(\mathbf{z})_j = \frac{e^{z_j}}{\sum_{k=1}^{K} e^{z_k}} for j = 1...K$$

This similarity score was correlated against the semantic similarity scores commonly used in WordNet[6]. Following table contains the similarity scores for a few target words with the primal word as "*good*". Resnik and Lin similarity measures were reported to be null because the underlying Information Content file had no contents for this part-of-speech. Clearly, even though the similarity scores of most of these near-synonymous words are close-enough, experimentally only "*adept*", "*well*" and "*thoroughly*" are synonymous in a "*true*" sense.

Target	Path	LCH	WUP	Experimental
estimable	0.092	2.157	0.112	0.024
adept	0.370	3.152	0.471	0.421
dear	0.033	1.156	0.079	0.003
dependable	0.081	1.132	0.143	0
well	0.493	3.051	0.312	0.319

3.2 Second Psycholinguistic Experiment

For the second experiment, we sampled around 10000 pairs of lemmas from WordNet. Choosing one of them as the prime, the other word acts as the target. As depicted in the figure below, P_i denotes the ith *prime* and T_i denotes the corresponding *target*. We record the response times in a manner similar to the first experiment. Subjects of this experiment are expected to press one specific button to imply that the *target* is *synonymous* to the *prime* (type Y), otherwise another button (type N). We follow a similar evaluation procedure for the 'Y'-type *prime-target* pairs as the first experiment. Table below highlights the results obtained for this experiment. Although *dear* occurs in the same synset as *good* as *adept*, but it is reported more similar to *good* than *adept*. We also evaluated the True Positives and True Negatives (defined in Section 2). Also, by looking at the confusion matrix below, we can draw that although 50.8% of the 10000 words considered words belong to the same synset, but according to subjects they should not.

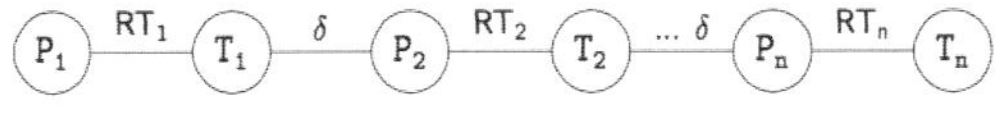

Primal	Target	Path	LCH	WUP	Experimental
good	adept	0.370	3.152	0.471	0.372
good	dear	0.032	1.026	0.079	0.002
happy	felicitous	0.011	1.132	0.143	0.008
happy	glad	0.489	2.357	0.290	0.401

	Type Y	Type N
Same synset	4920	5080
Not in same synset	2340	7660

4 Conclusion

Through this paper, it was shown that the proposed experiments performed sufficiently well in the task of establishing near-synonym differences among near-synonyms derived from the WordNet corpus. The semantic similarity scores obtained would help extending the English lexical knowledge base in a computationally feasible fashion.

References

[Edmonds and Hirst, 2002] Philip Edmonds and Graeme Hirst. Near-synonymy and lexical choice. *Computational Linguistics,* 28(2): 105-144, 2002.

[Foss and Hakes, 1978] Donald J. Foss and David T. Hakes. Psycholinguistics – An Introduction to the Psychology of Language. *Prentice Hall, Englewood Cliffs, NJ*, 1978

[Miller et al., 1990] George A. Miller, Richard Beckwith, Christiane Fellbaum, Derek Gross and Katherine Miller. Introduction to wordnet: an online lexical database. *International Journal of Lexicography,* 3(4): 235-244, 1990

[Sun et al., 2011] Koun-Tem Sun, Yueh-Min Huang, Ming-Chi Liu, et al. A Wordnet-based Near-synonyms and Similar-looking Word Learning System. *Educational Technology & Society*, 14(1):121–134, 2011.

[Traxler, 2011] M. J. Traxler. Introduction to psycholinguistics: Understanding language science. *John Wiley & Sons*, 2011.

[Pederson et al., 2004] Ted Pederson, Siddharth Patwardhan and Jason Michelizzi. WordNet::Similarity: measuring the relatedness of concepts. *In Demonstration papers at HLT-NAACL 2004. Association for Computational Linguistics*, 2004.

Can AI Reason over Representations?

Matthew Wyss, Aaron Thieme, John Licato
Analogical Reasoning and Constructivism Lab
IPFW Department of Philosophy
Fort Wayne, IN 46805
wyssmd02@students.ipfw.edu, thieac01@students.ipfw.edu, licatoj@ipfw.edu

1 Introduction[1]

This poster investigates the possibility of an AI reasoning *over* representational systems. In artificial intelligence research, this marks a shift from an AI merely reasoning from *within* one. Given an AI and a set of representational systems, our question is whether an AI reasoner can choose between the representational systems for the purpose of some application. We begin by defining representational systems and recommending formality as a useful metric for choosing between them. Next, we provide a precise, general interpretation of formality as permutation invariance. We argue that more work will have to be completed on problems of AI and pragmatics (e.g., context sensitivity) before an account can be developed of how AI can fruitfully reason over representational systems.

2 Representational Systems

Taking our cue from object oriented programming and following Licato (2017), we define a representational system **R** as an ordered pair (**M**, **A**) where **M** is a set of typed elements (with or without values) and **A** is a set of methods. A representation ***R*** is a pair ($\mathbf{R}_v$,*f*) where $\mathbf{R}_v$ is an instantiated representational system (i.e., every element has a value) and *f* is a semantic evaluation function from $\mathbf{M} \cup \mathbf{A}$ to set **S**. Intuitively, **S** is a set of semantic values that correspond to each element and method in $\mathbf{R}_v$.

Our question is whether, given a set of representational systems, an AI reasoner can choose between them in order to solve some problem. Because different applications will require different levels of representational formality in making this decision, an AI must be able to reason over the formality of different representational systems.

3 Formality as Permutation Invariance

There are a variety of precise interpretations of formality, e.g., the formal as computable, the formal as de-semantification. (See Dutilh Novaes 2011 for a survey.) Following Sher (1991, 1996), van Benthem (1989), McGee (1996), McCarthy (1981), and MacFarlane (2000), we interpret formality as *permutation invariance*. The two historical inspirations for this approach are the success of Klein's Erlanger program (1893) in delineating different geometries and Tarski's work on logical notions (1986). Klein indicated how the concepts of Euclidean geometry are invariant under similarity transformations while the concepts of topology are invariant under bicontinuous transformations. Tarski (1986) writes "we call a notion 'logical' if it is invariant under all possible one-one transformations of the world onto itself" (149). On the permutation invariance interpretation of formality, formal structures do not depend on the individual identities of their elements. Formality as permutation invariance, then, captures the sense in which the formal is general and abstract.

The permutation invariance interpretation also offers technical utility. Following MacFarlane (2000) and van Benthem (1989), we can make permutation invariance precise in the generalized setting of type theory, though we lack space to do this here. Barring the interpretation of formality as computability, this kind of technical precision and generality is lacking in other interpretations of formality.

MacFarlane (2000) argues that permutation invariance is always relative to some intrinsic structure on the objects being permuted; equivalently, a definition of permutation invariance requires delimiting what kinds of transformations are permitted. In Euclidean geometry, these are only similarity transformations, a subset of bicontinuous transformations under which topological concepts are invariant. In spelling out the permutation invariance of logical concepts, Tarski permits every permutation of the set of objects while holding rigid the set of truth values, the structure Tarski is interested in preserving. In some concrete application, if an AI is to choose between representational systems, it must decide what structure is intrinsic to the concepts in **S**; that is, it must decide what kinds of permutations should be permitted on the concepts of **S**.

2 Conclusions and Future Work

In sum, reasoning over representational systems for the purpose of effectively employing a representation requires determining the level of permutation invariance of the representations. This determination depends on the intrinsic structure on **S**, the set of semantic concepts of the representation. Our claim is that the choice of an intrinsic structure on **S** must depend on how the representation ***R*** is to be *used*. In this way, it is a *pragmatic* choice.[2] But developing an AI that can take into account context-sensitive pragmatics is currently an intractable problem in AI research that does not appear to be solvable in the foreseeable future. Hence, an AI considering formality as permutation invariance to reason over representational systems for the purpose of effective applications is not a foreseeable prospect.

Future work may, first, attempt to address the problem of AI taking into account pragmatic assumptions in order to choose between representational systems as a special case of the more general problem of developing AI that is sensitive to pragmatic context.[3] Second, future work may attempt to avoid the problems raised by pragmatics by developing non-pragmatic, context insensitive criteria for AI to choose between representational systems. For example, computability is a criterion that does not require pragmatic assumptions to the extent that permutation invariance does; assuming an amount of resources available for computation is the only pragmatic assumption required by a computability criterion. This criterion would be of the following form: given two systems, if one requires more resources than available, choose the other system. However, it is precisely because this computability criterion does not take into account more pragmatic information that it is of minimal use in choosing between representational systems.

Other possible criteria may be borrowed from Rudolf Carnap's (1950) criteria for the process of explication. Following Licato (2017), future research may explore similarity, exactness, fruitfulness, and simplicity as criteria. Carnap suggests these conditions as criteria for a scientifically useful explication of inexact, informal concepts. Because of the extreme contextual sensitivity of these criteria, they presuppose much more pragmatic information than computability and even permutation invariance. Further, these criteria are not as open to a generalized, technical formulation. For them to function as criteria for an AI choosing between representational systems, more work will have to be completed on contextual pragmatics and AI.

In short, choosing a representational system is not an isolated choice but a choice *for some end*. To avoid making an arbitrary decision and to maximize utility, pragmatics must be considered. Given this difficulty, we propose that future research follow the first direction of working on contextual pragmatics and AI for the problem of representational system choice.

References

Carnap, Rudolf. 1950. *Logical Foundations of Probability*. Chicago: University of Chicago Press.

Klein, Felix. 1893. Vergleichende Betrachtungen ¨uber neuere geometrusche Forschungen (Das Erlanger Programm). [A Comparative Review of Recent Researches in Geometry.] *Mathematische Annalen 43*, 63–100.

Licato, John. 2017 (under review). "Two Paradoxes and Their Implications for AI-Assisted Analysis." International Association for Computing and Philosophy Conference. Stanford University, Stanford, California.

MacFarlane, John. 2000. *What Does It Mean to Say that Logic is Formal?* Dissertation. University of Pittsburgh, Pittsburgh, Pennsylvania.

McCarthy, Timothy. 1981. "The Idea of a Logical Constant." *Journal of Philosophy 78*, 499–523.

McGee, Vann. 1996. "Logical Operations." *Journal of Philosophical Logic 26*, 567-80.

Sher, Gila. 1991. *The Bounds of Logic: A Generalized Viewpoint*. Cambridge: MIT Press.

—. 1996. "Did Tarski Commit 'Tarski's Fallacy'?" *Journal of Symbolic Logic 61*, 653-86.

Tarski, Alfred. 1966. What are Logical Notions? Ed. John Corcoran. *History and Philosophy of Logic 7* (1986), 143–154.

van Benthem, Johan. 1989. "Logical Constants Across Varying Types." *Notre Dame Journal of Formal Logic 30*, 315–342.

[2] For example, if ***R*** is to represent the space of all possible representations in general, then there will be no assumptions on the structure of **S**. In contrast, if ***R*** is to represent scientific reasoning, then one might presupposes that the elements in ***S*** obey fundamental physical laws.

[3] A reviewer suggested that weaker notions (e.g., a forgetful functor from category theory) might be more appropriate than permutation invariance for thinking about abstraction and formality. Future research should be done on a comparative or relative conception of permutation invariance such that one system of concepts can be more permutation invariant than another.

Syntactic Differentiation in Oscar Wilde's "Dorian Gray"

Melissa Wright, Reva Freedman
Northern Illinois University
DeKalb, Illinois 60115
meliswright16@gmail.com, rfreedman@niu.edu

Abstract

This study analyzes the syntax and constituents in Oscar Wilde's *The Picture of Dorian Gray*, looking for syntactic differences between quoted and narrative sections. We investigate sentence length, parse tree height and the frequency of various coordinating conjunctions in the text. We show that Wilde's character dialogue uses shorter sentences and less subordination than narrative passages. We also show frequency differences among the conjunctions studied. We hypothesize that these differences relate to the difference in working memory load between speaking and reading.

1 Introduction[1]

The aim of this study was to analyze differences in the syntactic form of sentences in two different types of running text. As a case study, we analyzed the syntactic structure of each sentence in Oscar Wilde's *The Picture of Dorian Gray* (1890). We distinguished between two types of text in the novel, dialogue and narrative. We analyzed three hypotheses: 1) that there was a difference in sentence length in the dialogue and narrative sections of the novel, 2) that there was a difference in the average height of parse trees, and 3) that there was a difference in the frequency of use of the conjunctions *and*, *but* and *or*.

A series of Python programs were created to clean up the input and make the text readable for the Stanford Parser[2] (Klein and Manning, 2003). The syntax trees provided by the parser enabled us to see how often certain parts of speech occurred and at what level of syntactic structure they were found. A CSV file was created with this information and fed to a final program to evaluate the hypotheses and calculate statistical significance.

2 Data Source and Cleanup

The input for this study, containing 57,673 words, was retrieved from the Project Gutenberg website.[3]

A few items had to be manually changed before preprocessing. The text contained poetry in both French and English, as well as entire paragraphs in French. Not only were these irrelevant to the hypotheses, but a parser trained on English prose could obviously not parse them. Furthermore, when these items were preceded by a colon (e.g., "He said: ..."), the colon had to be replaced by a period so that the introductory phrase would not appear to refer to the text after the deleted material, which might not even be a quote.

Since the Stanford Parser treats every period as final sentence punctuation, ellipses ("...") gave rise to empty sentences. As the material after an ellipsis can start with a capital letter (e.g., a proper noun), it was necessary to decide manually whether each ellipsis was intra-sentential, in which case it could be deleted, or terminal punctuation.

Following the manual phase, the second phase consisted of mechanized preprocessing. Periods and other terminators (e.g. !, ?, etc.) that occurred elsewhere than at the end of a sentence were dropped so that abbreviations such as "Mr." would not cause false sentence breaks. Similarly, we removed the periods that Oscar Wilde used after Roman numerals. Wilde's use of the unusual punctuation string ",--" was replaced by equivalent modern punctuation. Front and back matter, chapter headings (e.g., "CHAPTER XII"), and page numbers, formatted as [12], or [...12] when a chapter started mid-page, were also removed.

3 Methodology

The preprocessing phase enabled us to split sentences at the final punctuation mark. The text contained standalone quotations which were complete sentences, as well as narrative sentences which contained no quotations. However, it also contained sentences with an initial narrative portion introducing a quotation ("He said, '...'"), with a terminal narrative portion ("'...,' said Lord Henry"), or with a variety of more complex sentence structures, such as the following:

> "Oh, there is really very little to tell, Harry," answered the young painter; "and I am afraid you will hardly understand it. Perhaps you will hardly believe it."

To separate quoted from narrative material, we broke each sentence into segments, separating quoted and non-quoted material. Since the Stanford Parser parses sentences, a new

[2] http://nlp.stanford.edu/software/lex-parser.shtml.
[3] https://www.gutenberg.org/.

record was created when either a sentence break or a change in text type (from quote to non-dialogue or vice versa) occurred. For example, the above sentence was split into the following four segments:

Q: Oh, there is really very little to tell, Harry,
N: answered the young painter;
Q: and I am afraid you will hardly understand it.
Q: Perhaps you will hardly believe it.

We replaced segment-final punctuation with periods so that the parser would treat each segment as a complete sentence. As can be seen in the third segment above, or the segment "said Lord Henry", not all segments were sentences according to prescriptive English grammar; however, since the Stanford Parser is probabilistic, it could generally handle the segments we gave it. We verified some unusual cases before settling on this approach. For example, the parser could handle "said Lord Henry" but not "Said Lord Henry", which fortunately did not occur in the corpus.

Note that this decision does not affect the length or tree height of sentences in the quoted material but reduces both variables for narrative segments, since, for example, "answered the young painter" has a sentence length of 4 and contains no nested clauses, while the original sentence is obviously longer and contains coordination.

Figure 1 provides a sample output from the parser, showing examples of the extensive Penn Treebank tagset (Santorini, 1995). The parser output was used to calculate segment length, parse tree height and the frequency of *and*, *or* and *but*. We then conducted a two-tailed t-test with unequal variances on each of these variables, applying the Bonferroni correction in each case.

4 Results and Discussion

With regard to sentence length, the t-test showed that there is a significant difference ($p < .001$) in sentence length between the two types of text; narrative sentences are significantly longer. This result is even more striking when one considers that the length of the narrative segments was artificially depressed by the splitting mechanism employed.

Two extreme examples of sentence length are the two longest sentences in the book, both of which are pure narrative. One contains 198 words and the other contains 448 words. Although the rest of the book could be parsed in one batch, each of these sentences needed five times the default memory size of the Stanford Parser and had to be parsed separately.

```
(ROOT
  (S
    (NP (NNP Lord) (NNP Henry))
    (VP
      (VP (VBD stretched)
        (NP (PRP$ his) (JJ long) (NNS legs))
        (PRT (RP out))
        (PP (IN on)
          (NP (DT the) (NN divan))))
      (CC and)
      (VP (VBD shook)
        (PP (IN with)
          (NP (NN laughter)))))
    (. .)))
```

Figure 1: Sample parse from "The Picture of Dorian Gray"

Similarly, with regard to height of the syntax trees, the t-test showed that there is a significant difference ($p < .001$) in tree height between the two types of text; the narrative text also had significantly deeper trees. This finding is consistent with the previous one, providing further evidence that the narrative portion of the text is significantly more complex than the quoted portion.

This pattern could be due to Wilde's attempt to mirror real-world conversational style: if there are "limitations in human working memory and processing capacity [which] force reliance on a number of syntactic heuristics in order to make a provisional parse of a sentence as it is being processed" (Elman, 2009, p. 556), then it would be intuitive as an interlocutor to utilize less complex sentences within a discourse.

The findings illustrated in this study illustrate the importance of context when studying linguistic features. Within a conversation, there may be a subconscious expectation that speakers will utilize simpler constructions due to working memory load; however, when reading a descriptive passage in a written work, such limitations may not apply.

We examined three coordinating conjunctions, *and*, *but* and *or*. In the quoted text, *and* occurs approximately five times as often as *but*, while in the narrative text, it occurs approximately 25 times as often. Similarly, in the quoted text, *or* occurs approximately twice as often as *and*, while in the narrative text, these conjunctions have similar rates of occurrence. These data provide evidence that coordinating conjunctions play different roles in different types of text.

The relative rarity of *but* in the narrative text may result from the fact that *but* is most frequently used to show a contrast between two propositions. Therefore it would be less useful in longer sentences containing multiple propositions. *But* may also be more useful in dialogue, where it frequently occurs sentence-initially, allowing one character to signify disagreement with another. Further evidence from a text where *but* would be likely to occur in a non-quoted context, such as a deductive or argumentative context, would be useful in extending our understanding of *but*.

These patterns in Wilde's work may also display the author's linguistic thumbprint (Nolan, 2001). Previous research has been done on examining whether speakers and authors can be identified by unique linguistic patterns, and this study may indicate that there are indeed such patterns. Further evidence, from other works by Oscar Wilde and from other authors, would be required to evaluate this hypothesis.

5 Related Work

Coh-Metrix (Graesser et al., 2004) uses parts of speech, word frequency statistics and other features to measure cohesion. Wang et al. (2014) used syntactic features to differentiate conference papers from workshop papers. Freedman and Krieghbaum (2014) used syntactic features to differentiate early essays from revised ones by the same student authors, while Freedman and Krieghbaum (2015) used syntactic features to differentiate two faculty authors. Freedman (2017) used both syntactic and semantic means to differentiate sections of the book of Isaiah. Further information about the current study can be found in Wright (2017).

6 Conclusions

In this paper we analyzed the differences between quoted and narrative portions of Oscar Wilde's *The Picture of Dorian Gray*. Through parsing every sentence and analyzing the results, we showed that there are significant differences ($p < .001$) in both sentence length and parse tree height between quoted text and narrative portions. We also showed major differences in the frequency of various coordinating conjunctions between these two types of text.

Perhaps the most significant implication of this study is the possible intuition speakers and authors may have when taking part in or creating a conversation – if interlocutors instinctively know that shorter structures are to be employed in a conversational context, this may indicate underlying unconscious conversational syntactic principles.

The methods used in this study may enable future researchers to investigate linguistic components specific to an individual's written and oral speech patterns that will allow differentiation between personal style and unconscious conversational syntactic principles. Further research is also needed on the relationship between choice of conjunction, depth of clause embedding and discourse context, such as speaker quotation or other prose forms, including narrative, descriptive, explanatory and argumentative text.

There is also room for further analysis of the variation in sentence length between dialogue and narrative text. Such research has the potential to illustrate the strength of working memory load theories concerning real-time sentence processing, giving discourse psychologists a more solid foundation for investigating cognitive processing during conversation and reading.

Acknowledgments

Dr. Gulsat Aygen and Dr. Betty Birner, Department of English, Northern Illinois University provided advice on this study. The tree analysis code was based on code written by Doug Krieghbaum.

References

Elman, J. (2009). On the meaning of words and dinosaur bones: Lexical knowledge without a lexicon. Cognitive Science, 33: 547-582.

Freedman, R. 2017 (to appear). Can Natural Language Processing Help Identify the Author(s) of the Book of Isaiah? In Proceedings of the 30th Annual FLAIRS Conference.

Freedman, R., and Krieghbaum, D. 2014. Effects of Rewriting Essays on Linguistic Measures of Complexity. In 25th Annual Meeting of the Society for Text and Discourse.

Freedman, R., and Krieghbaum, D. 2015. Comparison of Expert Tutors through Syntactic Analysis of Transcripts. In Proceedings of 17th International Conference on Artificial Intelligence in Education (AIED 2015).

Graesser, A., McNamara, D., Louwerse, M., and Cai, Z. 2004. Coh-Metrix: Analysis of Text on Cohesion and Language. Behavior Research Methods, Instruments and Computers, 36: 193-202.

Klein, D., and Manning, C. 2003. Accurate Unlexicalized Parsing. In Proceedings of the 41st Meeting of the Association for Computational Linguistics, 423-430.

Nolan, F. 2001. Speaker identification evidence: Its forms, limitations, and roles. Proceedings of the conference "Law and Language: Prospect and Retrospect", December 12-15, 2001, Levi (Finnish Lapland). Available from http://www.ling.cam.ac.uk/francis/LawLang.doc.

Santorini, B. 1995. Part-of-Speech Tagging Guidelines for the Penn Treebank Project. University of Pennsylvania, Natural Language Processing Project. Technical Report MS-CIS-90-47, LINC LAB 178.

Wang, H., Di Eugenio, B., Lin, S., and Yu, C. 2014. Distinguishing Different Types of Conference Submissions: The ACL Case Study. Chicago Colloquium on Digital Humanities and Computer Science. Available at http://www.nlp.cs.uic.edu/PS-papers/dhcs_2014_manuscript.pdf.

Wilde, O. 1890. *The Picture of Dorian Gray*. From http://www.gutenberg.org/cache/epub/4078/pg4078.txt.

Wright, Melissa. 2017. Natural Language Processing and Syntactic Differentiation: A Corpus Case Study. M.A. thesis, Northern Illinois University.

AUTHOR INDEX